PLURALISM AND DEMOCRACY IN INDIA

PLURALISM AND DEMOCRACY IN INDIA

Debating the Hindu Right

Edited by Wendy Doniger

Martha C. Nussbaum

OXFORD
UNIVERSITY PRESS

Oxford University Press is a department of the University of
Oxford. It furthers the University's objective of excellence in research,
scholarship, and education by publishing worldwide.

Oxford   New York
Auckland   Cape Town   Dar es Salaam   Hong Kong   Karachi
Kuala Lumpur   Madrid   Melbourne   Mexico City   Nairobi
New Delhi   Shanghai   Taipei   Toronto

With offices in
Argentina   Austria   Brazil   Chile   Czech Republic   France   Greece
Guatemala   Hungary   Italy   Japan   Poland   Portugal   Singapore
South Korea   Switzerland   Thailand   Turkey   Ukraine   Vietnam

Oxford is a registered trademark of Oxford University Press
in the UK and certain other countries.

Published in the United States of America by
Oxford University Press
198 Madison Avenue, New York, NY 10016

Library of Congress Cataloging-in-Publication Data
Pluralism and democracy in India : debating the Hindu right / Edited by Wendy Doniger
and Martha C. Nussbaum.
pages cm
Based on presentations at a conference at the University of Chicago Law School in November 2005.
Includes bibliographical references and index.
ISBN 978-0-19-539553-2 (pbk. : alk. paper)—ISBN 978-0-19-539482-5 (hardcover :
alk. paper)—ISBN 978-0-19-938092-3 (ebook)—ISBN 978-0-19-938093-0 (ebook)
1. Hinduism and politics—Congresses.   2. Democracy—Religious aspects—Hinduism—
Congresses.   3. Hindutva—Congresses.   4. India—Civilization—Congresses.   5. Pluralism—
Congresses.   I. Doniger, Wendy, editor of compilation.   II. Nussbaum, Martha Craven,
1947– editor of compilation.
BL1215.P65P63 2014
322'.10954—dc23
2013043629

9 8 7 6 5 4 3 2 1
Printed in the United States of America
on acid-free paper

CONTENTS

CONTRIBUTORS

Amrita Basu is the Paino Professor of Political Science and Women's and Gender Studies at Amherst College. Her main research interests are in social movements, religious nationalism and political violence in South Asia. She is the author of *Two Faces of Protest: Contrasting Modes of Women's Activism in India* (1994) and *Violent Conjunctures: Hindu Nationalism in Democratic India* (forthcoming), and has edited several books.

Akeel Bilgrami holds the Sidney Morgenbesser Chair in Philosophy at Columbia University and is the author of the books *Belief and Meaning* (1992), *Self-Knowledge and Resentment* (2006), and *Secularism, Identity, and Enchantment* (2014). He is currently working on a long project on the nature and scope of practical reason, and two short books, both forthcoming: *What is a Muslim?* and *Gandhi, The Philosopher*.

Paul B. Courtright is Professor Emeritus in the Department of Religion and the Graduate Division of Religion at Emory University, Atlanta, Georgia. He is the author of *Gaṇeśa: Lord of Obstacles, Lord of Beginnings*, and coeditor of *From the Margins of Hindu Marriage*. His current research focuses on historical study of representations of and controversies around religion in early colonial India.

Gurcharan Das is the author of *India Grows at Night: A Liberal Case for a Strong State*, as well as two other nonfiction works, *The Difficulty of Being Good* and *India Unbound*. He has also written a novel, *A Fine Family*, and an anthology, *Three Plays*. He studied philosophy at Harvard and was CEO of Procter & Gamble India before he became a full-time writer. He writes a regular column for *Times of India* and four Indian-language papers, and periodically for the *Financial Times*, the *New York Times*, and the *Wall Street Journal*. He lives in Delhi.

Antara Dev Sen was senior editor with the *Hindustan Times,* New Delhi, when she went to Oxford as a fellow with the Reuter Foundation. She founded the *Little Magazine* when she returned to India and is its editor. She has worked with the Anand Bazaar Patrika Group in Calcutta and with the *Indian Express* in Delhi, where she was senior assistant editor. She is a columnist for the newspapers *Asian Age*, the *Deccan Chronicle,* and *DNA*, and earlier wrote columns for *The Week* and Sify.com, among other publications.

Nabaneeta Dev Sen is a creative writer in India, and an academic. While her academic work is in English, her creative writing is in Bangla. Retired as professor of comparative literature, Jadavpur University, Kolkata, Dev Sen has more than eighty publications in a variety of genres, consisting of poetry, novels, short stories, travelogues, plays, belles lettres, memoirs, literary criticism, translations, and children's literature. She has received national and international acclaim, including the Padmashri from the President of India, the Sahitya Akademi Award, the Bangla Akademi Lifetime Achievement Award, and the Publishers and Booksellers' Guild Lifetime Achievement Award. She represented Indian writing at the India Festival in the United States, the Frankfurt Book Fair, the Munich Book Festival, the Edinburgh Book Festival, the Moscow Book Fair, and the NSW Poetry Festival, Sydney. She was the Radhakrishnan Memorial Lecturer at the University of Oxford and held the Maytag Chair of Comparative Literature and Creative Writing at Colorado College. She is the president of *Soi* Women Writers, Association of West Bengal.

Wendy Doniger [O'Flaherty] (PhD, Harvard University; DPhil, Oxford University) is the Mircea Eliade Distinguished Service Professor of the History of Religions at the University of Chicago and the author of forty books, most recently *The Hindus: An Alternative History* (2009), *On Hinduism* (2014), and *Hinduism* in the Norton Anthology of World Religions.

Mushirul Hasan is a Padmashree awardee, former vice chancellor of Jamia Millia University, and director general, National Archives of India. He was awarded Officer of the Order of Academic Palms by the Prime Minister of the French Republic in 2009. He has authored *Legacy of a Divided Nation: India's Muslims Since Independence* (1997), *From Pluralism to Separatism: Qasbas in Colonial Awadh* (2004), and recently *Faith and Freedom: Gandhi in History* (2013). He has edited *Exploring the West: Three Travel Narratives* (2009).

Zoya Hasan is professor of political science and former dean of the School of Social Sciences at Jawaharlal Nehru University. Her recent books include *Congress After Indira: Policy, Power and Political Change (1984–2009)* and *Politics of Inclusion: Castes, Minorities and Affirmative Action*.

Pratik Kanjilal was chief operating officer of Indian Express Online Media before he joined the *Little Magazine* as coeditor and publisher. He has been a leader writer and senior assistant editor of the *Indian Express*. He has also worked with the *Economic Times* and *Business Standard*. He has received the first New York University Prize for Hyperfiction (1998) and the Sahitya Akademi Translation Prize (2005). He is a columnist with *Time Out,* New Delhi, *Hindustan Times,* and *Free Press Journal.*

Mona G. Mehta is an assistant professor of political science at the Indian Institute of Technology, Gandhinagar. She previously taught comparative politics and politics of South Asia at Scripps College in Claremont, California. Her research interests include democracy, civil society, ethnic conflict, and identity politics in India. She has coedited, with Nalin Mehta, *Gujarat Beyond Gandhi: Identity, Conflict and Society* (2010). She received her PhD from the University of Chicago in 2010..

Ritu Menon is a publisher and writer who has been active in the South Asian women's movement for over twenty years. She is cofounder of Kali for Women, India's first and oldest feminist press, and founder of Women Unlimited, an associate of Kali for Women. She is coauthor of *Borders & Boundaries: Women in India's Partition* (1998). Her edited book *No Woman's Land: Women from Pakistan, India & Bangladesh Write about the Partition of India* was published in 2004. Also recently published are *Educating Muslim Girls: A Comparison of Five Indian Cities* (2005), *Unequal Citizens: A Study of Muslim Women in India* (2004), and *In a Minority: Essays on Muslim Women in India* (2005), all coedited with Zoya Hasan. As part of the Core Group of Women's WORLD, India, Menon has coedited *Just Between Us: Women Speak About their Writing* (2004) and *Storylines: Conversations with Women Writers* (2003). Her latest book (coauthored with Kalpana Kannabiran) is titled *From Mathura to Manorama: Resisting Violence Against Women in India* (2007).

Ved P. Nanda is John Evans University Professor at the University of Denver and Thompson G. Marsh Professor of Law and director of the International Legal Studies Program at the University of Denver Sturm College of Law. From 1994 to 2008 he also served as vice provost for internationalization at the university. He currently serves on the board of trustees of the Iliff School of Theology, as honorary president of the World Jurist Association, an elected member of the American Law Institute, as a councilmember at large for the American Bar Association Section of International Law and Practice, and honorary vice president of the International Law Association–American Branch. Nanda has received honorary doctorates from Soka University in Tokyo, Japan, and Bundelkhand University, Jhansi, India. He is widely published in law journals and national magazines, has authored or coauthored twenty-five books in the various fields of international law and more than 225 chapters and major law review articles, and has been a distinguished visiting professor and scholar at a number of universities in the United States and abroad.

Martha C. Nussbaum is Ernst Freund Distinguished Service Professor of Law and Ethics at the University of Chicago. She is appointed in the law school and the philosophy department and is a member of the Committee on Southern Asian Studies and of the Steering Committee of the University's new Center in Delhi. Her books include *The Clash Within: Democracy, Religious Violence, and India's Future* (2007), *The New Religious Intolerance* (2012), and *Political Emotions: Why Love Matters for Justice* (2013).

Malini Parthasarathy is Editor of The Hindu, a leading English language daily. She is also founding director of the Hindu Centre for Politics and Public Policy. She has been a political journalist for three decades. She has an MS in journalism from Columbia University's Graduate School of Journalism and a PhD from the Centre for Political Studies, Jawaharlal Nehru University. She has won two awards for excellence in journalism, the first Bank of India Award (1997) and the Haldighati Award from the Maharana Mewar Foundation, Udaipur. She has been a member of South Asian Association of Regional Cooperation (SAARC) election observer groups during elections in Pakistan and has participated in several Track II dialogues on India and Pakistan, particularly under the auspices of BALUSA (a joint India-Pakistan initiative) and Pugwash. She has been a member of the Governing Board of the Auroville Foundation since September of 2004, and has served on the executive committee and project approval committee of the National Literacy Mission Authority.

Prabhat Patnaik has taught at the University of Cambridge and at the Centre for Economic Studies and Planning (CESP) of the Jawaharlal Nehru University, New Delhi, where he held the Sukhamoy Chakravarty Chair in Planning and Development at the time of his retirement and is currently Professor Emeritus. He has written a number of books and articles, including *Time, Inflation and Growth* (1988), *Economics and Egalitarianism* (1990), *Whatever Happened to Imperialism and Other Essays* (1995), *Accumulation and Stability Under Capitalism* (1997), *The Retreat to Unfreedom* (2003), *The Value of Money* (2008) and *Re-envisioning Socialism* (2011). He is the editor of the journal *Social Scientist*.

Arvind Rajagopal is a professor in the Department of Media, Culture and Communication, and an affiliate faculty in the Department of Sociology, and the Department of Social and Cultural Analysis, at New York University. His book *Politics After Television* won the Ananda Kentish Coomaraswamy Prize from the Association of Asian Studies in 2003. In addition to two other collections, he edited *The Indian Public Sphere* (2009). His recent articles include "The Emergency and the New Indian Middle Class" in *Modern Asian Studies*, 2011, and "Special Political Zone" on the anti-Muslim violence in Ahmedabad, Gujarat, in the *South Asian Multidisciplinary Academic Journal* from the Ecole des Hautes Etudes en Sciences Sociales, Paris. In 2010–11, he was a fellow at the Center for Advanced Study in the Behavioral Sciences at Stanford University. He is currently completing a book on state formation and publicity in relation to India.

Tanika Sarkar is professor of Modern History at Jawaharlal Nehru University, Delhi. Her monographs include *Bengal 1928–1934: The Politics of Protest* (1987), *Words to Win: A Modern Autobiography* (1999), *Hindu Wife, Hindu Nation: Community, Religion, Cultural Nationalism* (2001), and *Rebels, Wives, Saints: Designing Selves and Nations in Colonial Times* (2009). She is a coeditor of *Women of the Hindu Right* with Urvashi Butalia (1995) and *Women and Social Reform in Modern India (2008)* with Sumit Sarkar, and a contributor to *Khaki Shirts and Saffron Flags: A Critique of the Hindu Right,* edited by Tapan Basu (1993). She has taught at the University of Chicago, Yale University, Grinnell College, and the University of Witswatersrand in South Africa. She has been a visiting fellow at the University of Cambridge, the University of Keele in the United Kingdom, Zentrum Moderner Orient in Berlin, the University of Washington, and a number of other institutions.

Amartya Sen is Thomas W. Lamont University Professor and professor of economics and philosophy at Harvard University, and was until 2004 the Master of Trinity College, Cambridge. He has served as President of the Econometric Society, the American Economic Association, the Indian Economic Association, and the International Economic Association. Sen's research has ranged over social choice theory, economic theory, ethics and political philosophy, welfare economics, theory of measurement, decision theory, development economics, public health, and gender studies. His books have been translated into more than thirty languages, and include *Choice of Techniques* (1960), *Collective Choice and Social Welfare* (1970), *Choice, Welfare and Measurement* (1982), *Commodities and Capabilities (1987), The Standard of Living* (1987), *Development as Freedom* (1999), *Identity and Violence: The Illusion of Destiny* (2006), *The Idea of Justice* (2009) and *An Uncertain Glory: India and its Contradictions* (2013).

PLURALISM AND DEMOCRACY IN INDIA

INTRODUCTION

Wendy Doniger and Martha C. Nussbaum

Postscript, July 2014

While this volume was being copyedited, Narendra Modi was elected prime minister of India in a landslide, and with an outright majority of Parliament. The election of May 2014 marked a sharp turning point in the history of India's democracy whose meaning is as yet unclear. Modi is clearly identified with the Sangh Parivar (family of Hindu Right groups), and, as Chief Minister of Gujarat, is widely thought to bear some responsibility for the terrible events in that state in 2002— events that were a major part of the inspiration for this book. Since that time he has been denied a visa to enter the United States, because the US State Department judged that evidence of his complicity in the pogrom was convincing, even though he has not been convicted in court. It is too soon to tell whether Modi will govern on his announced platform of economic growth and efficiency or whether he will eventually introduce a more divisive sectarian agenda. The electorate repudiated the years of inefficiency and corruption under the leadership of the Congress Party. They did not opt in any clear sense for Hindu Right politics, and it is likely that any attempt to foreground such an agenda would lose Modi at least some of the support he currently has. Nonetheless, the moment is an ominous one, for pluralism and amity between groups, for the freedoms of press and scholarship, and for India's very future as a democracy.

Our volume originally framed the events of 2002 from the point of view of democratic survival, and the body of this introduction tells a basically optimistic tale of a threat surmounted. We have decided to retain the original text of this introduction, written early in 2013, before the sudden ascent of Modi, and to allow current events themselves to comment on the qualified optimism of that time. We do not feel confident about what the future holds, and the future itself, as it unfolds, will frame the historical studies contained in this volume.

India, the world's most populous democracy, is also, by any standard, its most diverse. With its twenty-two official languages and over three hundred that are actually spoken; with enormous regional differences in history and culture; with stunning inequalities in basic nutrition and health care between rich and poor, male and female, urban and rural, higher castes and lower, and also between Hindu and Muslim; and with a politics that embodies a range of influential caste, ethnic, and minority identities, it is a tapestry of stunning complexity and has been so not only since Independence, but throughout its long previous history. Although at times one hears phrases such as "Indian values" and "Indian culture," anyone who talks that way, without immediate qualification, is either confessing ignorance or pushing a party line. Wherever one looks—whether to a Bollywood movie, to a cricket match, to a fashion show, or to the Lok Sabha—diversity is likely to be among the first things that strike the ear, the eye, and the mind.

Most salient, perhaps, is India's religious diversity. About eighty-two percent of its citizens are Hindus, eleven percent Muslims. Parsis and Christians are also given special recognition under the system of personal laws, although their percentage of the population is far smaller. Nor is each of these groups internally homogeneous. The Hindu tradition was always highly diverse, containing wide regional and caste differences. Sikhs, Jains, and Buddhists, although counted as Hindus under the Census, hardly think of the Hindu identity as their central self-conception. (Many, like the Constitution's primary architect, Dr. B. R. Ambedkar, may feel that affirming a Buddhist identity is a way of protesting against aspects of Hindu tradition.) Muslim lives, too, vary greatly along lines of region and class. Christians are Protestant and Catholic, influenced by the national traditions of Portugal, Germany, Britain, and other nations. Atheists and agnostics abound, although most of these are classified for legal purposes under the religion of their ancestors.

The wonder is not that India is diverse, but that India, sixty-seven years after Independence, is a single nation—and a thriving democratic nation at that, with high rates of political participation; a strong commitment to ending discrimination along lines of caste, religion, and gender; cultural and artistic achievements that are known the world over; an expanding economy; and growing achievements in education.

In recent years, however, India's democratic future has been threatened by the rise to power of the Hindu Right or Sangh Parivar (Family of Groups), a complex network of political and social organizations that have many faces, but that aim, in the long run, at changing the very nature of India's constitutional democracy. The social organizations of the Sangh Parivar, which include the Rashtriya Swayamsevak Sangh (RSS; National Corps of Volunteers), the Vishva

Hindu Parashad (VHP; All-Hindu Council), and the Bajrang Dal (Strong Group), are closely linked to the highly successful political party, the Bharatiya Janata Party (BJP; National People's Party). The BJP, despite having many faces, retains a deep commitment to implementing the Sangh Parivar's central goals. Instead of a nation that celebrates pluralism, the Sangh Parivar seeks a Hindu nation, which will allow others to remain and flourish only if they acknowledge the fundamentally Hindu nature of India's culture and assimilate to that. In effect, they seek to implement a Hindu-first vision of India that existed long before the founding, and that was strongly repudiated by both Gandhi and Nehru: that of a Motherland that has an ethnoreligious identity at its heart. Instead of an India unified by political commitments to equality and a decent living standard—the vision of the Constitution—they seek an exclusionary India. They also seek an exclusionary Hinduism, recasting the plural and tolerant religion as a unified set of doctrines and as a militant force that seeks to dominate various "others." Particularly antagonistic toward Muslims and Christians, they frequently foment acts of violence, and they did so famously in 1992 when angry Hindu mobs destroyed the Babri Masjid, a mosque in the city of Ayodhya that rests—they asserted—over the remains of the god Rama's birthplace, which they represent as *the* central holy place of Hinduism, through considerable historical and religious simplification. The shock waves that this event sent through the nation are still reverberating, as the legal issues deriving from it continue to be litigated.

The incident that was the catalyst for the present volume, however, was more recent: the massacre of Muslim civilians in the state of Gujarat in 2002, after a fire on a train carrying Hindu pilgrims killed fifty-eight Hindus. Blame was immediately put on Muslims—although subsequent forensic investigations strongly suggest that the fire was a tragic accident caused by the kerosene stoves carried on board the train and stored beneath the seats. Violence swept the state, and the call to violence was issued not only by the VHP and Bajrang Dal, but also by government officials, who ordered police not to suppress the rioting and who offered support to the rioters. Efforts to prosecute these officials continue, but witness intimidation has prevented some prosecutions from going forward.[1]

Gujarat was a single event, but it was part of a larger tapestry of events that showed the fragility—and, ultimately, the resilience—of India's constitutional values. The Hindu Right proved highly effective, for a time, in spreading its message of division and fear, in part through its temporarily successful attempts to impress its values on public education and scholarship, and through its highly successful youth movement. The value of respect for others across religious differences was not as successfully disseminated at the grass-roots level. The expatriate Hindu diaspora community in the United States played—and still plays—an influential role, funding the politicians who were at the center of the riots and fueling attacks on scholars who do not toe the Hindu Right line on history and religion.

The story of the Hindu Right has often been told. So has that of the Gujarat riots. The present volume tries to dig beneath the crisis to understand how values of pluralism and toleration have been implemented in the society as a whole—in a way that made the crisis possible, but in such a way, too, that the democracy has surmounted it—at least up to the present moment. How does a decent constitution become a working political reality? What mechanisms did the founders put in place to effect the transition between ideal and reality, how have these mechanisms evolved over time, and what are their strong and weak points? How do governmental institutions such as public education, political parties and movements, and national economic policy function in transmitting (or blunting) national ideals? How do a variety of other institutions, from poetry and religion to the media culture, play their part, when protected by constitutional guarantees? What role do gender norms play, as they interact with explicitly political and legal aspects of society? Finally, how does the presence of a wealthy community of Indians in the United States influence India's political culture? What was it about all of these aspects of Indian society that made the events of Gujarat possible, and yet enabled India to repudiate that call to hatred?

The volume derives from a conference at the University of Chicago Law School in November 2005, sponsored by the Law School's Center for Comparative Constitutionalism and the Divinity School's Martin Marty Center. When the conference was held, the BJP had recently gone down to defeat in the election of 2004; in the intervening years, with another defeat in 2008, the resilience of democratic institutions became more evident. But then, in 2014, the BJP rose to power once more. We felt that it was wise to create a distance between immediate political events and our scholarly reflections: thus we gave our authors several years to ponder the unfolding events and to situate their immersed reflections in a wider historical framework. They have taken advantage of this distance in some cases incorporating discussion of subsequent related events such as the 2008 Mumbai bombings.

The moment this volume studies is now part of the past—in a sense. But it remains relevant for three reasons. First, the Hindu Right has come to power again. Between Gandhi's death and the 1980s, the Sangh Parivar was in eclipse—but then it gathered force, controlled the government for many years, and now has won with an outright majority. Second, the moment we study is an important part of India's history, and a part that can best be studied, we believe, at some distance from immediate events. Finally, it is a moment that has importance for all nations, as they seek to implement values of pluralism and mutual respect. The volume poses a question about India, but it is also a question for all democracies: How can values of toleration and mutual respect be implemented in such a way that they govern people's real lives, becoming more than the words on paper in a nation's constitutional and legal documents?

India has a rich tradition of critical argument, and it also has a rich humanistic tradition. These two interweaving strands in India's identity become salient themes throughout the volume, which examines their history and their present fate, pondering their respective roles in democratic public culture. The idea of an "argumentative Indian," so vividly described by Amartya Sen in his book of that name and in his contribution to the present volume, has a long history and forms part of the explanation for India's success in establishing a working democracy that has withstood many threats.[2] One contribution of the volume is to document the sources of this idea in India's political culture. Another, however, is to document current threats to public dialogue, as argumentative transparency has been repeatedly compromised by propaganda and incitements to hatred.

As for humanistic public culture: emotion and religious or quasireligious commitment played a large part in Gandhi's movement, as in his thought about what Indian democracy should be. But mistrust of these forces on the part of India's subsequent leaders led to their neglect, and the Hindu Right quickly seized this opportunity, filling a cultural void with resonant appeals to nationalistic emotion and to exclusivist ideas of the polity. Many contributors to this volume regret the neglect of religion, culture, and the humanities generally on the part of India's tolerant and progressive leadership, as a narrow notion of scientific rationality came increasingly to dominate the public realm, estranging many citizens from the values of pluralism. If there is one shared conclusion emerging from these essays, it is that democracy needs both a head and a heart, both arguments and emotional commitment. If people who favor religious pluralism and toleration do not offer their ideas in ways that appeal to the imagination of ordinary people, searching for meaning in life, those people are likely to turn elsewhere for spiritual guidance. The Hindu Right has understood all too well how to feed people's emotional hunger—with a diet of exclusion and hate.

Any investigation into this complex requires interdisciplinary cooperation, and we have been lucky to assemble a remarkably diverse set of scholars from history, political science, economics, philosophy, law, religious studies, media studies, and literature. But we have also turned to journalism, publishing, and the arts for insight. The resulting conversation is unusually rich and probing.

I

We begin with history, since the past leaves its marks on the present day. "India: Large and Small," by Nobel Prize–winning economist and philosopher Amartya Sen, portrays the longstanding commitments of Indian traditions to both argument and toleration, showing how the former supports the latter. A populace given to public deliberation through argument is less easily manipulated by propaganda than one not trained in critical thinking. It will question stereotypes and inflammatory appeals to a single religious identity. An uncritical electorate, correspondingly, will have a hard time resisting propaganda and peer pressure, and can easily be hoodwinked into thinking that only a single identity matters for a person and for the nation.

Such ideas of respectful toleration and pluralism are often associated with the Hindu and Buddhist traditions of India. (The emperor Ashoka, who drew upon a number of Buddhist ideals in his rock edicts in the third to second century B.C.E., was the first ruler to proclaim these values.) They are less frequently associated with India's Muslim traditions, and in today's world we frequently hear the canard that Islam is the only major world religion that has never had an "enlightenment." Mushirul Hasan's rich historical paper shows readers that such claims are in error: an Islamic enlightenment did take place, in India at least, in the form of internal criticism of religious norms and practices, during the nineteenth century, on the part of an influential group of Muslim intellectuals who, active over several generations, ultimately joined with Gandhi and played a leading role in the independence movement. (This same group founded Jamia Millia Islamia, the pluralistic Muslim-majority university of which Hasan, a noted historian, was, until recently, the Vice-Chancellor—so he is writing as the living heir of the tradition he describes.[3]) These people were genuinely religious, but they argued that their religion, correctly understood, required a secular and tolerant nation, equal education for women, and a range of progressive values. They did not lack opposition, but their "side" prevailed in most respects in today's India, where Muslims, though typically poor and vulnerable to many forms of discrimination, are active democratic citizens who for the most part strongly support the goals and institutions of the pluralistic secular state.

With Martha Nussbaum's essay we turn to the ideas of Jawaharlal Nehru, the primary architect of the institutions of modern India and a democratic leader of undoubted greatness. If India has become a thriving democracy, as Pakistan did not, it is in large part because of Nehru's uncompromising defense of values of equality and fraternity, his refusal to seek personal profit, and his vision, shared with Gandhi, of a democratic nation built on firm protections for religious pluralism and freedoms of speech, press, and assembly. And yet Nehru's thought and work contained, Nussbaum argues, a large gap: a failure to understand the importance of humanistic and emotional values in the lives of most people, and his consequent denigration of the humanities in the broadest sense, in favor of a narrow conception of scientific rationality. Examining his arguments against religion and in favor of science in *The Discovery of India*, she finds them flawed as arguments, and she shows that confidence in these flawed arguments led Nehru to turn his attention away from creating a public symbolic and artistic culture that would put flesh on the bones of national ideals.

Philosopher Akeel Bilgrami concurs in this critique of an excessive reliance on science. Examining Gandhi's critique of the Enlightenment, Bilgrami agrees with Gandhi that Enlightenment science urges us to view the world in a "disenchanted" way and therefore to use nature as a mere tool for our own ends. (Bilgrami does not equate this view with science itself, although Gandhi did.) He argues that these same values contributed to colonial exploitation, since the colonizers infantilized conquered people and claimed it was proper to dominate them because they allegedly lacked scientific rationality.

The five essays in this section contain many points of disagreement. Sen would probably be skeptical of Nussbaum's account of the role of emotions in a decent political culture. Although his view of rationality is broader than Nehru's, embracing the literary and philosophical humanities, his dislike for religion is as great. Nussbaum, on the other hand, while utterly in agreement with Sen in his call for a critical public culture, would not agree with him that religious violence is caused primarily by intellectual error. She sees the failure of culture to nourish strong emotions connected to pluralism and toleration as among the primary sources of recent troubles. In writing elsewhere about education for democratic citizenship she has emphasized that both Socratic critical thinking and the expansion of the empathetic imagination are crucial for democracy's success. Hasan seems to agree with these twin goals, given the figures he admires.

Thus while agreeing with Bilgrami that scientific rationality is not sufficient for a successful democracy, Nussbaum does not concur with his repudiation of the Enlightenment. Her critique of Nehru calls for a partnership between science and humanistic public culture—and Nehru always insisted that both traditions were thoroughly at home in India. (He said that it was the British who discouraged India from scientific development, because it would threaten their power.) Nor would Nussbaum accept the idea that Enlightenment values themselves caused colonial domination. The seventeenth-century thinkers of concern to Bilgrami made a strong distinction between the human being and the rest of nature, arguing that all human beings had souls and no nonhuman creature did. Every human, therefore, must be treated as an end, and no nonhuman being is more than a means. While such views do explain many deplorable aspects of Europeans' treatment of nonhuman animals and the environment, they can hardly explain humans' domination over other humans, which involved a betrayal, rather than an application, of Enlightenment values. Indeed, if any single aspect of the British treatment of India was most salient, it was the utter failure of the Raj to treat humanity as an end.

So the essays in this section leave readers with options, as they think about India's future: Sen's idea of public dialogue without much reliance on emotion, poetry, or humanistic public culture; Nussbaum's and Hasan's idea of scientific and Socratic rationality in conversation with poetic and, in the broadest sense, humanistic resources; or Bilgrami's idea of a more thoroughly spiritualized or "enchanted" world.

II

Any successful democracy needs a free press dedicated to the uncovering and dissemination of truth. Amartya Sen's Nobel Prize-winning work on famines has shown the importance of a free press in generating constructive thinking that leads to the avoidance of famine, in situations of food shortage. But history shows us many other areas in which the press sustains democracy: deliberations about war, the unmasking of corruption, the defense of national ideals (for example pluralism and nonracism) against disinformation and propaganda. India's media have won widespread admiration for their high quality of dedication and courage, and the nation has wisely protected its freedom. Even when this freedom, like many others, was under assault during the Emergency, the Indian public rallied on the side of freedom, and the subsequent actions of the Supreme Court have made a return to those days of diminished freedom unlikely. As Malini Parthasarathy writes, a free press is a "key element in the continuing vitality of India's democratic structure."

It is then with considerable alarm and regret that we should read the essays by Parthasarathy and Antara Dev Sen. Parthasarathy is one of India's leading journalists, for a long period the leading editor of *The Hindu*, generally acknowledged to be India's best newspaper, and also a member of the family that owns it. She thus speaks as an immersed insider—but also as an outsider, in that at the time of the conference she had stepped outside her job to write a doctoral thesis in political studies at Jawaharlal Nehru University. She agrees with Amartya Sen that India's press has long been one of the glories of the democracy. But during the crisis brought on by the rise to power of the Hindu Right, she argues, it did not live up to the high standards of its past. Major sections of the media uncritically absorbed the themes and issues of Hindu nationalists, without questioning their formulations. Indeed, she argues that the media, by employing charged stereotypes of Muslims and Christians, contributed to legitimizing violence against them. Most newspapers were filled with "a barrage of propaganda assaults by overzealous Christian missionaries even as Muslim terrorists were sneaking up to plant bombs in public spaces." Along with an increase in incendiary reporting, there was a decrease in factual scrutiny; both involve culpable abdication of fundamental journalistic principles. Parthasarathy calls on the press to return to its true function as democratic watchdog.

Antara Dev Sen is a different sort of journalist: the founder (along with her husband, Pratik Kanjilal) of the *Little Magazine*, a twice-yearly journal of culture and politics that offered, inter alia, sustained analysis of the Gujarat violence. She examines the achievements of India's media by looking at coverage of Hindu-Muslim issues beyond Gujarat, focusing on several ethnically charged murder cases and on the 2008 Mumbai bombings. Her findings agree with those of Parthasarathy: sensationalism and stereotyping. Like Parthasarathy, she sees a decline from an era in which the press saw its function as "to educate, entertain, and inform" to a new era in which its function is primarily "to excite, entertain, and titillate." She blames commercial pressure, which leads to a focus on the sensational, combined with excessive deference to privileged middle-class readers. Like Parthasarathy, she issues a call to the media to return to older standards of journalistic ethics and older aspirational norms.

Arvind Rajagopal is an expert on Indian television. His influential book *Politics After Television* examined the Hindu Right's clever use of the medium during its rise to power, painting an ominous picture of a credulous populace, eager to be entertained by serialized versions of classical epics and unwilling to investigate their accuracy. His article in the present collection offers a more complex assessment. In a study of television advertising between 1992 (the year of the destruction of the Babri Masjid) and 2003 (the year after the Gujarat riots), asking how advertising both reflects and changes social values, he finds a marked democratization of television, which both reflects and empowers a newly influential set of social groups, poor as well as middle-class. Having begun by catering to an elite rich audience that was represented as if it stood for the entire nation, advertising, during the period he studies, evolved to reflect and represent the values of the poor as well—thus helping to lead the nation beyond the Nehruvian assumption that progress would come from the educated middle and upper classes and that the poor would emulate these models. Rajagopal finds that in marketing to the poor consumer, television portrays this consumer as clever, thrifty, and hard to trick, capable of seeing through the brand image. His picture, however, is not entirely positive. Not too surprisingly, advertising expresses consumerist values and encourages acquisitiveness, detaching its audience from political issues. Even an ad for the newspaper *Times of India* portrays political corruption humorously, treating the potential reader as "postcivic."

III

Political parties and movements are not mandated, as such, in any nation's constitution, but they are omnipresent in democracies, and their functioning is a big part of the story of the functioning of the democracy itself. In "The Long March from Ayodhya," political scientist Amrita Basu examines the functioning of the BJP in the context of a range of state and civil society institutions, seeking to understand why democracy in India has failed to prevent regular episodes of violence against minorities. She finds failures at the level of national government, such as the failure to invoke President's Rule in crisis situation, and at the level of state and local government, as police and municipal officials, dominated by Hindu activists, repeatedly encouraged or failed to suppress violence. A large part of the story, however, lies in the link between Hindu social activism and the BJP. Despite the fact that a radical party must broaden its agenda in order to achieve national power, focusing on economic growth as well as on ethnoreligious issues, this tendency to softening is lessened by militant activism within the party itself, through its link to social organizations. Basu also examines a range of civil society institutions that have contributed to the violence.

One might think that one way national government could promote the interests of vulnerable minorities would be through the creation of commissions with minority interests as their charge. Political scientist Zoya Hasan studies two such commissions: the National Commission for Scheduled Castes (NCSC) and the National Commission for Minorities (NCM), of which Hasan was until recently a member, which focuses on religious minorities, especially Muslims and Christians. Looking at the early years of the democracy, Hasan compares the governmental awareness and willingness to combat discrimination against Scheduled Castes (SCs) and Scheduled Tribes (STs) with the lack of political support for special treatment of (religious) minorities. Created in 1992 as part of a network of institutions aimed at implementing constitutional protections against discrimination, the NCSC has a number of weaknesses, but it has effectively promoted the political empowerment of SCs and STs; other areas (education, employment) show less improvement. The NCM, first launched in 1978 but achieving statutory status in 1992, has been relatively ineffective. Hasan argues that the rise of the Hindu Right is the primary reason why forward momentum in securing equality and nondiscrimination for minorities has been stalled. She argues for a stronger policy framework for the NCM, one that would ensure that it would really "act as a protector of the rights of minorities."

The management of the economy is one of the most important functions of any democracy, and choices made in this area have enormous impact on the standing of vulnerable groups. Economist Prabhat Patnaik examines government policy in the area of food, arguing that official claims of a decline in rural poverty are inaccurate: they cannot be squared with figures for actual foodgrain consumption per capita. Furthermore, urban poverty has also been worsening, measured by per capita calorie consumption. Patnaik then argues that neoliberal economic policies are to blame for the decline, together with increasing reliance on foreign investment and the increasing stranglehold of a few large corporations over the economy. Patnaik champions a revival of the role of the State as protector of peasant agriculture.

IV

Our historical essays all pointed to the critical importance, for democracy, of the institutions of civil society and the general shape of public culture. Returning to the theme of Bilgrami's and Nussbaum's essays, Gurcharan Das, an influential businessman, novelist, playwright, economic analyst, and commentator, laments the defensiveness about India's humanistic heritage that pervades secular society, including the schools. People everywhere associate an interest in the Hindu tradition with a right-wing ideological position. But the great texts of India's past, he argues, are not ideological weapons, but rich sources of deliberation and understanding for all citizens. (Subsequent to his essay for this volume, he has published *The Difficulty of Being Good*, a study of the Mahabharata that emphasizes its contribution to ethical reasoning and its tolerant and pluralistic elements.) Drawing on his own early education, Gurcharan Das argues that the study of the past nourishes a questioning and tolerant spirit. Indians need to learn about this heritage, both literary and historical, so that it will not be hijacked by the fanatical and ideological Hindu Right.

Nabaneeta Dev Sen is one of India's leading poets and writers, and she offers a vigorous and vividly written reflection on the importance of poetry in India today and its role in fostering a culture of pluralism. Drawing on her work with a group of women writers, *Shoi*, she discusses the group's response to the Gujarat massacre, as the women vigorously defended the freedom of speech and issued calls to courage and outspokenness. All writers, she then argues, are activists, and she illustrates the transformative power of art by discussion of a controversial political play. She further illustrates these themes from her own career, both as a poet and as a prose writer.

Like Gurcharan Das and Nussbaum, journalist and translator Pratik Kanjilal laments the decline of the humanities in the public culture. He begins by discussing the polarization of debate, as positions are squeezed into sharply opposed ideological camps and moderate positions are either ignored or misrepresented. Kanjilal blames the BJP for this polarization, but he also finds fault with prior governments, which have deemphasized the study of India's past in the schools and have not shown respect for moderate positions. Describing his experience as translator of the Hindu conservative writer Nirmal Verma, Kanjilal shows that a voice that is conservative but not ideological can all too easily be represented as part of a monolithic "Hindu Right" entity, and its subtle recommendations ignored. He blames this misunderstanding on a lack of education about religion, and argues (echoing Bilgrami) that India needs to recapture the pluralistic and humanistic public culture of Gandhi's movement. He worries that the marginalization of religion and the humanities leaves moderate citizens nothing to love or identify with: the secular state has become too cold and remote from people's real lives, unloving and unlovable.

The study of India's history in schools is an indispensable building block of a healthy democratic culture. It is here that young people learn skills of inquiry that they will carry with them into the political realm; and it is here that they learn the struggles for a pluralistic Indian identity that characterize the formation of the nation. Mushirul Hasan's essay on textbooks shows how this terrain has become a battleground between the Hindu Right and its adversaries. Chronicling the rewriting of national-level history textbooks during the ascendancy of the BJP, Hasan shows that the substitute books were marred by falsification and ideological slanting—as well as by sloppiness and incompetence. The details of this essay are alarming, for they show the ease with which an utterly slanted view of history can be purveyed as correct if historians do not stand up and protest. Fortunately, they did protest, and this essay (which has been previously published) forms part of the critical public culture that eventually unmasked the enterprise and contributed to the survival of a healthy pluralism.

V

Women constitute almost half of India's population, and their role in the democracy has been enormous, since before the founding. Although women continue to suffer from great inequalities and deprivations, the nation, from its beginnings, dedicated itself to the full inclusion of women as equal citizens, and has aggressively pursued that goal—for example in the constitutional amendments that guaranteed women one-third representation in the *panchayats*, or local village councils. It is well known that women's organizations of many types play an important role in the democracy, and our essays illustrate that diversity. Ritu Menon, founder of a women's publishing house and its lead editor, as well as an author of several books of history and empirical social science, looks at women's work for peace. Studying a variety of women's groups, but focusing on the Naga Mothers' Association (NMA), she shows how they attempt to deal with a range of social problems, but particularly with ethnic and tribal violence. The NMA argues that violence against women will never stop unless these other forms of violence are also stopped. The group has brought international attention to human rights violations in the Naga Territory, particularly sexual violence. From this basis, Menon then develops a more general analysis of gendered power relations in South Asia, showing that women ubiquitously play an important role in conflict resolution. Their practice of a "politics of understanding" provides, Menon argues, a model of how the democratic process ought to be carried out, and also of the importance of inclusion in democratic dialogue.

Historian Tanika Sarkar turns her attention to the Hindu Right, finding two contrasting patterns. On the one hand, the Hindu Right has been responsible for a large amount of violence against Hindu and Christian women. Its violent ideology includes a strong note of gender domination. However, the Hindu Right also contains its own women's groups, and these groups create an ideology of female aggression and violence. Offering as background a more general history of the Sangh Parivar and its rise to power, she describes its paradoxical operations in the area of gender, showing how the female Samiti participated in the violence at Ayodhya, and share the obsession of the men of the Hindu Right with alleged overbreeding by Muslims. They even defend the rape of Muslim women as a patriotic act.

VI

Many Indians currently live outside India. Non-Resident Indians (NRIs) include people who retain their Indian citizenship and a far larger number of expatriates with strong loyalty and family ties to India. This community—known as the Indian Diaspora—is very wealthy, and therefore capable of having immense influence over the direction of Indian politics. In the United States, where forty percent of people of Indian origin are from Gujarat, ties to the Hindu Right are strong, and the problematic actions of this NRI community form the topic of our final section. Paul Courtright is a scholar of Hindu religion at Emory

University who faced over a thousand death threats in response to his scholarly book on the Hindu god Ganesha, since members of the Hindu Right were not pleased by his depiction (based closely on ancient texts) of the nonwarlike and childlike sexuality of that god. His experience is not atypical: his essay examines links between Indian studies, religious studies, and Hindu nationalism in fostering attacks on scholars. Although Hindu studies were once practiced in a denigrating manner, through a Western lens, contemporary religious studies promotes a nonjudgmental historical and comparative investigation that does not have a normative agenda. And yet people unacquainted with the scholarship easily believe that Western-trained scholars are trying to denigrate their religion and humiliate them. This tendency is exploited by the Hindu Right, particularly within the United States, who rely on the fact that most of their Internet audience have not actually read the works in question. In conclusion, Courtright uses his own personal connection with Ganesha to illustrate the way in which myths cross national and religious lines: stories have no owners.

Wendy Doniger, a historian of religions and translator of ancient Sanskrit texts, discusses the effect of the rise of Hindutva (an extreme nationalist view of Hinduism) upon the writing of Indian history both in India and in the United States. Recent successful attempts to suppress the publication of textbooks and books that tell a story which conflicts with the BJP party line on Indian history (including Doniger's book *The Hindus: An Alternative History*) have already discouraged other authors and publishers from producing such books. India after Independence could boast of robust protections for freedom of speech and press; it remains to be seen how those protections will survive under the new regime. And in America, the increasingly vocal Hindu American community continues to argue that only Hindus have a right to read and teach about Hinduism—an agenda that Doniger, like Courtright, sees as posing a serious threat to the study of Hinduism within the Enlightenment traditions of the American academy.

A political scientist whose scholarship focuses on Gujarati civil society, Mona Mehta studies the political links between the Gujarati diaspora in North America and Gujarat, focusing on the events of 2002. She studies how the diaspora, a powerful source of funding for Narendra Modi, Gujarat's chief minister, creates a vision of the homeland, realizing it through social activities and financial support. This group supported Modi even after evidence of his complicity in the riots was revealed, and sought to bring him to the United States, although the State Department eventually denied him a visa on account of his complicity in religious violence. Mehta studies the outraged reaction to the visa denial, which enhanced Modi's appeal in India. Mehta then examines Modi's post-2002 reelection campaign, called "vibrant Gujarat," which portrayed Modi as a hero of economic development seeking to erase the stigma of the riots and the visa denial. She concludes that the Gujarati diaspora is different from other diasporas around the world because of its ambition to control political events back home.

Ved Nanda's "The Hindu Diaspora in the United States" is different from all the other essays in this volume, because it is written by a leading member of the Hindu Right, broadly conceived. Nanda, a law professor at the University of Denver, is a recognized scholar in the area of international human rights law. At the time of the conference he was the head of the HSS, which is the American version of the RSS, the leading social organization of the Hindu Right. (HSS stands for Hindu Swayamsevak Sangh, "Hindu Corps of Volunteers," since Rashtriya Swayamsevak Sangh, "National Corps of Volunteers," would make no sense in the US context.) As reported in Nussbaum's *The Clash Within: Democracy, Religious Violence, and India's Future* (2007), which drew on a taped interview with Nanda, he assumed leadership of the group in part to urge them in a more constructive and less polarizing direction. In the essay he clearly speaks as an advocate, both for the group and for Hindus in the United States. Our decision to include him in the conference and the volume reflects our belief that a diversity of perspectives serves understanding, and that Nanda is in good faith and seeks a constructive role for his association, although he is obviously highly constrained in what he can say about recent events. Nanda's paper describes the achievements of Hindus in the United States and the activities of various organizations of the Hindu diaspora in founding religious and social institutions in the United States. He then describes charitable work done by these organizations in both India and the United States. He explicitly denounces violence as "not an acceptable solution," but he does maintain that some of the attacks on Hindu organizations in the United States have been based on misinformation. He concedes that some Hindus have "perhaps reacted rather too harshly" to what they perceive as negative stereotypes of Hinduism, and argues that the solution is to focus on the good work these organizations can do in establishing human rights education programs. And yet he continues the line that Courtright and Doniger found problematic, by claiming that Hindu studies need to be taught more often by practicing Hindus, and by alleging that portrayals of Hinduism by non-Hindus are unbalanced. He urges the Hindu diaspora to take the initiative to "enter into a respectful dialogue with scholars to exchange ideas, present views, and find common ground."

VII

Our volume concurs in a number of urgent conclusions. First, democracy can be kept healthy only by a vigorous and argumentative critical culture, and this culture, in turn, must be supported by a courageous press, unrestricted by either political pressure or fashion. To the extent that journalistic values of bold investigation and truth-telling have been compromised in recent years, a renewal is badly needed. A critical culture must also be fostered by good teaching in schools, which should present history accurately and teach students how to assess historical evidence. More generally, students should learn to think inquisitively and critically, using argument to probe the political messages that are brought their way.

Second, there are a number of concrete steps that the State itself can take to foster a healthy democratic public culture: it can nourish multiparty competition, insist on holding state officials accountable for misdeeds, and use President's Rule sparingly but wisely in times of violence. Furthermore, in addition to commissions established to foster the interests of lower castes and minorities, government can and should also take concrete steps to empower these groups in education and employment. Economic policy should foster democracy by empowering the rural poor and working aggressively to raise the standard of basic nutrition and health enjoyed by India's poorest citizens.

Third, public culture must also take thought for the humanistic and emotional aspects of democracy, feeding the heart as well as stimulating the mind. This goal can be accomplished in many ways: by public support for the humanities and the arts, both in schools and universities and as aspects of the public culture, and by encouraging civil society institutions that provide a counterweight to the rabid but highly effective groups organized by the Hindu Right. At the same time, true religious freedom must be defended against the forces of chauvinism.

Women are key players in a healthy democracy, and government must show respect for their role by protecting them from violence, in the home and abroad, by criminal law reform that promotes speedy and fair trials for sexual crimes, and by making it clear that a female citizen is neither a victim nor a tigerish aggressor. Since women's movements are effective in the struggle for peace and for intergroup reconciliation, government can support them in their work. Finally, at a deeper level, political leaders can encourage all citizens to think of Indian masculinity in a way that does not link being a "real man" with aggression against the "other" (whether female or Muslim), and that shows compassion and restraint as essential attributes of manly strength. Gandhi began this rethinking of masculinity, but it has gotten lost somewhere, and a revival of his critical spirit is badly needed.

The US community of Non-Resident Indians plays an important part in India's future. It is unfortunate that so much of this community is organized along sectarian lines, both Hindu and Muslim: one should encourage nonsectarian groups where people of Indian origin can meet in a climate of respectful exchange. Within the groups that currently hold sway it is urgent to encourage a climate of respectful dialogue, in which scholars are no longer demeaned or threatened and their good faith and expertise are respected. In this way, both scholars and group members may increasingly join in a fruitful dialogue about the past and the present that will make a positive contribution to the Indian democracy's future.

Borrowing Nehru's words, we can add that "these dreams are for India, but they are also for the world." The analysis this volume offers illuminates not only the past and future of one nation, but the prospects of democracy in all.

Notes

1. These events have been analyzed in many places: see, for example, Martha Nussbaum's *The Clash Within: Democracy, Religious Violence, and India's Future* (Cambridge, MA: Harvard University Press, 2007).
2. Sen, *The Argumentative Indian* (New York: Farrar, Straus, and Giroux, 2005).
3. See Martha Nussbaum, "Land of My Dreams: Islamic Liberalism Under Fire in India," *The Boston Review* 34 (March/April 2009), 10–14. Reprinted in *The Idea of a University: Jamia Millia Islamia*, ed. Rakhshanda Jalil (New Delhi: Aakar, 2009), 13–28.

THE PAST AND THE PRESENT

1 THE POLITICS OF HISTORY

Amartya Sen

This chapter, and the lecture presented at a conference in Chicago in November 2005 on which it is based, are moved by two main concerns.[1] One is the need for clarity in understanding the relevance of history in our thinking about contemporary affairs. Some of our prominent intellectuals are critical—rightly I think—of citing Indian history as a reason for doing anything in contemporary India, and they see in this, appropriately enough, a danger of being imprisoned in history. And yet we cannot ignore the fact that history has a profound influence on our thinking and on our concerns, and to take note of those connections, with critical assessment, is not the same as being a prisoner of the past.

In discussing this issue I shall illustrate the arguments involved by considering and commenting on the views on this subject expressed by one of the leading intellectuals of India, Ramachandra Guha, in the course of his extremely engaging—and enlightening—review of my book, *The Argumentative Indian*.[2] Guha's forcefully presented contention that I attach too much importance to history, and also make anachronistic use of modern ideas by making them look older (he thinks) than they actually are, certainly deserves serious attention.[3] And related to that personal disagreement there is the much larger issue of the relevance of history, if any, for our understanding and assessment of contemporary affairs.

When the Chicago conference took place in November 2005, Guha's paper, published earlier in the year, was much under discussion, which is perhaps less so now. However, despite the passage of time—in the period close to a decade that separates the conference and the publication of this volume—the relevance of the questions that Guha was raising has not gone away. Guha was, in fact, speaking for many Indian intellectuals in taking the invoking of history in contemporary policy discussions to be largely a distraction and an unfortunate diversion.

My other concern relates not so much to the importance of history, but to the *kind* of history that we invoke in discussing contemporary affairs. My focus here is on the need to have an inclusive and open-minded understanding of history, rather than taking a narrow and sectarian view. There is a serious danger in India, given the fact that a large majority of Indians are Hindus—in one sense or another—that the reading of Indian history might reflect the biases of majoritarian politics. This has, in fact, happened in recent decades, often accompanied by considerable sectarian belligerence, directly connected with the form that the powerful Hindutva movement has tended to take.[4]

The recognition of the pluralist character of Indian society and culture, including the value of respecting this plurality, has a strong historical background, stretching over a long period—more than two thousand years—including the political philosophy and jurisprudence emerging from the ethical and legal pronouncements of Ashoka and Akbar. There are serious threats both to epistemic veracity and to sound practical reasoning in the promotion of an artificially narrow Hindutva reading of India's past, downgrading other sources of Indian traditions, and ignoring the constructive interactions between distinct communities that give contemporary India the cultural and social richness it has. If the importance of critically assessed history is one of my concerns, the need for open-minded history is surely another. I start, in fact, with the second concern.

1. Independence and Beyond

When India became independent in 1947, the broad and inclusive concept of an Indian identity that had emerged during the long struggle for freedom tended to command a sweeping allegiance. There was a deep sense of tragedy associated with the partitioning of the subcontinent and the riots and violence that occurred at that time. There was a widely shared determination not only to have a secular democracy in what remained of India, after partition with Pakistan, but also to defend—and celebrate—India's multireligious and multicultural heritage. There was furthermore considerable pride, which was not altogether silly (as pride sometimes is), in the fact that despite the political pressure for what came to be called "an exchange of population," the bulk of the large Muslim community in the territory of independent India stayed on in India, rather than moving—or trying to move—to the new Islamic state of Pakistan.

The demographic basis of India's internal diversity has not, of course, changed. Even though more than 80 percent of Indians come from a Hindu background, there are large communities of Muslims, Sikhs, Christians, Jains, and Parsees, among other religious groups. In particular, India has one of the largest Muslim populations in the world—indeed it is the third largest Muslim country on the globe (behind Indonesia but neck and neck with Pakistan).

No less importantly, the interactions in everyday living and in cultural activities in India (in literature, music, art, science, cinema, theatre, or sports) are not divided along communal lines. For example, Ravi Shankar, the great musician and sitarist, may be contrasted with Ali Akbar Khan, the remarkable sarod player, on the basis of their particular mastery over different forms of Indian music, but never as a "Hindu musician" and a "Muslim musician," respectively. The same applies to other fields of cultural creativity, not excluding Bollywood—that peculiar pillar of Indian popular culture with unparalleled razzmatazz.

As it happens, just before the Chicago conference, I had published a book, *The Argumentative Indian*, in which one of the principal themes was the importance of understanding the long history and contemporary relevance of argumentative traditions in India. One of its ancillary themes concerned the contrast between that interactive tradition of tolerance and coprosperity championed for a long period in India and the more divisive sectarian view of India promoted by the narrow politics of one kind or another. What I discussed at the Chicago seminar drew on the analysis presented in my book published earlier in that year.

2. Hindutva and History

India's past has certainly become an ideological battleground. Political divisions in contemporary India are partly fought over India's antiquity. In the case of the particular influence of Hindutva politics, it can be asked: Why is the past so important to Hindutva activists? I would argue that the answer lies in two specific features of contemporary Hindu politics. The first is the need for the Hindutva movement to keep together its diverse components and to generate fresh loyalty for potential recruits.

The hard-core of Hindutva advocates is, in fact, relatively small in number—but around them cluster a much larger group who may be called "proto-Hindutva" believers, who are typically less zealous than the Hindutva champions but who could nevertheless be moved in the direction of Hindutva by a sense of pride associated with their Hindu identity. While the Hindutva movement is intellectually impatient and also politically compromised by its association with intolerance and violence, this broader group of proto-Hindutva believers are typically quite opposed to violence, and are much happier with cultural pride than with sectarian butchery.

The second reason for focusing on India's past is the large support for the Hindutva movement that comes from the Indian diaspora abroad, particularly in North America and Europe, for whom it is quite important to be able to retain their general Indian nationalist attachment along with any other loyalty they may be persuaded to have (such as Hindutva). The two can be harnessed together by a Hinduized view of Indian history, which fosters an imagined congruence of a Hindu identity with a more general Indian identity. I have discussed these issues in my book *The Argumentative Indian*. It is not hard to understand why having bendable history is important for Hindutva politics.

Of course, there have also been other sources of misunderstanding and misrepresentation of Indian history.

Aside from distortions coming from other sources in contemporary India reflecting different kinds of political bias, there is also a long tradition of grand imperial history—stretching from James Mill and Lord Macaulay to the pronouncements of Winston Churchill on India's past—crafting an imagined history far removed from the available evidence on the past of India (as I have also discussed in *The Argumentative Indian*). Mill's extraordinarily lopsided account of Indian history was backed by the state power of the Raj, and his peculiarly biased book on the history of India was compulsory reading for British civil servants being sent to govern India.

Distortions can indeed come from different parts of Indian politics, and continue to do so. In a pluralist democracy this is, to a great extent, inescapable. What was particularly jarring in the official rewriting of Indian history in the previous period of Hindutva-sympathetic political rule (during 1998 to 2005), however, was the mixing up of myths and facts (for example, taking the great literary epic *Ramayana* to be actual history, a confusion against which Rabindranath Tagore, among others, had warned), and then using governmental power to ram that dubious history home—in textbooks for students, in particular. Since there are some serious signs of such a danger resurfacing again right now (as I finalize this paper, in 2014), in view of the belligerent pronouncements of some Hindutva advocates, the need to draw attention to the problem may be particularly urgent at this time. The possible prospects of sponsored distortion, combined with the increasing use of legal threats to silence other readings of history by threatening publishers with legal suits (making skillful use of the outdated Indian penal codes, which badly need reform), poses a serious danger for intellectual freedom in general in India, and for open-minded historical understanding in particular.

The rewritten Indian history, which occurred in the earlier period of Hindutva power, was oddly at variance with the more traditional—and more inclusive—readings of the history of the country, which have had sustained support of serious scholars of Indian history both within and outside India. It was also greatly at variance with some of the thoroughly established understandings of India's past, including its ancient past (for example, the pre-Sanskritic nature of the Indus Valley civilization, placing it well before the emergence of the Vedic literature). Going against massive historical data to construct an official version at variance with overwhelming factual evidence is something that must be shunned.

I must, however, add here a note of optimism despite the grimness of the potential danger. We are getting conflicting signals from the government, which in the present context is not a bad thing. On the one hand, I must say that in my recent personal experience as the chancellor of the re-established Nalanda University, I have seen no attempt whatsoever on the part of the new BJP government to influence academic decisions, and there has been clear evidence of the inclination of the political leaders involved with this particular project to abstain from interference, and to support academic excellence. And yet there are signals coming from other parts of the government, for example in the organization of Indian historical records, that indicate no great reluctance to intervene in a narrowly Hindutva direction.

The fact is that any government in office tends to take note of different influences coming from different sources, varying from internal diversity *within* the ruling party to the threat of political opposition in a democratic country with a reasonably free media. Informed discussion of the potential dangers of sectarian history can make a contribution to resisting it, and must not be seen as a prognostication that the direst scenario of sectarianism is inevitable.

3. Has India Been One Country?

I have so far been talking about "India" as if it is a well-defined concept. Some see this as an illegitimate use of a concept that does not have such definiteness. In his thoughtful (and largely kind) review of my book, Ramachandra Guha complains: "Throughout this book, Sen uses the term 'India' anachronistically; speaking of a time long before its meaning was known or the political and cultural unity it presumes ever existed."[5]

Others—many of them aligned to the Hindutva movement—accept the legitimacy of the idea of India as a historical entity, but only on the ground of the unity provided by the overarching presence of Hinduism across the alleged country. The idea of India gets capsulated in the idea of Hinduism as a unifying force.

I shall argue against both these positions. The latter view is more easily challenged than the former general skepticism, if only because what we now call

India has always been mixed in its religious background. This applies not only to medieval and modern India, but even to ancient India. Indeed, for more than a thousand years of ancient history, India had a huge presence of—and for many centuries political rule by—Buddhists. The great fourteenth-century philosophical compendium *Sarvadarshana-samgraha*, by Madhava Acharya, devotes the first two chapters respectively to Lokayata (agnostic and atheistic materialism) and to Buddhism. Surely, Hinduism as a part of the cultural background in India would have had a role in the flourishing of a pluralist India—as did the advocacy of Buddha and Ashoka, and later Akbar—but to think of the unity of the country in terms of Hinduism alone (as Hindutva history tends to do) would be a serious mistake.

I turn now to the skepticism well-articulated by Guha, as I have just quoted. Can we really talk about India as a historical entity? The very idea of "India" or of "Indians" in premodern contexts appears to many observers as being basically a confusion—perhaps an amiable confusion, but confusion nevertheless. The issue of Indian unity has been problematic over the past. It is also easy to see that the formation of a specific state called the Republic of India has given the idea of India a definiteness now that it could not have enjoyed many centuries ago. Underlying a critique of the kind that Guha articulates is a search for a level of precision that the subject of historical unity may not readily provide. There is a huge methodological problem here of the viability and usability of an irreducibly complex and ambiguous concept in public discussion and communication.

I would resist this exclusion-oriented line of reasoning and would argue that if ambiguity gave us definitive ground for abandoning any concept (no matter whether the subject matter itself has a corresponding ambiguity or not), we would do some injustice not only to history but also to social analysis of nearly every kind. As Aristotle noted (speaking of political science), the "account of this science will be adequate if it achieves such clarity as the subject matter allows; for the same degree of precision is not to be expected in all discussions, any more than in all the products of handicraft."[6] We must make room for the inherent ambiguities of many political, social, and cultural concepts, such as poverty, inequality, class, or community. We have to reflect adequately the substantial concerns that make us use—and worry about—these issues, and we cannot sensibly seek a false precision that ends up making a concept the mechanical vehicle of a much impoverished idea. If a concept includes some ambiguity, then that is the kind of concept it is.

The potential unity of India despite so much historical—and persistent— diversity has baffled many observers. When, for example, Winston Churchill made the momentous announcement that India was no more a country than was the equator, it is evident that his intellectual imagination was severely strained by the difficulty of seeing how so much diversity could fit into the conception of what can be seen as anything like a country. The British belief—which was very common in imperial days and is not entirely absent now—that it is the Raj that has somehow "created" India reflects not only a pride in alleged authorship, but also some bafflement about the possibility of accommodating so much heterogeneity within the coherent limits of what could be taken to be, in some sense, one country.

And yet general statements about India and Indians can be found throughout history, beginning from the ancient days of Alexander the Great—and of course Apollonius (who was something of a regional specialist on India in Greek higher education). Megasthenes in the third century B.C.E. authored the highly influential (if somewhat embellished) account of India in his book *Indika*. This idea of a country of Indians continued through the medieval days of Arab and Iranian visitors. When an Iranian mathematician named Al Beruni, born in 973 A.D., visited India, learned Sanskrit, and wrote a remarkable book called *Ta'rikh al-hind* ("The History of India"), he was talking about a country that he saw as India—a thousand years ago. That tradition of talking about India continued all the way to the European Enlightenment, with heroic generalizations about India presented by Herder, Schelling, Schlegel, and Schopenhauer, among many others.[7]

It is also interesting to note that in the seventh century C.E., when the Chinese scholar Yi Jing returned to China after spending ten years in India (mostly studying at the old Nalanda university), he was moved to ask the question: "Is there anyone, in the five parts of India, who does not admire China?"[8] That rhetorical question incorporates a unity of attitudes in the country as a whole, despite its divisions, including its "five parts."

The idea of taking India as some kind of a whole (despite many acknowledged ambiguities within the idea), can be seen in generalizations made at home, and not just penned by foreigners. Emperor Akbar, whose ideas of the country I have discussed in some detail in my book, *The Argumentative Indian,* is one of the characters in Indian history who would not accept that their regime was complete until the bulk of what they took to be one country was under their respective rule. In this respect Akbar's sense of geographic integrity was not dissimilar to that of other ambitious and energetic emperors, like Chandragupta Maurya, Ashoka, and the later Chandragupta of the Gupta dynasty, among others.

Indeed, the wholeness of India, despite all its variations, has consistently invited recognition and response. This was not entirely irrelevant to the British conquerors either, who—right from the eighteenth century—had a more integrated conception of India than Churchill would have been able to construct around the equator. Indeed, even the *pre-imperial* travelers from Britain also

tended to see India as a country. This clearly applies, for example, to that determined English tourist Ralph Fitch, who roamed around India in the sixteenth
century, and also to a number of others who undertook similar explorations of
an exciting—if strange—country (on this see William Foster's *Early Travels in
India*).[9]

4. Science and Literary Pursuits

The features of India's unity vary greatly with the context. Some of them are
more often recollected than others, though they all have their specific relevance. To consider a less discussed feature, take the scientific and cultural
relevance of the city of Ujjain, in the early centuries of the first millennium
C.E. It came to be treated as the location of the principal meridian for Indian
calendars, serving as something like an Indian Greenwich.[10] It still, nearly
two thousand years later, serves as something of an approximation to the
base of the Indian standard time today, and it emerged a long time before
Greenwich itself became the basis of the Greenwich Mean Time (the GMT).
That technical development clearly had much to do with the location of the
imperial power dominant in India as well as that of scientific research at that
time. Ujjain (or Ujjayini, as it was then called), as an ancient Indian city,
moved from its role as the capital of Avanti (later, Malwa) in the seventh century B.C.E. to become the capital of the Shaka royalty, and most prominently
served as the base of the later Gupta dynasty in the period of the flowering of
Indian mathematics and science.

Ujjain was, as it happens, also the home of many leaders of India's literary
and cultural world, including the poet Kalidasa, in the fifth century. It was that
connection, rather than the scientific one, that attracted E. M. Forster—that
profound observer of India—to Ujjain in 1914. He was struck by the lack of
contemporary interest in the history of that ancient Indian city: as he noted,
with some sadness, "Old buildings are buildings, ruins are ruins."[11] In Kalidasa's
long poem *Meghadutam*, which presented a hauntingly united view of India as a
country with very rich variations within it, we hear a banished man, who asks a
cloud to carry across India his message of love and longing to his faraway partner.
Kalidasa makes the lonely lover insist that the cloud must undertake a detour to
see the magnificence of Ujjain—his own city.

Of course here, too—as elsewhere in his sensuous writings—Kalidasa cannot
resist dwelling on the seductive feminine charm that could be found there, something that the Hindutva movement might have found particularly objectionable.[12] When Forster visits modern Ujjain, he recollects Kalidasa's description of

the beauty of Ujjayini women and how the fifth-century city livened up in the evening as "women steal to their lovers" through "darkness that a needle might divide." The thundering cloud is firmly instructed:

> Though it diverts you on your way northward,
> Do not fail to see the roofs of Ujjayini's stuccoed palaces—
> If you are not enchanted there by the way the city women's eyes
> Tremble in alarm at your bolts of lightening,
> You are cheated.[13]

Kalidasa seem to combine his observation of diverse charms and beauties across India with a determination to provide a large view of the entire land that lies in its journey from one end of India to another, on a route that the poet determines for the messenger cloud.

Similarly, Akbar not only noted the variations across India, but made serious attempts at some standardization also. Indeed, both his abortive move to initiate an integrated calendar for India, the Tarikh-ilahi, and his unsuccessful efforts to have a synthetic religion, the Din-ilahi, drawing on the different religions known in India, reflected a constructive search for an overarching unity, combined with a firm acknowledgment of plurality. The recognition of heterogeneity has much to do with an understanding of India's qualified solidarity that emerges in these diverse literary, scientific, and political efforts. Neither a homogenous conception of a unitary India (linked with Hinduism or any other allegedly overarching unity), nor a view of isolated fragments, could take the place of the ambiguous but coherent idea of India that had emerged well before the establishment of the British Raj in India.

5. Is History Relevant?

Another question of significance concerns the relevance of history in the context of political and social discussions in contemporary India. The Hindutva theorists do, of course, base their view of India on a certain reading of Indian history, but the question can be raised as to whether it makes sense to spend time and effort in showing that particular reading of history to be factually erroneous. Guha goes further to dispute what he takes to be my view that "the distant past must somehow guide how one acts in the present"—a view that he repudiates.[14]

I would repudiate that view as well, and I fear the view attributed to me by Guha is *not* mine.[15] We have reason to take note of our past, both because it influences our sense of identity and because those with whom we argue may attach huge importance to a particular reading of history—or alleged history. But there is no reason at all why this understanding should take us to the extreme position view that the distant past must somehow guide how one acts in the present.

Guha is right to refer to the fact that not only did Mahatma Gandhi reject a full dependence on history, but also "Bankim Chandra Chatterjee had pointed to the hazards, in fighting battles of the present, of invoking ideas and individuals from a very distant past."[16] Not only do I not dissent from that judgment, I am also pleased to find a generalization made by Bankim with which I can readily agree (there are topics on which I fear this is not easy for me to achieve, given Bankim's very special reading of Indian culture, despite the greatness of his literary contributions).

Guha's attribution to me is clearly mistaken, but his question is certainly important. How relevant is our understanding of history for contemporary discussions, and if it is at all important, why does it, in fact, have this significance? I have tried to address this question elsewhere, in an essay called "On Interpreting India's Past." The reasoning I have tried to present there drew on a general understanding that while we cannot live *within* our past, we cannot live *without* it either.

> We live in the present, but that is a tiny bit of time—it passes as we talk . . . . Our identities are strongly influenced by the past. The self-perceptions that characterize a group are associated with, and to a great extent defined by, the shared memories and recollections of the past, and by the agreed priorities and implicit allegiances that draw on those evocations.[17]

The interpretation of India's past cannot but be sensitive to the concerns of today. Our identities cannot be defined independently of our traditions and past, but this does not indicate a linear sequence whereby we interpret our past first, and then arrive at our identity, equipped to face contemporary issues. On the contrary, our reading of the past and understanding of the present are interdependent, and the selectional criteria that are central to interpreting the past have to take note of the relevance of the different concerns in the contemporary world.

Central to the role of history in contemporary affairs is the way our understanding of history makes us see ourselves—and others—in terms of our self-conception, which is deeply influenced by what we think actually happened.

6. Muslim Conquest and India

Consider the way the Muslim conquest of India is viewed in different readings of Indian history. A particularly narrow view, emphasizing only the brutalities that went with the wars and conquests, has received championing—not only from the Hindutva school, but from many other writers. For example, in his engaging study of the history of Hinduism, Nirad C. Chaudhuri notes that his chosen point for concluding his historical survey is the end of the twelfth century, since by then "the structure of Hindu religious life was fully erected, and the later changes only extended it without in any way modifying the character of the system."[18]

I had to address this issue and examine the veracity of Nirad Chaudhuri's diagnosis, while writing a foreword to the reprint of my grandfather Kshiti Mohan Sen's book *Hinduism*, originally published in 1960.[19] Kshiti Mohan's account devotes a good deal of time to the constructive intellectual and cultural influences of Islamic thought on Hindu ideas and practices, especially through the interactions between the Hindu Bhakti movement and Islamic Sufi beliefs, and these interactions became very intense from the sixteenth century onward, particularly in the poetry of Kabir, Dadu, Mirabai, and others—and elsewhere, for example in Bengal in the form of the integrated culture and poetry of the Bauls. In the difference between Chaudhuri and Kshiti Mohan Sen, factual issues are quite central: Did such interactions, in fact, occur after Chaudhuri's closure, in the twelfth century, of the history of Hinduism?

That question is not hard to settle; they did. But it is not the only aspect of this debate, since the existence and the nature of these interactions cannot but be relevant to contemporary concerns, including political and social issues related to the acknowledgement of Muslim contributions to Indian culture, including—in this case—even Hindu traditions and literature. The importance of what Chaudhuri chooses to omit (in fact, firmly excludes) must depend on how we link our reading of the past with our contemporary concerns.

Chaudhuri's view of Indian history thus has relevance to both practical reason and epistemology. In discussing what he sees as the effect of the Muslim conquest, Chaudhuri concentrates not on the interactions of ideas, but instead on the destruction of Hindu temples by Muslim assailants: "Over seven centuries from the eleventh to the end of the seventeenth all the great cities of northern India dating from Hindu times were sacked by Muslim invaders and conquerors of India."[20] There is, of course, much truth in this statement (even though there is some exaggeration as well). However, to take this to be the preeminent truth and to ignore the constructive interactions between Hindus and Muslims in religious thinking (in addition to the creative interrelations in literature, music, painting, architecture, science, and medicine) not only raises questions of veracity, but also of the significance of divorcing one bit of reality from others importantly present in a fuller picture.

7. A Concluding Remark

In terms of our conception of ourselves and of others around us, there is a clear need to link our present with our past—not in the sense that the past must guide our present, but in the sense that references to the past are relevant to our contemporary reflections, and also because the interest we take in different features of the past are influenced by our contemporary concerns.

To consider a different kind of example, the fact that the work of Hindu mathematicians became known in Christian Europe through the efforts of Muslim Arabs and Iranians is relevant not only to the history of science, but also to our present-day concerns about the relation between Hindus and Muslims. Again, consider the fact that it was Al Beruni, the Muslim mathematician from Iran, who provided the earliest overall assessment of the achievements of Indian mathematicians and of their importance for the world of mathematics—beginning with Arab and Iranian mathematics, which would later help to reshape European mathematics. There are many such constructive interactions in Indian history, and their factual veracity is not, in fact, irrelevant to the way history has to be assessed in the context of our contemporary social and political concerns.

It is the miniaturized view of India in the sectarian accounts that makes it particularly important to see India's past in an adequately broad light. My disagreement with the Hindutva reading of history does not lie in any belief that they are wrong to see history as relevant to our present-day concerns; they are certainly right there. The disagreement lies, rather, in the lack of veracity, as I have illustrated, in the particular view of Indian history that Hindutva presents. There is something to argue here, and I am ready to join that argument. But we cannot reasonably take the view that history is irrelevant for our present-day concerns—a kind of weakness of the will.

I end by restating my thesis that we do not have to live *within* history to be able to understand that we cannot live *without* history either. It is necessary for us to have open-minded history, taking note of the evidence that exists. And this is because history is important—and not irrelevant.

Notes

1. "India: Implementing Pluralism and Democracy," conference at the Center for Comparative Constitutionalism and the Martin Marty Center of the University of Chicago, November 11–12, 2005.
2. *The Argumentative Indian* (London: Penguin, and New York: FSG, 2005).
3. Ramachandra Guha, "Arguments with Sen," *Economic and Political Weekly*, 40, October 8–14, 2005.
4. "Hindutva" is a newly coined Sanskrit word that literally means "the quality of Hinduism," or "of Hindu culture." But in the practical context, it represents a school of thought and a set of political priorities, seeing India in primarily Hindu terms.
5. Guha, "Arguments with Sen," p. 4422.
6. Aristotle, *Nicomachean Ethics*, Book One, section iii; in the translation by J.A.K. Thomson, *The Ethics of Aristotle: The Nicomachean Ethics* (London: Penguin, revised edition, 1976), pp. 64–65.
7. For references to these literatures, see *The Argumentative Indian*.
8. See J. Takakusu's translation of Yi Jing's book, *A Record of the Buddhist Religions as Practised in India and Malay Archipelago* (Oxford: Oxford University Press, 1896), p. 136.
9. William Foster, ed., *Early Travels in India* (Oxford: Oxford University Press, 1921).
10. Ujjain had to compete initially with Benares, which is an older city. The early astronomical work *Paulisha Siddhanta*, which preceded Aryabhata's major break-through in the fifth century, focused its attention on longitudes at three places in the world: Ujjain, Benares, and Alexandria. On this see chapter 15 ("India through Its Calendars") in *The Argumentative Indian*.
11. E. M. Forster, "Nine Gems of Ujjain," in *Abinger Harvest* (Harmondsworth: Penguin, 1936, 1974), pp. 324–27.
12. There was an attempt by some militants of Hindu politics even to ban Valentine Day cards in India. Given the mundane nature of these cards, I am not able to determine readily whether Kalidasa would have found the cards to be almost as disappointing as the censorship.
13. Translation from Barbara Stoler Miller, *The Plays of Kalidasa* (Delhi: Motilal Banarasidass, 1999), pp. 5–6.
14. Guha, p. 4424.
15. On this see my "Our Past and Present," *Economic and Political Weekly*, 41 (2006); this was largely a response to Ramachandra Guha's critique of my book *The Argumentative Indian*.
16. Guha, p. 4424.
17. "On Interpreting India's Past," in Sugata Bose and Ayesha Jalal, eds., *Nationalism, Democracy and Development* (New Delhi: Oxford University Press, 1996), p. 10.

18. Nirad C. Chaudhuri, *Hinduism: A Religion to Live By* (Oxford: Oxford University Press, 1979), p. 100.
19. Kshiti Mohan Sen, *Hinduism* (Harmondsworth: Penguin, 1960); new edition with an introduction by me (London: Penguin, 2005).
20. Chaudhuri, p. 125.

2 PLURALISM ON TRIAL IN LATE NINETEENTH-CENTURY INDIA

Mushirul Hasan

No one can fathom the mystery of another person.
Each individual in the world is like an undeciphered manuscript.[1]

—GHALIB

Seldom is one allowed to see a pageant of history whirl past, and partake in it too. Ever since becoming the capital in the early thirteenth century, imbibing knowledge and ideas and imparting cultures, becoming homogeneous and cosmopolitan in spite of the origins and ethnicity of its rulers and inhabitants, [Delhi] had remained the embodiment of a whole country, free of the creedal ghosts and apparitions that haunt some of modern India's critics and bibliographers chased by the dead souls of biased historians of yesterday.[2]

—AHMED ALI

We have created you from a male and a female, and We have made you into peoples and tribes so that you may come to know one another. The noblest among you in the eyes of God is the most pious, for God is omniscient and well informed.[3]

—QURAN 49.13.

1. Introduction

Long ago, the British Orientalist H. A. R. Gibb (1895–1971) discussed "the atomism, the discreteness, and the intensity of the Arab imagination, its resistance to synthetic constructions and, above all, its aversion to rationalism."[4] His conception of the "Arab imagination" is untenable, for the reformist and traditionalist strands are so mingled that any period in history must be considered and judged as a whole. This is best illustrated by the expression of deep-seated convictions by sections of the Muslim intelligentsia in nineteenth-century Delhi. Even though 1857 left indelible scars and ruins and the best men were seized with despair, the second half of the nineteenth century appears to be fairly creative in the evolution, articulation, and dissemination of modernist thinking. While the cramped sphere in which its proponents moved stifled intellectual activism, the historian must recognize that it was due to them, and to their impressive scholarly output, that upper India's Muslim communities, notably in Punjab and Uttar Pradesh (United Provinces), were held together.

The noteworthy point is that there was among them, with the notable exception of Altaf Husain Hail and a few more writers, no quest for a lost or submerged past whose ideal images and exemplars would serve as prototypes and models for social and cultural innovation. Whether it is the poet Ghalib or the historian Zakaullah, there is no attempt to establish the Mughal glory of the past to evoke in Muslims a parochial consciousness. Instead, they explained the reasons for Europe's strength to demonstrate that Muslims could adopt European concepts and methods without being untrue to their faith. They stubbornly maintained, while exalting the place of reason and freedom in Islam, that true Islam teaches the family virtues, the application of reason, and true equality; they argued that it was important to restore the rights, not of an outward and fossilized orthodoxy, but of the inward reason of Islam, and to reaffirm Islam's social values and cultural ideals in a world in which science and technology progressed. This could be done in such a way as to build a stable society endowed with a vigorous social order capable of playing an active and constructive role. The breadth of their appeal lay in their ability to reflect the aspirations of their time, as much as of their own people, and to speak in their own terms, both to the Urdu readers in their thousands and to educated elites of the cities.

Let us consider for a moment the kind of intellectual temper and inclinations that were widely diffused through the vast corpus of Urdu literature that Delhi alone produced. There is no consensus on defining modernism, a term used by Muslim thinkers such as Muhammad Abduh and Western scholars like C. C. Adams and Gibb, or on delineating sharply the contours of a modern way of life. Part of the problem lies in the philosophical predilections of those who regard themselves as *islahi* or modernists, their difficulty in seeing their own time in historical perspective, and the complexity of disentangling reform issues from the community's political entanglements and preferences. Under the circumstances, even when they rallied ordinary citizens to the banner of civic engagement to promote the public good, their position suffers from ambiguities. This is the burden of Sayyid Ahmad's arguments;[5] in fact, there are certain respects in which his own stance, a hybrid of liberalism and reform, is avowedly elitist, authoritarian, and indifferent to even friendly censure. Yet he and his colleagues, though maligned as apostates or unbelievers by some, read the signs of the times and used their sound critical judgment with a nice historical sense. They moved with the times, uncontrolled by theology, attacked the mumbo-jumbo of Muslim theologians, and nurtured a moral and transcendental vision of Islam.

In another work,[6] I have discussed certain prominent figures whose achievement differed so widely. They range from people like Sir Sayyid, who moved heaven and earth to convince his community of the importance of Western education; to historians like Zakaullah, novelists like Nazir Ahmad, writers like Hali, and to poets like Ghalib. While none of them achieved quite the recognition or gained quite the luster that surrounded their counterparts in other regions, their scholarly output was indeed impressive, and of some originality. Without being reformers of the type who go to the stake for their convictions, they each significantly affected the thoughts, feelings, and actions of a significant number of people in north India. In fact, even though historians have showed Sayyid Ahmad, Ghalib, Zakaullah, Nazir, and Hali a condescension they do not deserve, they stand as principled, conscientious individuals with the promise and perils of a new colonial modernity.

Broadly speaking, each of them was different from the others in their background, thinking, and aims. In the final reckoning, though, the spirit of Delhi's renaissance was present in each of them. When placed side by side, they appear to be in tune with the newer tendencies, not out of sympathy with them. Yielding to necessity and pointing to how 1857 brought the Muslim communities to the precipice, they engaged with changing Muslim attitudes toward modern education, reforming the Muslims from within, and creating a viable moral structure to fortify their confidence in their heritage, their present, and their future. Despite being sometimes vague and evasive in their recommendations, they were strongly and consistently wedded to the ideals of abnegation, self-sacrifice, and service, the basis of *adab*.

What legacy did such men leave behind? What was the impact of their main beliefs and their general outlook on life? To this, the answer is many-sided. In the first place, moderation was an essential part of their outlook, and without it they would not have survived. Their type of devotion was therefore well fitted to become the model for thinkers and reformers and publicists whose members were increasing rapidly in early twentieth century.

If we regard twentieth-century poet-philosopher Muhammad Iqbal as their most prominent interlocutor, it will not take long to discover that some of his ideas represent not only a departure from the traditional methodological prescriptions, but also contravene his previously declared principles. At the same time it is hard to dispute his stature or to deny his role as one of the key exponents of the most sweeping modernist reformulation of Islamic doctrine. Besides elaborating and refining Sayyid Ahmad's views on *ijtehad*, he talked of *ijma* or "consensus," one of the bases (*usul*) of the Islamic religious law, to revive and give the legal system an evolutionary character, and stated that "the claim of the present generation of Muslim liberals to reinterpret the foundational legal principles, in the light of their own experience and the altered conditions of modern life, is, in my opinion, perfectly justified."[7] Author of the chronogram inscribed on Sayyid Ahmad's tomb in the university mosque at Aligarh, Iqbal set its great reformer apart "as probably the first modern Muslim to catch a glimpse of the positive character of the age which was coming." According to him,

> The real greatness of the man consists in the fact that he was the first Indian
> Muslim who felt the need of a fresh orientation of Islam and worked for
> it. We may differ from his religious views, but there can be no denying the
> fact that his sensitive soul was the first to react to the modern age.[8]

In like manner, Nazir Ahmad and Ameer Ali shared certain views on polygamy, divorce, and widow remarriage. They shed disquieting light on the seclusion of women, and on their soul-destroying burdens of joyless domesticity. Ameer Ali held that the Prophet secured to women rights they had not previously possessed,[9] and that he restrained polygamy by limiting the maximum number of contemporaneous marriages to four. He regarded polygamy not only as "an unendurable evil," but hoped that a general synod of Muslim doctors would declare the practice, like slavery, as abhorrent to Islam.[10] He drew comfort from the ninety-five men out of every hundred Indian Muslims who were monogamists, either by conviction or by necessity, to conclude that polygamy did not find much favor among the educated classes.[11]

Purdah retarded Muslim advancement, observed Ameer Ali.[12] But this British-trained lawyer and jurist lapses into the familiar apologetic tone and rhetorical device with the remark that purdah had many advantages for the "unsettled and uncultured communities."[13] In the same narrative, though, he points out that "to suppose that [the Prophet] ever intended his recommendation should assume its present inelastic form, or that he ever allowed or enjoined the seclusion of women, is wholly contrary to the spirit of his reforms." He concludes with the rhetorical flourish: "The Koran itself affords no warrant for holding that the seclusion of women is a part of the new gospel."[14] The truth of the matter is simple: in general, Muslim reformers wanted to unveil women's mind without unveiling their faces.[15]

Although Ameer Ali did not strike a responsive note in the heart of his generation—for he was a Shia and an anglicized one—his arguments are far more advanced, if not progressive, than Sayyid Ahmad's stance on Muslim women's education or Iqbal's denunciation of the modern Western woman as heartless and devoid of womanhood.[16] What is more, their followers construed the views of these two men, especially during the high noon of the Pakistan movement in the 1940s, in an antirational direction.[17] Even though some adamantly hold the opinion that amid the ups and downs of politics Iqbal's "politics-mongering followers"[18] distorted his perspectives, the crux of the problem, one that confronted the Muslim modernists generally, is their inability to formulate a basic synthetic attitude and resolve the contradictions between things "Islamic" and otherwise. Shibli Numani mentioned this, though in general terms, while speaking at the Aligarh College in 1913.[19] A year earlier, he had been more explicit at his home turf in Nadwat al-ulama, when he told the assembled:

> If we remain inflexible in our attitudes rigidly and adhere to taqlid (*taqlid-i jamid*), we will be destroyed. In our trying times, we will not be able to compete with any one. Hence, we must take into account the changes in the world and, accordingly, the demands of religion. [We have] to consider the resources we can marshal to meet the requirements of the faith.[20]

The tension between the position of Iqbal, Ameer Ali, and the neomodernists and that of the religious orthodoxy assumed, for the most part, different forms in different periods. Yet common to their basic predicament was to decide what elements in the history of Islam should they emphasize and recombine for an effective self-statement to the existing challenges. What should they modify, and what should they reject?[21] Despite anxious heart-searching, reformers and thinkers like Sayyid Ahmad and Iqbal found it extremely tricky to make their mind up. This, in part, explains their ambivalence on the status of Muslim women.

> However dynamic his outlook life might have been, in the female question he remained bound to a very narrow interpretation of the Quran and did not even share the modernist view according to which, for instance, polygamy is regarded as permitted only under the condition that the man treats his wives with complete equality, i.e. as an implicit order for monogamy; nor has he ever mentioned the view launched by Syed Ameer Ali and his followers that Islam has freed the weaker sex and has given her a most exquisite rank in the society which could be proved by the long lists of ladies who had played a leading role in the religious or cultural life since the beginnings of Islam.[22]

Unlike Turkish and Egyptian educators who placed changing the status, education, and roles of women at the core of national advancement,[23] their Indian counterparts did not have the same degree of commitment. This is not all. Even when explored through the prism of nationalist educational discourses in other regions of India, notably Bengal and Maharashtra, one does not see the intersection of educational nationalism (not in the narrow but in its broad sense) and gender in north India's Muslim communities. Muslim educators, reformers, and creative writers quite often espoused traditional notions in terms of modesty, domestic centrality, self-sacrifice, and self-abnegation. The emancipation of women emerges in their writings and public stand as a lost option, a road tragically not taken.

Moving to a more recognizable and ideologically more cohesive entity, the ulama created their own structures and insulated themselves, at least on contentious issues, in their imagined world of piety. So long as they were not too visible in the public domain as agitators, as some had become in 1857, they were left alone within the confines of their theological seminaries. In addition to not disturbing the status quo, a lesson learned from the 1857 experience and succinctly expressed in the Queen's proclamation, the colonial government even made concessions to religious sentiments or negotiated with religious orthodoxies that the Deobandis and Barelwis embodied.[24] No longer a set of specific rights, and no longer a privilege to be enjoyed by a body or people in specific circumstances, religious freedom now became an open-ended entitlement. This arrangement suited the men of religion, especially because it enabled them, from the time Deoband's *dar al-ulum* came into being, to define the frame of reference and the terms of the religious discourse with a view to controlling its outcome.

In general, the imperial policy on critical social issues stemmed from a broad consideration of how best to curb the influence of the traditional Muslim groups, particularly theologians, beyond their own self-defined boundaries. After the horrors of the 1857 Rebellion, the imperial claim to social reconstruction in the Victorian image appeared to be a discarded project. No wonder, then, the government usually lent its weight, as a tactical step, to a traditionalist interpretation of the Shariat. To give one example, the courts' rulings very often worked to deny women access to property even though the Koran asserts that women are entitled to inherit a portion of a parent's or husband's wealth. Like the courts, the political arm of the Raj pursued no consistent policy with regard to women's property rights. This suited the theologians, who took little or no interest in issues of women's property rights.

In sum, if a mark of modern society was improvement in the status and rights of women, then neither the administrative nor the legal arms of the Anglo-Indian government were engines of modernization. What they gave to women with one hand, they often took away with the other.[25]

Being deeply sensitive to the religious susceptibilities even of those who were neither custodians of the Shariat nor certified by any person, body, or institution as its qualified interpreters, the government made concession after concession to muftis, mujtahids, and maulvis. Even before 1857 it had fought shy of modifying Muslim criminal law, even when some of its features were demonstrably not suited to the notions of justice entertained by the British themselves.[26] Not only was there a dual court system; Hindu and Muslim criminal law continued to operate, albeit often without British participation or permission.[27]

In this rather complex process the government sanctified the men of religion, while secular intellectuals, public figures, and other Westernized elites encountered exclusion and denial of official recognition. Indeed, officials either ignored or discarded their concerns on the presumption that they were uninfluential, unrepresentative, and not quite attuned to the so-called Muslim/Islamic way of life. As in the case of specific social reform issues such as widow immolation, and also in relation to the growing liberal opinion, they secured "an insistence on their own view by ignoring, marginalizing, domesticating, and exceptionalizing whatever did not accord with their presumptions."[28] To say the least, this had a devastating impact on liberal processes as well as the secular nationalist projects.

In the end, colonial perceptions of where the liberal intelligentsia stood influenced the sum and substance of the colonial agenda, as well as its strategy toward the Muslims. Soon enough public discourse was polarized—as evident from Sayyid Ahmad's tortuous reform career—between a wide variety of perspectives that often converged on certain matters. Moreover, because their platform was gradually narrowed by the government and their stature lowered within imperial structures, executive and judicial, liberals and modernists of all hues felt inhibited fighting their battles on an enlightened plank. Some pressed on, as evidenced from the career of various progressive literary movements from the 1920s onward; others joined the revolutionary struggles. To keep their heads above water, the in the late 1930s the Communist Party of India acknowledged and ultimately yielded to the growing demand for cultural self-determination in terms of a Muslim collective identity. This was a fatal mistake.

In a more general way, the Muslim public at large, especially in the 1930s and 1940s, was faced with only one choice: to shore up the variegated Islamist groups who presented themselves as the protectors and the authentic interpreters of the Islamic codes. As the decades rolled on, more and more reformers conceded the high religious ground to their opponents on education of women, their property rights, and purdah. This opposition came not so much from traditional thinkers as from those steeped in modern learning.

Thus, the failure of Muslim modernism lies as much in colonial mentalities as in the resistance to reform and innovation from Muslim orthodoxies: Shia, Sunni, the Ahl-i Hadis, the Barelwis, and the Deobandis. This is probably what

Shibli meant while decrying his community as "blind," in the lifetime of Sayyid Ahmad and his own (*Qaum haqiqat mein Sir Sayyid Marhum ke waqt mein bhi andhi thi aur ab bhi hai*).[29] Blind or not, large segments of it were decidedly ill-equipped to value or promote democratic aspirations of the kind that became so central to the powerful reformist currents engendered by Brahmo Samaj in Bengal and Arya Samaj in Punjab.

2. Living in a Pluralist Society

In my book on Delhi's Muslim intelligentsia in the nineteenth century (*A Moral Reckoning*, 2005), I have analyzed the opinions of certain key figures that found vent in various directions. By and large, we have tried to show how best they took a crack at reconciling and integrating the religious and secular discourses, minimizing disharmony around them, and giving a secularized twist to communitarian debates. I want to emphasize just a few points at the end, especially because of a certain analytical blindness or blockage in the learned world, particularly in relation to Delhi's intellectual and academic discourses and their impact on north India generally. The points I draw attention to are not only among the most engrossing themes of the historians, but are of the highest value to all who wish to know what advocates of pluralism were saying, and why their appeal diminished in the 1920s and 1930s.

First and foremost, Sayyid Ahmad, Zakaullah, Nazir Ahmad, Hali, and Ghalib hardly ever dreamed of a unified society where everyone shared the same belief and practices. Without advocating the cultural merging of religious traditions or the dissolution of religious boundaries, they were content to let the hundred flowers bloom. They found wisdom in numerous religious traditions,[31] built bridges of understanding and mutual respect between them, and balanced, on the strength of their reading of Persian *akhlaq* literature (notably the works of Nasiruddin Tusi), the interests of different religious communities. While Islam was a necessary cultural and spiritual ingredient of the national culture, they viewed religion as a matter of personal choice and disposition. Again, while adhering to the personality paradigm of the Prophet, they drew on non-Muslim religious figures so as to develop a conception of coexistence between religious institutions and the men of faith in different religions.

In this way, all five put across, despite dissimilarity in emphasis, a maximally inclusive notion to make the various segments of the two communities become parts of a whole.

Zakaullah's moral structure and his overall worldview served as a resource of engagement with other communities, and he extended the basic premises, conceptions, and values of Islam to them. These included moral education, kindliness, and a sense of justice. "All men are equal, but it is the goodness of the person that makes him superior to the other," he wrote.[32] Knowing full well how the world around him was charged with hatred and filled with sectarian animus, he explored the ways to move diverse cultural and religious traditions toward intercommunity cooperation. He avoided theological controversies to become "one of God's peacemakers who brought unity among the children of men by his goodness and love."[33] Breaking decisively with the Arya Samaj's tradition of exclusionary nationalism, he made cultural pluralism—an idea previously associated with Sayyid Ahmad Khan and Ghalib—an article of faith. Delhi College, the main source of his early intellectual energy, may not have created a new form of liberalism, but it helped to invigorate liberal values and to imbue its members with a more pluralistic understanding of north Indian society. Critics referred to Zakaullah disparagingly as a "free-thinker," but, as Andrews put it:

> If the phrase "free-thinker" means, that he thought freely and sincerely and with an open mind about religion, and regarded the spirit of his Islamic faith to be more important than the letter, then the phrase is nobly true concerning Zakaullah, and he well deserves the title. For it would have been hard to find a man more free from formalism and bigotry, more open-minded and tolerant. It was this fact that made him a close friend and associate of earnest Hindus all through his long life. It was this also which was one of the things that drew me instinctively to him from the first, and has remained rooted in my memory ever since.[34]

No wonder, when Pandit Tulsi Ram's family lighted the lamps to worship every evening, they included his name in their prayer at that time, along with those of other close family members. Andrews amplified this viewpoint:

> What most struck the imagination of us, Englishmen, who used to be present (at the Reading Room in Delhi), was the exceeding kindliness of toleration, unsullied by a touch of religious bitterness—an atmosphere in which political wisdom could mature and social friendships ripen. In all the many years during which I knew Munshi Zakaullah (and during the last years of his life I used to see him almost every day) I cannot once remember hearing a bitter or uncharitable word spoken by him concerning any Hindu religious custom. On the other hand, I have continually heard him speak with a deep respect for those who differed from him fundamentally in matters of belief. Wherever he went his influence always made for peace and goodwill.[35]

Nazir Ahmad ascribed his own experiences to a senior, or *buzurg*, in his student days: "In short, sometimes I was a Christian, sometimes a Muslim, and sometimes not at all."[36] The source of Hindu-Muslim fracas, according to him, lay in the values instilled in youth and in the phobias created in them. But it was still possible to resolve disagreements through education and reconciliatory methods (*sazgari aur sulahkari*). Using the metaphor of a cloth merchant and the sweet maker, he remarked: "After all, the sweet maker does not object to the cloth merchant not producing sweets like him; nor does the cloth merchant get angry with the sweet vendor for not selling cloth." He referred to Zauq,[37] the poet, to point out that differences were the essence of creation, the gift of God that created people with diverse social and cultural habits and religions. Nevertheless, divergences had to be reconciled with the aid of British structures and the secularized educational curriculum, also a British gift, and not allowed to explode into violent conflicts.[38] In this, the great Urdu novelist tried shifting the self-image of the Hindu and Muslim ideologues to create new possibilities in which communal violence is not the core of the country's ethos. The choice had to be made, and then fought for.

If social identities and differences are constructed, fluid, multiple, and over-lapping, then every group has a right to its own history and myth making that embodies and strengthens their identity. The key is to enable "mythic struc-ture and future dreams to embody the erstwhile enemy other in a benign way, even in loving embrace."[39] Marc Gopin, a scholar writing on the long-standing Israeli-Palestinian conflict, concludes with this plea:

> It is our job to enter into the damaged and strange world of enemies and enemy systems, to suspend judgement, to see truths on all sides, to see justice and injustice on all sides, to engage in a level of empathy that is enormously demanding, all to help evoke peace processes that reso-nate at the most profound level of human consciousness and experience. If enough of us, on all levels of intervention, do this persistently and patiently, I do believe that we can stimulate a fundamentally new path to peace.[40]

Some of the late nineteenth-century Delhi's best men, Hindus and Muslim alike, reflected much the same sentiment. Nazir Ahmad, who was consistently impatient with demagogic religious leaders, did not want fellow Muslims to demonize non-Muslims but to discover, through regular processes of self-examination, their own faults and weak points.[41] In *Taubat-an Nasuh*, he narrates the story of a missionary preaching and distributing books, like a member of a theatrical cast, at the Chandni Chowk bazaar. This was not an uncommon occurrence. The missionaries did not merely read the Bible to their listeners, but rather demonstrated its purpose. In their street sermons they took the Bible with them and used it to emphasize the truth of their message. On that fateful day, so runs the story, a boy used an opprobrious epithet for the preacher. This agitated many of the bystanders, but not the preacher. He did not want the boy to be hurt by anyone. This act charmed Ulleem [Alim], Nasuh's second son. He approached the same missionary for the Bible, which he read with great interest. Unlike his elder brother who disapproved of such reading habits, Uleem was struck by the fact that if Christians followed the teachings in that religious text, they could not be so bad as his people painted them. Nasuh, who listened to this story, remarked:

> There is no doubt some opposition between the doctrines of Islam and Christianity, but then no two religions have so much in common. The Koran speaks well of Christianity and its professors, and their Gospel is held to be the word of God. The Mosalman may lawfully eat and intermarry with the Christian, and the alienation which now characterizes their relations is not sanctioned by the canon law. The best of our religious books could hardly have benefited you more than the missionary's volume. But you said just now you had learned sympathy for others from its maxims. Tell me, have you ever put this teaching into practice?[42]

The performance by the missionary, almost like a rehearsal of a text rescued from the Biblical records somewhere, and the reaction of the audience, open for us a panoramic window into the then Delhi's world and encapsulate an entire culture that was so much more tolerant than the following decades.

As detailed above, the process of entering into other cultures is daunting in any period of history and in any situation, but Zakaullah and Nazir Ahmad showed appreciation of whatever they read of Hindu and Christian texts. The former, having spent a lifetime of intellectual friendship with Hindu scholars, held firmly the view, right up to the day of his death at the advanced age of eighty-seven, that harmony and reconciliation between Islam and Hinduism were always possible.[43] "Reconciliation," he contended, "sustains faith [iman] and brings in its wake generous [fayyazana] behaviour."[44] No wonder Nazir Ahmad fervently applauded him for being "far-sighted" in avoiding painful religious disputes. The fact is that Zakaullah observed toleration in every detail, in spirit as well as in letter, in religious matters.[45] "What is the use of argument and controversy?" he told Andrews. "Tell me your Beautiful Names for God, and I will tell you mine."[46]

The account sketched above suggests that the dialogical element signaled a crucial step toward avoiding paradigms of encounter—and undermining religious violence. The point is not to exaggerate its limitations or to debate whether or not such men were authentically modern, but to highlight their inventiveness. As people who had no conception of pacts and unity conferences that became the métier of peace in the 1920s for the sake of immediate political goals, they talked of building on the overarching shared ethical values and practices, and acknowledging each other's common visions. Andrews, who was moved by such thoughts, concluded with a paean of praise to Zakaullah's kindness, courtesy, confidence, and friendship. He deserved a place among the great Indians of the nineteenth century, so he wrote, as a "singular and beautiful example of the combination of the past and the present, of the East and West," and also as a "true prophet of the future."[47] He owed something more to Nazir Ahmad—an idea of the power of Islam at its best, in molding character and creating an atmosphere of reverence.[48]

Zakaullah's outward manners and customs were a part of Delhi's sharif ethos. His dress, his habits, his domestic life, and his religious life—all that he valued most dearly—remained unchanged.[49] *Makhzan*'s editor, Shaikh Abdul Qadir, who knew him well during 1907–1908,[50] wrote that while sticking to the old-fashioned style in dress and manner of living, he held progressive views. Progressive or not, he remained true to the same social and cultural ideals that informed many others in his generation. While Islam provided them a universal frame of identity and considerable freedom to retain their regional, linguistic, and class identities, the historically conditioned symbiosis between region, language, and faith enabled the educated elites—if not the masses—to pursue a high degree of cultural and historical continuity to transform it into a modern national identity.

Whatever their difference in emphasis, Sayyid Ahmad, Ghalib, Zakaullah, Nazir Ahmad, and others planted the seeds of a pluralist vision that could eventually become a touchstone of a liberal and secular polity. With Hakim Ajmal Khan and Mukhtar Ahmad Ansari, another prominent Dilliwala, providing depth and acceleration to the process in the early 1920s, their home—Sharif Manzil in Ballimaran and Dar-us Salam in Daryaganj (now Ansari Road)—became powerful and living symbols of a new awakening.

This essay would have served its purpose if the sagacious and memorable admonitions of such men stimulated writers to reconstruct this heritage in South Asia. Moreover, it would be intellectually fruitful to foreground the submerged story of social and cultural invigoration and not just concentrate on, as is often the case, the inadequacies, contradictions, and paradoxes of the Muslim intelligentsia and plumb the deep and hidden meanings of their "failure."

The wind has blown away the dust of men
unnumbered from your lane:
Yet your true lovers are not daunted: men
come to your threshold still.[51]

Reasonable as these conclusions are, we cannot escape the consequences of serious Hindu-Muslim disputes in the lifetime of Zakaullah, Nazir Ahmad, and Andrews. Indeed, it was their misfortune that the prospect of interfaith dialogue was to chill and then freeze the conditions needed to maintain the climate. Yet as the new century begins, the peoples and countries of South Asia are striving toward greater cooperation in shaping their destinies. Nobody can predict the ultimate fate of such trends. All one can hope is that studying Delhi's past will be a source of knowledge of a cultural and intellectual heritage that belongs to all of South Asia. When the history of ideas of the countries of the subcontinent is better explored and better known, the historian will recognize the currents of influence which, from Pakistan to Bangladesh, constitute the very fabric of the history of Islam in the region. We may not have it in our power, as Thomas Paine (1737–1809) proclaimed in 1776, "to begin the world again." But we can provide an adequate language for comprehending the twenty-first century, and we can decide for ourselves the importance of living together, understanding each other, and interpreting each other's lifestyle and value systems. Arnold Toynbee sums up this message candidly in the following words:

In order to save mankind we have to learn to live together in concord in spite of traditional differences of religion, civilization, nationality, class and race. In order to live together in concord successfully, we have to know each other's past, since human life, like the rest of the phenomenal universe, can be observed by human minds only as it presents itself to them on the move through time . . . . For our now urgent common purpose of self-preservation, it will not be enough to explore our common underlying human nature. The psychologist's work needs to be supplemented by the archaeologist's, the historian's, the anthropologist's and the sociologist's. We must learn to recognize, and as far as possible, to understand, the different cultural configurations in which our common human nature has expressed itself in the different religions, civilizations, and nationalities into which human culture has come to be articulated in the course of its history . . . . We shall, however, have to do more than just understand each other's cultural heritages, and more even than appreciate them. We shall have to value them and love them as being parts of mankind's common treasure and therefore being ours too, as truly as the heirlooms that we ourselves shall be contributing to the common stock.[52]

Notes

1. Ghalib, cited in M. A. Sadiq, *A History of Urdu Literature* (Delhi: Oxford University Press, 1984, 2nd edition), p. 203.
2. Ahmed Ali (1910–94), *Twilight in Delhi* (Delhi: Rupa, 1940, 1991 rpt), p. viii.
3. H.A.R. Gibb, *Modern Trends in Islam* (Chicago: University of Chicago Press, 1945), p. 109.
4. Quran 49.13.
5. Thus, he wrote: "What a great pity it is that the Muslims of this age have not only failed to discover any way to preserve the exercise of intellectual scrutiny, but have even discarded those methods that had been discovered in the past! In acquiring every kind of knowledge the condition of Muslims for a long time has been such that they hardly read in any area of learning in order to find out the reality and truth in it. Their purpose is simply to know all that is written in a given book, regardless of whether it be true or false . . . . If discussion occurs, it is not on the question of whether a principle written in a book is true or false, but simply on whether that particular principle is recorded in the book or not . . . . This method has destroyed freedom of opinion and broken the way of life that used to afford protection against falling into error. All their learning and wisdom has fallen into error." Sayyid Ahmad Khan, "Azadi-i Rai," M. Moaddel and K. Talattof (eds.), *Contemporary Debates in Islam: An Anthology of Modernist and Fundamentalist Thought* (London: Macmillan, 2000), pp. 119–20.
6. *A Moral Reckoning: Muslim Intelligentsia in Nineteenth Century Delhi* (Oxford: Oxford University Press, 2005).
7. Muhammad Iqbal, *The Reconstruction of Religious Thought in Islam* (Oxford: Oxford University Press, 1934), pp. 159–60.
8. Muhammad Iqbal, *Speeches and Statements of Iqbal* (Lahore: Al-Manār Academy, 1945), p. 131.
9. "If Moslem woman does not attain in another hundred years, the social position of her European sister, there will be time enough to declaim against Islam as a system and a dispensation. But the Teacher who in an age when no country, no system, no community has any right to woman, maiden or married, mother or wife, who, in a country where the birth of a daughter was considered a calamity, secured to the sex rights which are only unwillingly and under pressure being conceded to them by the civilized nations in the twentieth century, deserves the gratitude of humanity. If Mohammad had done nothing more, his claim to be a benefactor of mankind would have been indisputable." Ameer Ali, *The Spirit of Islam* (London: Chatto and Windus, 1967 rpt., 1st ed. 1922), p. 256.

10. Ibid., p. 232.
11. Ibid., p. 231.
12. Ibid., p. 248.
13. Ibid., p. 249.
14. Ibid., p. 249.
15. Gail Minault, "Other Voices, Other Rooms: The View from the Zenana," Nita Kumar (ed.), *Women as Subjects: South Asian Histories* (Charlottesville: University Press of Virginia, 1994), p. 119.
16. For Sayyid Ahmad Khan, *Tahzibul Akhlaq* (Uttar Pradesh: Aligarh Muslim University), Vol. 1, pp. 71–4.
17. Fazlur Rahman, *Islam* (London: Weidenfeld and Nicolson, 1966), pp. 225–6.
18. Vice-President of India, Mohd. Hamid Ansari, in his 30 October 2007. Address at the Annual Convocation of Jamia Milia Islamia.
19. Sayyid Sulaiman Nadwi (ed.), *Khutbat-i Shibli* (Azamgarh, 1965), p. 185.
20. Ibid., p. 131.
21. Rahman, *Islam*, p. 235.
22. Annemarie Schimmel, *Studies in the History of Religions* (Leiden: E. J. Brill, 1963), Vol. 6, p. 245.
23. Barak A. Salmoni, "Women in the Nationalist-Educational Prism: Turkish and Egyptian Pedagogues and their Gendered Agenda, 1920–1952," *History of Education Quarterly*, Vol. 43, No. 4, Winter 2003.
24. For Deoband, Barbara Metcalf, *Islamic Revival in British India: Deoband 1860–1900* (Delhi: Oxford University Press, 2002 edn); Usha Sanyal, *Devotional Islam and Politics in British India: Ahmad Riza Khan Barelwi and his Movement, 1870–1920* (Delhi: Oxford University Press, 1996).
25. Gregory C. Kozlowski, "Muslim Women and the Control of Property in North India," *The Indian Economic and Social History Review*, Vol. 24, No. 2, 1987, p. 181.
26. M. P. Jain, "Challenges of Indian Legal System"; Raman, "Utilitarianism and the Criminal Law in Colonial India," *Modern Asian Studies*, Vol. 18, No. 4, 1994, p. 746.
27. David Skuy, "Macaulay and the India Penal Code of 1862: The Myth of the Inherent Superiority and Modernity of the English Legal System in the Nineteenth Century," *Modern Asian Studies*, Vol. 32, No. 3, p. 522.
28. Lata Mani, *Contentious Traditions: The Debate on Sati in Colonial India* (Delhi: Oxford University Press, 1998), p. 193.
29. Shibli to Abdul Majid Daryabadi, 15 November 1913, *Makatib-i Shibli*, Vol. 1, p. 292.
31. *Jitne mazajib duniya mein hain waqt aur maqam ke lihaz se sab ke sab aadmi ki islah aur uske faide ke liye chale hain aur har ek mein kuch na kuch faide aur sadaqat aur neki ke ansh maujood hai.* Nazir Ahmad, *Lekcharon ka Majmua* (Agra: Mufid-e Aam Istemar Press, 1918), Vol. 2, p. 154.

32. Zakaullah, *Mahasinul Akhlaq*, vol. 1 (Delhi 1891), p. 209.
33. C. F. Andrews, *Zakaullah of Delhi* (with introduction by Mushirul Hasan and Margrit Pernau, Delhi: Oxford University Press, 2003), p. 98.
34. Ibid., p. 109.
35. Ibid., p. 107.
36. Oesterheld, "Nazir Ahmad and the Early Urdu Novel," *Annual of Urdu Studies* (Madison: University of Wisconsin), p. 40. 2001.
37. *Gulha-i rang rang se hai raunaq-i chaman/Ai Zauq is jahaan ko hai zeb ikhtilaaf.*
38. Nazir Ahmad, *Lekcharon ka Majmua*, Vol. 2, pp. 420–1.
39. M. Gopin, *Holy War, Holy Peace: How Religion Can Bring Peace to the Middle East* (Oxford: Oxford University Press, 2002), p. 91.
40. Ibid., p. 228.
41. Speech at Anjuman Himayat-i Islam, Lahore, December 1888, Nazir Ahmad, *Lekcharon ka Majmua*, Vol. 2, pp. 117–8.
42. Nazir Ahmad, *The Repentance of Nasuh* (Delhi: Permanent Black, 2004), pp. 33–5.
43. Andrews, *The True India* (London: Hodder & Stoughton, 1939), p. 198.
44. Ibid., p. 199.
45. Andrews, *Zakaullah of Delhi*, p. 10.
46. B. Chaturvedi and M. Sykes, *Charles Freer Andrews: A Narrative* (London: George Allen & Unwin, 1949), p. 40.
47. Andrews, *Munshi Zaka Ullah: A Great Educationist, Modern Review* (Calcutta, 1911), pp. 351–7.
48. C. F. Andrews, *North India* (Oxford: A. R. Mowbray, 1908), p. 135.
49. Ibid., p. 92.
50. For Abdul Qadir's career, see *Auraq-i Nau* (Lahore): *Abdul Qadir Number*, 1951.
51. Ralph Russell, *The Pursuit of Literature: A Select History* (London: Zed Books, 1992), p. 48; translating Kulliyât, Vol. I, p. 259.
52. Arnold Toynbee, *A Study of History*, quoted in Richard C. Martin (ed.), *Approaches to Islam in Religious Studies* (Oxford: Oneworld Publications, 2001), p. 105.

3 NEHRU, RELIGION, AND THE HUMANITIES

Martha C. Nussbaum

1. The Culture Gap

At the time of Independence, a large proportion of Indian citizens, invited to reflect on religion's role in the new nation, would probably have been inclined to identify religion in general—and Hindu religion in particular—with Gandhi's moral and spiritual commitments. Hinduism, so understood, was an inclusive movement that supported equal citizenship for Muslims, an end to caste and to the subordination of women, and an unswerving dedication to "the pursuit of truth by nonviolent means."

People could hardly help knowing that there were other faces to Hinduism: traditions that enforced the caste hierarchy and the subordination of women; antagonisms between Hindus and Muslims, Hindus and Christians; and a radical Hindu political and cultural movement built upon a highly selective reading of such traditions. The Hindu Right had been around for a long time, in the form of the politically aggressive Hindu Mahasabha and the more recessive Rashtriya Swayamsevak Sangh (RSS), which claimed to be apolitical. V. D. Savarkar, a key figure in the Hindu Mahasabha, was politically influential, a hero to many; his *Hindutva: Who Is a Hindu?*, published in 1923, offered an account of the tradition that was utterly opposed to Gandhi's emphasis on nonviolence and inclusiveness. Who could have failed to know about the Savarkar ideology, when Nathuram Godse, after shooting Gandhi at point-blank range, offered at his sentencing hearing a book-length statement of self-justification that blamed Gandhi for compromising the manhood of the new nation by his devotion to nonviolence and his indulgent stance toward Muslims? Godse made no secret of his devotion to Savarkar, though he denied that Savarkar had any role in planning the assassination.

Even if Godse's statement was not allowed publication at the time, its sentiments were widely known, and they had changed the face of history.

Still, if people reflected seriously about matters religious and spiritual, they would not have been so likely to identify Savarkar's views with religion or spirituality. Savarkar had little interest in religion; nor had Godse. For both men, Hinduism was a source of cultural traditions that could become the basis for an aggressive ethnocentric nationalism. They never suggested that one would have to have the slightest interest in spiritual matters to follow their call to Hindutva. Golwalkar and the RSS were more religious, and part of Golwalkar's appeal, like that of other RSS leaders, was surely that of a religious guru. Still, his writings focus on ethnicity and attachment to the land far more than on religion as such. Nor were his ideas widely known at the time of Independence, since the RSS was keeping a low profile, quietly pursuing grass-roots organization through the creation of innumerable *shakhas* for boys.

In the early years of the nation, therefore, people would be justified in associating Hindu religion, and religion more generally, with a deeply passionate liberal movement. It must have seemed obvious that Gandhian religion was a major force in winning India's freedom and in creating the nation as an inclusive, equality-pursuing, caste-denying, rights-protecting nation. Even the great Dalit legal thinker B. R. Ambedkar, profoundly skeptical of Hindu traditions for obvious reasons, did not denounce religion as such, or even abandon it: instead, he became a Buddhist, pursuing spiritual commitments similar to those of Gandhi by a different route.

Today, none of this is true. When progressive young people in India think of religion and its role in Indian society they typically think of the Hindu Right, and so they associate religion with the hatred of Muslims and Christians, with traditionalism about women's roles, and even with support for the caste hierarchy. (The Hindu Right, while officially eschewing caste and while organizing among the lower castes, remains in essence an upper-caste movement, and its leaders often express contempt for the lower castes.) Gandhi's religious movement may be alive in South Africa and (through the legacy of Martin Luther King, Jr.) in the United States; in India it has long been a thing of the past. Gandhi's face is on the currency, but whether it is in people's hearts may be doubted. If someone remarks that it is a good idea to learn about Hindu traditions or to study the classic religious texts, people immediately conclude that the person is a reactionary, probably in league with the policies of the Hindu Right. In progressive, feminist, and inclusivist circles—particularly in the universities, but beyond them as well—religion is profoundly unfashionable, almost unmentionable. (It is not even recognized as a subject of academic study in Indian universities.)

Even when they think about world history, Indian university students rarely imagine that religion might be a force for good. When I've visited political science and women's studies programs and spoken about the role of organized religion in the United States in ending slavery and achieving racial equality, when I mention the fact that (until very recently, when several states have legalized same-sex marriage) the largest organized groups of Americans who approve and practice same-sex marriage are several religious bodies, Reform, Reconstructionist, and, more recently, Conservative Judaism, along with Unitarian Universalism and the tentative posture of the Protestant Episcopal Church (which has ordained two openly gay bishops, but does not perform same-sex marriages as such), my statements are typically greeted with astonishment—despite the fact that the US civil rights movement owes its inspiration to Gandhi.

What accounts for this remarkable shift? Giving discredit where it's due, a major factor has been the cleverness of the Hindu Right, who, with great dedication and selflessness, purvey a narrow sectarian version of Hinduism—through the *shakhas*, through creative use of media, and through grass-roots organization all over the nation. Because they have done their job so carefully, millions of people all over India identify Hinduism with what this ideological movement says Hinduism is. Another major factor, clearly, has been the influence of Marxism on India's educated elites: many still cannot think of religion—even Gandhian religion—as anything but an opiate, and they shrink from it in much the way that some secular American academics do, as if it's embarrassing and almost contaminating.

Still, the Hindu Right could not have succeeded so thoroughly had they not encountered a cultural void into which they could pour their stories without effective resistance. So the question must be: How, after Gandhi's death, did this void arise? Why were there no other powerful public stories of Hinduism to counter the stories purveyed by the Sangh Parivar? Why did no liberal inclusivist grass-roots organizations with an emotional and spiritual dimension address the young, countering the appeals of the RSS *shakhas*? In short, why did liberal religion and liberal spiritual culture fall silent?

It's really worse than that. In the United States, because of constitutional constraints that protect minorities against the domination of a religious orthodoxy, children cannot be taught religious doctrines as correct values in the public schools. All, however, learn about the civil rights movement, and they learn those values as correct political values, the values on which their nation is founded. The celebration of Martin Luther King, Jr.'s birthday as a major national holiday is not centrally a celebration of religion, but it is a celebration of ideas that King connected to religion, and it is more generally a celebration of the imagination, of the emotions of the struggle for equality, of the spiritual in its largest sense. In India, the silence that has grown over the years is not just a silence of liberal-religious voices; it is a silence of liberal emotion-culture, liberal spirituality.

This silence is not total: Bollywood is a major purveyor of images of Hindu-Muslim friendship and amity, and the world of cricket has its own ways of portraying India (with emotion, certainly) as an inclusive society. Furthermore, there are important regional differences: Bengali culture, for example, is still influenced by Tagore's powerful humanism, and his legacy continues to instill, through poetry and music, the message of a diverse and richly plural nation. Nonetheless, in the nation as a whole there is an absence of cultural ritual, of ethical and humanistic learning—in the schools, in civil society, and in the space after school that the *shakhas* so cleverly fill.

This culture gap enormously helps the forces of the Hindu Right, who fill the void with attractive, ultimately addictive propaganda. Golwalkar said that if he saw a beautiful peacock and wanted it to come to his garden every day, he would feed it little bits of opium until it became addicted. Then it would come every day. He said that that was how the *shakhas* work: lure boys by fun and games, and once they are addicted they will be yours to work on. If that peacock had had some competition for its attention, the outcome would have been less certain. In government schools, however, where rote learning rules, there is no competition: no creative use of the arts to teach the values of an inclusive society, no rituals of antisubordination. An Indian acquaintance of mine was struck by the fact that his young nephew, in school in North Carolina, was learning about the US civil rights movement by putting on a play in which some children play the roles of African Americans forced to sit in the back of the bus, and they then all discuss how those people felt about the stigma of second-class status, and why they protested. I had absolutely nothing like that in India, he said with regret.

So little do the vast majority of India's talented children internalize the values of mutual respect and inclusiveness through humanistic instruction in school that the prestigious Institutes of Technology and Management now report that they encounter severe social problems of both caste and religion-based discrimination and exclusion. They have wisely concluded that they need to introduce courses in the humanities to open students' minds and to strengthen their imaginations. Why, though, did it have to come to that? Why didn't every little child grow up with the words of Gandhi on her lips, with the songs of Tagore (or someone akin to Tagore) in her ears, with countless civic rituals expressing the values of a decent society? Why the culture gap, in a nation that was created not so long ago on a foundation of inclusivist spiritual culture?

The question is huge, but it seems likely that at least a part of the answer can be found in the complicated psychology of Jawaharlal Nehru. Nehru's attitudes about both religion and the humanities played a very powerful role in setting India on a course, after Gandhi's death, that valorized science and devalued the spiritual in all its forms. My aim is to pursue an analysis of Nehru's convoluted and often apparently contradictory attitudes, asking how far such an analysis can help us think about how things got to their present state.

2. Nehru on Religion

In one sense, a more unlikely adversary of spiritual culture could hardly be found. Jawaharlal Nehru was in his own way a deeply spiritual man and a great humanist, with a huge heart and a poetic imagination almost unique among world leaders—not to mention an English prose style equaled by no other politician of the twentieth century. In his will, asking that his ashes be thrown into the river Ganges, he writes:

> Smiling and dancing in the morning sunlight, and dark and gloomy and full of mystery as the evening shadows fall, a narrow, slow and graceful stream in winter and a vast, roaring thing during the monsoon, broad-bosomed almost as the sea, and with something of the sea's power to destroy, the Ganga has been to me a symbol and a memory of the past of India, running into the present, and flowing on to the great ocean of the future.[1]

That passionate response to the mystery of nature, if not religious, is surely spiritual and poetic. That a man who saw his own life as a spiritual journey— who had such a deep sense of life's mysteries and such courage in confronting them—should so often have slighted the religious form this search took in the vast majority of his fellow citizens, is a strange fact. One might think it simply the result of Nehru's elitism, which always kept him distant from those whom he so often called "the masses," combined with the influence of Marxism, which made him believe that religion was precisely what those masses did *not* need.

Such an account, however, would be far too simple. Nehru devoted a great deal of thought to the topic of religion, and his arguments on this score are complicated. We certainly are not dealing with the unthinking prejudice of a Marxist intellectual. (Indeed, in one of the discussions of religion we shall shortly examine, while acknowledging the influence of Marxism on his view of the world, he expresses impatience with a dogmatic Marxist approach to questions of ultimate reality: "Life is too complicated and, as far as we can understand it in our present state of knowledge, too illogical, for it to be confined within the four corners of a fixed doctrine" [DI 31].) So we must look further.

Given Nehru's voluminous writings, the sources touching on the topic of religion are virtually innumerable; an exhaustive study would require a lengthy book. Therefore, rather than pick bits from here and from there, I propose to focus on only one text, *The Discovery of India*, and, within that, on two sections in which Nehru confronts the topic of religion head-on. One, near the start of the work, is a section called "Life's Philosophy," in which he describes a variety of influences on his approach to life (24–33). The other section, near the end, is entitled, "Religion, Philosophy, and Science" (509–15); here Nehru discusses the role of those three forces in India's future. The two sections are largely consistent, though each is internally complex. Together they provide us with a picture of attitudes that I believe to be basically constant throughout Nehru's life, although I shall not be able to demonstrate that here.

As we study Nehru's arguments, we should bear two things firmly in mind. First, these passages occur in a work in which Gandhi is a central figure. Thus it could not be said that Gandhi, as an example of a spiritual life and leader of a quasi-religious movement, was not present to Nehru's mind throughout. Second, the work includes detailed discussion of the history of Hinduism as a tolerant and inclusive religion. One of its other heroes is the Buddhist emperor Ashoka, whose policies of religious toleration and pluralism Nehru warmly praises (in a way that anticipates the central role of Ashoka in Amartya Sen's recent writings about Indian traditions). He even says of Hinduism, "Its essential spirit seems to be to live and let live" (75), and he speaks of the Upanishads as having "produced that atmosphere of tolerance and reasonableness, that acceptance of free-thought in matters of faith, . . . which are dominant features of Indian culture" (91). We must, then, ask how far his objections to religion square with these very positive characterizations of key manifestations of Indian religion.

The second thing we must remember as we analyze is that in both discussions, religion is closely associated with philosophy and other humanistic approaches to life. Indeed, Nehru writes, "Religion merges into mysticism and metaphysics and philosophy" (26). He later mentions in the same connection "art and poetry and certain psychic experiences" (31). What Nehru sets over against all of these approaches to understanding is science. Indeed, his repeated encomia of science verge on the starry-eyed: "The methods and approach of science have revolutionized human life more than anything else in the long course of history, and have opened doors and avenues of further and even more radical change, leading up to the very portals of what has long been considered the unknown" (31); "Science . . . made the world jump forward with a leap, built up a glittering civilization, opened up innumerable avenues for the growth of knowledge" (511); and "There is no visible limit to the advance of science, if it is given the chance to advance" (512). The two sections are as much a passionate outpouring of attachment to science as they are a critique of other avenues to understanding.

Attachment, indeed, propels the argument. For in both sections, Nehru argues as follows. Science has offered understanding of many things, but it has not offered understanding of the ultimate values and purposes of life. ("Science does not tell us much, or for the matter of that anything about the purposes of life" (26)—an uncharacteristically ill-written sentence that seems to betray a mental tension.) To confront life's mysteries, he then says it would at least appear that other disciplines and approaches are needed:

> The ultimate purposes of man may be said to be to gain knowledge, to realize truth, to appreciate goodness and beauty. The scientific method of objective inquiry is not applicable to all these, and much that is vital in life seems to lie beyond its scope—the sensitiveness to art and poetry, the emotion that beauty produces, the inner recognition of goodness. (513)

The methods of science, so well adapted to the visible world, seem "not wholly adapted" to the "invisible" realm of meaning and purpose (26). Other disciplines seem to go further in these mysterious domains (512).

Nonetheless, Nehru concludes, we had better cling to science and the scientific temper and trust it as far as it can go, leaving the other disciplines aside. Who knows? Science may yet have something to say about ultimate meaning. And even if it does not, we should stick to it anyway, even though we have a deep need to confront the mysteries about which it is silent:

> Often, as I look at this world, I have a sense of mysteries, of unknown depths. The urge to understand it, in so far as I can, comes to me: to be in tune with it and to experience it in its fullness. But the way to that understanding seems to me essentially the way of science, the way of objective approach, though I realize that there can be no such thing as true objectiveness. (28)

The conclusion seems to be a nonsequitur. If all our evidence to date is that science cannot say much about ultimate meaning and other disciplines can, why is the right conclusion a trust of science, even in the realms where it has heretofore been unhelpful? What we need to try to understand, then, is what Nehru loves in science—what characteristics explain his willingness to follow it even where it does not appear to him, up until now, to offer understanding.

Science, says Nehru, is based on observation. It looks "at fact alone" (511). It is "precise" (32) and rigorous, with "hard discipline" (512). It is also dynamic, flexible, and experimental. Its temper is "adventurous yet critical" (512). It refuses to accept anything "without testing and trial" (512). It is willing to alter received conclusions in the face of the evidence (512). On account of these features, science has reached great technical achievements that have yielded increasing control over nature, and, even more important, techniques for the amelioration of poverty (31).

It is to Nehru's credit that he acknowledges that the power of science may also be used for evil and "instruments of destruction," if pursued in a way that is "unconnected with and isolated from moral discipline and ethical considerations" (33); here he alludes to the unleashing of destructive technology during the then-ongoing World War. In the later passage as well, he notes that "some vital element was missing" (511) when people pursued science without understanding of ultimate purposes. These passages appear to grant that science can at most tell us about means, not ends, and that its power can be used for good only if directed by some insight from a different source.

And yet, acknowledging all this, Nehru keeps on returning to the same conclusion: it is the scientific temper that we need to rely on, "not merely for the application of science but for life itself and the solution of its many problems" (512). The twistings and turnings of the argument suggest an unresolved inner debate about how far we really can trust scientific method, and yet an almost dogmatic commitment to science that—ironically—is not based on evidence or logic. How did Nehru, the great rationalist, get himself into a position of trusting science with, one might almost say, the blind faith of a lover?

Let's see whether we can understand the position better by beginning from the other side, with Nehru's objections to religion and its allied disciplines. His position would be consistent if he could argue that the other disciplines have flaws so great that we would not be well advised to trust them, even though they offer avenues of understanding that science does not; science, with all its limitations, is a more reliable guide to life. I think that something like this is Nehru's view, although the tensions in the argument are by no means easy to resolve, particularly if we keep reminding ourselves that he knows about Gandhi and Ashoka.

Nehru grants that religion supplies something without which most people cannot live, and that religions have helped a great deal in laying down moral standards. Nonetheless, he finds five flaws in religion that make it unworthy of the trust of India's people. Let's see how far each one goes, and against what type of religion each is plausible.

First, some religious leaders are bad people. Nehru immediately admits that this argument is not very strong, since not all religious leaders are like that (26). However, second, even when their leaders are not bad people, they rule by authority and ask people not to criticize. Notice that this second argument in part rehabilitates the first, since it suggests that the religious temper discourages the sort of critical scrutiny that would enable people to decide whether their leaders are good or bad—a major problem in the case of the Hindu Right then and now, clearly. The point would then be that even if not all religious leaders are bad, the posture of mind that all such leaders promote in their followers militates against their making reliable judgments of goodness and badness.

How good is this argument as an objection to Gandhi's religious movement? It cannot be said that it is worthless. Gandhi was not exactly an authoritarian, but he did exert control over people by his personal example, and he certainly did not always encourage critical thinking. Early on, when he set up a school in Bengal, Tagore, a great defender of Socratic and critical methods in education, found the degree of submission in Gandhi's method of instruction somewhat alarming. This theme persisted throughout the uneasy relationship between the two men. In a published exchange with Gandhi in 1921, Tagore questioned the role of "unquestioning obedience" in the noncooperation movement, concluding acerbically, "So easy is it to overpower, in the name of outside freedom, the inner freedom of man."[2] Tagore is right: although Gandhi certainly does ask people to dig deep into themselves and to criticize their own erotic and aggressive desires, he certainly did not favor Socratic reasoning or critical thinking as key elements of politics. His way of bringing people over to his own way of thinking had much more to do with force of example and moral authority than rational critique, and the type of democracy he projected did not make rational deliberation central.

We must be careful here. Gandhi was one of history's most powerful critics of tradition, and he certainly urged his followers to learn to stand alone against the power of authority and peer pressure. (Here he turned to Tagore: his favorite song was Tagore's "Ekla cholo re," which we shall study later, a song that urges solitary dissent.) His writings, moreover, are full of critical arguments. Nonetheless, it remains true that his conception of dissent gave conscientious objection the central role, and rational argument a role that was at best subsidiary. Nor was he afraid to appeal to peer pressure, or to use the force of his moral authority to summon his followers to follow.

Why is submission dangerous, if the moral authority is good? Well, first, there remains the problem of identifying the good without the use of critical reason. But there is another issue, which brings us to Nehru's third argument: religions are based on dead tradition, and they tend to take a part of the truth that they see and to "petrif[y]" (513) it into a dogma—with the result that people who are ruled by religious authority are ruled by the dead hand of the past. Nehru is particularly concerned with this issue: the later section begins with the insistence that a good future for India requires no longer being dominated by the past. Religion, he clearly thinks, encourages people to be ruled by that dead hand.

Now it might seem that this is a very weak objection to the type of religion that Gandhi constructed, since it was radically new and involved breaking with the dead hand of the past in matters of caste, gender, and interreligious relations. Indeed, we can hardly imagine India overthrowing the past in those areas without the deep emotional appeals of Gandhian religion. Critical argument had done something in these areas, but Gandhi's passionate movement went much further, and with many more people. Nonetheless, we can still appreciate the force of Nehru's objection if we put it this way: A good relationship to social problems as they unfold requires a temper that is experimental, free, creative, always ready to criticize and innovate. Gandhi's greatness was surely not of that sort. He was a dogmatist, and he did not encourage experimental thinking. Thus even if his movement was entirely good at the time when it began, it encouraged a temper of mind that did not prepare people well to confront the challenges of the future. Nehru would then be arguing that even when organized religion takes its most radical form, the dogmatism characteristic of all organized religion cannot equip India well to face new problems. Indeed he explicitly makes this point, saying that the frozenness of religion does not prepare people to adapt to the changing needs of humanity (513).

We can deepen this point by observing that the good charismatic leader is still bound to die at some point. If he rules by moral authority, rather than by encouraging independence of mind, his movement may become petrified after his death. Even if he himself can adapt to new conditions, and lead the movement to adapt, his passive followers are not being prepared to do so.

Fourth, Nehru continues, religions teach people to believe in an eternal order, and to care less about improving things in this world. People become less self-reliant (513), and more submissive to bad conditions in the present (511). Once again, this might at first blush seem to be a very weak objection to Gandhi's movement, which was all about compassion for the poor. But of course we know that Gandhi and Nehru had utterly divergent views of what that compassion required. In Nehru's view, Gandhi's romanticization of village simplicity encouraged people to submit to bad economic conditions, when real compassion for the poor would require improving those conditions. And Nehru would have been right to think that the spiritual and the material were profoundly at odds in Gandhi's thinking.

I have left for last an objection that may be the deepest, getting to the root of Nehru's aesthetic and personal distaste for religion: its arguments are mush, "soft and flabby" (27), difficult to understand and hence to criticize. The method relies on intuition and emotion rather than reason (513). It is not made clear why this is supposed to be bad, but it is clear that Nehru doesn't like it.

3. A Public Poetry?

Nehru seems to have some powerful objections to common forms of organized religion, particularly in the face of India's problems. Even Gandhi's movement may be guilty of encouraging conformity and passivity, and of reconciling people to bad economic conditions. Religious movements have often transcended the fourth criticism—think of liberation theology, of Martin Luther King, Jr.'s Gandhian demand for radical social and economic change. They have less often evaded the third objection, since most have sought cohesion through authority rather than through rational assessment. And yet even here there are profound differences among the religions that Nehru might have investigated. Some (e.g., Judaism, Kantian rational religion) strongly encourage critical rational argument: a rabbi is not an authority figure, but a scholar who leads the argument. Reform Judaism in particular has emphasized the autonomy of each person's reason as the core of what religion is about. Others (e.g., Buddhism) have no organized rituals and no authority figures. So even though there may be dangers of the type Nehru sees in the mere fact of organized religion, it seems occasionally possible for the right type of more or less organized religion to avoid these dangers.

More important, perhaps, criticizing organized religion does not mean criticizing all public spirituality. We have plenty of examples of spiritual and quasi-religious approaches to life that are even more antinomian than Buddhism. Tagore's humanistic "religion of man," for example, takes as its key historical source the Baul tradition, imagining the solitary poet and singer as the prototype of what spirituality should be. Nehru does not investigate such possibilities— although Tagore's *The Religion of Man* was a famous text by that time, as were texts of a similar sort by Auguste Comte (very influential in India) and John Stuart Mill (influenced by Comte, and thus an intellectual cousin of Tagore). So the failure to look into humanist religion is surprising, and a great gap in Nehru's argument.

More generally, Nehru might have pondered the idea that there is a public role for poetry and the humanities in constructing the emotional underpinnings of a decent democratic culture—an idea that by that time had exercised a large influence in many different places. Tagore in India, Walt Whitman in the United States—to cite just two examples—used poetry and (in the former case) also music and dance to express a vision of life's meaning that was intended to have a public role. Whitman's poems passionately champion the idea that a new democracy needs poets as well as laws and arguments. Tagore's humanistic religion suggests a similar conclusion, though with less political concreteness. Poetry is needed, they believe, in order to bring people together in a way that is respectful of the complexity of their humanity: the poet, as Whitman puts it, "sees eternity in men and women, he does not see men and women as dreams or dots."[3] Furthermore, the arts are emotionally deep, and this emotional depth is necessary to keep abstract ideas alive.

Particularly in songs devoted to patriotic themes, Tagore (using melodies drawn from the Baul tradition) emphasizes strongly the theme of critical and experimental spiritual searching, indicating that this is the religion that a nation would require:

> If no one answers your call, then walk on alone.
> (walk alone, walk alone, walk on alone.)
>
> If no one says a thing, oh you unlucky soul,
> If faces are turned away, if all go on fearing –
> then opening up your heart,
> You speak up what's on your mind, you speak up alone.
>
> If they all turn back, oh you unlucky soul,
> If, at the time of taking the deep dark path, no one cares –
> then the thorns that are on the way,
> O you, trampling those with bloodied feet, you tramp on alone.
>
> If a lamp no one shows, oh you unlucky soul,
> If in a rainstorm on a dark night they bolt their doors –
> then in the flame of thunder
> Lighting your own ribs, go on burning alone.[4]

This is the spirit of the Baul way of life that Tagore later develops into the "religion of man." It is critical, experimental, daring. It insists on breaking with the dead hand of the past. And yet it is also poetic, spiritual, and emotional.

Might one not suggest that this poetic quasi-religion offers resources that science, all by itself, does not? Here is an argument that should have interested Nehru—all the more since that song was famous as Gandhi's favorite song.

What, then, does Nehru have to say about forms of spirituality and humanistic searching outside of traditional or even not-so-traditional organized religion? Very little indeed. Nehru does spend some time with philosophy, finding that it is somewhat more rigorous and critical than organized religion, but still too vague and otherworldly (27), ill adapted to the problems of the real world (511). An ethical approach such as Gandhi's idea of "right means" deeply attracts him, he says—but he is troubled by the fact that he cannot find a logical justification for it (28). As for poetry and the other humanities, he owns to being drawn by them (514), and he even imagines that a poetic nature-religion might have been the only sort that could win him (28). But he says no more, and goes straight to his conclusion about the need to rely on science.

Very oddly, moreover, Tagore plays a small part in *Discovery* as a whole, and no part at all in the sections dealing with religious and quasi-religious approaches to life—despite the fact that Nehru knew the Shantiniketan school well, since his daughter Indira (later to become Indira Gandhi) spent her happiest school days there. (A photo of her there, dressed up for a dance performance, recently published in Mushirul Hasan's *The Nehrus*, shows a sensuous, happy Indira, looking more free than we ever see her, at least in public.) *The Discovery of India* does include a brief comparison of Tagore and Gandhi (340–41), calling them "the two outstanding and dominating figures of India in this first half of the twentieth century" (340), and Nehru does credit Tagore with the "tradition of accepting life in the fullness thereof and going through it with song and dance." He does not, however, even suggest that this engagement with the arts has a public purpose. He does not mention Tagore's songs (two of which later became the national anthems of India and Bangladesh). Nor does he acknowledge the tradition of radical experimental religion with which Tagore engages in *The Religion of Man*, or the connection of that project with the humanist quasi-religions of Comte and Mill. Never once does Nehru try to connect his own poetic and experimental side to those projects. Never does he suggest that such projects could have their own dividends for a democratic public that (by his own account) cannot live by science alone.

In short, Nehru is already busily at work constructing the culture gap, in his silence about just those forms of spirituality that might have survived his first four arguments.

It is here that the fifth argument (or, really, assertion of taste) comes into view. Nehru is uneasy about any utterance that cannot be cast in the form of a logical argument. Although his arguments justify a rejection only of religion's more dogmatic and authoritarian side, his taste seems to push him in the direction of a more sweeping reductionism. He doesn't believe in the idea of justification in ethics, because he thinks like a logical positivist: justification takes place only by appeal to empirical fact. He comes close, even, to accepting something like the verificationist conception of meaning, when he suggests that anything that can't be so verified, anything poetic or emotional, is "soft and flabby," and perhaps in the end nonsensical. We can't pursue understanding in such ways.

It is this lurking positivism—this hunch that metaphorical, emotional, and even ethical utterances are in the end too "soft" to help us, this embarrassment before the spiritual, even in its most extended sense—that explains the odd conclusion of *Discovery*, the conclusion that we ought to follow science even where we have no reason to think science can give us any illumination. Nehru was profoundly drawn to poetry, but he cannot justify his love, so he spurns it. Poetry is for him a guilty pleasure, not a source of sustenance for a nation.

4. The Need for More

What might a leader have done? Surely a wise leader of India should not have fostered any particular religious sect as a national religion. Even Gandhi, inclusive though he was, connected so deeply to Hindu traditions and symbols that one might have grave doubts about the suitability of his movement as the source of a "civil religion" for a pluralistic society. Nehru could certainly have pointed to India's basic constitutional commitments and observed that some forms of Hinduism are compatible with those traditions and others are not, and to a degree he did this, with his constant criticisms of the Hindu Right. He also could urge Indians to learn more about the tolerant and pluralistic elements in Hindu tradition, and that, too, he did, both by writing *Discovery* and in other writings.

He could also, however, have done things he did not do. He might have created public rituals expressive of the pluralistic commitments of the nation, focused around its history and its key struggles (as, for example, the United States has done with the life of Martin Luther King, Jr.). He might have encouraged or even created grass-roots movements centered around moral values consistent with the nation's core ideas (Gandhian movements, for example). Above all, and more important than this, he might have encouraged educational institutions to focus on instilling the habits of mind that a Tagorean religious humanism requires: an antinomian imagination, a critical yet soaring poetic spirit. That this could be done in the schools we know, because Tagore—and many others—did it. India had a thriving progressive education movement, from the elementary level on up through the liberal arts college or university (Visha-Bharati, Jamia

Millia Islamia)—until state control brought standardization and an end to the humanistic mission. When Tagore's Visha-Bharati needed money, it asked the government in—and then the government killed it. Jamia Millia similarly lost its progressive component (and the entirety of its elementary education program) when it accepted state assistance and therefore control. So: Nehru could have had a different posture toward what government should support in early and higher education. He could have fostered the idea that the arts and humanities are key ingredients of the good citizen. He could have made it clear that a citizen who only knows technology is incomplete: the imagination also requires cultivation. As Tagore said of education in his time:

> History has come to a stage when the moral man, the complete man, is more and more giving way, almost without knowing it, to make room for the . . . commercial man, the man of limited purpose. This process, aided by the wonderful progress in science, is assuming gigantic proportion and power, causing the upset of man's moral balance, obscuring his human side under the shadow of soul-less organization.[5]

Nehru might have taken thought for that balance, in thinking about public culture and, above all, about education.

He did not do so. The result of his lack of support for the humanities is that they quickly became disfavored. By now they are even held in contempt. Everyone is doing what Nehru told them to do: trusting science even where we have no reason to think that science offers insight. The upshot is the cultural vacuum I described earlier. Into that vacuum the Hindu Right has poured its baneful propaganda. But it's worse than that: for the void is not just out there, in a public space, it is in the hearts of so many of India's students, as they learn technical skills without a corresponding development of the spirit, the emotions, and the imagination.

As a man, Nehru longed for poetry and derived sustenance from it. As a leader, however, he could not see his way clear to honoring it, because it seemed just too "soft and flabby." But of course this soft part is a part of him, as anyone who reads what he writes can immediately see. So it is a part of his own personality that he views as too soft, and cannot publicly recommend. The rejection of a deep element in himself is, psychologically, of a piece with other things about Nehru: the fact that he could express love more easily at a distance than in the person's presence; the profound loneliness that so many observed in him, even in the midst of a life of action; the sense people had that this funny, kind, witty conversationalist, always the life of the party, was at the same time wandering in those deep woods of which the poet Robert Frost speaks. Nehru always was somewhat embarrassed about the emotional, about human connection. (If we should ever gain access to his correspondence with Edwina Mountbatten, we might learn a great deal more about how this struggle unfolded in later years of his life.) And so, being embarrassed, he was unwisely attracted to the logical-positivist view that the forms of discourse expressing these things are soft and unilluminating.

What his positivism fails to see is that the emotions have their own precision, and poetry its own clarity. What prose treatise, for example, could express the goals of the new nation as clearly as this great song of Tagore—greater even, in its comprehensiveness, than "Jana Gana Mana," though no doubt the latter is, in its brevity, better suited for its function:

O my mind, in this sacred spot of pilgrimage awake gently
On the shore of this Bharat's ocean of the great Humanity.
Standing here, raising both arms, I salute god in human form –
In sublime joy, I sing in an open rhythm my worship song.
These mountains in meditation absorbed, this land the rivers' prayer-bead
    strands hold,
Right here witness each day the sacred earth, *dhoritree* –
On the shore of this Bharat's ocean of the great Humanity.

Nobody knows at whose call people in how many streams
Came from where on unstoppable currents and merged in the seas.
Here the Aryan, here the non-Aryan, here the Dravidian, the Chinese –
Hordes of Shakas and Huns, Pathans and Mogals, in one body they mixed.
Today the West has opened its gates, from there they bring presents,
Will give and take, match and mix, not turn back with hands empty.
On the shore of this Bharat's ocean of the great Humanity.

Come you Aryan, you non-Aryan, come Hindu, Mussalman.
Today, welcome you English, welcome you Christian.
Come you Brahman, purifying your mind, hold all their hands.
Come you Outcaste, dispelled be the burden of all insults.
Come quick to mother's coronation, still to fill the pitcher for consecration
With holy water made sacred by the touch of everybody.
On the shore of this Bharat's ocean of the great Humanity.[6]

There's a poem that every school child in India might have been taught to sing—no doubt with accompanying dance and theatrics of a sort that would reinforce its meaning. It is religious, although it expresses no known organized religion, religious in the sense of Tagore's experimental humanism. But it is not just for the lonely poet: it can be loved and sung by many. It might have helped bring a nation together in dedication to fine ideals.

There's a poem Nehru might have honored—consecrated even—had he not been ashamed of his own heart.

Notes

1. Quoted in Tharoor, *Nehru*, 216.
2. Tagore, "The Call of Truth," in *The Gandhi Reader*, ed. Homer A. Jack (New York: Grove Press, 1956), p. 152.
3. *By Blue Ontario's Shore*, section 10.
4. From the section of "songs on patriotism" in *Of Love, Nature, and Devotion: Selected Songs of Rabindranath Tagore*, trans. and ed. Kalpana Bardhan (Delhi: Oxford, 2008), song Swadesh, *Gitabitan*, pp. 305–6, tune in the *Baul* mode, composed 1905. I have not reproduced her spacing inside lines, which is part of her interpretation of the songs' rhythm.
5. Tagore, *Nationalism* (London: Macmillan, 1917).
6. Tagore, songs, Bardhan p. 316, composed June 1910.

4 GANDHI, NEWTON, AND THE ENLIGHTENMENT

Akeel Bilgrami

Salman Rushdie once said, no doubt under duress, that secular humanism was itself a religion, thereby selling short both religion and secular humanism in one breath. I reckon (this is a conjecture) that he made that equation so that he could repudiate the charge of apostasy. One cannot, after all, be committing apostasy if one is only opposing one religion with another. Under the threat of execution, one may be allowed a confused thought, but with a clear mind no one with even a vestigial understanding of the mentalities and the realities of religion *or* the aspirations of secular humanism would be tempted by Rushdie's equation.

Though his equation itself may be quite wrong, I want to briefly pursue with some variation a theme it opens up. What I want to ask is really a familiar question, and trace some of the philosophical attitudes and intellectual history that makes it familiar, the question of whether there can be in the secular a form of continuity with something in the religious, in my view a continuity that actually stands for a particular form of humane radical politics that was very early on thwarted by a very specific notion of scientific rationality, which in this essay I will call a "thick" notion of scientific rationality. By constantly appealing to this notion of scientific rationality, a dominant orthodox strand in thinking about the Enlightenment has consistently tarnished a certain kind of radical questioning of this orthodoxy with charges of irrationalism. It is worth exposing a sleight of hand in all this.

A good place to begin is with Gandhi, a humanist and secularist yet by open declaration opposed to the Enlightenment and also avowedly a Hindu—even if by the lights of high Hinduism, a highly heterodox one. I will be focusing, and focusing selectively, only on

Gandhi's thought and writing and not his political interventions during the long freedom movement. I have said this before and will say it again at the outset of this essay: there is something particularly thankless about writing an interpretative essay on someone as intellectually and politically creative, perverse, and prolific as Gandhi.

I have hardly ever spoken on him in public (or indeed in someone's drawing or dining room) without someone offering a refutation by citing either some action or proposal of his during the freedom movement, or by mentioning some attitude of his toward his wife or children or ashram companions, or, more soberly, reminding me of some passage in his writing that is in tension with what I have just said. That is why I am keen to say at the very outset that I will be doing *merely* what I say: focusing selectively on some of his thought and writing with a view to offering a partial (but I hope interesting) interpretation that frees us of some of the standard, clichéd ways of thinking of him, as a saint on the one hand or a shrewd politician on the other; a nostalgist and traditionalist; or more specifically, a reactionary holding back the progressive, modernist tendencies in the nationalist movement, and so on.

The idea is not—not by any means—to write anything even approximating a definitive interpretative essay, as if that could be any sensible person's idea. The fact is that Gandhi, remarkable philosopher though he was, was not a systematic thinker, not a philosopher in the sense that the academic subject of philosophy circumscribes. So it is tiresome to demand of him that he be entirely consistent in all his writing. Not only would he have had to be a much less interesting thinker than he was to have that rightly demanded of him, he would have had to be born all over again.

What Gandhi says about the Enlightenment, as well as what he often omnibusly called "the West," relates closely to his view of science. In careless moments, Gandhi often said that it was a *predisposition* of science from its earliest days that it would lead to a way of thinking that was disastrous for politics and culture in ways that he outlined in great detail. This notion of a predisposition is obscure because general claims about the predispositions of something like science (something that is at once a theoretical pursuit as well as a practice, something that is defined in terms that are at once conceptual, methodological, and institutional) are hard to pin down and study, let alone confirm or refute, if they are intended to be empirical hypotheses. So I will instead sympathetically read his hunch about such a predisposition by situating it in a certain intellectual history. At the end of this exercise, it will emerge that a far better way to put his point would be in terms not of an empirical hypothesis about "science" as a self-standing human cognitive enterprise, but rather as a critique of a certain very specific notion of scientific "rationality."

The notion of rationality as it has governed our thought about history and politics and culture has in the past—famously—taken an idealized form, with a progressivist or developmental conception of these subjects; and for a few decades now that has been under a thoroughly critical scrutiny, as is the notion of modernity with which this idea of "progress" is so often coupled. Much more often than not the *telos* that defines the progressivist trajectory is in terms of an envisaged ideal or *endpoint* and the dialectic by which the end is (or is to be) realized is the large subject of the relevant historiography. Yet it is sometimes more fruitful to focus on the *beginnings* of such a sequence, since it may give a more truthful sense of the notions of rationality that are at stake than those defined by an idealized statement of the normative end.

Why, in the study of ideals of progress, do I stress the idea of a beginning rather than the end or rather than the accumulation and convergence of a progressive narrative toward that end? Because, in general, a sequence, especially when it is consecutively narrativized and dialectically and cumulatively conceived, as progressive ideals are bound to conceive it, cannot have started from the beginning of thought and culture itself. If a sequence is to aspire to conceptual and cultural significance (as the very idea of progress suggests) it cannot have *its* beginnings at the very beginning of conceptual and cultural life. That would trivialize things—evacuate the notion of sequence of any of the substance and significance that progressivist narrative aspires to. It cannot be that we have been converging on this significant progressive end from the random inceptions of our intellectual and cultural existence. One assumes, rather, that there were many strands at the outset, endless false leads, but then at some point (what I am calling the *beginning* of the progressivist trajectory) we got set on a path, which we think of as the *right* path, from which point on the idea of cumulative steps toward a broadly specifiable end began to make sense, a path of *convergence* toward that end. Accumulation and convergence toward a progressive endpoint, then, does not start at the beginning of thought, but starts rather at some juncture that we think of as the *start* onto a *right* path.

This point has many implications for historiography, some of them highly critical. Let me convey this concept with an example somewhat distant from our immediate concerns.

I think the point about a right path being essential to the idea of progress implies a real difficulty for philosophers such as, for instance, Hilary Putnam, when they say that scientific realism is true because it is the only explanation of the fact that there is accumulation and convergence and progress in scientific theories—that is to say, the posits of science ("gravity," say, or "electrons") must be *real* properties and things in the world (that is, the doctrine of "scientific realism") because it is only their reality which would explain the cumulative nature of the claims of scientific theories over time. In other words, for Putnam and many other philosophers, science, unlike other intellectual enterprises, has cumulative and convergent knowledge, with present research constantly building on past results in a progressive advancement of knowledge; the only explanation of this progression is that science's claims and science's terms are tracking reality itself. Thus electrons can't be dismissed as lacking a reality, as mere theoretical tools and constructs deployed for the sake of explanation, in a way that we might dismiss the idea of a social contract or even the idea of the unconscious. It is *because* science's terms ("gravity," "electron") refer to *real* properties and things in the world that scientific knowledge has this uniquely cumulative and convergent character that no other knowledge possesses.

What is the difficulty with this that I have in mind? Let us for the moment grant that science is cumulative and convergent and progressive in this way. Let us grant even that it is unique among forms of knowledge in being so. But even if we grant these as true, the fact is that these converging and cumulative trends of science have not existed since the beginning of theorizing about nature. In fact, Putnam would be the first to say that it is only sometime in the seventeenth century that we were set on the right path in science, and only from *then* on there has been an accumulation and convergence that is best explained by the corresponding reality of what the cumulative and converging scientific theories posit. But now a question arises. What makes it the case that *that* is when we were set on the "right" path? What is the notion of rightness, here? If we have an answer to this last question (about what makes the path the "right" path at *that* starting point), then that notion of "rightness" would already have established scientific realism and we don't need to wheel in scientific realism to explain the subsequent convergence, as Putnam and others claim.

Well, my subject is neither the merits of such well-known arguments nor even scientific realism, but the point I am making is generalizable to efforts that characterize modernity in progressivist terms. Indeed, it is even generalizable to interesting recent efforts to characterize modernity in sequential terms that are *not* progressivist.[1] These too cannot avoid the hard question of the sequence's starting point, which may have the greater power to illuminate than the sequence itself. That is why I am stressing the importance of the points where progress is supposed to *begin*. These reveal much more about what is invested and what is at stake in the idea of progress and ideals of rationality and modernity. Thus there is no avoiding the fact that if we even so much as accept the idea of "modernity" as a genuinely distinctive descriptive and analytical category (whatever side we take on the normative issues of whether modernity is a good thing or not), then we cannot but focus on the genealogy of its beginnings in Early Modernity.

So let me explore these beginnings briefly by recording the detailed affinities between Gandhi's ideas about science and the metaphysical, political, and cultural anxieties that first surfaced at the very site and time of the new science as it first began to be formulated in the seventeenth century in the West. There are many passages in Gandhi's dispatches to *Young India* and also in some passages in his book *Hind Swaraj* that suggest the following line of argument.[2]

Sometime in the seventeenth century we were set on a path in which we were given the intellectual sanction to see nature as—to use a Weberian notion—"disenchanted." This coincided with the period of the great revolutionary changes in scientific theory, so Gandhi crudely equated it with science itself and its newly and self-consciously formulated experimental methods. He saw in it a conception of nature whose pursuit left us disengaged from nature as a habitus, and which instead engendered a zeal to control it rather than merely live in it. And my claim is that these criticisms by Gandhi have extraordinarily close and striking antecedents in a tradition of thought that goes all the way back to the second half of the seventeenth century in England, and then elsewhere in Europe, simultaneous with the great scientific achievements of that time. It goes back, that is, to just the time and the place when the outlook of scientific rationality that many place at the defining center of what they call "the West" was being formed, and it is that very outlook with its threatening cultural and political consequences that is the target of that early critique.

It should be said emphatically at the outset that the achievements of the "new science" of the seventeenth century were neither denied nor opposed by the critique I have in mind, and so the critique *cannot* be dismissed as Luddite reaction to the new science, as Gandhi's critique is bound to seem, coming centuries later, when the science is no longer new and its effects on our lives, which the earlier critique was warning against, seem like a fait accompli. What the critique opposed was a development in outlook that emerged in the philosophical surround of the scientific achievements. In other words, what it opposed is the notion of what I will call a "thick" rationality that is often described in glowing terms today as "scientific rationality." What do I have in mind by calling it a thick notion (a term I am recognizably borrowing from Clifford Geertz)?

To put a range of complex, interweaving themes in the crudest summary, the dispute was about the very nature of nature and matter and, therefore, about the role of the deity, and of the broad cultural and political implications of the different views on these metaphysical and religious concerns. The metaphysical picture that was promoted by Newton (the official Newton of the Royal Society, not the neo-Platonist of his private study) and Boyle, among others, viewed matter and nature as brute and inert. On this view, since the material universe was brute, God was *externally* conceived with all the familiar metaphors of the "clock winder" giving the universe a push from the *outside* to get it in motion. In the dissenting tradition—which was a scientific tradition, for there was in fact no disagreement between it and Newton/Boyle on any serious detail of the scientific laws, and all the fundamental notions such as gravity, for instance, were perfectly in place, though given a quite different metaphysical interpretation—matter was *not* brute and inert, but rather was shot through with an *inner* source of dynamism responsible for motion, that was itself divine. God and nature were not separable as in the official metaphysical picture that was growing around the new science, and John Toland, for instance, to take just one example among the active dissenting voices, openly wrote in terms he proclaimed to be "pantheistic."[3]

The link with Gandhi in all this is vivid. One absolutely central claim of the freethinkers of this period was about the political and cultural significance of their disagreements with the fast developing metaphysical orthodoxy of the Newtonians. Just as Gandhi did, they argued that it is only because one takes matter to be "brute" and "stupid," to use Newton's own terms, that one would find it appropriate to conquer it with nothing but profit and material wealth as ends, and thereby destroy it both as a natural and a human environment for one's habitation. In today's terms one might think that this point was a seventeenth-century predecessor to our ecological concerns, but though there certainly was an early instinct of that kind, it was embedded in a much more general point (as it was with Gandhi too), a point really about how nature in an ancient and spiritually flourishing sense was being threatened, and how this was in turn threatening to our moral psychology of engagement with it, including the relations and engagement among ourselves as its inhabitants.

Today, the most thoroughly and self-consciously secular sensibilities may recoil from the term "spiritually," as I have just deployed it, though I must confess to finding myself feeling no such self-consciousness despite being a secularist and indeed an atheist. The real point has nothing to do with these rhetorical niceties. If one had no use for the word, if one insisted on having the point made with words that we today can summon with confidence and accept without qualm, it would do no great violence to the core of their thinking to say this: the dissenters thought of the world not as brute but as *suffused with value.* That they happened to think the source of such value was divine ought not to be the deepest point of interest for us. The point, rather, is that if it were laden with value, it would make normative (ethical and social) demands on us, whether we was religious or not, normative demands therefore that did not come merely from our own instrumentalities and subjective utilities. And it is this sense of forming commitments by taking in, in our perceptions, an evaluatively "enchanted" world which—being enchanted in this way—therefore moved us to normatively constrained engagement with it, that the dissenters contrasted with the outlook that was being offered by the ideologues of the new science.[4] A brute and disenchanted world could not move us to any such engagement since any perception of it, given the sort of thing it was, would necessarily be a detached form of observation; and if one ever came out of this detachment, if there was ever any engagement with a world so distantly conceived, so external to our own sensibility, it could only take the form of mastery and control of something alien, with a view to satisfying the only source of value allowed by this outlook—our own utilities and gain.

We are much used to the lament that we have long been living in a world governed by overwhelmingly commercial motives. What I have been trying to do is to trace this (just as Gandhi did) to its deepest *conceptual* sources and that is why the seventeenth century is so central to a proper understanding of this world. Familiarly drawn connections and slogans, like "Religion and the Rise of Capitalism," are only the beginning of such a tracing.

In his probing book *A Grammar of Motives*, Kenneth Burke says that "the experience of an impersonal outlook was empirically intensified in proportion as the rationale of the monetary motive gained greater authority."[5] This gives us a glimpse of the sources. As he says, one had to have an impersonal angle on the world to see it as the source of profit and gain, and vice versa. But I have claimed that the sources go deeper. It is only when we see the world as Boyle and Newton did, as against the freethinkers and dissenters, that we understand further why there was no option but this impersonality in our angle on the world. A desacralized world, to put it in the dissenting terms of that period, left us no other angle from which to view it but an impersonal one. There could be no normative constraint coming upon us from a world that was brute. It could not move us to engagement with it on *its* terms. All the term-making came from us. We could bring whatever terms we wished to such a world; and since we could only regard it impersonally—it being brute—the terms we brought in our actions upon it were just the terms that Burke describes as accompanying such impersonality, the terms of "the monetary" motives for our actions. Thus it is, that the metaphysical issues regarding the world and nature, as they were debated around the new science, provide the deepest conceptual sources.

The conceptual sources that we have traced are various but they were *not* miscellaneous. The diverse conceptual elements of religion, capital, nature, metaphysics, rationality, and science were tied together in a highly deliberate integration—that is to say, in deliberately accruing worldly *alliances*. Newton's and Boyle's metaphysical view of the new science won out over the freethinkers' and became official only because it was sold to the Anglican establishment and, in an alliance with that establishment, to the powerful mercantile and incipient industrial interests of the period in thoroughly predatory terms. Terms that stressed that how we conceive nature may now be transformed into something, into the kind of thing that is indefinitely available for our economic gain by processes of extraction—processes such as mining, deforestation, and plantation agriculture intended essentially as what we today would call "agribusiness." None of these processes could have taken on the unthinking and yet systematic prevalence that they first began to get in this period unless one had ruthlessly revised existing ideas of a world animated by a divine presence. From an *anima mundi*, one could not simply proceed to take at whim and will. Not that one could not or did not, till then, take at all. But in the past, in a wide range of social worlds, such taking as one did had to be accompanied by ritual offerings of reciprocation which were intended to show respect toward as well to restore the balance in nature, offerings made both before and after cycles of planting, and even hunting.

The point is that in general, the revision of such an age-old conception of nature was achieved in tandem with a range of seemingly miscellaneous elements that were brought together in terms that stressed a future of endlessly profitable consequences that would accrue if one embraced this particular metaphysics of the new science and build, in the name of a notion of rationality around it, the institutions of an increasingly centralized political oligarchy (an incipient state) and an established religious orthodoxy of Anglicanism that had penetrated the universities as well, to promote these very specific interests. These were the very terms that the freethinkers found alarming for politics and culture, alarming for the local and egalitarian ways of life, which some decades earlier the radical elements in the English Revolution such as the Levellers, Diggers, Quakers, Ranters, and other groups had articulated and fought for. Gandhi, much later, spoke in political terms that were poignantly reminiscent of these radical sectaries and, in *Hind Swaraj* and other writings, he wrote about science and its relations to these political terms in ways that echoed the alarm of the somewhat later scientific dissenters.

These scientific dissenters themselves often openly avowed that they had inherited the political attitudes of these radical sectaries in England of about fifty years earlier and appealed to their instinctive, hermetic, neo-Platonist, and sacralized views of nature, defending them against the conceptual assaults of the official Newton/Boyle view of matter. In fact, the natural philosophies of Anthony Collins and John Toland and his Socratic Brotherhood (and their counterparts in the Netherlands drawing inspiration from Spinoza's pantheism, spreading to France and elsewhere in Europe, and then, when strongly opposed, into secretive Masonic Lodges and other underground movements) were in many details anticipated by the key figures of the radical groups in that most dynamic period of English history—the 1640s—which had enjoyed hitherto unparalleled freedom of publication for about a decade or more to air their subversive and egalitarian views based on a quite different conception of nature.

Gerard Winstanley, the most well known among them, declared that "God is in all motion" and "the truth is hid in every *body*" (emphasis added).[6] This way of thinking about the corporeal realm had for Winstanley, as he puts it, a great "leveling purpose." It allowed one to lay the ground, first of all, for a democratization of religion. If God was everywhere, then anyone may perceive the divine or find the divine within him or her, and therefore may be just as able to preach as a university-trained divine. But the opposition to the monopoly of so-called experts was intended to be more general than in just the religious sphere. Through their myriad polemical and instructional pamphlets, figures such as Winstanley, John Lilburne, Richard Overton, and others reached out and created a radical rank-and-file population that began to demand a variety of other things, including an elimination of tithes, a leveling of the legal sphere by a decentralizing of the courts and the elimination of feed lawyers, as well as the democratization of medicine by drastically reducing, if not eliminating, the costs of medicine, and disallowing canonical and monopoly status to the College of Physicians. The later scientific dissenters were also very clear that these were the very monopolies and undemocratic practices and institutions which would get entrenched if science, conceived in terms of the Newtonianism of the Royal Society, had its ideological victory.

Equally (that is to say, conversely), the Newtonian ideologues of the Royal Society around the Boyle lectures started by Samuel Clarke saw themselves— without remorse—in just these conservative terms in which the dissenters portrayed them. They explicitly called Toland and a range of other dissenters "enthusiasts" (a term of opprobrium at the time), and feared that their alternative picture of matter was an intellectual ground for the social unrest of the pre-Restoration period when the radical sectaries had such great, if brief and aborted, popular reach. They were effective in creating with the Anglican establishment a general conviction that the entire polity would require orderly rule by a state apparatus around a monarch serving the propertied classes and that this was just a mundane reflection, indeed a mundane *version*, of an *externally* imposed divine authority that kept a universe of brute matter in orderly motion, rather than an *immanently* present God in all matter and in all persons, inspiring them with the enthusiasms to turn the "world upside down," in Christopher Hill's memorable, eponymous phrase.

To see God in every body and piece of matter, they anxiously argued, was to lay oneself open to a polity and a set of civic and religious institutions beholden to popular, rather than scriptural and learned, judgment and opinion. They were just as effective in forging with the commercial interests over the next century, the idea that respect for a sacralized universe would be an obstacle to taking with impunity what one could from nature's bounty. By their lights, the only obstacles that now needed to be acknowledged and addressed had to do with the difficulties of mobilizing toward an economy geared to profit. No other factors of a more metaphysical and ideological kind should be allowed to interfere with these pursuits once *nature* had been transformed in our consciousness to a set of impersonally perceived *natural resources.*[7]

It was this scientific rationality, seized upon by just these established religious and economic alliances, that was later central to the colonizing mentality that justified the rapacious conquest of distant lands. The justification was merely an extension of the connections that I have outline to colonized lands, which too were to be viewed as brute nature that was available for conquest and control—but only so long as one was able to portray the inhabitants of the colonized lands in infantilized terms, as a people who were as yet unprepared, by precisely a mental lack of such a notion of scientific rationality—to have the right attitudes toward nature and commerce and the statecraft that allows nature to be pursued for commercial gain. It is this integral linking of the new science through its metaphysics with these attitudes that I am calling the thick notion of scientific rationality.

There is a fair amount of historical literature by now on the intellectual rationalizations of colonialism, but I have introduced the salient points of an earlier precolonial period's critique here in order to point out that Gandhi's criticisms had a very long and recognizable tradition going back to the seventeenth century in the heart of the West that anticipated in detail and with thoroughly honorable intent, those lamentable developments around the thick notion of scientific rationality. What he called, perhaps confusedly, a "predisposition" of science itself is exactly what was being expressed in these prescient anxieties that these early freethinkers were voicing about how these alliances around a certain outlook generated by the new science was "thickening" what should otherwise have been an innocuous (and "thin") conception of science and rationality.

Once that point is brought on to center stage, a standard strategy of the orthodox Enlightenment against fundamental criticisms raised against it, is exposed as defensive posturing. It would be quite wrong and anachronistic to dismiss this initial and early intellectual and perfectly *scientific* source of critique, from which later critiques of the Enlightenment derived, as being irrational, unless one is committed to a very specific orthodox understanding of the Enlightenment, of the sort I am inveighing against. It is essential to the argument of this paper that far from being anti-Enlightenment, Gandhi's early antecedents in the West, going back to the seventeenth century and in recurring heterodox traditions in the West since then, constitute what is, and rightly has been, called "the Radical *Enlightenment*."[8]

To dismiss the pantheistic tendencies that I cited as unscientific and in violation of norms of rationality would be to run together in a blatant slippage the general and "thin" use of terms like "scientific" and "rational," with just this thick notion of scientific rationality identified above, which had the kind of politically and culturally disastrous consequences that the early dissenters feared. The appeal to scientific rationality as a defining feature of our modernity trades constantly on just such a slippage, subliminally appealing to the hurrah element of the general and thin terms "rational" and "scientific," which we all applaud, to tarnish critics of the Enlightenment such as Gandhi, while ignoring the fact that in their critique, the opposition is to the thicker notion of scientific rationality that was defined in terms of very specific scientific, religious, and commercial alliances.

Were we to apply the thin conception of "scientific" and "rationality" (the one that I imagine most of us embrace), the plain fact is that *nobody* in that period was getting prizes for leaving God out of the worldview of science. That one should think of God as voluntarily affecting nature from the outside (as the Newtonians did) rather than sacralizing it from within (as the freethinkers insisted), was not in any way to improve on the *science* involved. Both views were therefore just as unscientific, just as much in violation of scientific rationality, in the thin sense of that term that we would now take for granted. What was in dispute had nothing to do with science or rationality in that attenuated sense at all. What the early dissenting tradition as well as Gandhi were opposed to is the metaphysical orthodoxy that grew around Newtonian science and its implications for broader issues of culture and politics. This orthodoxy, with all of its implications, is what has now come to be called "scientific rationality" in the thick sense of that term, and in the pervasive cheerleading about the West and about the Enlightenment, it has been elevated into a defining ideal, dismissing all opposition as irrational, with the hope that accusations of irrationality, because of the general stigma that the term imparts in its thin usage, will disguise the very specific and thick sense of rationality and irrationality that are actually being deployed by the opposition. Such (thick) *ir*rationalism is precisely what the dissenters yearned for; hindsight shows just how admirable a yearning it was.

So the dismissals of Gandhi's critique of the Enlightenment ideals as a kind of irrationalism and nostalgia have blinded us to making explicit the interpretative possibilities for some of his thinking that are opened up by noting his affinities with a longstanding, dissenting tradition in the most radical period in English history. I am not suggesting for a moment that what was radical then could be retained without remainder as being radical today or even at the time when Gandhi was articulating his critique. But I am saying that it opens up liberating interpretative options for how to read Gandhi as being continuous with a tradition that was clear-eyed about what was implied by the disenchantment of the world, to stay with the Weberian term. It is a tradition consisting not just of Gandhi and the early seventeenth century freethinkers, but any number of remarkable literary and philosophical voices in between, such as Blake, Shelley, Godwin, not perhaps all of Marx but certainly one very central strand in Marx, William Morris, Whitman and Dewey in America, and countless voices of the nontraditional Left, from the freemasons in the early eighteenth century down to the heterodox Left in our own time, voices such as those of E. P. Thompson and Noam Chomsky, and the vast army of heroic but anonymous organizers of popular grass roots movements: in a word, the West as conceived by the "radical" Enlightenment, which has refused to be complacent about the orthodox Enlightenment's legacy of scientific rationality that the early dissenters in England had warned against well over three centuries ago.

To move away now from the specific sacralized formulations of Gandhi and his antecedents in intellectual history, we should be asking in a much more general way what their view amounts to, once we acknowledge that we have our own intellectual demands for more secular formulations. This is a tractable, historically situated version of the question I began with: is there something interesting in the secular that is continuous with something in the religious? Even so situated, it is a very large question that requires a far more detailed inquiry than I can give in a brief essay, but I do want to say something now to give at least a very general and preliminary philosophical sense of what I think is the right direction for its answer.

I had said earlier that our own secular ways of reenchanting a world made brute by the rampant adoption of the ideologies around the thick notion of scientific rationality, turns on seeing the world as suffused with value, without any compulsion to see this as having its source in the pantheistic terms of a divinity.

Here, then, is how I've allowed myself to think toward that idea.

Spinoza, in a profound insight, pointed out that one cannot both intend to do something and predict that one will do it, *at the same time.* Predicting what one will do is done from a detached point of view, when one as it were steps outside of oneself and looks at oneself as others would, from a third person point of view. But intending is done from the *first* person point of view of agency itself. And we cannot occupy both points of view on ourselves at once. Now, I want to claim that there ought to be an exactly similar distinction, not on the points of view that we have *on ourselves,* which was Spinoza's concern, but the points of view we have *on the world.* The world too can be seen, on the one hand, from a detached, third person point of view (science being the most systematic version of such a point of view) and, on the other, it can be seen from an engaged, first person point of view, the point of view of practical agency. And it is the availability of the world to us through its value properties (which move us to our first personal engagement with it) that provides the minimal continuity with the sacralized picture—the rest of which we cannot find palatable any longer.

Thus, putting it in the most abjectly simple terms, one might for instance find, from a certain perspective of the study of populations and disease and so on, that this or that segment of a population has a certain average daily caloric intake and that they, as a result, die of old age at an average in their late forties, an indication of their malnutrition. But that is only one perspective that I could take on the matter, one of detached, roughly scientific, study. I could then switch perspectives and see those very people as being in *need*. And the crucial point is that need is a value notion quite unlike the notions of caloric counts and, therefore, it makes normative demands on me. To view the world from this quite other perspective is, as I said earlier, to view it from the point of view of engagement rather than detachment. To be able to perceive the evaluative aspects of the world, one therefore has to possess practical agency, one has to have the capacity to respond to its normative force. In fact, we experience ourselves as agents in the practical sense partly in the perceptions of such a value-laden world.

Our agency and the evaluative enchantment of the world, then, are inseparably linked. That is why Spinoza's insight about ourselves can be extended outward onto the world. In a long and unsatisfactory philosophical tradition of moral psychology (deriving from philosophers such as Hume and Adam Smith), values are said to be given to us in our desires and moral sentiments. This is precisely the tradition that values are properties in and of the world, to which our practical agency responds. So here, then, is the absolutely crucial point. If my extension of Spinoza's point is right, the objects of our desires must be given to us as desir*able*, that is, as desir*abilities* or value elements in the world itself. If they were not, if the objects of our desires were given to us, not as desirable but as desir*ed* (as Hume and Adam Smith's moral psychology claims), then they could only be given to us when we step outside of ourselves and perceive what our desires are from the third person point of view. But that is precisely to abdicate our agency, our first person point of view. Agency is possible only if we take the desirabilities or evaluative properties in the world itself as given to us in the experience of our desires.

Compare my two statements "This is desired" and "This is desirable." The first is a report by me of something in my psychology. I have to step outside of myself and view myself as an object to make the report. In the second, I am not an object to myself, I am a subject expressing (not reporting) what I desire. And it is only the second which has it that the world contains desir*abilities*, or values. So for us to be agents and subjects rather than mere objects, we have to not only have desires, but our desires have to be responses to desirabilities or values in the world.

I have said that these evaluative properties are contained in the world and can be perceived or apprehended as such. But I have also said that this evaluative aspect of the world is nothing, it is darkness, to subjects that do not possess agency, a capacity for normative engagement. One reductive confusion to watch out for here is to think that because subjects capable of agency and engagement alone are capable of perceiving values in the world external to them, that values must therefore *not* be external after all and ultimately come from us. Another related confusion is to think that because some people may see some values in the world and others may not (you may see someone as being in need and be moved normatively by it; I may not), it is wrong to think that values are in the world at all and that we respond to them normatively—rather the world is indeed brute and value-free as Newton and Boyle claimed, and it is we who through our moral sentiments *make up* values and project them differentially onto the world. This is as confused as saying that because observation of things, of objects in the world, is theory-laden—that is, because when we hold different physical theories we will perceive different objects in the world, we must therefore in some sense be making up physical objects. These confusions may be natural but they are elementary and are easy to identify and resist.

A more ideological confusion that all this amounts to something unscientific is no less elementary, but being ideological it may be harder to resist. I have said that even irreligious people committed to scientific rationality in the thin sense of the term can embrace this way of thinking of the enchantment of the world because I insist that there is nothing unscientific about it.[9] To view nature and the world, not as brute, but as containing value that makes normative demands on our agency, is not by any means unscientific. It only means that natural science does not have full coverage of nature. In general, it is not unscientific to say that not all themes about nature are scientific themes. It is only unscientific to give unscientific responses to science's themes—as hypotheses about creationism or intelligent design do (being, as they are, responses to scientific questions about the origins the universe).

The point here is not the point often made by so many that we do not know very much scientifically. One can say that science knows only a very little bit of what might be known without in any way upsetting the scientistic naturalist picture that I think a reenchantment of nature would and should upset. The point is not just to be humble about how little we have managed to come to know and may ever come to know, but to say that nature consists of more than what science (at least as we know and understand it now) can know, because it is not the business of science to cover all that is in nature.

Nor is the point the same as the perfectly good point many have made before, which is that science has told us how to study nature but not how to study the human subject. The point is rather that there is no studying what is special about human subjectivity *unless we see nature and the world itself* as often describable in terms that are not susceptible to the kind of inquiry that natural science or even social science provides. There is a revealing point here about someone like Weber and his legacy. He, among others, is seen as having directed us to what is now fairly widely accepted as an undeniable truth, viz., that what makes the study of *human beings* stand apart from the natural sciences is that such study is value-laden. But, bizarrely, he never linked this now-familiar point explicitly with his own remarks about the disenchantment of nature. The fact is that there is no understanding what makes the study of human society stand apart by its value-ladenness unless we see that fact as being *of a piece* with an equally fundamental insight about a value laden natural and human environment, in virtue of which our agential engagements with it are prompted. Without that further link the insight that the study of human society stands apart from scientific study in its value-ladenness is incomplete, and the claim to the naturalistic irreducibility of the human subject is shallow.

I don't want to give the slightly misleading impression that in order to gain a secular enchantment of the world that is continuous with something in the religious, all I am concerned with is denying the scientistic picture, which has in it that *natural* science has total coverage of the world and nature. In fact, that will not suffice and that is not all that I am concerned to say. This is because the scientistic picture accommodates much more than *natural* science.

Under the influence of a familiar orientation in the social sciences, we might aspire to a certain picture of the world that concedes that we do not have to view it as brute. In other words, we can allow that it may contain more than what natural science studies, it contains opportunities for us to satisfy our desires. Thus, I might say, if I were to take a purely impersonal and scientific perspective on the world, I would see the water in the glass in front of me as H_2O, but with the social scientific broadening of this perspective to include a certain expanded notion of scientific rationality, I could also see that very glass of water as an opportunity to satisfy a desire of mine, to quench my thirst. This loosens things up a bit to allow the world to contain such strange things as opportunities, something the physicist or chemist or biologist would never allow nor could study, since opportunities, whatever they are, are not the subject matter of these sciences.

Rather, they are the subject matter of economics and more broadly the social and behavioral sciences which could now be seen to be, among other things, the science of desire-satisfaction in the light of (probabilistic) apprehension of the desire-satisfying properties in the world—that is, opportunities that the world provides to satisfy our wants and preferences.

But this is not the loosening up of our understanding of the world that is needed for a secular *enchantment* of the world that is continuous with the religious. Though it grants that the world is not entirely brute and it grants that the world contains something (opportunities) that escapes the purview of the natural sciences, it doesn't grant enough. It may be a first step, but to stop there is merely to extend the reach of scientific rationality in the thick sense—it is not to show its limitations in its conception of nature and the world. Nothing short of seeing the world as containing *values* (an older Aristotelian idea, if recent writers such as McDowell read him rightly) does that limitation get revealed, for it is values not opportunities that put *moral* demands on us.

Thus, even if we respond to others with a view to gratifying our moral sentiments of sympathy toward them, we are not quite yet on board with the depth of the demand that what a perception of others needs is the perception of something that puts normative *demands* on our individual and collective agency. It is in this deep respect that Marx's talk of needs in his slogan "From each according to his abilities to each according to his needs" went beyond the moral psychology of Hume and Adam Smith. Perceiving opportunities in the world merely tells us that the world is there for satisfying our desires and preferences, however filled with sympathy for others those desires are, but it doesn't conceive of the desires themselves as responding to what I have described as desir*abilities* in the world. (This has impoverishing implications for how one may think of more specific questions relevant to politics and political theory, implications I cannot pursue in this essay.[10]) Nothing short of perceiving in the world *values* that move our agency to respond in ethical terms, then, will reenchant it and help to arrest our alienation from it,[11] providing the initial steps to a *secular* version of what Gandhi and the freethinkers of the seventeenth century were struggling to find.

That the deliverances of their struggles yielded sacralized and pantheistic conceptions of the world with which we have little sympathy today, does not at all imply that those struggles were not honorable. But to say that their struggles are honorable is to say that they must be the antecedents to our own philosophical struggles to recharacterize the world and nature, and in doing so to reorient our entire range of social scientific and historiographic interests away from the obsessively causal explanatory methods that dominate them. This disciplinary reorientation based on such a review of nature may have some chance of laying the ground of resistance to the ubiquitously narrowing effects of the orthodox Enlightenment's legacies, not just in the universities, but in our moral and political lives generally.

In a previous essay of mine called "What is a Muslim?" I had tried explicitly to locate the forms of political pacification that come from a loss of agency owing to a picture of things in which a third person, rather than a first person, point of view dominates our conception of ourselves and our cultural and political identity.[12] In the present essay, I have tried to integrate those ideas with the politics that grew around the new science for the first time some centuries ago as a result of an increasingly third-person conception not of ourselves, but of the world and nature. Many more deep connections between metaphysics, moral psychology and politics and culture still need to be drawn—which I could not possibly have drawn here and likely don't have the intellectual powers ever to do—before anything of genuinely theoretical ambition is constructed on the subjects of identity, democratic politics, and disenchantment. But even without them it is possible at least to state the issues and aspirations at stake.

What Gandhi's and the seventeenth century radical sectaries' and the somewhat later scientific dissenters' intellectual efforts made *thinkable*, and what I am trying to consolidate in secular terms in my last many remarks, is something that goes measurably beyond what recent scholars have started saying is our best and only bet: the placing of constraints on an essentially utilitarian framework so as to provide for a social democratic safety net for the worst off. Salutary though the idea of such a safety net is (how could it fail to be given the wretched conditions of the worst off?), it is a project of limited ambition, in which Adam Smith and Hume remain the heroes, and Condorcet (among others) is wheeled in as the radical who proposed the sort of requisite constraints we need. In a recent book, Gareth Stedman Jones, chastened by the failures to put into practice more ambitious intellectual frameworks, comes to just these modest conclusions about our world as we have inherited it from these more ambitious theories and their failures.[13] By contrast, the heroes of this lecture, Gandhi and the key radicals as well as later dissenting figures of the seventeenth century, through whose lens I have been reading him, wanted it to be at least thinkable that the world could be "turned upside down"—not entirely, not all at once, but in places where the reach of "thick" rationality has not been comprehensive and where there might be scope for some reversal and secular reenchantment.

Gandhi in many of his writings had passionately aspired to the argument that India as it first struggled for its freedom and then later came to be poised to gain independence from colonial rule, was just such a place. It would be a reflection both of our moral complacence and our failure of political will to say that what Gandhi aspired to for his times can no longer be an aspiration for ours. I can think of no more urgent task for a political philosophy in India (the governing theme of this volume of essays) than to aspire to some form of intelligently and judiciously adjusted theorization of what such a "radical" Enlightenment (within which I am placing Gandhi) amounts to for our own time and place.

Notes

1. For a very interesting such effort see Sudipta Kaviraj's "An Outline of a Revisionist Theory of Modernity," in *Indian Political Thought: A Reader*, edited by Aakash Singh Rathore and Silika Mohapatra (London: Routledge, 2010).
2. M. K. Gandhi, *Hind Swaraj and Other Writings* (Cambridge: Cambridge University Press, 1997).
3. In a series of works, starting with *Christianity Not Mysterious* in 1696, more explicitly pantheistic in statement in the discussion of Spinoza in *Letters to Serena* (1704) and then in the late work *Pantheisticon* (1724). These writings are extensively discussed in Margaret Jacob's extremely useful treatment *The Radical Enlightenment: Pantheists, Freemasons, and Republicans* (London: George Allen and Unwin, 1981). In case it is a source of confusion, I should make clear that the metaphysical and scientific debate about the nature of matter and nature, whose centrality I am insisting on, should not be confused with another debate of that time, perhaps a more widely discussed one, regarding the "general concourse," which had to do with whether or not the deity was needed after the first formation of the universe, to keep it from falling apart. In that debate, Boyle, in fact, wrote against the Deists, arguing in favor of the "general concourse," of a continually active God. But *both* sides of that dispute take God to be external to a brute nature, which was mechanically conceived, unlike Toland and his "Socratic Brotherhood" and the dissenting tradition I am focusing on, who denied it was brute and denied that God stood apart from nature, making only external interventions. The dispute about "general concourse" was only about whether, the interventions from the outside of an *externally* conceived God were or were not needed after the original creative intervention.
4. I have written at greater length about this conception of the world as providing normative constraints upon us and the essential links that such a conception of the world has with our capacities for free agency and self-knowledge, thereby making both freedom and self-knowledge thoroughly normative notions, in my book *Self-Knowledge and Resentment*, chapters 4 and 5 (Cambridge, Mass: Harvard University Press, 2006). For the idea that values are perceptible external qualities, see John McDowell's pioneering essay "Values and Secondary Qualities," in *Morality and Objectivity*, edited by Ted Honderich (London: Routledge and Kegan Paul, 1985).
5. University of California Press, 1969.
6. Cited by Christopher Hill in his *The World Turned Upside Down* (New York: Penguin, 1975), p. 293, from *The Works of Gerard Winstanley*, edited by G. H. Sabine (Ithaca, NY: Cornell University Press, 1941).

7. The conceptual links between 1) the democratization of religion that is possible when one has a sacralized view of nature and body and 2) the resistance to the cast of mind that rationalizes the commercial plunder of the bounties of nature by the very same sacralized conception of nature, is essential to the reading I am giving of Gandhi through the affinities he has with the seventeenth century dissenters. As Utsa Patnaik acutely pointed out in a discussion after my verbal presentation of this lecture at Jawaharlal Nehru University, if 1) were emphasized without 2), other movements such as Bhakti, which are commonly cited in the Indian context could also be assimilated with the critique of thick scientific rationality being presented here. Thus 2), or more accurately, 1)'s *necessary and conceptual links* with 2), are indispensable to the argument being made here.

8. See Jacob, *The Radical Enlightenment*.

9. By rationality in the "thin" sense I mean just the standard codifications of deductive rationality and inductive rationality or confirmation theory, and decision theory.

10. In a forthcoming essay in *Economic and Political Weekly*, tentatively entitled "Value, Disenchantment, and Democracy," I pursue some of those implications.

11. Actually the relation between opportunities in the world and values in the world is a close, complicated and interesting one. It is arguable that values in the world cannot be acted on unless we also see the world as containing opportunities. All that I am opposing is that it is *sufficient* to repudiate the picture of a brute nature and world by pointing out that the world contains opportunities. I am not denying that seeing the world as containing opportunities is *necessary* for that repudiation.

12. See "What Is a Muslim," *Critical Inquiry*, Summer 1992.

13. Gareth Stedman Jones, *An End to Poverty? A Historical Debate* (New York: Columbia University Press, 2005).

DEMOCRATIC MEDIA

5 LEGITIMATING MAJORITARIAN CHAUVINISM: THE INDIAN MEDIA AND THE HINDUTVA CAMPAIGN

Malini Parthasarathy

1. A Key Player in India's Democracy

The Indian press has been widely celebrated for its catalytic role in the success story of India's democracy. In a sense, the Indian media has had a historic advantage in comparison to many of its counterparts elsewhere in that having been in the vanguard of the struggle against British colonial rule, it can rightly claim to be one of the principal stakeholders in India's democratic republic. Testifying to the deep sense of engagement that the Indian press had with the birth of India's democracy was the lively reporting and perspectives that journalists, columnists, and editors brought to India's freedom struggle, the intense public debate in editorial columns over the shape and direction of the future independent state, and the impassioned arguments over the political and economic issues facing the future Indian state.

Yet when India became independent in August 1947, the joy was tinged with sadness. There was exhilaration on the one hand at the prospect of freedom from colonial rule and eager anticipation of the future India wherein it was hoped that the best of liberal values would be realized. But there was also the sobering thought that the disastrous politics of hatred and polarization, stoked by cynical and partisan political interests, had resulted in the harrowing and disintegrating experience of Partition that unleashed terror and destruction in its wake. The two new states of India and Pakistan, which came into being that August, had this painful legacy to contend with. In India, this translated into a political determination to insulate the new state from such potential sectarian conflicts, which could threaten its very survival.

Fortunately for those who were entrusted with the task of writing India's new Constitution, their moral authority was greatly strengthened by a broadly supportive and enthusiastic discourse in the public sphere, with most of the press urging India to usher in a democracy founded on sound liberal values such as pluralism and secular governance. It thus lightened the burden of the Constitution framers, enabling them to be assertive in their acknowledgment that the new Indian state would have to be emphatically secular and affiliation-free if it were to survive as a cohesive national entity.

It became a matter of public recognition and even axiomatic that India's parliamentary democracy would necessarily have to be anchored to the postulates of secularism, pluralism, and democracy if India's diverse cultural, religious, ethnic, and linguistic strands were to cohere together as a single national unit. The Indian press found it easy to slip into the role of a custodian of this new democratic framework. Thereby was developed a robust tradition of independent reporting and relatively unfettered editorial analysis, all of which had the implicit objective of strengthening the normative functioning of India's democracy. It followed that the press in India was perceived by the wider public as a key player in the democratic arena, with expectations of it as playing the role of a referee and blowing the whistle whenever the government was perceived as straying from its normative obligations.

It would be a fair claim to make that a free and independent press is a key element in the continuing vitality of India's democratic structure. When Indians point proudly to the resilience and durability of India's democratic project, it must also be noted that the prior conditions of a vibrant civil society, knit together primarily by the Gandhi-Nehru vision of civic nationalism and an active and politically well-tuned public sphere which fostered the collective spirit of a democratic Indian nationalism privileging civic identity over every other affiliation, paved the way for the success of Indian democracy. As political philosopher Charles Taylor has pointed out, the rise of the public sphere is a crucial feature of the shift in the social imaginary to a horizontal direct access society, in other words, to a modern democratic state, which would be the case with India after 1947 too: "Modernity has involved . . . a revolution in our social imaginary, the relegation of these forms of mediacy to the margins, and the diffusion of images of direct-access. . . . This has come about in a number of forms: the rise of a public sphere, in which people conceive themselves as participating directly in a nationwide (sometimes even international) discussion."[1]

Taylor's description of the transition to a modern social imaginary that manifests in a democratic state that is inescapably secular can be seen to apply to India's own emergence as a secular democracy in 1947. The rise of a horizontal direct-access society is given political form by an act of the people, and "this forms the background to the contemporary sources of legitimate government in the will of the people." Democracies, Taylor points out,

> therefore require a relatively strong commitment on the part of their citizens. In terms of identity, being citizens has to rate as an important component of who they are . . . . In other words, the modern democratic state needs a healthy degree of what used to be called patriotism, a strong sense of identification with the polity and a willingness to give of oneself for its sake. That is why these states try to inculcate patriotism and to create a strong sense of common identity even where it did not previously exist. And that is why one thrust of modern democracy has been to try to shift the balance within the identity of the modern citizen, so that being a citizen will take precedence over a host of other poles of identity, such as family, class, gender, even (perhaps especially) religion.[2]

Taylor argues that this has been one of the motivations for secularism of the independent ethic mode: "State builders reached for it as a potential common point of allegiance for citizens, above and beyond their other differences, in the recognition that the democratic state requires such a common allegiance."[3] This, in essence, was at the heart of the efforts of the nation-builders in the early years of independent India and the media was a willing ally in the pan-national project to build a new vision of a secular pluralist democracy, which would have equal resonance for every citizen.

Given that India's independent press has historic linkages with the democratic system and is seen as an integral part of the democratic framework, I argue that the Indian press continues to be a major stakeholder in the democratic process and cannot afford to abandon its role as a custodian of the core democratic values—secularism, equality, and pluralism. Further, it cannot and should not be deterred by the argument that such values might have less salience in the context of changed market realities or different corporate priorities. As has been pointed out, Indian democracy has been fundamentally enriched by the historical presence of a lively argumentative tradition. Philosopher and economist Amartya Sen has observed that India "has been especially fortunate in having a long tradition of public arguments, with toleration of intellectual heterodoxy," thereby enabling it to make a particularly effective connection with democracy and choose a resolutely democratic constitution.[4] Democracy, notes Sen, is "intimately connected with public discussion and interactive reasoning . . . And to the extent that such a tradition can be drawn on, democracy becomes easier to institute and also to preserve." The role of the argumentative tradition of India "applies not merely to the public expression of values, but also to the interactive formation of values, illustrated for example by the emergence of the Indian form of secularism."[5]

As a crucial component of the larger democratic framework, the media which can be said to be enjoying an intellectual dominance of the Indian public sphere, at least currently, cannot escape the fact that its institutional credibility and its ever expanding reach vests it with a responsibility to the wider audience of civil society and nation. In this chapter, I seek to demonstrate how perilously close the media (by examining some samples of the writings and reports in the English language dailies of the period at which the Hindutva campaign was at its peak) came to abdicating its responsibility as a guardian of the fundamental democratic values, allowing itself to be co-opted in a dangerous project to scuttle the basic premises of governance of the Indian nation.

India has had a narrow escape from being engulfed by the tides of fundamentalism as a result of the abrupt halt to the steady ascent of Hindu nationalism. Until the elections of 2004 and the emergence of a secular coalition, which later called itself the United Progressive Alliance, shattered the myth of an all-conquering Hindu nationalism, a high-voltage campaign to enshrine a Hindu nationalist ethos of governance had unfolded with piercing intensity. So confident were these self-proclaimed arbiters of India's national destiny that they seized the center stage of the political discourse with the effect that the entire public agenda appeared to be polarized around their claims and demands. That the Hindutva ideological campaign which insidiously gathered momentum through the 1990s managed to capture so much space in the public discourse was largely the result of the failure of the media to scrutinize their claims with the necessary rigor.

Substantial sections of the media absorbed uncritically the themes and issues tossed out by the Hindu nationalists aiming to enlarge their own political space in the public discourse. They appeared to have been co-opted in the spinning out of spurious dreams of an "India Shining," in hindsight so grossly disconnected from the ground reality that there was disillusionment and alienation from what was seen as empty political rhetoric. This explains why despite the fact that there was a significant penetration of the themes and rhetoric of Hindutva into the media, it did not really help turn the electoral tide in favor of the forces of Hindu nationalism. Yet if not for the fact that influential columnists and several publications appeared to legitimate the specious claims of Hindutva, it could not have acquired the momentum it did, in such a short space of time.

I point out in this chapter the elements in the media response to the Hindutva campaign, which served to aid the partisan political agenda of Hindu majoritarianism. Led by a group of highly ideological columnists like Arun Shourie, Swapan Dasgupta, and S. Gurumurthy, whose writings were featured prominently in leading national dailies and newsmagazines, there was a tendency to glorify the Hindu nationalist leaders and exaggerate their popular appeal, to give play to unsubstantiated themes and claims, thereby forcing tendentious and partisan issues onto the national political agenda at the expense of more crucial governing and developmental priorities and, most dangerously, providing the political legitimization for sectarian leadership and conflict of the worst kind.

The disinclination to resist the abrasive propaganda tide, seen as attracting scores of Hindu middle-class voters and newspaper readers, led to a surprising blindness as to where and how this majoritarian fervor was going to end, thus failing to anticipate the horrifying climax of the Gujarat pogroms in early 2002.

2. Implicit Sanction for Hate Politics?

It is important to note that the periodic featuring of the politically tendentious themes of Hindutva—and more disturbingly the repeated peddling of the worst kind of ethnic stereotypes of Christians and Muslims, of the former as rabid evangelists out to "convert" Hindus, of the latter as "fundamentalist terrorists"—provided incendiary political justification and the implicit legitimization of hate crimes such as what happened with the Australian missionary Graham Staines, burnt to death in Orissa and the Gujarat pogroms against Muslims. For instance, the writings of columnists like Arun Shourie and Gurumurthy, both regarded as influential voices with the Indian middle classes, appeared to provide a strange kind of moral sanction for these dark episodes.

One example would be the case of the Report of the DP Wadhwa Commission of Inquiry released in August 1999, which was widely criticized as having failed to have exposed the real truth behind the brutal murder of Graham Staines by shying away from probing the killer Dara Singh's links to the Bajrang Dal and other Hindu extremist groups operating in Orissa at the time. On a matter that had evoked widespread public horror and worldwide revulsion, Arun Shourie came to the defense of the Wadhwa Commission in his article "Who Killed Australian Missionary Graham Staines?" but more pertinently, used the Staines murder to reassert the tendentious Hindutva suggestion that tensions were mounting because of "conversions." In this article, the first target of Shourie's ire was the Minorities Commission: "The Minorities Commission sent a team, and declared that the genesis of the trouble lay in Bharatiya Janata Party (BJP) men inflaming feelings of the local Hindus and instructing them to covert the Cross into a Trishul. As for the incidents and tension, it came to the conclusion it always does: the Hindus had created the trouble."[6] Shourie mocked the press for rushing to conclusions before investigating the facts.

His observations on the Minorities Commission were particularly stinging and with a debilitating impact, given that as a nationally reputed columnist, Shourie's words would have been taken very seriously by large sections of the reading public: "The second institution which comes out most poorly is the Minorities Commission. For quite some time now, this Commission has been putting out patently partisan reports, reports so partisan as to appear to be designed to inflame."[7]

Shourie went on to paint a picture of Staines as an aggressive missionary, almost as if to say "well, he asked for it!" Noting that Staines had "the typical concerns of a typical missionary—harvesting souls for the Church," Shourie even subtly seemed to exonerate Dara Singh: "Several witnesses testified that Dara Singh had been engaged in rescuing cows . . . Cows are revered by Hindus. The man trying to save them becomes an outlaw in the eyes of the police and a hero in the eyes of the people." On the other hand, noted Shourie, "Staines and his associates are left free to go on converting Hindus to Christianity."

To top it all, Shourie's final pronouncement, of considerable political value to the Hindu majoritarian project but which would have sent intimidating signals to minority citizens who were being told subtly that there was a justification for the violence directed against them, was: "That is the key lesson if the State is going to persist with double standards in regard to the sentiment of Hindus and non-Hindus on the one hand, and with a deliberate shutting of eyes on the other, it is paving the way for such crimes."[8]

It was clear that the writings of these leading columnists whose articles ran almost daily in mainstream national dailies provided a springboard for the main ideological assault by the Hindu majoritarian campaign in the political arena. The propaganda offensive was barely concealed in some of the arguments that were unveiled in major national dailies. For instance, writing after the Tamil Nadu Chief Minister Jayalalithaa's remarks following the Godhra train carnage, wherein she had caustically noted the failure to condemn violence against the majority community, columnist S. Gurumurthy, writing in the *New Indian Express*, praised her for showing "the courage to speak out on the malaise in our secular polity." He went on to express regret that "the malaise runs deeper . . . it extends to the entire secular class. And a large intellectual class. It is founded on pseudointellectualism and pseudosecularism that presently form the foundation of the public discourse."[9] Amid his sarcastic jibes at the "seculars," Gurumurthy's piece laid out all the politically loaded components of the majoritarian offensive:

As chance would have it, those killed were only Hindus, irrelevant to secular India. If a Christian church in thatched roof were attacked, Christian

governments in the West would pounce on us. If it were Muslims, the
entire Muslim world would converge on us.

Compare the Godhra carnage with what happened when some tribals torched
Staines and his children in Orissa. Hell broke loose. The entire country was set
upon and came to a halt. "Hindu Fundamentalists, RSS-VHP-Bajrang Dal"
goons have snuffed out a great social worker, shouted the secular megaphones—
the media, leaders and parties, Gurumurthy wrote. "The same was the case in
Jabhua rape. It was established to be an intratribal and intra-Christian affair.
But the secular media and the minorities blamed the Hindus and the RSS . . . .
This is the real face of secularism as practised in India, of the secular media, of
the secular leaders . . . if Gujarat is on fire today and the country is witnessing fits
of communal outburst, the secular class has to accept its own share of blame."[10]

It would be easy to dismiss such outpourings as the rants of an extremist but
for the fact that such writings were showcased in major national dailies on the
op-ed pages and sometimes as front-page anchor news pieces, which vested this
provocative rhetoric with undue respectability. It must be also noted that the
highlighting of this kind of provocative and sectarian propaganda in the context
of a sensitive issue such as the Godhra incident would have added a fillip to the
orgy of bloodletting and violence unleashed in the subsequent pogroms against
Muslims in Gujarat after Godhra. In other words, this sort of writing provided
an incitement to these genocidal binges.

It was striking that Hindutva propagandists managed to have several leading
dailies, not all necessarily sympathetic to the Hindu nationalist point of view,
publish their blatantly sectarian and provocative pieces virtually goading pro-
spective middle-class audiences to engage in civil war with their fellow citizens.
Given the high standards of professional rigor and ethics that marked mainstream Indian journalism over the more than fifty years since Independence,
it might be asked how such incendiary propaganda passed muster with newspaper editors or other such gatekeepers. The answer to that question would be
that for at least a decade preceding the BJP's ascent to power in New Delhi in
1998–1999, the orchestrated campaign by Hindutva chauvinists in the public
arena aimed at breaking down some of the fundamental axioms of the prevailing
political discourse, notably the ideas of secularism and pluralism, had begun to
make headway.

The Hindu majoritarian campaign needed to demonize Muslims and
Christians and to portray these minority citizens as "Sinister Others" with
extraterritorial loyalties, in order to mobilize public support for its assault on the
doctrines of pluralism and secularism. But it was inexplicable why the media,

which had a strong tradition of evaluating its sources of information and had also developed over the years a certain degree of healthy skepticism about political authority, allowed itself to be manipulated by these peddlers of hate.

Looking back at the content that filled the newspapers during the height of the BJP's sway in the late 1990s and until 2002, it might appear that little else was happening in an India reeling from a barrage of propaganda assaults by overzealous Christian missionaries even as Muslim terrorists were sneaking up to plant bombs in public spaces. In a sense, by lending newspaper and magazine space to these specious arguments and tendentious stereotypes, the media helped create a political environment that was hospitable to the ascent of Hindu majoritarianism.

The tendency to echo whatever were the themes and issues highlighted by the Hindu nationalists, predictably "forced conversions" and "Islamic terror rearing its head," had the media giving undue editorial weightage and respectability to these "problems" as though these were critical points in the national discourse, requiring urgent redressal. Instead of making an independent scrutiny of the claims made by Hindu nationalist activists, many major publications and television channels were mindlessly co-opted into painting a picture of a society on the brink of a major ideological transformation, as if events were moving inevitably to the grand climax of the Indian nation-state finally connecting with its Hindu essence. This uncritical assimilation of political propaganda cut the media off from the actual political and social realities, so different in its contours.

The second feature of this pattern of uncritical absorption of the political agenda of the Hindu majoritarianists was the highlighting of alarmist reports, the tone and tenor of which often bordered on xenophobia, based on unverified details and statistics, the sources of which were never made transparent, on various themes that were so dear to the Hindu chauvinist heart. Needless to say, such reports were the delight of the various Hindutva votaries who wrote columns in the same newspapers and magazines. For instance, regarding the issue of forced conversions, a stream of news items appeared almost daily in major newspapers taking note of the so-called connection between Christian groups and churches and foreign funding. It was evident that preceding the propaganda blasts from the columnists, the ground was being laid by seemingly innocuous news reports matter-of-factly pointing out numerous instances of the "foreign hand" at work behind the activities of Christians in the country.

There was a clear sectarian bias in the proposition that Christian groups or churches were being funded from abroad and no professional news organization or editor could in all conscience let such writings pass for news. But despite the fact that such reports had strange congruity with the main themes of the Hindu majoritarian political agenda, these reports were featured in many dailies almost on a routine basis, thus entrenching particular negative stereotypes about particular communities in the minds of the reading public.

One example was a report in the *Times of India* of August 16, 1999, written by Inder Sawhney. It asserted:

> Christian missionaries and allied groups continue to be largest recipients of foreign funds. They received Rs 15.88 crore (75.69 percent of the total foreign funds) in April–June this year compared with Rs 11.41 crore during the corresponding period last year and Rs 12.67 crore in the first quarter. A study of the receipt of foreign funds by religious/non-political organisations and other groups in April–June, based on Intelligence reports gathered by the Home Ministry, indicates a sharp increase to Rs 20.98 crore compared with Rs 14.02 crore during the corresponding period in 1998.[11]

It is obvious that the source for this report was the Home Ministry, presided over then by the leading ideologue of Hindu nationalism, L. K. Advani, whose political priorities reflected clearly in the focus on such a scrutiny of foreign funding by the Indian intelligence agencies. Yet the news report should have gently drawn the reader's attention to this important detail, which it did not, that these figures emanated from a source that had a vested interest in the propagation of such details. Predictably, the foreign connection that was repeatedly suggested in this kind of news reports triggered bouts of sneering from the Hindutva propagandist-columnists.

So strong was the pressure of the Hindutva campaign on the discourse that even a newsmagazine like *Outlook* widely regarded as having impeccable liberal credentials thought it fit to publish a taunting harangue by the RSS ideologue Seshadri Chari, then the editor of the RSS journal *Organiser* about the allegiance of Christian churches in India to the Vatican: "Today, half a century after Independence, if the present generation of the Church leaders in India want to free themselves from their foreign 'yoke,' will they be able to do so? The Vatican has not concealed its agenda . . . . The Vatican will prevail over the churches in India through their working order that in matters political, as well as spiritual or temporal, the view of the Vatican is final and binding . . . The question here is: are the church leaders, who are devout Indians going about their 'normal business' in a harmless manner, be ever out of the control of the Vatican?"[12] The invidious and politically loaded jibes at the Christian community had strong echoes of another familiar slur hurled time and again at Indian Muslims whose national loyalties are perennially questioned, even as they are taunted for their "greater allegiance to Mecca."

There were no dearth of commentators jumping into the fray, many with no clear *locus standi* in the issue making wild allegations about the activities of Christian social workers and groups that could kindle feelings of xenophobia and religious chauvinism among the reading public. For instance, Francois Gautier, a French journalist settled in Auroville in southern India and a prominent voice in the campaign for Hindutva, writing in the *Indian Express* in November 2000 on "Christ and the Northeast," alleged that it was in the Northeast that the Papal drive for "evangelisation" was meeting with most success "as it is peopled with simple, poor and uneducated tribals, who make easy targets." Gautier's lurid account pointed ominously at Tripura, where "there were no Christians at Independence, the maharaja was a Hindu and there were innumerable temples all over the state. But from 1950, Christian missionaries (with Nehru's blessings) went into the deep forests of Tripura and started converting the Kukis. Today, according to official figures, there are 120,000 Christians in Tripura, a 90 percent increase since 1991. The figures are even more striking in Arunachal Pradesh where there were only 1710 Christians in 1961 but 115,000 today . . . What to say of Mizoram and Nagaland, where the entire local population is Christian!"[13] The rest of Gautier's essay, published in the *Indian Express*, a national daily of considerable influence, sketched a scenario that was meant to set the alarm bells ringing not only among the Hindus but also to trigger national security fears. "Isn't it also strange," mused Gautier, "that many of the Northeast's separatist movements are not only Christian dominated but also sometimes have the covert backing of missionaries? The Don Bosco schools, for example, which are everywhere in the Northeast, are known by the Tripura Intelligence Bureau to sometimes harbor extremists at night."[14] The essay finally ended with an appeal to Indians to awake to "the threat of Christian conversions here." The argument "mostly put forward by 'secular' thinkers that Christians are only 3 percent of the population in India, and therefore cannot be a threat, is totally fallacious: the influence Christians exercise in this country through their schools, hospitals and the enormous amount of money being poured in by Western countries for the purpose of converting Hindus is totally disproportionate."[15]

Similar invective was hurled at Muslims on the basis of unsubstantiated theories and statistics that inevitably found their way to the newspaper columns. As with the stereotype being relentlessly and steadily built up over months of the Christian community as a bunch of fanatical evangelists with foreign money in their pockets, Indian Muslims were being painted as potential terrorists and fundamentalists. News reports clearly sponsored by the Advani-led Home Ministry subtly stoked fears of Islamic fundamentalism rearing its head in the country. One such report noted that Islamic *madrassas* were mushrooming on the Indian borders. The report in the *Times of India* in December 2002, basing itself mysteriously on unnamed sources, hinted that "concerted efforts were being made by Pakistan to generate a feeling of alienation among people living in border areas through allurements, subversive propaganda and religious fundamentalism." In this context, said the report, there was an "indiscriminate growth" of *madrassas* along the international border, which were liable to "misuse for fundamentalist and other antinational activities." Hence the Central Government was now considering legislation to regulate the activities of these places.[16] What was intriguing in this report was the fact that apart from its being based on an unnamed source, most likely a Home Ministry official, there was absolutely no clear explanation for the sudden focus on an issue such as *madrassas*, and there was no substantiation of the linkages with Pakistan or "antinational activities" that were alleged. Such items were carried regularly by national dailies resulting in the entrenching of a dangerously negative portrayal of the Muslim community, rendering them vulnerable targets.

Newspapers appeared to pick up the pet themes of the ruling BJP and even editorially endorse them. As is well known, one of the BJP's main political rallying points is its xenophobic response to the illegal immigration particularly from Bangladesh. While it is certainly an editorial prerogative for newspapers to express their opinions on all major policy issues, and those opinions might happen to coincide with that of the ruling establishment, for newspapers to give intellectual respectability and weight to points that are basically part of ideological propaganda would be to abdicate their responsibility to their readers. An editorial in the popular newsmagazine *India Today* headlined "Passage to India" is a case in point. The editorial started dramatically: "Throw them out." It went on to note that "When Deputy Prime Minister LK Advani says so about Pakistani and Bangladeshi nationals who have overstayed in this country, it is easy to see it as extreme rightwing xenophobia. It is not. He has only given voice to a dangerous national reality."[17] The editorial had no statistics or data to show the reader why one of the BJP's favorite talking points had suddenly become an issue of overwhelming national importance.

It was clear that the publication of such articles and opinions in major newspapers and magazines lent a dangerous credibility to pernicious and incendiary rhetoric. The linkage between the continual highlighting of Hindu sectarian themes designed to drive the minorities into a corner, by painting them as antinational and disloyal, a tactic typical of all majoritarian campaigns, and the shocking spurt in hate crimes, the most prominent being the slaying of Graham Staines and the massacre of Muslims in Gujarat in early 2002, was painfully evident. Yet these new horrors did not seem to stop the dangerous trend of legitimization of the politics of hate. Undeterred by the brutal murder of Staines and the obvious damage to India's credibility as a secular country, columnists and writers continued to thunder away in the major dailies about the danger of conversions and the falsehood that Christians were being harassed. The *Times of India* ran a column by M. V. Kamath, known widely to have Hindutva sympathies, in October 1999, barely nine months after the Staines episode, which implicitly shifted the onus of responsibility for Staines' slaying from the Hindu extremist groups to the activities of the Christian missionaries. Standing the Indian Constitution on its head, Kamath argued:

> The Constitution clearly says (Article 25, Freedom of Conscience, etc.) that "all persons are equally entitled to freedom of conscience and the right freely to profess, practice and propagate religion" but what is forgotten is that this right is "subject to public order, morality and health." If conversions or attempts at conversion lead to public disorder, the government has a duty sternly to deal with guilty missionaries. If the government does not step in on liberal pretenses, then violence can be predicted even justified by insulted citizens. It is time that Christian missionaries understand that India—and Hinduism—cannot be taken for granted.[18]

In other words, Kamath's suggestion that violence could be justified against Christian missionaries if government did not stop their activities was a blatant incitement of hate crimes, and for a leading daily to feature this kind of suggestion amounted to tacitly endorsing such incitement of violence.

3. Declining Normative Standards?

The trend of repeatedly giving respected editorial space to such unsubstantiated calumny against minority citizens was in effect a betrayal of the framework of India's secular democracy. To allow such blatantly sectarian propaganda to masquerade as news or informed opinion was to mislead the public—but worse was the space that was provided for the vitriolic rhetoric of Hindutva columnists, which suggested tacit editorial approval for these sentiments. This had the disastrous effect of desensitizing the reading public and lowering the collective guard against the sectarian onslaught on India's democratic fabric. What was of concern in this permissiveness toward such an incendiary discourse was that it raised questions about the media's own professionalism. There seemed to be a disinclination to scrutinize the factual authenticity of the themes inspired by Hindu nationalist campaigners, a discernible reluctance to ask the hard questions required in any journalistic appraisal and a tendency to accept the terms of debate as set by the BJP and the Sangh Parivar leaders, regardless of whether these conflicted with the existing norms of the Indian democratic framework. This in turn raised a more troubling question as to whether there was a breaching of another elementary journalistic ethic—the requirement to maintain independence and distance from governmental and political authority.

Perhaps some of India's darkest moments might not have happened had the media been more watchful and more vigilant, instead of allowing the campaign of demonization of minority groups and the raising of imaginary threats to unfold on the large public canvas. Ayodhya is a case in a point. There were few questions asked as to the validity of the political framework that the BJP had set for the Ayodhya dispute, as for example its argument for a temple at the disputed Babri Masjid site, an overtly political demand from one group, which was being encouraged by the mainstream political parties for their own electoral compulsions. Instead of stepping back and examining the genesis of the new demand in the larger context of India's existing political and constitutional scheme, many in the media were quick to provide space for what was a blatantly sectarian impulse, even proceeding to give this a veneer of respectability. Inexplicably, newspapers and magazines gave undue legitimacy to the negotiations between the Vishwa Hindu Parishad (VHP) and the All India Babri Masjid Action Committee (AIBMAC) on the disputed Ayodhya site, under the aegis of the Prime Minister's Office during the Narasimha Rao era (1991–1992), just before the Masjid was destroyed by Hindutva fanatics. Few pointed out the untenability and unconstitutionality of such a governmental action in a secular democracy wherein there was a clear prohibition of the involvement of the state in religious activities. That these "negotiations" between self-appointed spokespersons for the respective communities were certainly not privy to these confidential talks was given credibility in the public eye was in large part due to the detailed media coverage of this event. The media attention given to the dispute also allowed the Ayodhya issue to move to the center stage of the public discourse. Meanwhile, the disproportionate attention to the revanchist urges of a group of chauvinists, hardly representative of the general sentiment of the wider community, also gave room to the Hindutva propagandists to make the Ayodhya temple issue a major rallying point in their campaign.

Another striking aspect of the successful penetration of the media discourse by the Hindu majoritarian campaign was the manner in which the BJP leader and then Prime Minister, Atal Behari Vajpayee was built up and hailed as a legend and a statesman in the league of Jawaharlal Nehru. Not many would doubt Vajpayee's natural inclinations toward moderation, his personal affability and the sincerity of his intentions to bring about peace with Pakistan. But there was little to suggest that he had an approach different from other Hindu majoritarianists in regard to the core issue of national identity and the perception that minorities had to live in a "Hindu India." It was Vajpayee, and not any trishul-wielding Hindu extremist, who had helped undermine the sense of collective horror over the burning of Graham Staines by suggesting a week after the grisly murder, a national debate on the matter of forced conversions. It was the same Vajpayee who, after the trauma of the bloodbath in Gujarat in early 2002, had, in a partisan vein, and despite the fact that he was the Prime Minister of a secular republic, pointed an accusing finger at the Muslim community, hinting darkly that the ghastly pogrom against Muslims was a consequence of the Godhra incident.

On each such occasion that Vajpayee lapsed into these partisan binges, the media did dutifully register the sectarian implications of these remarks. But surprisingly, none of all this added up to casting a shadow on the image being assiduously projected of Vajpayee as a national leader with a healing touch. Significant sections of the media continued to unquestioningly subscribe to the high-decibel nationwide campaign claiming that Vajpayee was India's "tallest leader." This iconic buildup of Vajpayee led to hasty and absurd conclusions. Newspapers argued that with a strong leader like Vajpayee being projected, the National Democratic Alliance (NDA) would coast to victory in the Lok Sabha elections of 2004. The "Vajpayee factor," as it was dubbed, did not have the political weight ascribed to it by an overeager media, which had overlooked the signals from the ground.

Indian journalists and editors need to ponder on why the media was so wrong in overestimating the persuasive appeal of the Hindu majoritarian political campaign, incorrectly concluding that there was a collective yearning for a new national cultural ethos and completely missing out the ground reality that the ordinary Indian had no interest in labels and identities, but was completely disconnected from this so-called Hindu cultural renaissance. The failure of the media to provide the Indian public with an intelligent and factual scrutiny of the claims of the Hindutva propagandists and the willingness of a large number of journalists and columnists to buy into the orchestrated campaign that a Hindu nation was India's natural destiny waiting to be fulfilled, helped legitimize the sectarian political agenda of Hindutva. This also had the unhappy effect of presenting a picture of Indian civil society that did not reflect the authentic ground reality. More chilling is the thought that by having been mindlessly co-opted in the political sloganeering of the Hindu nationalists, the news media unwittingly provided the legitimization and political space in the public discourse for the worst kind of hate politics exemplified by Narendra Modi's genocidal binge in Gujarat in early 2002.

4. Conclusion

The Indian press has its moorings in the finest traditions of Indian democracy and is the product of India's most liberal inclinations. It is also a major stakeholder in the democratic framework, and if it is not to lose its place as a credible interlocutor in the democratic process, it cannot make the mistake again of abandoning its traditional role as a vigilant observer. It would have to ensure that its functioning adheres to the highest professional and ethical standards, scrupulously ensuring that its reporting and analysis distinguishes between the wishful and fanciful thinking of self-serving propagandists and the actual aspirations and expectations of Indian citizens. The press cannot abdicate its responsibility to the process of strengthening India's secular democracy. A free press can function only within a democratic structure and a liberal society and so too in India, where there is no escape from the acknowledgment that the best journalism cannot flourish and the truth cannot be pursued where there is intolerance and the crushing of dissent.

Notes

1. Charles Taylor, "Modes of Secularism," in Rajeev Bhargava (ed.) *Secularism And Its Critics* (Oxford: Oxford University Press, 1998), p. 38. The argument that the public sphere has a normative status that helps supervise and check political power is developed more fully in Taylor's essay "Modernity and the Rise of the Public Sphere," part of the Tanner Lectures on Human Values, Stanford University, February 25, 1992. Summing up the potential of the moral authority that is implicit in the existence of an independent media, Taylor points out that the public sphere "is a space of discussion which is self-consciously seen as being outside power. It is supposed to be listened to by power, but it is not itself an exercise of power . . . just because public opinion is not an exercise of power, it can be ideally disengaged from partisan spirit and rational."

2. Ibid., pp. 43–4.
3. Ibid., p. 44.
4. Amartya Sen, *The Argumentative Indian* (London: Allen Lane, 2005), p. 12.
5. Ibid., pp. 13–14.
6. Arun Shourie, "Who Killed Australian Missionary Graham Staines? The findings of the Justice Wadhwa Commission of Inquiry." http://arunshourie. voiceofdharma.com/articles/wadhwa.htm.
7. Ibid.
8. Ibid.
9. S. Gurumurthy, "Madam, Will They Be Shamed By Your Blunt Words?" *New Indian Express*, Chennai, March 2, 2002.

10. Ibid.
11. Inder Sawhney, "Christian Organizations Get Lion's Share of Foreign Funds," *Times of India*, August 16, 1999.
12. Seshadri Chari, "Lord, Pardon Them," *Outlook*, October 30, 2000.
13. Francois Gautier, "Christ and the Northeast," *Indian Express*, November 20, 2000.
14. Ibid.
15. Ibid.
16. "Law to Check Madrassas in the Offing," *Times of India*, Pune, December 30, 2002.
17. Editorial, *India Today*, January 20, 2003.
18. M. V. Kamath, "Mission Impossible: Putting An End to Conversion Activity," *Times of India*, October 13, 1999.

6 CLARITY BEGINS AT HOME: TO NURTURE PLURALISM AND DEMOCRACY IN INDIA, THE MEDIA NEEDS TO FIRST INCULCATE THESE TRAITS WITHIN ITSELF

Antara Dev Sen

Periodically, the Indian media battles the government's exasperated attempts to apply guidelines and regulations to it. And every time, it wins hands down. In India, which enjoys one of the world's largest and best media presences, the freedom of the press is sacred.

But as a faithful member of the Indian media, I must admit that sometimes you can't blame the government for trying to contain our unbridled enthusiasm—like during the spirited jingoism and reckless television coverage of the Mumbai terror attacks. We were going boldly where no responsible journalist had gone before—into premises where soldiers were fighting terrorists or trying to rescue hostages, into the private space of the grief-stricken, even into the "mind of the terrorist." We were the valiant mutant ninja hacks, scoffing at the rules of the game, bowing only to the god of audience ratings.

Such militancy, among other worrying habits, does not exactly foster democratic freedoms. And it may be a good time to rethink the role of the Indian media in nurturing pluralism and democracy.

Even 62 years after Independence, with an exemplary Constitution and an energetic, free and largely fair media, our public sphere fails to adequately reflect a plurality of values. This is because of (a) commercial pressure and (b) the fact that our media community reflects India in microcosm, where the values and emotions of the powerful often rule at the cost of democratic principles, pluralism, and individual freedoms. Together, these make Indian media not the voice of the people, but the voice of the privileged middle class.

Around the world, the media's original plan to educate, entertain, and inform has been replaced by the frenzy to excite, entertain, and titillate. This trend is reflected in Indian media, too. It is increasingly catering only to its target audience and failing to recognize issues that do not directly concern them or media producers. This self-indulgence, along with brazen prioritizing of commercial gain over social duty, can actually erode democracy and pluralism.

To recognize this disquieting trend, I will look at some news stories that have dominated Indian print and television in the last few years. I will also look at newspaper headlines from one randomly selected week. And I will discuss what I regard as errors of omission and commission, which seem particularly disturbing because the Indian press is generally mature, combative, balanced, and fair.

1. Mumbai *Meri Jaan*

The Mumbai terror attacks of November 26, 2008 triggered rabid patriotism in a Hindu-dominated, elitist media. Television news ran riot, snatching sound bites and indiscriminate footage in hysteric frenzy. While excited reporters crowded around the security forces and broadcast hostage rescue strategies live, anchors and other talking heads concentrated on drumming up mob hysteria. Pakistan is the enemy, they shouted. Bomb them! Kill them! Bring in the army! Throw out the politicians! Let the battle commence!

To pump up their diatribe, news channels gathered celebrities who glamorously raged against politicians and Pakistan. It was star-studded jingoism. The people of India will no longer tolerate this, they roared, stop paying taxes! And they focused squarely on the attacks on two five star hotels—the Taj and the Oberoi—ignoring the shooting at the CST train station, the real lifeline of Mumbai, where scores of ordinary mortals were killed.

To be honest, it was not mass murder that drove the media wild with grief and rage. It was the deaths of friends and family. The devastation playing out on live television in favored restaurants and familiar hotels brought terror home. The killing of the rich and powerful in five-star settings shattered the image of terrorism as something that happens to the less privileged—in Kashmir, or in the Northeast, in buses and trains, in mosques, in crowded, sweaty marketplaces.

"Enough is enough!" screamed 24-hour news channels as they replayed footage of the attacks ad nauseam, falsely flashing the ubiquitous "Breaking News" logo. Microphones were thrust into the faces of the recently bereaved: "What are you feeling now?" The media carried on its savage attack, powered by mindless questions and shameless scrutiny and the unwavering, obscene stare of the television camera at the very private moment of grief.

Then there were the citizen journalists, the wannabe news-gatherers who help channels cut costs. Eager novices ran wild, seeking a newsworthy shot or two, completely ignorant of journalistic ethics or security concerns—which was not far from what regular reporters were doing. But with no police cordon, it was perhaps natural for any adrenaline-charged reporter to sniff around for more. Editors and producers, who are supposed to draw the line and present a coherent picture out of the flood of raw data, were missing in action.

So every move of the security forces was broadcast live, with strategic details. The forces complained that the terrorists were getting all their tactical information from the media. It was an unequal fight which endangered the lives of security men and hostages. Some hostages later said that live coverage disclosing where they were hiding (TV reporters fished it out of distraught friends/relatives who were in touch over the phone) prompted the terrorists to find them.

If most English news channels made you cringe, most Hindi channels made you want to flee. They pulled lustily at the heartstrings: Why oh why did they do it? Who are these heartless terrorists? What did they have against these innocent victims? Look at her—where will this poor little orphan go? Do they have no pity, these cold-blooded killers from Pakistan?

Drumming up hysteria against Pakistan and manipulating public opinion to encourage war between two nuclear powers is not just unprofessional and unethical; it is unbelievably foolish. It is bad enough to air our intolerance and irrationality; it is surreal to exhibit our glee at playing the brainless ringleader whipping a hurt nation into a lynch mob. Patriotism and nationalism were bandied about, and the national flag stared at you relentlessly as the talking heads bayed for Pakistani blood.

Sure, Pakistan-backed terrorism has been a serious problem for decades, and we must defend our right to life. But suspending democratic rights, as war-footing demands, is not the way to do it. Yes, almost two hundred were killed in Mumbai. But in our unfortunate land, thousands die in sectarian violence, and in caste and gender atrocities. There are many faces of human insecurity, and terrorism is only one of them. The lives lost in luxury hotels in Mumbai are precious, but so are the lives lost in the streets and villages of India. In the interest of democracy, the media needs to look beyond the urban privileged classes, at the India of the underprivileged.

Mumbai, refusing to be cowed by terrorism, reflects the resilience of an India powered by deep-seated democratic principles. Ironically, a frenzied media came close to damaging those very foundations and compromising on social justice and civil liberties. It almost helped terrorism win the battle. Because in the end, India will survive every terror attack, but it will not survive the slow death of democracy.

2. Operation Batla House

Such patriotic frenzy was evident even before the Mumbai terror attacks. Take the coverage of the police raid on Batla House, a private residence near Delhi's Jamia Millia Islamia University, on September 19, 2008. Two Muslim boys were shot dead along with encounter specialist M. C. Sharma, the policeman leading the operation. And the media went berserk. The dead boys were instantly declared terrible terrorists while Sharma was frenetically deified. In its hysteria, the media propagated the stereotype of Muslims being terrorists and ignored the various questions that were being raised by the locals challenging the police version.

The Indian police have a terrible track record in human rights and ethics. And encounter specialists are the most distrusted. Nevertheless, in troubled times we need heroes in uniform, which explains the media's glorification of Sharma. The much-awarded Sharma had killed 35 terrorists and arrested 80 more. With his inseparable senior, the dreaded Assistant Commissioner of Police Rajbir Singh, Sharma had swiftly nabbed terrorists following the Parliament attack and the Diwali blasts, and shot dead terrorists in the Ansal Plaza shopping complex. The media were delighted. The more conservative were jubilant, baying for the blood of those in custody. Today, the Ansal Plaza shooting is widely accepted as a fake encounter. The main accused in the Parliament attack, S.A.R. Geelani, has been pulled out of death row and honorably acquitted by the court. And both Singh and Sharma are dead. Singh was shot dead months before Sharma, apparently by criminals he worked and killed for.

Any untimely death, like Sharma's, is tragic—especially for the family. But endlessly glamorizing such encounter specialists can inflame passions. Privileged civil society is guided more by convenience than correctness, and lionizing cops who become street killers gives us a false sense of protection. Sadly, the media has generally not been responsible while handling the shootout at Jamianagar.

For example, the boys killed and arrested were all branded as terrorists—even as "India's Bin Ladens"—without a shred of evidence. There was no hesitation, no "alleged" or "terrorist suspect." The police version was accepted as god's truth, suspending common sense, and fed to the audience nonstop.

The media were not interested in questions raised by local residents, activists and others who visited the site of the shooting. Any question challenging the police version was rubbished by big media. Like the illustrious Prannoy Roy's paternal chiding on NDTV's 9 o'clock news, sighing at conspiracy theories, expressing horror at questions about Sharma's killing: "You can't get lower than that!" The days of questioning and probing, of not taking anything at face value, of not going by a one-source story, are clearly numbered. What started as lazy journalism, as reporters warmed to PR handouts and saved on legwork, is now the culture of news.

Irresponsible coverage encourages censorship. It would be tragic if our admirable media—always free, generally fair, routinely confrontational—is shackled because of the irresponsible behavior of some TV channels. Besides, media needs credibility and hysteria devalues it.

Unfortunately, such judgmental coverage was not really an aberration. We often whip horror-struck viewers into a lynch mob. We will discuss two cases here—the murder of the schoolgirl Arushi and her family's domestic help Hemraj, and the mass murder of slum children—both in Noida, a posh Delhi suburb.

A 2006 media study showed how violence dominates television news and 50 percent of TV news space goes to crime, entertainment, cricket, and the supernatural. The police are most frequently quoted, while lawyers and activists have almost no voice. So crime stories are presented from the police angle, obsessing on irrelevant details and missing the larger picture.

3. Arushi: Multiple Murders

The morphing of news as information into news as entertainment has blurred both our vision and the once inviolable line between reality and drama. In the Arushi murder case, our media presented the father as the monster who kills his own daughter and his domestic help. And through a dubious sex angle, incessant repetitions, curious graphics, high drama, and low morals, it dangerously incited the audience against him. Later, the Central Bureau of Investigation cleared his name.

On a bright May day in 2008—when police firing killed 15 demonstrators of the Gujjar tribe demanding Scheduled Tribe rights, when farm loan rates were raised sharply and oil prices soared—our media focused firmly on the arrest of Dr. Rajesh Talwar for murdering his daughter Arushi, 14, and domestic help Hemraj, 45. "It was the Father!" screamed leading dailies in banner headlines; "Murderer" and "Murder Most Foul" dominated the front pages, and the press ripped the father apart. As the police offered several contradictory theories, the media gleefully aired several opinions, photographs and illustrations.

The Hindi channels splashed their screens with blood, undulating knives, the child's smile, and the father's grim face. One channel even ran a "*Dhongi* Papa" ("Sham Dad") segment, where they kept repeating a clip where the police were taking away Arushi's shrouded body with Rajesh Talwar tottered behind, mumbling, looking every bit the shattered father. "Look how he walks, the murderer, the hypocrite, pretending to be shocked!" barked the presenter. "Look how he hangs his hands as if he has no control over his body!" (For graphic effect, Talwar's hands are swiftly circled in red.) "What a fraud!"

You hear the grief-stricken father mumbling: "Arushi, my child!" The presenter gets quite frenetic. "Look how he chants: *'Arushi bete, Arushi bete!'* [A speech bubble pops up, saying, *'Arushi bete, Arushi bete!'*] What a fake!" says the presenter, inciting the audience against the *dhongi* or sham father. When the police tries to lower the body to the ground, the father says, "Don't put my daughter on the floor." The presenter is now ready to reach into the screen, drag out Talwar and lynch him: "Look how he pretends to be so caring, this killer father, look how he says *'Mere beti ko neechey mat rakho!'* [speech bubble pops up, saying *'Mere beti ko neechey mat rakho!'*] What a terrible phoney, what grand acting!" The drama continues as the news channel runs this same clip over and over again with dancing speech bubbles.

When Arushi's mother finally broke her silence and spoke to the media, saying her husband was innocent, the media pounced on her. Hindi news channel India TV got an "expert" to answer philosophical queries: "Do you believe this woman? Could she be lying?" The expert announced: "Of course she could be lying. She must be thinking, my daughter is gone, now if I lose my husband too, then who will I live with?" And the shock and horror over how the father could have killed his daughter continued over various channels.

This lynching by media is distressing. Yes, Talwar may have killed Arushi. Fathers regularly kill their daughters in our country. The week Arushi died in Noida, in Vadodara, Vandana, 19, was axed to death by her father, a retired army man, for marrying against his wishes. Vandana's mother and sister helped him. The point is not whether Talwar could have killed his daughter, but whether he actually did. And the media's assumed role of investigator, jury and executioner is unacceptable.

The media's job is to help in getting justice, not to incite the public against the accused. Especially when there are so many loopholes, and when the accused is the father. A responsible media would provisionally give the parents the benefit of the doubt and allow them to grieve in peace. Instead, our media brutally attacked a parent and violated the child further by harping on imaginary sexual dalliances. And of course Hemraj, the domestic help, was almost forgotten as this double murder became just the "Arushi murder case."

4. Nithari's Serial Killers

Delhi began the New Year of 2007 with news of the mass murder of children in the suburb of Noida dominating media and mind-space. Moninder Singh Pandher and his domestic help Surendra Koli were accused of raping and killing at least 20 boys and girls in Noida.

The bribed cops had refused to register the complaints of the missing kids' parents, who were slum dwellers, gave false reports and acted as the killers' private army, until they were removed. As the media went to town on stories fed by investigators, Surendra the servant morphed into a monster who apparently raped and killed children, had sex with their corpses, tore out their livers and ate them. And Moninder the master became increasingly refined, a globe-trotting connoisseur of fine wines, expensive cognacs, and spirits flavored with flakes of gold. Because Moninder was one of us: a Westernized businessman with upper-class habits.

Within days, the horrific Noida murders that involved a rich businessman, his servant and the local police changed into a grotesque drama almost entirely centered on a psychopathic servant—an appalling rapist, pedophile, necrophile, and cannibal. It became a bizarre theatre of the absurd played out among the lower classes, the unfathomable Other.

First, the "Noida killings" became the "Nithari killings." It was distasteful to have Delhi's fashionable suburb sullied by pedophiles and serial killers. Let it happen in "Nithari Village," full of poor "villagers." In reality, these were slum dwellers, mostly migrant labor, in the Nithari neighborhood of Noida. This was clearly an urban tragedy in the National Capital Region and should have been treated as such.

Then the alleged killers metamorphosed magically. As explained earlier, Surendra morphed into a monster as Moninder became increasingly classy. The news stories were based solely on the confessions of the alleged killers extracted in police custody. The domestic had done it all alone, we were told, the master was not involved.

What a relief. The whole drama was then neatly restricted to the lower classes. We no longer needed to think too deeply about the real issues, like the role of the police. For two years, they had aided and abetted the serial killers by inaction. They had shooed parents away, asked why they had so many children, declared that the missing girls had eloped, accused the older girls of being prostitutes and asked for bribes. Finally, a distraught father moved court to stir the police into action. In all, 38 children had gone missing in two years. Allegedly, the police were being paid by Moninder.

The media's single-source stories focusing squarely on salacious details changed the nature of the crime. Instead of a big pedophilia or organ trade racket that could expose a web of greed and corruption within the administration, we had a neat package: one pervert servant raped, killed, and ate scores of slum kids.

Primitive societies needed such scapegoats, the "Other," to bring their fractured community together. A twenty-first century democracy should not. But the media excels in it. And it is not always a class thing. Here are six examples of the media's stoning the Other: the cases of Khushboo, Uma Khurana, Geetanjali Nagpal, Santhi Sounderajan, Gudiya, and Imrana. Not surprisingly, all of them are women.

5. Khushboo: Courting Trouble

Since 2005, Khushboo the Tamil film star has been plagued by numerous legal cases (26 were stayed in 2008) filed by various protectors of Tamil culture and Hindu values. Her crime: to comment in a magazine article responding to a survey of sexual habits of Indians, that educated men should not expect their brides to be virgins, and premarital sex was okay if it was safe. Horrified Tamilians pounced on Khushboo for a legal honor killing. She was propagating loose morals, they screamed, as they fell over each other to stone the devil woman.

Then the actress found her face on a half-naked woman's body, framed by suggestive sexual comments, on the cover of the Indian edition of *Maxim*, the men's magazine. Sick of such sensational self-discovery, Khushboo sued the magazine. *Maxim* apologized instantly.

The fact is that Indian society is still very conservative. And instead of trying to encourage liberal thought, media plays on this conservatism, hitting out at people who break conventions. In a crazed world, we love those who allow us to be our unwashed, unshaved, unclothed Neolithic selves in a flashy twenty-first century ambience. So picking on the weak is the media's selling point. We like to publicly humiliate people on television shows as the "weakest link" in a team. We like being bullies, and encourage our audience to feel righteous and powerful.

But *Maxim* made a serious error of judgment by picking on a besieged victim who was being savagely attacked for taking an honest, responsible, and tolerant stand on sex. In effect, it responded to a closed society's fanatical attack on a woman with liberal values in the way that feudal societies are expected to act—by stripping her in public and hitting her with asinine sexual comments. Of course the picture was morphed—*Maxim* had no access beyond public photos of this public figure—but it used her identity. Even with a "100 percent fake" disclaimer stamped on the image, it was Khushboo who was being offered to the reader's eyes.

6. Uma Khurana: The Sting in the Tale

In August 2007, when an exasperated government was again pondering a content code for the disturbingly carefree broadcast media, a fake sting operation by India Live TV exposed Delhi schoolteacher Uma Khurana supplying schoolgirls for prostitution. The story was replayed incessantly and was picked up by other channels. A huge lynch mob attacked Uma. The police snatched her out of their grasp, put her in hospital, then clapped her in jail.

This drama was dutifully recorded by the media. They cheerfully repeated visuals of her public stripping and thrashing by the mob. Uma was swiftly sacked, and her husband and children went into hiding. The media came alive with speculations about Uma's unholy life as it established her as a terrible monster.

A week later, the police announced that Uma had been framed. The sting was fake. How shocking, said the media. But we still don't need your content code, thanks. Keep your blipping Broadcast Bill away from us. Some channels merely shrugged, while India Live continued as if nothing had happened. There was no apology, no effort to set the record straight and clear Uma's name.

7. Geetanjali: Model Failure

Unlike Uma's story, which was not journalism but plain fiction, the media's coverage of Geetanjali Nagpal's story was dreadful journalism. In September 2007, the former model was spotted, unkempt and confused, begging in Delhi. Instantly, she became headline news on every newspaper and TV channel for days, portrayed as a drug addict. The media ripped the last vestige of dignity off the unfortunate woman, invading her privacy, sensationalizing, and offering imaginary details of her private life. What a shame, we sniggered, see what happens to women who walk the ramp and do drugs!

Later, Geetanjali was revealed to be mentally disturbed, not a drug addict. Sadly, the media could not look beyond her as a gossip item, and refused to move on to larger issues of mental health, social security or homelessness. We have 18 million kids, and possibly as many adults, on the street. Some of them are beggars, some daily wage earners, widows, old people thrown out of home, the mentally ill. But only an ex-model is sexy enough for our media.

8. Santhi: The Gender-Bender

Also in September 2007, remarkable athlete Santhi Sounderajan attempted suicide, and the media found another victim to violate publicly. It dwelt shamelessly on her intersex identity and speculated that the humiliation must have led to her suicide attempt. Headlined customarily as "Tainted athlete" or "Sex-test failed athlete," Santhi's identity of excellence as a sportsperson was wiped out by her identity as a curiosity of unspecified gender.

In 2006, when Santhi's failed sex test robbed her of her silver medal at the Asian Games, our media had shown no sensitivity, labeling her "abnormal," detailing her physical inadequacies, robbing her of self-respect and dignity. And barring one or two notable exceptions, journalists didn't reach beyond the curiosity factor to look at the rights of the third sex, or the lack of opportunities and sympathy that force them to fake their gender identity. The closest they came to sympathy was reporting her coach's explanation that because Santhi's family was so desperately poor, she had not had a proper meal until 2004, which may have caused the sexual imbalance.

Both times our media harped on sexual features and lost a fantastic opportunity to empower the third sex, by focusing on Santhi's remarkable athletic achievements and underlining how our citizens can make India proud, whatever their gender. And now that Santhi is back in sports as a sought-after coach, with her own training academy in Tamil Nadu and hordes of students, the media has lost all interest in her.

9. Gudiya: Whose Doll?

Gudiya was married to Arif, a soldier who was captured by Pakistan during the 1999 Kargil war and was presumed dead. So finally, young Gudiya married Taufiq. Then, in 2004, when she was eight months pregnant with Taufiq's child, Arif returned.

Thrilled, a news channel whisked the pregnant Gudiya and her two husbands away to their studio, where an impromptu village court or *panchayat* was organized with community leaders, to decide who would get the wife. The show was called "*Kiski Gudiya?*" or "Who owns Gudiya?"—literally, "Whose doll?" Zee News declared that it would resolve the conflict and held opinion polls through cell phone text messaging, so everyone watching in their homes could decide the woman's fate. Arif and Taufiq were repeatedly asked what they wanted. Like a gentleman, Taufiq said he would go by what his wife decided, but first husband Arif, sparkling with a Kargil hero's resolve, won. Nobody was interested in Gudiya's preference. The impromptu *panchayat* decided Gudiya's fate on national TV: she had to go back to her first husband, and the second husband would take the child when it was born. As a personal crisis was milked dramatically on public television, it endorsed the view that women, especially Muslim women, are commodities and have no say in their own destinies, or on their reproductive rights.

Gudiya never recovered from the trauma of her husband and child being snatched from her. She died soon after in January 2006. She was 26.

10. Imrana: Punishing the Victim

In July 2005, another Muslim woman dominated the news. In Uttar Pradesh, Imrana was raped by her father-in-law, Ali. Instead of the rapist, the *panchayat* of community elders tried the victim and found her *haram*, unfit for her husband.

The Darul Uloom Deoband issued a *fatwa*: she must leave her husband, consider him her son, and marry her rapist. She refused but changed her mind after death threats. And under the excited glare of the media, a secular crime, rape, became a religious issue, with the All India Muslim Personal Law Board (AIMPLB) endorsing the bizarre verdict.

The media, clearly shocked, reported that the National Commission for Women had appealed for Imrana's case to be treated on "humanitarian grounds." It did not find the defensive, pleading attitude out of place, or demand justice on strict legal grounds, as Imrana's basic right. And the old pattern of blaming the victim returned with rape presented as consensual sex. "Do you think a woman who can come out in the open and talk about being raped by her father-in-law would have given in so easily?" asked the AIMPLB. The media did not flinch. Or point out that personal laws cannot rule on criminal matters like rape. Or that this was not just about Imrana, or about Islam, but about basic civil rights guaranteed to all Indians.

Thankfully, the press stuck to the story, diligently reporting the outrage that followed, and giving enough space to opinion and analysis pieces against the *fatwa*. It helped in getting Imrana speedy, secular justice. In October 2006, the court sentenced Ali Muhammed to 10 years in jail for rape.

But the media did trample on sensitivities. A rape victim's name is not supposed to be revealed, yet Imrana's was, while the rapist Ali Muhammed's name was hardly mentioned. Our prejudices are often revealed by what we disclose and what we don't.

Sadly, sensitivity toward the underdog is not our media's strength. And we saw it clearly during the protests against caste-based reservation in education.

11. No Reservations

In 2006, when the government decided on 27 percent caste-based reservations for Other Backward Classes in higher education, students of elite institutions rose in furious protest—though their general category seats would not be affected, since the government had promised to increase seats in the reserved category in order to accommodate more candidates from the backward castes. The media—dominated by upper-caste members of the privileged classes—was brazenly supportive of these illogical antiquota protests, passionately highlighting every move the protestors made. It stoutly ignored the proreservation demonstrations by the lower castes, who felt the antiquota protestors were denying them a chance of social justice and access to education that could help overcome a tradition of upper-caste abuse and historical wrongs.

The press almost glorified the protesting medical students and doctors as they crippled the health system for weeks on end with their endless strikes, spurning olive branches from the president and prime minister. Their message was that of a terrorist hostage taker: unless you meet our demands, innocent people will die. Government doctors paid by the taxpayer, students being educated on the taxpayer's money, living in a bubble subsidized by the taxpayer, decided that they would not treat the taxpayer or the common Indian. And they had the mainstream media's support.

The media presented their every move. Stethoscope-adorned doctors dramatically swept the streets with brooms. If the low-caste do our jobs, they were saying, then we would have to do theirs. Horror! We would become sweepers! They also pulled rickshaws, to send out the same message. They offered to commit mass suicide, wrote protest letters in blood, shaved their heads in symbolic mourning, buried themselves in the soil for further effect, fainted in the heat while on hunger strike and collected millions of rupees to fund their privileged protest.

The media mostly did not point out the deep caste bias in their actions. Or the unethical, inhuman act of turning away thousands of sick people—including the gravely ailing who travelled long distances from villages to get to a good city hospital—and leaving them to die. Instead, they highlighted banners screaming "Doctors are next to God" as the deluded souls held a gun to the nation's head. Human interest stories of the sick and the dying were reported much like a natural disaster, as inevitable. And the proreservation side of the story was almost never presented.

12. The Shaming Game

Almost as dangerous as this subtle upper-caste bias of Indian mainstream media (though it plays up sensational stories about Dalits and the lower castes) is its male bias.

A 2006 study by the National Commission for Women in Delhi showed how television structures news stories so that males represent authority. Even in crimes against women, the male voice was dominant. For example, in 32 such crimes, they quoted 11 relatives, three social activists and six members of the public, and each category had only one token woman. Similarly, there was only one woman among the 55 police officers quoted in all.

This patriarchal prejudice was vividly visible in the front-page lead visual of the *Telegraph* on July 18, 2009. It flaunted a digitally modified photograph of five men—West Bengal Chief Minister Buddhadeb Bhattacharjee and his top four administrators—draped in colorful saris. Clearly, the paper wished to shame the administrators by suggesting they were not man enough to do their jobs. The caption read: "We apologise to women who may feel the elegant sari has been wasted on our administrators."

Not just the visual, even the apology was an insult to women. This liberal Calcutta paper with intellectual aspirations was unashamedly perpetuating the gender stereotype of women being weak, unfit for public office and only interested in clothes. In reply to reader outrage, the paper gave a lengthy but confused justification and half an apology, including: "In yesterday's paper, the five top administrators were depicted as men in saris to illustrate the paralysis of government draped in humour . . . It is possible some may have associated the administrators in the graphic with women, which was not the intention of the visual device at all." It is not clear what the intention of the visual device was, of course, nor what the *Telegraph* regards as humour. What is clear, however, is the blatant sexism.

Such crude chauvinism is rare at least in our English language press. But general prejudice, most flagrant in the language press, is not hard to find. Here are some examples from national English papers of just one random week—the seven days preceding November 11, 2005, the day the original version of this paper was presented. I will also refer to other examples of similar media prejudice.

13. The Menacing Muslim

"At least four terror modules behind blasts" says the headline. The *Hindustan Times* goes on to talk about how the police are homing in on these terrorist groups. The man in the photograph is only mentioned in the caption: "Does he resemble the terrorist in the sketch?" Our prejudices fill in the gaps in textual knowledge, and the reader, with her ever-shrinking attention span, will hold this young man guilty.

At least four terror modules behind blasts

FIGURE 6.1

'Cops are the only ones who haven't beaten me today'

Ghaziabad mob mistakes 19-yr-old for blast suspect

GOPAL SATHE
GHAZIABAD, NOVEMBER 3

DAILY wage labourer Mohammed Nawab, 19, was today beaten up by a mob at Vaishali in Ghaziabad because he looks like the man police suspect triggered Saturday's Govindpuri blast.

Thinking him to be the same man as the one whose sketch police have distributed, a large crowd gathered and beat up Nawab and then took him to the police station at nearby Indirapuram. He was there the rest of the day — for his own safety.

"So far we have found no connection between him and the blasts. We have kept him here as people outside were beating him. We will release him to his parents soon," an officer said.

"I met someone last week who told

Md Nawab. Right: Sketch of suspect

me to meet him here (saying) he had a job for which I would get Rs 100 a day," said Nawab.

"Then people started pointing to a sketch in the papers and beat me. I don't even know what crime they think I've committed, I think people shouted I started a fire. My face looks nothing like the sketch. Just because I am poor, people are beating me. The only people who haven't beaten me today are the police," he added.

FIGURE 6.2

A WILD GOOSE CHASE

All Delhi joins in hunt for bomb blast suspects

Frantic phone calls all day – and cases of mistaken identity galore....

Staff Reporter

NEW DELHI: The Delhi police were flooded with endless phone calls on Thursday from people all over the city and around claiming they had information about the Govindpuri bomb blast suspect whose computer-generated portrait was released by Police Headquarters on Wednesday. Such was the extent of public involvement in the case that a 21-year-old man bearing resemblance to the suspected terrorist was actually overpowered, beaten up and handed over to the police by residents of Vaishali in neighbouring Ghaziabad. The young man was later released after a thorough verification of his identity.

"People are coming forward to provide details about the Govindpuri blast suspect after we released the portrait. We are taking these calls seriously and following them up," said a senior police officer, adding that the police were expecting more cooperation from the public in identification of the terrorists involved in the weekend

MISTAKEN IDENTITY: *Delhi weekend blast "suspect" Mohammad Nawab Khan in police custody at Ghaziabad on Thursday before he was found to be innocent.* – PHOTO: V. SUDERSHAN

blasts that left nearly 60 innocent citizens dead and over 200 injured.

The police authorities in various districts across the Capital have been instructed to intensify their ongoing tenant verification drive to find out if there had been any suspicious movement in their areas. "Since we cannot cover all the residential pockets in such a short period, we request the public to come forward and provide us valuable inputs," said the police officer.

Different teams of the Delhi police Special Cell are continuing to mount raids across the city in search of clues. A number of people have already been questioned.

The incident in Ghaziabad took place around 8-30 in the morning when office-goers noticed a young man loitering about in Sector IV of Vaishali under seemingly suspicious circumstances. As he seemed to bear some resemblance to the portrait

released by the police, the bystanders took no chance and overpowered him. When he offered resistance, he was beaten up and taken to the local police station.

As soon as news about detention of a "terrorist" spread, senior officers of the Ghaziabad division rushed to the police station and also informed their Delhi counterparts. During interrogation, the young man identified himself as Mohammad Nawab Khan, a native of Dasna. He said he had been staying with his father in a one-room accommodation in the Ghaziabad Development Authority flats.

Nawab said he had gone to the Vaishali Sector IV area to meet one Saleem who had promised to get him a job. "He was waiting for Saleem when on suspicion that he was the one behind the blast inside a Delhi Transport Corporation bus at Govindpuri in South Delhi, the bystanders caught him and handed him over to us," said a police officer.

A Delhi Police sub-inspector was sent out to check the identity of the detainee. After verification of his antecedents, Nawab was let off.

See also Page 3

FIGURE 6.3

The fact is, this man is innocent.

"Ghaziabad mob mistakes 19-year-old for blast suspect" says the *Indian Express*. It tells us how young Mohammed Nawab, a daily wage laborer, was beaten up by people who thought he looked like the computerized picture of the suspect published in newspapers. The police have cleared his name.

"All Delhi joins in hunt for bomb blast suspects" says *The Hindu*. The caption mentions that he was found to be innocent.

So not only is the *Hindustan Times* keeping you uninformed, it is actually misleading you and falling back on the new stereotype of the dangerous Muslim, the Islamic terrorist. Although India has had terrorism for decades, and much of it has involved Islamic terrorists, the terrorist stereotype of the Indian Muslim is relatively new and borrowed from the West, particularly evident since September 11, 2001.

While demonizing the Other in a media dominated by the celebrity cult, it is best to seek out a celebrity Other—like film star Salman Khan.

In July 2005, the *Hindustan Times* launched its Mumbai edition with excerpts from a taped telephone conversation of 2001, allegedly between Salman and his former girlfriend, film star Aishwarya Rai. "I am connected with the underworld," declares a drunk male voice. "I know Abu Salem and Chhota Shakeel. I know Chhota Rajan." Mob fury followed, especially at the movie theatre where Salman's new film was being released that day. Since we have a vigilant media, and alcohol is not exactly a logic-enhancer, the drunk's every incoherent hiccup needed to be explained to a furious Parliament and a nationwide lynch mob. Hungry for sensationalism, the *Hindustan Times* had fished out a four-year-old dubious tape of a chat between lovers and used it to launch a city edition. It set the ferocious hounds thirsting for the blood of

FIGURE 6.4

the "Other" on Salman, an excellent Other as a Muslim who has been jailed twice (for hunting blackbuck, a protected species, and for rash driving that killed a man).

In fact, when Salman was arrested in October 2002, after his car killed a man, the media swiftly changed his image from the suave, idolized star to a hunted, caged Muslim.

We saw close-ups of Salman, the emphasis on his prayer-cap. This was telling and particularly offensive in an atmosphere of confused, imagined fears of Muslims—shortly after the Gujarat pogrom against Muslims and a year after 9/11. He had morphed from a hero into a villain, from a bratty idol into a representative of a community being projected as terrorists. With the caged man in the prayer cap, the media moved the focus away from the alleged wrongs of the privileged class, to the assumed wrongs of a minority stereotype.

Then we tried to brand Salman as a terrorist—a grave allegation—based on a tape that is not admissible as evidence in court, on which the police had not acted for four years. We disregarded public sentiment, fanned the fire of sectarian violence, badly hurt the film industry and happily sold some newspapers and TV time. Trial by media had given way to a new level of irresponsible behavior—conviction by media, skipping the trial altogether.

It turned out that the tape was fake. Salman was innocent. The media swiftly dropped the story.

Traditionally, the Indian mainstream media has kept politicians in check, toppled unsatisfactory governments, sought justice and educated the public about relevant issues. Now it increasingly keeps truth in check, topples value systems, confuses justice, and educates the public about completely irrelevant issues.

The power of the media is based on its credibility, which is defined by responsible behavior. Pushed by enormous competition, we are losing our grip on truth and our perspective on news. Drab, nonentertaining news is being slowly turfed out. As sensationalism and personality cults, once sniffed at by serious media as the stuff of tabloids, take over sensible media, we lose credibility.

14. Sex and the Second Sex

Take the papers of November 9, 2005. Almost all the papers had as their front-page anchor the report of a study regarding sexual habits. The *Times of India* said: "Greeks are the Gods of Love: Global hard facts." The *Hindustan Times* declared, "Indians start late, take few risks, still have fun: survey shows Greeks most sexually active, Norwegians most adventurous."

The *Asian Age* went straight to the point—"Sex: Indians safest, most satisfied." The *Times of India* actually had two sex anchors, one in each section. The front page of its international section importantly announced details of the sexual habits of the Chinese.

It wasn't as if nothing else had happened that day. There were political scandals. And the *Indian Express* had an anchor on the riots in France. Then there were the usual no drinking water, death in police custody, and husband-burns-wife stories cleverly hidden away.

Only *The Hindu* had a different report as the main anchor, also about our reproductive habits, this time closer home: "Religious leaders join hands against female foeticide: they express grave concern at the declining birth ratio of the girl child in the country." Not surprisingly, this event was ignored altogether by the other papers—except the *Times of India*, which reported in an inside page on how its proprietor's Guru had risen in astounded anguish to stop foeticide.

Though not particularly interested in our reproductive habits, the Indian mainstream media is very interested in women. We are dominated by the dream woman. Enamored by the beautiful, rich, classy, empowered, fantasy woman of glossies, page three and advertisements, the Indian media has been steadily turfing out the harassed Indian woman who makes up the appalling statistics in our human development indices. The malnourished, underfed, underpaid, overworked woman, deprived of family fortunes, health care, and decision-making authority, is the Indian woman we see in short, single-column news reports. She figures mostly in stories of sex and violence—in stories that can be sensationalized—because drama is an integral part of news as entertainment. It triggers public interest, but doesn't create reasoned opinion. Besides, we use the underprivileged only to tell anecdotal stories of suffering. Considered opinion, analysis, and solutions come strictly from urbane experts.

We are so disinterested in the people behind the anecdote that we even forget to name them. Take this happy story from *Asian Age* on 5 November 5, 2005: "Gambled wife bashes husband." Ram Singh got drunk, gambled, lost money and put his wife at stake. He lost again, and the jubilant winner rushed to his home to claim his winnings. The wife heard the story, picked up a burning log from the fire and thrashed the man who had come to claim her, chasing him to the police, who got Ram Singh to settle the matter with money. But when Ram Singh went home that night, his wife beat him up good and proper, in public, and made him vow never to gamble again.

So who is the hero of the story? She remains the unnamed "gambled wife." While women are consistently named as victims, as heroes we dim their visibility.

We do this because victims are easier to sensationalize. We did it stunningly when Pushkin Chandra, a USAID officer, and a male friend were murdered in Delhi in 2004. "In a double homicide that threatens to 'out' Delhi's upmarket homosexual culture, two men, one naked and the other seminude, were found murdered," declared the *Hindustan Times*. "Investigations into the Pushkin Chandra murder are throwing considerable light on the capital's dark underbelly," said the *Times of India*. Headlines like "Gay murders tip of sordid sleazeberg" (*Times of India*) or "Double Murder Outs Delhi's Gay Culture" (the *Hindustan Times*) and ghastly details of the killings, homosexual pornography, and speculation about Pushkin's sexual life dominated the news. Once again the victim—along with the entire gay community—was on trial by media.

15. Power Politics

Slipping into prejudice is easy, as media operates within a culture and uses its symbols, including prejudices and stereotypes. A media dominated by male, urban, middle-class, Hindu, heterosexual media producers therefore largely reflects dominant social values and often perpetuates stereotypes—as the Gujarati press did, under Chief Minister Narendra Modi.

The Editors Guild Fact Finding Mission's report says that sections of the Gujarati press had helped inflame passions during the 2002 Gujarat carnage. If it had not been for responsible and ethical coverage by national media and the local English press, the riots could have well spread to other parts of India.

But then, national newsweekly *India Today* was dominated firmly by Modi, who had four cover stories lovingly dedicated to him over 10 months. The magazine also carried propaganda material for him marked out as an advertisement feature, along with a multimedia CD. Modi, the new mascot of Hindutva, owes much to the media.

Bowing to the demands of political and economic power groups and the market, mainstream media becomes largely exclusionary, elitist, aspirational and self-centered. And this homogeneous media leads to a systematic lack of information necessary for a healthy democracy. It targets demographically narrow groups as their chosen audience and treats them to the news they want, passing it off as all the news that's fit to print. This customization leads to segmentation, lack of understanding of the other, and systematic silencing of voices that do not have buying power. Thankfully, with the growth of groups and institutions that are interested in such people, and who can also buy the paper and what it advertises, these voices are occasionally aired.

An increasingly self-centered media presenting news as entertainment ignores debilitating endemic threats and obsesses on dramatic developments. We sprang to attention for the world's biggest industrial disaster in Bhopal in 1984, but have no interest in its toxic waste, which continues to poison generations. We ignore the hundreds of millions who are affected by arsenic in ground water in the Ganga plain, from Uttar Pradesh to West Bengal and in Bangladesh. But we raise a media storm when pesticide is found in our own middle-class drinks—bottled water and Coke and Pepsi, clearly the lifeline of civilization.

This homogenization of news according to our own limited interests harms pluralism. It is necessary to understand all the value systems that weave different colors into our social fabric. This is the pluralistic tradition that we carry in our genes and in our cultures, in our rituals, our lifestyles, our thoughts, and our languages. And when our media becomes too self-centric, we miss the larger picture.

Which is why we were stunned when the BJP-led National Democratic Alliance government was voted out of power in the 2004 Parliamentary elections. Immersed in our very stylish navel-gazing in the media, we missed the basic issues that haunt the country where 70 percent of people live in villages. And except in a few rare cases (like the *Indian Express* or *The Hindu*), our national English dailies steered clear of the unappealing side of "India Shining"—the National Democratic Alliance (NDA)'s advertising campaign. They focused on how India should "Feel Good," a concept borrowed from aspirational media. But most Indians still lacked basic necessities. They did not feel good. They just felt excluded, and marked their protest at the 2004 polls.

As long as our media, especially news media, is focused on the interests of the middle-class, urban, Hindu, male majority, their prejudices will define truth for the future. Thankfully, our regional and linguistic diversity (we have 22 official languages) prevents our mainstream media from becoming monolithic. Adding to this pluralism in media are the conscience keepers—the independent media.

But shouldn't all media be independent, at least in principle? The independent journalist is the bedrock of responsible media, as opposed to embedded journalists, enlisted by dominant political, ideological or business interests.

Happily, the line between mainstream and independent media is blurring as independent media seeks a larger audience while the mainstream occasionally champions long-neglected social and cultural issues. This is an excellent beginning, and those of us in independent media who feel cheated when we see our efforts being filched and flaunted grandly by big moneyed big media need to applaud its larger significance. This may stop the Indian news media, the reliable watchdog, from turning completely into a lazy little lapdog, waiting to be fed, hyperventilating in excitement, madly wagging its tail in slavish gratitude. For we need to boost pluralism and democracy in every way within media if we hope to nurture these traits more effectively in our magnificently multicultural, pluralistic, and democratic nation.

7 THE EMERGENCE OF A NATIONAL-POPULAR TELEVISION AESTHETICS: SURVEYING IN THE 1990S THROUGH ADVERTISEMENTS

Arvind Rajagopal

Far from suppressing criticism of every day life, modern technical progress realizes it.

—HENRI LEFEBVRE[1]

1. Introduction

Secularism was built into the Indian Constitution, and was justified on the basis of its philosophical principles rather than in terms of its historically proven effects. Whereas in the United States and in France, there was a lengthy historical experience of secular governance before the establishment of universal franchise, in India the historical test of secular governance was inaugurated with universal franchise. Democratic participation through elections and the relatively free public exchange of information applied pressure on secular ideas, and resulted in compromises that were largely tacit. Secular governance involved a series of gaps between principle and practice that until the 1980s, were not subject to much scrutiny, but had a taken-for-granted status.

For example, while election campaigns tended to mobilize voters along caste lines, editors and news reporters seldom wrote about it, or reflected on its implications for the government's claims of secular rule. Nor did national leaders tend to acknowledge such dynamics in their election speeches. Government decisions that involved intervention into religious matters, whether in affairs of personal law, religious endowments or charitable trusts, were largely confined to expert bodies, and rarely escalated into political disputes. When communal incidents occurred, the news media refrained from mentioning the names of religious communities. Even when particular groups or parties were known to have instigated violence, such knowledge remained within oral culture, or was confined to publications that did not circulate very widely. In the media, as in most other spheres of public life, despite the overwhelming predominance of upper caste Hindus, and a disproportionate scarcity of Muslims in particular, claims of secularism did not get seriously contested, except in very limited ways. The Hindu right's opposition to secularism had, in fact, such a fringe aspect to it before the 1980s.

In 1980, the Congress Party returned to power after being humbled by an unprecedented national defeat in 1977, largely in response to Mrs. Gandhi's imposition of a National Emergency (1975–1977). While the media industry congratulated itself and its audiences on the resilience of India's democracy, and on the indispensability of the media itself, a far-reaching set of political transformations were under way. The defeat of the Emergency signaled that the ruling party needed to find new ways of establishing political consensus, and could not assume that reasons of state could be put forward as such, and win popular approval. Without any explicit acknowledgment until more than a decade later when the balance of payments crisis occurred in 1991, there was a gradual move away from state-led economic development, and toward reliance on private initiative. The middle classes began to be seen as the key agent of progress, and were manifestly the state's surrogate. But now it was middle class consent that had to be managed and won, with the media industry serving as both ring and ringmaster in this process. The consent of the majority was obviously important too, but mass media were not assumed to be crucial for this purpose; in fact such an assumption was never apparent till only recently.

The expansion of television in the 1980s irretrievably complicated this plan. The assumption underlying the plan was that it would be possible to insulate the mechanisms and procedures of consent formation according to class. Conceived in an era when print was dominant, when the reading public was small, and stratified by language, such a scheme did not envision a time when audiences across class, language, and region could unite before a familiar narrative on television, as happened once the Ramayan epic was serialized on Doordarshan. Once this was shown to be possible, the metrics of political calculation changed. Mass political strategies had to be formulated in which the middle class and not the poor were most prominent; strategies targeted specifically at the poor thereafter had the tacit status of a niche.

Advertising is a revealing place to gain insight into these changes because it is not considered to be a space for enunciating political principles, and is as such hardly a bastion of orthodoxy. Rather, it is seen to be a form of expression that is aspirational and fanciful, within a space where sectional appeals can safely be made without provoking objection, provided of course that no overt offense is expressed. Advertising is also a form of communication singularly unburdened by its own history, and even unconscious of it. As such, it is a helpful indicator of historical dynamics, although interpretations of advertisements have to be suitably contextualized.

For instance, the first few decades of advertising in India witnessed the extensive use of Hindu god pictures by manufacturers small and large, native and foreign. Such god pictures continue to be present in Indian bazaars and in a majority of Indian homes today. But they have become downmarket while acquiring the status of historical artifacts for the educated elite. Today, when national and multinational companies invoke Hindu religiosity or culture, the form of appeal tends to be far more discreet, and avoids images of deities as such. And thereby hangs a tale.

Very briefly, Hindu gods were used as a means of communicating across markets irretrievably fragmented by language and region, caste and sect. Deity-worship itself mirrored caste divisions rather than transcending them, and therefore, to utilize images of deities for commerce was not only innovative, but provoked few objections even from the orthodox. This confirms Louis Dumont's observation that caste was in fact prior to god in Hindu practice.[2] Seen from this perspective, the nationalist invention of Bharat Mata followed the logic of an expanding market, albeit for political purposes. As with Bharat Mata in nationalist mobilization, the importance of Hindu god pictures in advertising tends to be ignored by standard accounts, treated at best as a mute artifact rather than as a reflection of deliberate strategy.[3]

An important difference of course is that the appearance of Hindu imagery from the late 1980s onwards is an audiovisual phenomenon, not only experienced directly but multiply mediated through print, film, television, and the built environment, with social and political consequences that are before and ahead of us and not consigned to a voiceless past.

The growth of daily television and of the urban middle classes made it possible to establish a national-popular aesthetics that political campaigns improvised on, and that the market in turn adopted. Television provided the hardware that bridged the gulf between the premium market of the urban department store and the downmarket bazaar of the small towns. But it was through electoral politics that the electric current began to flow, that demonstrated the possibility of their interlinkage. It is to advertising that I will now turn, to seek the unselfconscious reflections available there, of the shifts and changes in this interlinkage across the decade of the 1990s.

In this essay, I offer readings of a selection of television advertisements screened between 1992 and 2003 as a means of tracing some of the cultural shifts witnessed in India during the period of economic liberalization inaugurated in

1991.[4] Nationwide television broadcasting began in 1982 with the advent of the 9th Asian Games held in New Delhi. It increased in scope and intensity as market reforms grew, bringing discrete regional markets within the country in contact with each other through a new audiovisual domain of representation. As the license-permit raj gave way to economic liberalization, the relatively isolated linguistic markets in the cultural sphere began to be subject to a tacit system of regulation achieved through television.

In their attempt to devise appeals to reach a mass market in the 1990s, Indian businesses found that all the decades of experience they had gained did not easily translate into an ability to represent mass consumers to themselves, so heavily had they focused on the premium market until the onset of nationwide television and the entry of multinationals. Hitherto, in selling consumer goods to the masses, utility had been the dominant theme of address, reflecting marketers' belief that these consumers focused on subsistence needs and could not afford to address their desires, or realize their ambitions. By contrast, the urban well-to-do were believed to be capable of self-realization, since they were understood to have satisfied their subsistence needs and therefore could benefit from an aesthetic of consumption. Deriving from Abraham Maslow's theories of humanistic psychology, presuming a hierarchy of needs with self-realization being at the apex of the hierarchy, accessible only to a few, these beliefs came to be institutionalized in consumer goods advertising and marketing.[5]

In the process, what arose was an image of the culture of Indian developmentalism, but it was a mirror image, one that reversed the visible tenets of Nehruvianism. Now, Nehruvian development was enacted as a largely expert-led initiative. Planners expected educated middle classes to act in rational, civic-minded ways to fulfill the objectives of national advancement, and stood in a tutelary relationship to the poor who, it was assumed, would benefit over the long run through economic growth and emulation of their betters. Left to themselves, the poor would stagnate in their abject poverty, blind faith and superstition. Advertisers enacted something like the opposite: the poor were treated as if they were too sensible to be fooled, whereas the well-to-do were more pliable consumers seeking cultural and material appurtenances and acquiring modes of self-presentation to bolster their progress through a changing world. Let me explain.

The marketing of consumer goods to poor, rural consumers assumed that their consumption choices were based on rational, utilitarian calculation, and that value for money appeals and adequate distribution to the hinterland would serve the purpose. By contrast, more affluent, educated consumers were intensively targeted, and absorbed the bulk of advertising budgets. The best creative minds, advertising agencies argued, exercised themselves in locating the secret triggers and servomotors of Indian culture, the better to appeal to its foremost representatives in their quest for betterment through the purchase of personal care products and other consumer goods.[6] "Creative" was in fact an imprecise description for the exercise. Advertisers understood their task to be one of modernization, and thus did not want to reflect existing culture so much as to transmute it into something more modern—and this usually meant variations on western culture, British or American.

Indian advertising thus reflected the absence of a popular aesthetic in the culture of Nehruvian development, and highlighted the extent to which attempts at devising a secular and modern national culture circulated largely in urban, well-to-do settings, at least as reflected in the consumer goods market. What allowed this set of assumptions to prevail until the 1990s was the existence of a protected domestic market that grew relatively slowly, and communication technologies whose use reflected the divides between the different market strata. English language print media addressed the premium segment, while radio and Indian language print media mainly addressed the lower market segments. Price and affordability were the practical means through which the various divisions of the market were administered. Economic divisions were thus translated into impermeable cultural divisions, with poor consumers understood to be able neither to afford premium goods nor capable of imagining they could, and vice versa with premium market consumers vis-à-vis goods for the poorer classes.

Small wonder then that when these barriers began to break down, and poor consumers began to demonstrate their interest in and capacity to buy premium goods, as did occur in the wake of television advertising, it led to a cognitive crisis for businesses, who found themselves unequipped to respond to consumer behavior that to their minds was unacceptably promiscuous. Arguably, intermingling caste milieus and imagining intimacy with the lower caste consumer were challenges that advertisers, who largely identified with upper castes, chose to avoid as far as possible.

I suggest that advertisers responded to the crises by relying on solutions arrived at in the political sphere. If during the Nehruvian era (which can be said to have lasted until the National Emergency of 1975–1977), popular participation in politics occurred mainly through nonofficial forms of appeal that were localized, and varied from state to state, Hindu nationalists capitalized on the absence of a viable national culture of political participation, with its transgressive introduction of religion into national politics. This absence of a popular political aesthetic was the counterpart of the absence of a popular aesthetic of consumption. In this sense, the consumer goods market accurately mirrored the political and cultural disposition of Nehruvianism. In the ways that advertisers resorted to Hindu forms of appeal and modified them, we can see the trace of emergent cultural patterns and trajectories of democratization and my readings of advertisements below will illustrate this.

2. A Certain Kind of Lens

When advertisers seek to persuade consumers of the virtues of their products, they do not merely sell goods.[7] Especially in as-yet nascent consumer markets, they simultaneously offer a particular mode of perception and a pattern of behavior commensurate with it while picking their way through prevailing social divisions, inhibitions, and proscriptions. By constructing scenes of desiring and desirability, advertisers create a sense of autonomy and independence as well as a perception of the achievability of individual wishes, which is critical in constructing the subject of consumption. Locally rooted relationships of dependence based on caste, community, and gender are gradually linked in generalized relations of commodity exchange, as more insular regional markets are transformed and consolidated within a more global market. In the process, advertisers transcribe fragments of local knowledges within a wider orbit of intelligibility.

There is a twofold character to this operation. Advertisers tend to seek appeals that are familiar and recognizable, and that avoid arousing the prejudices of their audiences. At the same time, ads inflect the socius with a new set of possibilities and connections, and offer new circuits along which individual desires might travel. In the process, existing ritual or community-centered bases for consumption become suffused with a new consciousness of publicity, and an awareness about the specific kinds of public they constitute, in a shift from earlier, more transcendentally rooted religious practice. If this is only part of a much larger process of social change, ads are at any rate useful in transforming "otherwise opaque goings-on," in Erving Goffman's phrase, "into easily readable form."[8] Advertisements constitute an archive of efforts at microecological changes in social orientation that—at least in the case of India—has only recently begun to receive scholarly attention.[9]

Here I do not treat advertising as a treasure trove of the popular as such; rather, it presents us with an archive of advertisers' and marketers' understanding of the field of their activity. Advertisements thus provide glimpses of the historical consciousness of those at the helm of the market, and of the shifts attempted and accomplished over time in their understanding about the internal social relations of the market. In other words, we can track the relationship of dominant conceptions of the market to politics over time, if we read the archive of advertising with suitable care.

To summarize my argument briefly, the counterpart of an elite secular consensus in the political sphere was a relatively westernized advertising culture, catering to a small urban middle class. As the character of this political consensus changed, and economic liberalization proceeded there developed a search for new sources of value within advertising, with local culture increasingly used to endow goods with symbolic distinction. If Indian advertising had evolved a set of codes to address a limited elite audience who fashioned themselves as standing for the nation as a whole, these codes now had suddenly to be brought into alignment with a truly nationwide market. What would be the terms on which this genuinely mass market would be included, into what had hitherto been an elite public, and what kind of public would be constituted as a result of this engagement? Although Indian advertising scarcely conceived of its mission in these grandiose terms, some of the burden of solving this vexing historical-political conundrum willy-nilly fell to its lot, in light of the failure of political elites to fulfill their own tasks. Doubtless, advertisers sought to maximize market share, and to win as many new consumers as they could. They were, however, limited by their long recalcitrance in refusing to perceive the enormous plurality of consumers that had for decades lain under their noses. Furthermore, they were constrained by their political timidity, in imagining alternative modes of configuring the socius that would disrupt the existing mode of distribution of capital.

3. The Indian Advertising Industry

Indian advertising grew in a protected economy, catering to a market that was relatively limited in terms of class and culture. For example, in a protected domestic market, there was little value in the theme of national cultural identity, whether expressed as national or as regional culture, as a marker of product difference; multinationals, who spent the most on advertising goods, were not anxious to draw attention to their origins. It should be noted that the ad industry itself hardly operated with exposure to the full rigors of a market, and was only poorly professionalized. Finally, the domestic market was itself understood as small and homogeneous, and this then further simplified the work of the ad industry. Advertising created an image of the market, as it could be expected to, reproducing certain assumptions about the market that dovetailed with the prevailing political consensus. With market liberalization, each of these assumptions came to be exposed, and its limitations revealed.

Marketers in India constantly refer to the homogeneous character of the market before liberalization, as opposed to its much more stratified aspect today. This is quite misleading unless we realize that what they refer to is a middle-class market—not the middle class per se but the middle class of the marketers' imagination, which was indeed homogeneous.

Until recently, advertisers did not attempt to go beyond highly patronizing modes of address in selling goods to lower income sections of society. As discussed above, one might say that utility was presented as the most salient aspect of consumer messages for the lower middle and working classes, while aesthetics remained the province of their betters, the middle and upper classes. It was for them that the finer particulars of appearance, individual satisfaction and self-actualization were important. Not that these aspects were entirely omitted in ads for lower income segments, but if we examined the amounts of money spent in creating those ads, a clear stratification would emerge. What occurs in recent times is that attention is finally paid to the insistent demand made by these (hitherto neglected) segments, a demand that was noticed because of competitive pressures, and a changed political context. As downmarket consumers wean themselves from unbranded and regionally branded goods, they enter a new regime of consumption whose contours are not self-evident or readily available. Rather, it had to be constructed, by dint of advertising and marketing effort, through new modes of signification and styles of reading that consumers must then learn to deploy efficiently. A selection of ads thus reveals not merely a class-stratified range of texts to match a price-stratified array of products. We can find, as well, appeals that can be distinguished in terms of different audio-visual semantics, according to the character of the publics sought to be addressed or constructed (the assumption of a particular kind of address tending over time to form its own object). If advertisers envision the establishment, sooner or later, of a universe populated entirely by international brands, the pathway forged for the purpose must still negotiate intractable national histories. Ads within a protected domestic market evinced a clear stratification, between a visual aesthetic for the upper classes and utilitarian appeals for downmarket customers. The distinction of the latter, more inexpensive ads emerged rather in the audio, through the jingle, which would be based on Hindi film or folk tunes. As the regime of consumption is resignified to manage an expanding class spectrum, the relationship between class-stratified appeals must be reworked, and indeed, takes on a different character with television.

Below, I analyze some recent ads from Indian television as exercises in pedagogy—that is, as exercises in the sentimental education of consumers. I will begin by discussing two ads for upmarket products, the first for Pepsi and the second for premium condoms.

3.1. Ganga Soap

The ad evokes the river Ganges, and by staging the scene at the Benares *ghats*, it indicates that the evocation is one of a particular approach to the river, traditional and ritualistic rather than say naturalistic or scenic merely.[10] The Ganga is of course, sacred in Hindu mythology, and bathing in its waters is considered redemptive and purifying not only physically but spiritually too; indeed the distinction between the two is not clear.[11] The sale of Ganga water is an old practice, one which Ganga soap repeated: a small percentage of the river water was claimed to be included in the soap's preparation.[12] However, the physical cleansing properties of the river have for many years now been held in doubt at least by rationalists, due to an extraordinary amount of industrial and human waste pouring into the river all along the length of the Gangetic plain. When the Congress (I) government led by Prime Minister Rajiv Gandhi came to power in December 1984, Rajiv's first address to the nation included a declaration of his intent to clean the Ganga river. The purification project was meant as a symbolic exercise of national renewal, with an ecological component for good measure. The relatively artless and ponderous nature of the effort, which went little beyond press releases and misspent public monies, was a lame follow-up to a skillful campaign by the Hindu nationalists. Only a few months prior to Rajiv Gandhi's campaign, the cultural arm of the Hindu nationalist party (the Bharatiya Janata Party, or Indian People's Party) had conducted a yearlong nationwide campaign, called variously the Ekatmata Yatra (Unity Journey), or Ganga Jal Yatra (Ganga Water Journey). Samples from local river water were mixed with Ganga water and taken on processions across the country, and as they were sold, people were asked to pay homage to Bharat Mata, Mother India, a synthetic nationalist icon portrayed as a Hindu goddess. It was the first nationwide test of a Hindu nationalist campaign in post-Independence times, and its success in drawing large crowds confirmed, for the Hindu nationalists, the timeliness of their approach, and sanctioned a continuation of religious mobilization.

3.2. Pepsi: Sachin's Love Letter

Sachin Tendulkar, India's cricketing star, is unable to compose a love letter to his fiancée Anita. Vinod Kambli, his teammate, spies his difficulty in the numerous crumpled notes scattered on the floor. Sachin's feelings have not found their vehicle, just as the litter has missed its proper receptacle. Picking a tall, cold Pepsi from a row of neatly arrayed Pepsis in the refrigerator, Kambli begins extemporizing, as he unscrews the lid and gazes at the foaming cola. There and then, he begins a soulful declaration of love, addressed to the Pepsi bottle. Sachin, raptly focused on the glass of Pepsi Kambli has poured for him, finds his own tongue loosening, and begins to chime in. Together, with hands crossed over their hearts, they avow eternal devotion to the *chulbuli, bulbulihaseen*—the frolicsome, bubbly beauty before them. Thus, a pair of muscular and normally inarticulate sportsmen begins to gush with the inspiration provided by the Pepsi, although in fact neither of them has tasted a drop yet. Intercut with this sequence are images of Anita and a friend of hers, doubled over in girlish merriment as they savor the letter from Sachin. The moments of the composition of the letter and its reception are placed side by side. As each phrase is composed, we are treated to the spectacle of its delighted consumption. Although a love letter has been simulated from a frank adoration of soda pop, it appears entirely to have fulfilled its purpose. Or has it? At the conclusion of the letter, Anita's friend remarks to her, "You must feel so special!" To which she replies, with a slightly disconcerted look on her face, "I feel like a . . . a Pepsi."

The ostensible message, albeit humorously delivered, is that the desire for Pepsi can be spoken without inhibition, and is a desire everyone can recognize. There are many reasons that might make it difficult to speak one's feelings, but perhaps the most obvious reason it could take a Pepsi to provoke this outpouring is that there can be no fear of rejection (meanwhile, of course, images of Pepsi's desirability are ubiquitous). Anyone can thus immerse themselves in a fantasy of acceptance and desirability. This is a privilege enabled in the private space of commodity consumption, and in a tongue-in-cheek manner, the ad dramatizes this point.

3.3. Kama Sutra Premium Condoms

The Sanskritic name stands out against the Westernized narrative and imagery of this ad, crudely colored to suggest its affinity with the genre of blue movies. This ad was notable as the first to boldly present condoms as instruments of sensual satisfaction rather than as burdens of a tedious civic duty. But the way in which passion is suggested is not by any expressed or visible desire for another, but by its opposite, a restraint of passion, on the expressions of the actors, and indeed on all the human surfaces before us. The house is gaunt and bare. Only nature is eloquent. The soundtrack suggests a sea in high tide, and spray scatters through the air. Then there are the taut, exposed bodies of the man and the woman, he walking toward the house and she in the shower. The rapid intercutting between the two sets up the expectation of an encounter. When they converge, however, amid the clouds of steam, they caress themselves rather than each other, although stills of the ad show him kissing her.

(She does not kiss back in any of the pictures, preserving a still-indispensable "Indianness" in her manner, it would seem.) As the music rises to a climax, the woman's hand turns on the cold water, indicating that the temperature within has achieved its peak, and the narrative concludes.

The name Kama Sutra of course evokes the legendary treatise on sensual pleasure and intimate etiquette, more often understood today as a sex manual. It is a paradoxical reference. The invocation implies that we were sexually liberated before the West, and the name of this essentially Indian text is proof of it. This goes along with the characteristic one-upmanship of cultural nationalism, which is to say that India was modern before today's moderns. The theme of the ad, however, brings up the limit condition of such claims, namely sexual behavior. Indianness is located in its traditions, even if they are traditions that are modern *avant la lettre*, and chief among them is certainly the purity of its women. No "good" woman could behave in explicitly provocative ways, therefore. We thus have an "Indian" sexuality where virtually all specifically Indian signs are erased from the scene, including clothing, decoration and caste marks of any kind. (The man, however, in one frame, is shown wearing a *yantra*, a protective amulet, around his neck, discreetly suggesting the legitimacy of a gendered [male] Indian sexuality.)

In the Pepsi ad, Sachin's letter is ostensibly addressed to Anita, but really it is admiring Pepsi. Or is it really to Pepsi and only ostensibly to Anita? The viewer is asked to hold these two possibilities in suspense as parallel narrative tracks, the pleasure of the text residing in part in the uncertainty of meaning, and in the equivalence suggested between two very unlike things. The viewers may at once learn to decode and enjoy the message, while complimenting themselves on their reading skill. Both ads place a question mark against the assurance of the reader's knowledge about the world, substituting for this certitude the pleasure of engaging with the text's own signifying process. It is this set of features that marks these ads as belonging to the premium segment. On the other hand, those ads addressed to lower reaches of the market seek to persuade consumers of the importance of new kinds of knowledge, and new habits of consumption. They tend to do this by extrapolating familiar signs in new directions, endowing old names with new meanings. As such, the character of screen-literacy invoked is different, as we will see in the following two ads.

3.4. Bajaj Scooters

Here we have a medley of shots that are all feature the Bajaj scooter, suggesting its insertion into the texture of the everyday. The sequence is accompanied by a background song: *Yehzameenyehaasman* (2) *Hamarakal, hamaraaaj* (2) (This earth, this sky, Our yesterdays, our todays). The words gesture and point without seeming to say much—this earth, this sky. But their brevity, and their repetition, suggest feelings that are perhaps too deep for words. They invoke a sense of shared destiny, linked to the horizon of a common territory. In the visuals, no narrative sequence is manifest except for the recurring appearance of the product: the words. But the lack of connection of disparate people and activities becomes the basis of their connection, asserted and repeated through the collective pronoun, in a characteristic paradox of nationalist argument. The ad concludes with the following words, sung, *Buland Bharat kibulandtasveer, Hamara Bajaj*: the great portrait/image of our great India, our Bajaj. Viewers are thus taught to see "India" in the diverse scenes presented, while moving between two senses of the word *tasveer*: both portrait (India's tapestry) and symbol (Bajaj).

The Hamara Bajaj campaign marked a moment of corporate defensiveness, signaling the market leader's unpreparedness for foreign competition. Bajaj scooters were based on an old Italian design from Piaggio, whose brand Vespa had earlier been licensed to the Indian company. Bajaj came to dominate the Indian market, marginalizing contenders, and handling waiting lists that were so long that a huge black market developed for its scooters. Once import tariffs were lowered, Piaggio and other companies, including Honda, began to offer products technically far superior to Bajaj, who had not invested their profits in upgrading the product or keeping it in any sense abreast of advances in the two-wheeler industry. The company (whose chairman was a vocal member of the Hindu nationalist Bharatiya Janata Party) derived an extended lease of life, a fact attributed in part to the success of this ad, and other ads made as variations on the same theme.

There is a liberal aspect to the ad's gesture of recruiting lower middle and rural classes in the making of a nationalist statement. However, we do not see these figures sharing an intimate, interior space. Rather, there is a sweeping inclusion of a motley cast of characters in the "grand tapestry" of India, one in which the prolific presence of Hindu imagery is noteworthy. We may understand this as a purely nominal gesture, in its failure to address the terms of inclusion other than through identity assertion. The power of this nominal gesture however is not to be understated, closing as it does the differences between urban and rural, rich and poor, scooter-riders and the scooterless, by invoking a collective identity. There is no indecision here, nor any suspense, about the parallel sets of meaning (Bharat and Bajaj)—unlike, say, in the Pepsi ad. The words instead merely teaches to perceive "Bharat" through a visual montage of its apparently dissimilar parts while offering assurance that the sum of these parts is something known and familiar.

3.5. *Charms Mini Kings Cigarettes*

The beat of a vigorous folk song inaugurates this piece (music associated with *Durga puja*, and hence signifying Calcutta-ness to those who know it). Each shot by itself is mundane and inconsequential, but a handheld camera and rapid cutting give it a documentary immediacy. We absorb the breadth and variety of urban life, and the simple pleasures that make it up, adorned, in nearly every frame, by a smoker. We see the masculine camaraderie of the crowded streets, the casual intimacy of its strangers, and the freemasonry of smokers who can wordlessly demand and be given a light. People make the space of the lanes and alleys their own, as they play cards or chess, chat and argue with one another. Here is an urban kaleidoscope too vast to be comprehended in its entirety, but here each part is like the whole. What is referred to is perhaps more audible than visible, in the festive exultation of the beat. The outdoors setting reinforces the coding of the product as male, tacitly relegating the feminine to the domestic sphere. The male intimacy we see in this ad is hence coded as "safe." The class coding of the characters is, however, firm. In the multitude of exchanges that the camera pans across, we see varieties of services being delivered to men as they smoke; the worker in each case is faceless, although their labor is visible. These efforts however come to fruition in the visages of their customers, whose serenity is confirmed in the white clouds of satisfaction they emit. The final flourish—"Charms Mini Kings—Calcutta's only cigarette," spoken in Bengali, associates the uniqueness of Calcutta's public culture with the quality of the cigarette. A story about the *beedi*, the indigenous hand-rolled cigarette used as a badge of identity by working classes, would be somewhat different, of course. The distinct Bengali beats help cue the reader to the message of "Calcutta-ness" sought to be conveyed across the variety of scenes, which share nothing more than successive shots of smokers.

In both the Charms Mini King and the Bajaj ads, we see a new process of reading being set up, as viewers see a series of disconnected frames whose synthesis needs to be secured at an abstract level, not necessarily transparent from the movement of the sequence itself. The fragmentary quality of modern experience is summoned, but an acknowledgment of the modern reader's self-consciousness would also require a suspension of the outcome of reading, and confer a more open quality to the text than in fact we are granted. Instead, there is an insistent audio track to each of these ads that closes its obvious gaps and slippages, claiming instead a coherence and unity to each of them, as Hindu/Indianness, or as "Calcutta-ness." The zealousness of advertisers' efforts to steer their readers is even clearer in the ads discussed below.

3.6. Avtar Washing Powder

The *dhobis* (washermen) are on strike, and are marching in procession, waving placards and shouting slogans, calling for a ban on Avtar washing powder. A fair-skinned, high-caste woman, hanging her wash out on the line in her front porch, watches the men go by. She explains to a neighbor that the *dhobis* are threatened by unemployment; since Avtar washing powder is so effective, no one requires the *dhobis'* services anymore. One *dhobi* passing by overhears her and comes closer to eavesdrop. The woman goes on to remark that for people to continue to patronize them, the *dhobis* should use Avtar. *Avtar ka kaamaurdhobiyon ka naam,* she sums up—the work of Avtar and (along with) the name of *dhobis.* The *dhobi,* a swarthy, mustachioed man, is visibly impressed by the wisdom, and in an aside to the camera, professes he had never thought of this. The woman abuses him, saying, "Sangat ka asar"—this is the effect of the company he keeps, a culturally coded reference to the donkey washermen use. In the next scene, the strike has been changed into a public service announcement, with the *dhobis* calling out,

> *Maaon, behenon, sunopukar*
> *Hamare pas bhihai Avtar*
> (Mothers, Sisters, listen to us!
> Avtar is now with us!)

From her front porch, the woman smiles to herself. Upper-caste rights to the *dhobis'* labor have now been taken away by Avtar washing powder. But it is the *dhobis* who are up in arms about it, since it is they who need patronage; their former customers appear more than satisfied with Avtar as replacement. The *dhobis'* march has the connotation of class insurrection, but any threat is deftly thwarted by high-caste feminine intelligence. What's in a name, after all? *Dhobis* should be content to stay in the background, and cede the place of honor to Avtar, which has swept the market, at least in this account. If they do so, *dhobis* can persuade customers to retain their services. Thus the laborer is reduced to his name, and his function is usurped by the brand, which is now itself held to perform the work. This ad neatly demonstrates how a brand name can be encoded with caste and gender connotations, with Avtar washing powder symbolizing the labor and the virility of *dhobis,* subordinated to the intellectual power of upper castes. At the same time, it is through a woman's superiority to men that the caste order is signaled. The hierarchy it represents is thus softened or sexualized.

John Berger has argued that advertisements express the culture of an industrial society that has moved "halfway towards democracy and stopped."[13] Thus social aspiration becomes widespread, even if often frustrated. Envy then becomes a widespread emotion, something absent in a society that has not known mobility as a routine possibility. As we can see in this ad, for example, envy is not considered possible between the *dhobi* and the high-caste women— or even for that matter sexual attraction—except when it registers as high-caste disgust. The gulf between them is too great to be bridged; indeed their differences are heavily accentuated; in terms of costume, complexion, demeanor, and tone. Although they occupy the same frame, they do not speak to each other. Cultural difference, for the audience imagined for this ad, is of the order of nature, dense, overwhelming, and immutable. It is interesting to note that overt social rivalry as a motive for consumption tends not to be used as a means of pitching new products. The explanation may be that advertisers are unsure how to handle the depiction of social difference in the lower castes. Are they to show it as something to be bridged and superseded, or as something consumers should strive to respect? In either case, there is the risk of running up against resistance, or of stumbling upon tripwires of caste or community boundary-maintenance. In this respect, the Avtar ad is striking in its portrayal of social inequality.

The Pepsi ad discussed above skirts any involvement with cultural difference: Tendulkar and Kambli, identifiable as light-skinned Brahmin and dark-skinned lower caste respectively, are teammates and comrades, and indeed it is Tendulkar who takes dictation from Kambli. In contrast, the ad sponsored by the indigenous company (JVC Group, an investment company having recently diversified into consumer products and entered the national market) appears relatively tactless in its social conservatism. By the same token, the Avtar ad has the virtue of candor, in suggesting how upper castes might envision the expansion of branded markets under their protection.

Market expansion by multinationals has perhaps been most fiercely challenged by indigenous manufacturers of low-cost laundry detergent. The ads resulting from this competition offer in a distilled form of the logic advertisers have sought to use in addressing new consumers.

3.7. Wheel Detergent Powder

Market research executives spoke of the extraordinary difficulty they experienced in researching the attitudes and tastes of women from low-income families, due to what they described as the extremely patriarchal and conservative nature of the households. The women would often decline to come out of the house, no matter what the inducement, even if invited by other women. Using the same strategy for them as for the consumers of premium detergents could be hazardous, then. There was then a shift from a didacticism of content to a didacticism of form. Subsequent ads became melodramatic, borrowing from Hindi film codes to structure the sequence, with histrionics and loud violins signaling each phase of the narrative. The practice of a man lecturing to the female consumer was dropped, and instead, the ad sought to make the message emanate from the progression of the story itself. But the device for introducing the new product (Wheel) remained to be settled. It could not be seen to emerge from any conflict within the family itself, because the man of the house would interpret that as a challenge to his authority.

The ad settles on a voice from heaven, offering Wheel as a solution to the intractable problem of the husband's dirty shirts, a difficulty threatening his survival as a salesman. The main narrative focuses on boosting the self-image of the working- or lower-middle-class housewife. According to market research, women in this class position rely heavily on the men of the house for reassurance, and never receive the affirmation they need. In the narrative, the man first abuses his wife and then turns adoring, at her successful accomplishment of household chores. In this way the ad attempted, improbably, to boost women's self-esteem within the terms of prevailing misogyny. Not surprisingly perhaps, it did little to address Wheel's competition. It was through the addition of lemons and *chakras*, spinning wheels, religious fetishes both, that the ads began to turn the sales of Wheel around, and helped to combat the challenge of Nirma. Tests were said to reveal that results were directly proportional to the number of lemons and the three-dimensionality and velocity of the spinning wheels. Neither are integral to the ad's overt narrative, although claims were made for lemon's cleaning power (these claims were merely notional, however). A rendition of a popular film song (*Arre aisa mauka phir kahan milega* [Oh when will we get a chance like this again?], from *An Evening in Paris*, starring Shammi Kapoor) was used for the happy ending, rephrased as *Arre aisi bibi aur kahan milegi* (Oh where would I find a wife like you?). Once the shirts were washed clean, the man stood ready to reward his woman. In one variation of the ad, the man went so far as to doff his turban on a ceremonial occasion and put it on her head, a sign of her symbolic accession to a status equivalent to her husband's, albeit as his favor to her. As businesses seek to educate new consumers in the transmissibility and substitutability of meanings, and so into the traffic in exchange value, the path before them is uncertain, since these consumers represent a market segment they have little experience with. Since these consumers are believed to be more conservative, and less suggestible to changes in lifestyle and habit, their habits of reading—that is of deciphering social codes—are thought to be decided by custom rather than by their own impulses. It is then by expanding the reach of familiar sign systems, and extending their applicability to new configurations of people and things, that the transition to a new regime of consumption is being indexed. In the process of this transition, a new scale of social legibility is achieved, creating a kind of transparency effect in communication, as the logic of the cultural realm and of the market swing into closer alignment. Such an effect is both the result of political change, wrought for instance by the Hindu nationalists, and has political outcomes of its own.

The following two ads are from the period when the Hindu nationalist Bharatiya Janata party had achieved power at the center; when not only some of the cultural turbulence of Hindu nationalism had settled, and Hindu imagery had acquired a more taken for granted quality, but as well, the advantage of the first users, who drew on Hindu imagery to make a break into the rural market had waned.

3.8. A Scene of Consumption: The Cup that Cheers

The ad is for Brooke Bond A-1 *kadak chaap* tea.[14] *Kadak chaap* indicates that this is strong tea (literally, the stamp of strength; *kadak* means strong, vigorous), and in India, the kind of tea favored by working and rural classes.[15] Tea stalls operating on city sidewalks would vend it. Staged in a melodramatic and filmi style, the ad shows a bulldozer, flanked by sinister-looking figures, demolishing undefined shanty structures on the street. The soundtrack is suggestive of a warzone, with helicopters and air-raid sirens loud in the background. A swarthy, bearded man wearing dark glasses sits in the shadowy interior of a white car, peering intermittently at his lawyer (or at any rate, a man in lawyer's costume) and his henchmen as they direct the demolition. Facing the bulldozer is a young woman in a white sari, drinking tea. Her costume suggests that she is a social worker or an activist. The camera pauses a moment to focus on the glass of tea in the woman's hand. On the street, tea is drunk in glasses, and at home, it is drunk in cups. A roadside tea stall is being demolished, and the woman has decided to resist it. Sitting in front of the bulldozer, the woman challenges the man at its wheel to run over her. A sharp exchange of words ensues in the bulldozer operator taking to his heels, while the crowd lies down prone, all around the machine. Brooke Bond A-1 *kadak chaap* works its magic, and an unarmed woman triumphs over a gang of toughs.[16]

The ad stages a typical scene in Mumbai and other cities in India, of the confrontation between the majority who dwell and make their livelihood on the street, and the minority, who view the streets as but the circuitry of the formal economy in which they themselves work. The ad offers symbolic redemption for the sidewalk residents and vendors who are invariably vanquished in such confrontations, but through the image of a consumer brand and the rhetoric of a young, female consumer. Now, everyday scenes of demolition are accompanied by police squads and city workers; as representatives of the only institution with usufruct in public space, namely the state. The ad boldly dramatizes the popular belief that the state is ruled by a class fraction partial to itself, or that it is hand-in-glove with criminals. The conundrum of a state undertaking illegal action is answered, appropriately enough, by a charismatic figure, a pretty heroine matching the goons' tough talk with her own fluent, idiomatic slang. Gendering the confrontation lowers the political threshold for its reception, we may note. And for the ad to feature real hawkers might perhaps distract from its aesthetic. Indeed, the life and work of hawkers themselves are nowhere to be seen here; their existence has to be inferred from the image of the bulldozer, the glass of tea, and Brooke Bond A-1 *kadakchaap*. Characteristically, the growing market for national and global consumer brands, which in part replaces the informal economy of roadside stalls, seeks to absorb the image of that which it replaces. But the audio track, shifting from a melodramatic announcement of the brand, to the soundscape of a battlefield, and the snappy repartee of streettalk, invokes the rhythms and lexical repertoire of popular cinema. The arcs of the visual and audio narratives both culminate in a global brand gone local, but in the ways they traverse the lexicon of popular culture, their moral economies overlap but do not coincide.

Despite its limitations, the ad offers more vivid acknowledgment of the rights of street vendors and of the depredations suffered by them in the terroristic regime of Mumbai city politics than is to be found in most news reports; the latter tend to regard street vendors as illegitimate or as anachronistic, and serve mainly as vehicles for middle-class and corporate campaigns against hawkers.[17] The ad excludes the faces and voices of hawkers, but a crucial aspect of their contemporary experience is portrayed: demolition is implied to be a violation of their rights. Aimed at a lower-income segment, but displaying high production values, the ad is a symptom of an expanding visual regime in which the viewing pleasures and consuming power of working class audiences have to be balanced against the interests of corporate sponsors.

3.9. Counterfeit Money

Party keheta hai ki woh police wala asli hai (roughly translated, this means "You think that policeman is a real one"). A uniformed policeman stands on a Mumbai street. A taxi driver is making a third, and illegal lane, driving on the wrong side of the road. He makes the characteristic pleading gestures to the alert policeman, who rebukes him. Both sides understand that their conversation is a negotiation over the amount of the bribe, not the wrongdoing. The taxi driver offers his driver's license, suggesting a submissive response to the reprimand. But in fact the reality lies behind this façade; in this case it is the currency note within, but it is a fake note.

The policeman pockets the bribe and walks off when a man bumps into him. Again we see a pleading gesture of the kind the taxi driver made to the policeman. Again, the gesture conceals something, since the man who bumps into him is a pickpocket and knows exactly what he was doing.

A song starts in the background here: *Rita!! Ta-ra-ta-ra. Ta-ra-ta-ra!* to the sound of trumpets. It is a cabaret song, from the 1972 film *Apna Desh* (My Country)—starring Rajesh Khanna and Mumtaz:

> *Duniya mein logon ko*
> *Dhokha kabhi ho jata hein.*
> *Annkhon hi annkhon mein*
> *yaaron ka dil kho jata hai.*
> In this world, every now and again
> Fools are made out of women and men.
> The eye can only see what it can see
> And friends just lose their hearts on what they see.

The pickpocket is in a state of high excitement, and runs into a dance bar—where bar girls are pirouetting on stage. He holds the currency note between his teeth, and one of the girls gracefully retrieves it from him. The camera cuts to the dressing room, where the girl hands the note over to the madam, who soon hands over to her boss a stack of 100 rupee notes, with documents indicating an official transaction. The boss, a well-oiled gentleman, smiles and receives the notes and the documents. Now it's the boss's turn. Traveling in a state vehicle, he arrives at a fancy beauty parlor. The girls go into a tizzy when they see him coming. The boss is given his special treatment, no doubt euphemistically portrayed in the ad, and he in turn hands over the payment, consisting of some hundred rupee notes, one of which reappears with one of the girls, who heads off after work in a taxi. The ride over, the girl hands over a 100-rupee note and the taxi driver from the earlier sequence, declares: *Shishter, yeh note to nakli hai*! (Sister! This note is fake!) A policeman comes running to apprehend the taxi driver for making a wrong turn, the same policeman as before, pursuing the same offense, and is about to receive the same response. After a moment's reflection, the driver hands over the note, realizing that this was the same note he had handed over to the policeman earlier that day. Time has progressed and events have elapsed, but nothing has changed.

Narrator voice-over:

Party kaisa aadmi hai! Jis note ne itna kaam kiya, bolta hai ki nakli hai! Pagal hai! Ehhh!

(What kind of a fellow is he! The currency note that has done so much work, he is calling fake! He's crazy!)

If the world is deceptive, we could not be expected to treat the revelation with solemnity, since the disclosure applies to the mediator as well as the object of his lesson. Truth and falsehood, like good and evil, are intermixed; in this world their coexistence is unavoidable.[18]

Cut to the brand logo:
The *Times of India*.
The Masthead of India.

The policeman (who may be real or fake) takes the money and walks off, in a sequence of images identical to the start of the film. Not only is the currency counterfeit, so perhaps is the incarnation of the law itself. The movement of money, like that of the narrative, is cyclical, and to assume these are progressive is to treat their fictions as fact.

"A day in the life of India" is what the *Times of India* claims to capture. But what does the newspaper of record do here? It makes no claims about civic virtue or serving the public interest. Its satisfaction is rather in letting viewers (who will presumably wish to be readers) witness an entire circuit of corruption, through images that the soundtrack reminds us are themselves illusions, emblems of our own desire and as illusory as the 100 rupee note that seems so real. But we are left with a conundrum. If the false works just as well as the real, for whom is the difference relevant? The ad is aimed at a public that appears postcivic, and is expected to relish the unveiling of corruption that lies beneath pretensions of good government. We see here a market where the velocity of illicit circulation is such that a fake note returns to its user within a day, provoking not indignation but a detached enjoyment.

The use of the image of a rupee bill in this context deserves comment. The tacit equation of money with the image, with its implications of universal adaptability and equivalence, of an absence of affiliation, available to the highest bidder so to speak, the omniscient spectator able to track the circulation of images and so arrive at both an analytic and a synthetic conception of the sociopolitical field, just as following the money would elicit the dynamic liaisons through which alliances were being fortified. What indigenous conceptions of vision are being drawn upon here, what native distrust of perception? In the context of an apparently naïve form of realism accompanying modern instruments of image documentation, with the democratization of access that they entail, what kind of interaction can we map here between these different modes of seeing?

The camera here of course, does not lie—or does it? We see everything, as privileged spectators, albeit in an MTV style of rendition. We see the *asli* (real) as well as the *naqli* (counterfeit); due to the privilege of an omniscient camera, we are actually able to tell the real from the fake. So in a sense the audio track, chiming in as it does with a time-honored piece of wisdom, is contradicted by the visual narrative. I suggest that what we see here is the attempted ascendancy of a visual regime, which can in fact be treated as transparent and unmediated, although also acknowledging its coexistence alongside an older oral culture that distrusts perception and relegates it to the realm of ephemera and deceit.

4. Conclusion

In the now-famous correspondence between Theodor Adorno and Walter Benjamin on the latter's work, Adorno wrote of the fruitful tension between the former's theory of the consumption of exchange value and the latter's theory about empathy with the soul of the commodity. Adorno understood commodity consumption as being not so much about the things in themselves as it was about the idea they stood for, of equivalence and the power this represented. Citing Adorno's remark, Benjamin observed that empathy with the commodity was nothing other than empathy with exchange value itself.[19] By this he meant that in consuming exchange value, ideas of equivalence and an open-ended availability were hardly apparent as conscious or palpable benefits of consumption. Rather, individuals could identify with the commodity and the sense of promiscuous possibility it connoted, of a many-sided and costless engagement with an infinitely various world.

I take the insight resulting from this debate as crucial in understanding the task of advertisements, which work by proferring identification with shifting objects of desire. Although the commodity opens out into an endless series of equivalences, the commodity cannot in fact be signified without mystification through particular images of longing. This is a reminder that although commodification is universalistic in conception, it can only be a phase in "the social life of things," becoming thereafter gifts in exchange, and/or objects in use or disuse, and part of affective networks of interdependence and domination. Advertisers, however, maintain the fiction that the space of the commodity is one of freedom, and that to draw consumers into the realms of branded goods is to set in motion a process of improvement. The more consumers are drawn up to the heights of upmarket privilege and sophistication, the more realized they are, in this view, as they learn how to perceive their own needs. But even if advertisers seek to improve consumers in the mass market as a whole, *they at the same time reproduce the cultural dynamics that maintain class differences, and thus act as a brake on any pedagogical process*. Thus, they tend to mirror a given configuration of consumption patterns without acknowledging their complicity in the political balance of forces that any such configuration must represent.

Advertising culture in India in the 1980s and before was marked by the absence, by and large, of a popular aesthetic for the majority of the consuming population. This was symptomatic of an elitist politics that Hindu nationalists both capitalized upon and overcame, as they drew on religion and ritual to indigenize the languages of politics, in an attempt to forge a new hegemonizing ideology. Advertisers in India, long identified with a colonial boxwallah culture, began to follow this lead. Religio-ritualistic imagery offered valuable resources in endowing brands with the aura they lack for new entrants into the global market.

I have indicated that the pedagogical project of making subjects into citizens is assumed not only by the state, but as well as increasingly by the market, in an age of economic liberalization. For the most part, advertisers' progress as pedagogues is limited given their parasitism on the prevailing political dispensation on the one hand, and their unsustainable conception of the market as an autonomous space of freedom, on the other.

What, however, are the contradictions enclosed and released through the circulation of images of hitherto excluded and degraded sections of society, of activities previously denied publicity, of realms of experience that suddenly acquire a kind of public legitimacy, however they may be regarded by advertisers themselves? Here I suggest we are witnessing both the potential energy being created by markets and media, as well as the limits placed on the expression of this energy by prevailing political understandings.

The postmodern crisis of experience, and the destabilization of the perceiving subject, were preceded by a different crisis of experience, namely the attempt to constitute an individual perceiving subject whose own sense perceptions are the only authoritative ground on which he or she can form knowledge, against the constraints of tradition. *I see, therefore I am.* This gained ground in its being succeeded by a series of social transformations, whereby the practical conditions for such new forms of perception were achieved even as they were being transformed. Briefly, even as perception was made an individual fact, it was rendered passive in conception, mechanistic in its operation, replicable and automatable in its design. From vision and hearing initially being modeled on human qualities, the development of techniques of mechanical reproduction led to seeing and hearing being patterned after their mechanical equivalents. That is to say, perception started to be conceived independent of the perceiving subject, as a physical process with its own dynamics. The emergence of panoptical systems of surveillance, beginning with Bentham in the eighteenth century, put the principle of transparency to work in a particular way: one's existence was proven and affirmed by being rendered available for surveillance. *I am seen, therefore I am.*

These two crises of experience—the crisis resulting from modernizing forces that constitute a locus of individual perception distinct from tradition, and the unsettling of this individual locus of perception itself, with the growing automation as well as the multiperspectival character of perception (briefly, the modern and the postmodern moments) follow in such rapid succession, as witnessed in these ads, that they virtually fuse together. In contrast to the kind of arguments Jonathan Crary has made, about the emergence of both expert and popular practices that helped socialize the destabilization of visual perception, and the way professional and managerial discussions sought to contain the effects of this crisis,[20] elsewhere such destabilization tends to reverberate upward and downward, yoking the existential together with the national-political. The most crucial distinction to be marked here is that the context Crary focuses on, the consolidation of western nation-states and the governmentalization of their populations is accomplished by the early twentieth century, at least in relation to the rest of the world, which remained under colonial rule during the period he focuses on (mid-nineteenth to early twentieth centuries). Elsewhere, changes in perception and in politics tend more directly to be read through each other. As a result, the crisis of the perceiving subject, in the different ways it is experienced outside the west, telescopes into more generalized cultural and political crises of governance.

So we witness both the attempts to contain the results of new modes of reading, and new styles of self-fashioning consequent on them, as well as the failure of these attempts, and their eruption in often paralegal or illegal acts of violence. It is therefore a paradox that even as we confront the apparent closure of politics, new kinds of violence, representing hitherto underconceptualized political struggles, erupt all around us.

Notes

1. Lefebvre, *Critique of Everyday Life*, p. 9.
2. Louis Dumont, *Religion/Politics and History in India: Collected Papers in Indian Sociology* (Paris: Mouton, 1970), p. 16.
3. For relevant discussion, see my essays "The Commodity Image in the (Post) Colony," in Sumathi Ramaswamy, Yousuf Saeed (eds.). *Visual Homes, Image*

Worlds. Essays from Tasveer Ghar, the House of Pictures. Delhi: Yoda Press, and "Politics and Media," Volume V of Brill's Encyclopedia of Hinduism, ed. Knut A. Jacobsen et al. 2013, pp. 750–769. http://www.brill.com/products/reference-work/brills-encyclopedia-hinduism-volume-five.

4. In 1991, census figures show 52.11 percent literacy. Information and Broadcasting figures indicate 121.5m newspaper readership, or 14.36 percent reach, and 154m TV viewership or 18.2 percent reach. In 1994, TV viewership had reached 228.4m. By 2001, population was 1.03 b. 65.8 percent counted as literates. And TV viewership was 395 m, with viewership being 38.4 percent. Data from *Mass Media in India.* Periodical compiled by Research and Reference Division, Ministry of Information and Broadcasting, Government of India. New Delhi Publ. Div. See also Jeffrey, *India's Newspaper Revolution.*

5. Maslow, *Motivation and Personality,* pp. 35–46.

6. I have described this at greater length in "Genealogies of the Consumer Subject: Advertising in India," in *Handbook of Indian Modernity,* eds. Saurabh Dube and Ishita Banerjee-Dube, Oxford University Press, forthcoming.

7. I discuss this topic, and some of the advertisements that follow, in my essay "Advertising, Politics and the Sentimental Education of the Indian Consumer," *Visual Anthropology Review,* vol. 14 no. 2, 1998–99, pp. 14–31.

8. Goffman, *Gender Advertisements,* p. 27.

9. Mazzarella, *Shoveling Smoke.*

10. The soap, released in 1992, was made by an indigenously owned company, Godrej; the following year Godrej was taken over by Proctor and Gamble, a new entrant into the Indian market. The campaign was then changed from a religious appeal to one based on celebrity endorsement, to the detriment of the product's market share.

11. To quote the well-known chronicler of Indian folklore, William Crooke, "Ganges water is carried long distances into the interior, and is highly valued for its use in sacrifices, as a remedy, a form of stringent oath, and a viaticum for the dying" (Crooke, *Popular Religion and Folklore,* 37).

12. Here and in the rest of this essay, I draw from fieldwork in the advertising industry in Mumbai, with interviews performed between January and March 1997. The names of executives have been withheld. Various ad executives I spoke to denounced this campaign for drawing on a reserve of imagery that ought to be proscribed from advertising, invoking as it did explicitly religious sanctions for promoting private consumption.

13. Berger, *Ways of Seeing,* 92.

14. I discuss this in my essay "The Violence of Commodity Aesthetics: Hawkers, Demolition Raids, and a New Regime of Consumption," *Social Text* no. 68, v. 19, No. 3, Fall 2001, pp. 91–113.

15. The ad was scripted by Piyush Pandey, and was made by Ogilvy & Mather. Thanks to Ashok Sarath for this information.

16. I thank Santosh Desai of McCann-Erickson for making a copy of the ad available to me.
17. In this connection, see Arjun Appadurai's important essay on contemporary Mumbai, "Spectral Housing and Urban Cleansing," in *Public Culture* 12(3), 2000, pp. 627–51.
18. Doniger O'Flaherty, *The Origins of Evil*, 357.
19. Benjamin, " Reply. 9 December 1938," p. 135.
20. Crary, *Suspensions of Perception*.

References

A&M [Advertising & Marketing], December 31, 1996.

A&M [Advertising & Marketing] magazine, January 1997.

Ashok, Roy (et al.) *Avenues of Advertising: The Blasphemous Bible for the Believers of Brand Building.* Mumbai: Advertising Club, 1996.

Benjamin, Walter. "Reply. 9 December 1938." In Theodor Adorno, Walter Benjamin, Ernst Bloch, Bertolt Brecht, Georg Lukacs, *Aesthetics and Politics.* Translation editor Ronald Taylor. London: Verso, 1977.

Berger, John et al. *Ways of Seeing.* London: Penguin, 1972.

Chatterjee, Partha. *The Politics of the Governed.* New York: Columbia University Press, 2004.

Crary, Jonathan. *Suspensions of Perception: Attention, Spectable, and Modern Culture.* Cambridge, MA: MIT Press, 2001.

Crooke, William. *The Popular Religion and Folklore of Northern India.* Delhi: Munshiram Manoharlal, 2d edition, vol. 1. 1972 [1896].

Doniger O'Flaherty, Wendy. *The Origins of Evil in HIndu Mythology.* Berkeley: University of California Press, 1976.

Goffman, Erving. *Gender Advertisements.* New York: Harper and Row, 1976.

Jeffrey, Robin. *India's Newspaper Revolution.* 2d edition. New Delhi: Oxford University Press, 2003.

Kapoor, Pragati. "Godrej Ganga in Trouble." *The Economic Times*, Mumbai, February 15, 1993.

Khalap, Kiran. "Chasing the Rainbow: A Two-Colour, One Decade Catechism on the Hunt for Advertising Excellence in a Pseduomature Market." *Advertising & Marketing*, June 30, 1995.

Kracauer, Siegfried. "The Mass Ornament." In *The Mass Ornament: Weimar Essays.* Tr. and ed. Thomas Y. Levin. Cambridge, Mass: Harvard University Press, 1995.

Lefebvre, Henri. *Critique of Everyday Life.* London: Verso, 1991.

Maslow, Abraham H. *Motivation and Personality.* New York : Harper and Row, 1970 [1954].

Mazzarella, William. *Shoveling Smoke: Advertising and Globalization in Contemporary India*. Durham, NC: Duke University Press, 2003.

Rajagopal, Arvind. "Thinking About the New Indian Middle Class." In Rajeswari Sunder Rajan ed. *Signposts: Gender Issues in Post-Independence India*, New Delhi: Kali for Women Press, 1999, pp. 57–100.

Rajagopal, Arvind. "Thinking Through Emerging Markets: Brand Logics and the Cultural Forms of Political Society in India," *Social Text*, No. 60, Fall 1999, 131–149.

III POLITICAL PARTIES AND MOVEMENTS

8 THE LONG MARCH FROM AYODHYA: DEMOCRACY AND VIOLENCE IN INDIA

Amrita Basu

Democracy has failed to prevent both quotidian and episodic violence against minorities in India.[1] Episodes of massive destruction of lives and property are often preceded and followed by routinized violence. The conditions for Indian democracy—namely a strong and vibrant civil society, multiparty competition, and a federal system of government—have also provided the conditions for violence. In the pages that follow, I question the widespread belief that violence in a democratic polity is an anomaly and that what requires explanation is how and why this deviation from democratic norms occurs. To treat massive violence as aberrant prevents us from explaining why antiminority bigotry and extreme violence have occurred in India's democratic context.

Violence is always anomalous relative to its before and after. Just so, the violence that Hindu nationalists organized around the temple in Ayodhya from 1989–1992 and in Gujarat in 2002 was preceded, separated, and followed by relative stability. The 2009 elections witnessed the return of a stronger, more secular Congress party to national power. The Gujarat violence was the only major incidence of violence against Muslims that occurred under the Bharatiya Janata Party (BJP)-led National Democratic Alliance (NDA) government (1999–2004). There has not been large-scale violence in Gujarat since 2002. Although Narendra Modi—widely regarded as an instigator of the violence—remains chief minister, democratic routines have resumed in Gujarat and India more generally. The *Sangh Parivar* or "joint family" of Hindu nationalist organizations, which includes the Rashtriya Swayam Sevak Sangh (RSS), the Vishva Hindu Parishad

(VHP), the BJP and their affiliates, is in ideological and organizational turmoil and seems ill equipped to orchestrate massive violence.[2]

However, to view the Gujarat violence as exceptional ignores the connections between repeated instances of violence that India has experienced in and around Ayodhya as well as in Gujarat. The same actors were involved in perpetrating violence over the same issue—namely the construction of a temple dedicated to Ram. The Gujarat violence belied predictions that the Ayodhya campaign would backfire. To the contrary, the Sangh Parivar sustained its campaign in Ayodhya for over twenty years. Much of the time it was working quietly in the trenches of civil society, where it was building the literal foundations for a temple and the symbolic foundations of a Hindu state. The fruits of its labor did not become apparent until the 2002 Gujarat violence. The period from 1992, when Hindu nationalists destroyed the mosque in Ayodhya, to 2002, when they organized what many regard as India's first pogrom, provides a ledger of their cumulative achievements.[3] Moreover, if mass violence did not occur under the NDA government, many smaller incidents of violence did. Hindutva (Hindu nationalist) forces also discriminated against Muslims and promoted Hindu domination through institutional means.

Most social scientists hold that stable democracy constrains mass violence. In his seminal essay "Perpetual Peace: A Philosophical Sketch" (1795), Immanuel Kant predicts that warfare is likely to diminish with the spread of democracy and commerce because democracies are unlikely to fight one another.[4] An extension of the "democratic peace" argument to domestic politics suggests that democracies place institutional checks on elite power and thereby prevent genocide and politicide (politically motivated mass murder). Democratic institutions protect minority rights and the inclusion of political opponents; competitive elections minimize the likelihood that candidates who uphold exclusionary ideas will be elected. But in the domestic, as in the international context, transitional democracies are violence prone for only at "the highest levels of democracy" are authorities constrained from engaging in repression.[5] Secure autocracies can limit domestic violence through their efficient, coercive state machineries, while stable democracies can divert protest into institutions. States closest to the "threshold of domestic democratic peace" are more prone to violence than strong autocracies or strong democracies.[6]

Confining attention to violence in imperfect, transitional democracies disregards extensive anti minority violence within stable democracies. There is Israel, with its large-scale destruction of Palestinian lives and territories, in both the 1940s and the present era. There is Sri Lanka, where the state suppressed the Sinhalese led Janathā Vimukthi Peramuṇa (JVP) movement in the late 1980s and subsequently, and more brutally, the Tamil separatist movement.

Israel, Sri Lanka, and India, which have been sovereign democracies for over sixty years, cannot be considered transitional democracies. Indeed, Israel in the Middle East and Sri Lanka and India in South Asia are often celebrated as model democracies in these regions. If the term "transitional democracy" refers to an evolutionary process that will culminate in stable democracy, can a transition follow a period of consolidation and stability? Alternatively, if these countries should not be characterized as stable, at what point should we cease to speak of a transition?

India provides an important case study because it has been democratic for all but two years since 1947. Its military is subordinate to civilian institutions and it possesses a strong bureaucracy, judiciary, and party system. Its vibrant civil society includes a range of social movements committed to human rights and social justice. Its democracy has neither been forced upon it nor subverted by international forces. Electoral participation is higher in India than in the United States. The 2013 Freedom House report on India places it at the highest level of poor- to middle-income countries by rating political rights 2 and civil liberties 3 out of a 1 to 7 scale in which 1 is the highest rating.[7] If India is considered a democracy despite its high levels of poverty and class inequality, it must also be considered a democracy despite periodic antiminority violence.

India, by most accounts, is more democratic today than it was at the time of Independence in 1947. What has been termed its second democratic revolution has expanded political representation to include low castes and regional and ethnic minorities.[8] Whereas the parties that emerged in the aftermath of Independence adopted centrist platforms that resembled those of the Congress party, over time parties have become more ideologically heterogeneous. The Communist Party of India Marxist (CPM) on the left and the Bharatiya Janata Party (BJP) on the right have grown, as have ethnic, regional, and caste-based parties. The federal system has become stronger as small regional parties have participated in national governing coalitions.. There has also been a steady growth in the number and autonomy of administrative states. Since three new states were formed out of existing ones in 2000, the federal system comprises twenty-eight states. As a result of economic liberalization, states have acquired rights and opportunities to develop economic policies independently of the national government. A constitutional amendment (number 73, in 1992 and finalized in 1993) enables state legislatures to treat panchayats (local administrative entities) as institutions of self-government. The government has made panchayats more representative along caste and gender lines. Civil society has burgeoned with the growth of NGOs, and the links between the state and civil society have grown. Yet all these indices of the growth of democracy have also furnished the conditions for violence.

In seeking to explain when democracy generates or enables antiminority violence, it is tempting to identify a single cause. However, a confluence of forces—namely, an ideologically driven and unified party, state, and civil society—has been the source of and conduit for violence in India. Even if we accept the characterization of the Gujarat violence as a pogrom, the state's power derived from its close links to a party and to civil society actors. This essay explores the ways in which elections, political parties, the state, and civil society—all normal and even essential institutional components of a democracy—have been the sources of both violence and stability at different moments in time.

1. The State

This section describes two developments that evidence India's democratic deepening and yet have also been associated with antiminority violence: first, the complicated implications of greater state autonomy from national government control and second, the creation of multi-party national coalitional governing arrangements. This is followed by a critical examination of the assumption the attainment of power moderates the stance of militant parties. I argue that the Hindu nationalist BJP has pursued many antiminority policies when it has occupied power in state governments.

2. Devolution of Power

One of the major flaws of post-Independence Indian democracy was the concentration of power in the Congress party and government. There has been significant devolution of power in recent years. State governments have acquired greater power and autonomy and the national government's ability and willingness to impose its rule on state governments has declined. The puzzle for students of democracy, for whom devolution of power is a key tenet of democracy, is how and why this has been accompanied by the growth of antiminority violence.

The devolution of power from the national to state levels has complicated implications for the central government's ability to restore order when violence erupts in the states. The constitutional provision for President's Rule (article 356 of the Constitution) enables the central government to remove state governments and rule directly in the presence of an external threat, severe regional instability, and the inability of the state government to form a government under constitutional guidelines. B. R. Ambedkar, the author of the Constitution, intended President's Rule to be used as only a last resort. However, by 1989 the central government had declared President's rule 67 times. Although it was only invoked eight times from 1951–1964, when Jawaharlal Nehru was prime minister, it was imposed thirty-nine times from 1975 to 1989, mainly under Indira Gandhi's leadership.

Exemplifying the self-correcting mechanisms of democracy, state-appointed bodies and courts challenged the excessive use of President's Rule. The Sarkaria Commission, which Indira Gandhi constituted in 1983 to review center-state relations, issued a report which claimed that President's Rule had been necessary only 26 of the 67 times it had been used and urged the central government to exercise restraint in imposing it. A landmark 1994 Supreme Court ruling (SR Bommai vs Union Government of India) affirmed the Sarkaria Commission findings, called for judicial review of central government decisions to impose President's Rule, and affirmed the possibility of the courts striking it down. On two occasions during his presidency (1997–2002), K. R. Narayanan questioned central government decisions to remove state governments from office and asked the Cabinet to review them; in both instances, the government revoked President's Rule.

Paradoxically, avoiding President's Rule has safeguarded one important democratic principle—namely the autonomy of elected state governments—at the expense of another—the protection of minority rights. The imposition of President's Rule in the states the BJP ruled in 1992 following the destruction of the mosque curtailed the growth of the BJP and its affiliates. In the immediate aftermath of the destruction of the mosque, a jubilant and unrepentant Kalyan Singh spoke of "an approaching revolution" and claimed that "no power on earth can now stop completion of the grand and majestic Ram temple."[9] Following national government sanctions, Kalyan Singh resigned from the post of chief minister of Uttar Pradesh, and L. K. Advani, describing December 6 as one of the most depressing days of his life, resigned as opposition leader. The BJP suffered electoral setbacks in subsequent state elections and could only attain power at the national level by moderating its stance.

By contrast, the national government's refusal to declare President's Rule in Gujarat and to call for Modi's resignation in 2002 strengthened RSS influence and the position of hardliners within the BJP. Fali Nariman, a distinguished lawyer and member of the upper house of parliament, questioned why the violence in Gujarat did not compel the central government to take action under article 356 of the Constitution. He pointed to the bias against invoking President's Rule when the party in power at the state level and national levels shared the same political views.[10] Former President of India K. R. Narayanan informed the press that Prime Minister Atal Behari Vajpayee had ignored his plea to order army troops to fire on the mobs.[11]

The BJP justified its opposition to invoking President's Rule in Gujarat as reflecting its commitment to federal principles.[12] Like the Congress party in the era of single party dominance and regional parties, BJP governments have called for President's Rule when it's in the party's interest to do so. In 2011 it called for President's Rule in Manipur, where a protest for the creation of a separate district was underway.[13] The BJP has also been reluctant to alienate its regional allies since it has been a beneficiary of the regionalization of politics.

One compelling reason to oppose the use of President's Rule and other forms of national government intervention to establish order is that they have backfired and contributed to the escalation of violent protest. Conversely, ethnic movements have ceased to employ violence when central governments have accommodated their demands.[14] Prime Minister Nehru accommodated regional demands for the reorganization of state boundaries along linguistic lines after some initial hesitation, and thereby encouraged groups to moderate their demands and express them through parties and institutions. By contrast, his daughter Indira Gandhi, who served two terms as prime minister, sought to undermine moderate opposition parties that challenged Congress dominance in Kashmir, Assam, and the Punjab in the 1980s. She thereby fuelled the growth of violent, militant oppositional movements.

However in contrast to ethnic minorities, Hindu nationalists have often escalated their militancy in response to government accommodations.[15] Indeed, Hindu nationalist militancy has been greatest when the state has been most acquiescent. The RSS and Jan Sangh were weak forces in Indian politics during the time that Nehru was prime minister because he severely circumscribed their activities. The BJP grew from the late 1980s on because successive prime ministers yielded to its demands and accepted the fusion of religion and politics. Indira Gandhi cultivated the support of the Hindu majority, and Rajiv Gandhi appealed to "Ram Rajya" in his election campaign. The left-of-center V.P. Singh drew on the BJP's support to form a government in 1991. Narasimha Rao allowed the movement around Ayodhya to grow until it he could no longer stop it.

What explains the different impact of government accommodations on ethnic minorities and religious majorities? One explanation has to do with the particular threats to democracy when majority groups align their interests with those of the nation as a whole. As Michael Mann suggests, murderous ethnic conflict is likely when demos is confused with ethnos.[16] If democracy is the rule of the people, it can easily be conflated with the rule of the majority ethnic group which seeks to eliminate ethnic minorities.[17]

Another explanation is that the leaders of ethnic and linguistic movements have made demands to which the state can concede without sacrificing its core principles and which actually make the system more democratic. By contrast, Hindu nationalist leaders, who include members of the RSS and VHP whose goals cannot be satisfied through institutions, have made demands which require the state to sacrifice secular principles. Thus the federal system was strengthened by central government concessions to Tamil demands for the creation of a linguistic state and Sikh demands for the devolution of power and resources. By contrast, Hindu nationalists have undermined democracy by engaging in violence that polarizes the electorate along Hindu–Muslim lines, violating constitutional procedures and ignoring court verdicts. The BJP has used violence strategically to achieve electoral gains, while the VHP and its affiliates have used it expressively to further their commitment to majoritarian nationalism.

Given the antidemocratic character of President's Rule, its invocation is a poor means of protecting democracy. Nonetheless, the failure to invoke it can increase the vulnerability of minorities. Paradoxically, the democratic principle of freeing state governments from central government constraints has enabled BJP controlled state governments to tacitly or explicitly support the violent antiminority activities of the VHP.

3. Coalition Governments

In every national election since 1989, parties based in a single state have joined coalition governments. Indeed, all national parties rely on regional parties to form governments. In principle, the coalition governments that have been formed since 1989 should be more inclined than one-party governments to curb the spread of violence. However this has not been the case when the NDA government was in office.

Many scholars have linked the BJP's increased centrism to the moderating effect of its coalition partners. Indeed, the twenty parties which allied with the BJP in 1999 demanded that it shelve its most contentious positions, including the construction of a temple in Ayodhya. However, during the NDA's tenure in office, its alliance partners were relatively ineffective in curbing the BJP's Hindutva commitments. Although the Dravida Munnetra Kazhagam (DMK), Telegu Desam Party (TDP), and Trinamul Congress protested the BJP's "saffronization" of educational institutions and textbooks, they have no impact on government policy. It was only when the Congress Party–led United Progressive Alliance government came to power that it attempted to stop the Sangh Parivar's takeover of educational institutions. The NDA did not hold the BJP to its promise of dropping the temple issue when the BJP conceded to some of the VHP's demands. Most seriously, the only party which resigned from the NDA in opposition to the BJP's role in the Gujarat violence was the Lok Jan Shakti, which held just four parliamentary seats. The other parties' criticisms of the Vajpayee and Modi governments were muted.

The failure of coalition members to check the BJP's actions is partly explained by their lack of programmatic and ideological unity and the opportunistic and fluid character of coalitional arrangements. In Karnataka the Ajanta Dal (U) and in Andhra Pradesh the Telegu Desam Party (TDP) allied with the BJP in 1999. In Uttar Pradesh (UP), the Bahujan Samaj Party (BSP) and the Samajvadi Janata Party (SJP), both powerful opponents of the BJP in the early 1990s, allied with the BJP to form coalition governments. Furthermore, regional parties supported the BJP at the national level in order to gain its support in state elections. Regional parties that are members of national governing coalitions have also been inclined to support state governments, which they lead. The DMK, Samata Party, Akali Dal, and Trinamul Congress had all fared poorly in the Legislative Assembly elections preceding the Gujarat violence and wanted the BJP's support at the state level. The BSP and BJP formed a coalition government in UP in 2002, and BSP leader Mayawati campaigned for Modi's reelection in Gujarat that year.[18] Although Mayawati rose to prominence as an opponent of the BJP, she played a major role in enabling it to weather the political crisis in 2002.

4. The BJP's Militancy in Office

Many scholars assume that once radical parties achieve power, they are drawn toward an invisible center. While militancy and violence might entail short-term electoral gain, it undermines ruling parties' interests in attaining broad-based support to foster economic growth and political stability. While this argument accurately describes certain broad tendencies, it neglects others. First, there are fewer pressures on state governments than on the national government to demonstrate centrism and moderation. Second, this argument assumes that activism is confined to extra parliamentary opposition, and it ignores the militant policies parties can pursue while in office. Third, the system of checks and balances has not curbed the militancy of the RSS and VHP either during elections or after the BJP has attained power. To different degrees, the states that the BJP ruled in the early 1990s, including Uttar Pradesh, Madhya Pradesh, Gujarat, and Rajasthan, all experienced some violence as a result of the joint activities of the RSS, VHP, and BJP.

Most BJP governments have sought to institutionalize antiminority policies. Even during the short period that the BJP was in office in UP in 1991–1992, it strengthened the rule of Hindutva by banning cow slaughter completely. It renamed towns which had Muslim names and gave them Hindu names. The BJP government had RSS members replace district officials, and the VHP appointed the head priest in Faizabad.

In the months before they destroyed the mosque, Hindutva organizations collaborated closely with one another and with the UP government. The government acquired 2.77 acres of land adjoining the Babri Masjid complex, ostensibly to plan a tourist complex there. Ignoring Supreme Court directives, the VHP began constructing a wall enclosing a large area, including the acquired land around the mosque. UP chief minister Kalyan Singh, national party president Murli Manohar Joshi, and many ministers and newly elected MLAs took an oath to build a temple at a ceremony that 100,000 people attended in Ayodhya on June 26, 1991.[19] At a meeting of BJP Legislative Assembly members at his residence on November 24, Kalyan Singh directed each MLA to send at least 500 people to Ayodhya to participate in a "kar seva" that the VHP was planning in Ayodhya. Advani asked all BJP MPs to remain in Delhi but allowed VHP MPs to be present, as were MM Joshi and Advani himself. On December 6, 1992, a group of Hindu activists wearing saffron head bands crossed the police cordons, descended on the mosque, and razed it to the ground. While a few BJP and VHP leaders weakly tried to stop them, most remained silent, and some, like Uma Bharati and Sadvi Rithambara, goaded the crowd on.

After the NDA took office in 1999, the BJP sought to demonstrate its nationalist commitments by testing nuclear devices, taking a strong stand on terrorism, and "saffronizing" educational institutions. But these measures were not sufficient to placate the RSS, which became openly critical of the BJP, especially after its poor performance in the 2001 Legislative Assembly elections. The RSS attributed these electoral set back to the BJP's deradicalization and directed the BJP to demonstrate heightened ideological commitments.

BJP-dominated state governments are especially free to sanction violence when the BJP is in power in the center and in the state, as was the case in Gujarat in 2002. The RSS sought to make Gujarat a laboratory for Hindu nationalism, since the BJP had ruled there continuously for all but one year since 1995. It worked assiduously to gain control over state institutions. It persuaded the BJP government to lift a ban prohibiting state government employees from participating in its activities. It deputized activists to work with the Home Guards, a police force that is deployed during riots. RSS candidates were appointed to senior positions in universities, public services and the courts. The RSS and BJP recruited its members to join the panchayats and municipal councils.

The RSS's most important feat was to take control of the BJP. It put an end to factional disputes in the party, supported Narendra Modi, a long-time pracharak, and ensured that he became chief minister of Gujarat in 2001. Modi's ideological worldview shaped his political decisions in a manner that was significantly different from the calculations of his career politician predecessor, Keshubhai Patel. Modi gained favor with the major national leaders of the BJP including Murli Manohar Joshi, L. K. Advani, and Atal Behari Vajpayee, and became the party's national secretary. By 2002, the BJP commanded a majority in the Legislative Assembly (with 117 out of the 182 seats). Gujarat's chief minister, Narendra Modi, and governor of the state, Sunder Singh Bhandari, were RSS *pracharaks*. At the insistence of Pravin Togadia, the international general secretary of the VHP, Gordhan Zadaphiya was made Home Minister.

Democratic institutions provided the conduits for the 2002 violence in Gujarat. Thanks to the close connections between Sangh-dominated municipal councils, Hindu activists had detailed information about the ownership of houses, shops, and even pushcarts in urban areas. Drawing on electoral rolls, they were able to single out Muslim shops in a row of Hindu-owned shops. They even destroyed the goods while leaving the shop intact in cases where a Muslim rented a Hindu's shop; conversely, they removed the goods and destroyed the structure when a Muslim owned it.

The chief minister, Cabinet ministers, the police, and bureaucrats all directly participated in the violence. Indeed there was no previous riot in which the government was as patently partisan as it was in Gujarat. It allowed a public funeral procession for the Godhra train victims, permitted the VHP to call a *bandh* on February 28, failed to arrest those who incited violence on February 27, made available voter registration and sales tax data that identified Muslim homes and property to the Hindu mobs, directed Hindu activists toward Muslim localities, and instructed the police not to assist Muslim victims. Witnesses testified that police officers often refused to aid Muslims—or participated in the violence, shooting and striking at Muslims as they ran from the mobs. Frantic calls for help to police and state government offices often resulted in little aid, or a betrayal: "We have no orders to save you."

The Chief Minister directed the Home Secretary to assume the powers of the Director General of Police and post suitable officers in key locations. Neither the police nor intelligence agencies protested this.[20] R. B. Shreekumar, the Indian Police Service officer who was in charge of the Gujarat state intelligence bureau between April and September 2002, filed a petition before the Central Administrative Bureau in March 2005 in which he stated that the chief minister, senior bureaucrats, and police officers had instructed him to conceal information about both lapses by government functionaries in preventing violence and their active role in promoting it, and to submit false reports about Muslim extremist leaders.[21] In spite of clear and well-documented evidence of their activities, the police were not prosecuted.

Shortly after the violence, Assembly elections were held in Gujarat, and the BJP swept back into power with 126 out of 181 seats—nine seats more than in the previous elections. The elections exemplified the links between elections and antiminority violence. The BJP claimed that the Election Commissioner's decision to postpone the Assembly elections by a few months violated democratic procedures. Its lead campaigner was the chief minister. In a display of Hindu nationalist triumphalism, Modi toured Gujarat as part of a "gaurav yatra" in early September and blatantly defended the worst violence. The state provided full support for the yatra and, with help from the RSS and VHP, mobilized 100,000 people, including students and teachers in government schools, to attend the yatra's launch in Phagvel.[22] The BJP won in 52 out of the 65 constituencies in which the violence had been most extreme. VHP candidates also scored some important victories in the Assembly elections. Most of them were elected to the Legislative Assembly for the first time, suggesting a link between their militancy and electoral success.[23]

The state continued to punish Muslims and favor Hindus long after the violence subsided. Bajrang Dal, VHP and BJP workers were not among the 2,500 people who were arrested in the weeks following the violence. The government ignored the First Information Reports (FIRs) that named 150 members of the Sangh Parivar. It tried Hindus under the Indian Penal Code, while branding Muslim terrorists and charging them under the Prevention of Terrorism Ordinance (POTO), which Vajpayee had passed some months before. Although the UPA government revoked POTO after it came to power in 2004, it did not release Muslims who had been arrested under its provisions.

In the aftermath of the violence, the state prevented Muslims from recovering the economic losses they had incurred. It did not make Hindus return to Muslims the grocery shops, STD booths, and *paan* shops they took over when Muslims fled. Many Muslims who returned to their villages were taunted, harassed, and beaten. Some were told they could only return to their homes if they withdrew the names of the Hindus from the FIRs they had filed. Muslim landowners, unable to cultivate their own land, often tried to work out sharecropping arrangements with Hindus, not always successfully. In many villages, Hindu landowners simply took over their land. Muslims were eager to sell their land at whatever prices they could get, and some left after returning for a short period. Having seen their neighbors killed, their homes looted and burned, many of them feared that they could never live there in peace.

The government's relief, resettlement and rehabilitation measures to the victims were seriously inadequate. Initially, the state government announced that the families of Hindus killed in Godhra would receive Rs. 200,000 (US $4,094), while Muslims who had lost family members in the subsequent violence would receive Rs. 100,000. Following public opposition to this double standard, it decided to provide all victims with a single sum of 100,000 rupees. However its disbursement of financial compensation was painstakingly slow and did not include all of those who were affected. Government authorities mainly provided rations and oversight to a few camps in Ahmedabad which housed displaced Hindus.

The Gujarat government provided meager facilities for Muslim survivors who had been rendered homeless. At a public function on September 9, 2002, Chief Minister Narendra Modi made a widely broadcast statement in which he asked, "What should we do? Run relief camps for them? Do we want to open baby-producing centers? We are five and they are twenty-five. Gujarat has not been able to control its growing population and poor people have not been able to get money." He went on to justify his statements by saying "There's a long queue of children who fix tire punctures. In order to progress, every child in Gujarat needs education, good manners and employment. That is the economy we need. For this, we need to teach a lesson to those who are increasing the population at an alarming rate."[24]

At the behest of Narendra Modi, the government ordered that all relief camps should be closed down by October 30, 2002, leaving 200,000 internally displaced people without resettlement and rehabilitation. Five years after the pogrom, 5,000 Muslims were still living in makeshift camps with limited access to schools, urban amenities, and jobs. Many families who wanted to buy homes in Ahmedabad were prohibited from doing so. Meanwhile, the Gujarat government still refuses to recognize them as internally displaced persons, thereby effectively treating Muslims as non-Gujaratis and denying them citizenship rights.

To summarize, the Gujarat violence entailed the state, allied with civil society organizations, planning and precipitating violence against minorities. Placed within the changing contours of Indian politics, this violence occurred amidst the growing autonomy of state governments. The NDA government that was in power in 2002 gave Modi a free hand because of the ideological affinities between the governments in both New Delhi and Gujarat. They were able to do so because they could call upon an understanding of democracy that opposed a strong interventionist central government and affirmed the autonomy of elected state governments.

5. Civil Society

An important body of literature suggests that stable democracies are apt to check the spread of violence by virtue of their strong civil societies.[25] From this perspective, civil societies create autonomous public spheres in which citizens acting collectively can express their interests, passions and ideas, exchange information, forge solidarities, achieve mutual goals, advance their interests and hold state officials accountable.[26] Civil society fosters democratic values and identities by challenging the centralization and abuse of power within political society. Cohen and Arato, for instance, conceive of civil society as "self-limiting, democratizing movements seeking to expand and protect spaces for both negative liberty and positive freedom."[27]

However, as Tocqueville famously argued in *Democracy in America,* civil society is not a realm of harmonious associational life. The most advanced democracies are fraught by tensions between individualism and majoritarian inclusiveness. Moreover, in most parts of the world, civil society is not insulated from political society. As civil society has grown in India, it has come to include more exclusionary groups. Moreover, civil society is intensely politicized, both in and of itself and by virtue of its links to the state.

Over the past three decades, Hindu nationalism has been able to establish a significant presence within civil society. The Sangh Parivar has formal or informal links with over a hundred civil society organizations. They are active in every conceivable sphere—education, science, technology, medicine, industry, commerce, governance, development, health, law, media, intellectual property rights, human rights, environment, the diaspora—and with every possible sector, including tribals, Dalits, women, producers, consumers, workers, students, teachers, lawyers, doctors, the handicapped, and retired soldiers.[28] The Sangh Parivar also has a huge transnational following. In 1989 the IDRF sought tax-exempt status from the US government for nine organizations in India that are affiliated with the Sangh Parivar. These organizations are linked in turn to 75 other organizations, including 60 that have established ties to the RSS.[29]

Many of these organizations employ the discourses and practices of left-leaning people's movements and voluntary associations. Some of them are located among poor and marginal segments of the population—urban slum dwellers, tribals in remote rural areas, and Dalits in poor urban neighborhoods.[30] Some, like the Swadeshi Jagran Manch, respond to the frustration, envy, and resentment provoked by rapid economic and social change with their antiglobalization campaigns. Others provide relief after disasters, including earthquakes, floods, and riots. After the 2001 earthquake in Gujarat, the Sewa Bharati funded the reconstruction of two villages and many schools in affected areas.[31] The VHP Ekal Vidyalayas runs schools in tribal villages, and the Vikasan Foundation raises funds for them.

Hindutva has also established a presence in civil society by engaging with the minutiae of people's daily lives. The RSS started *shakhas,* or training camps, in 1927, which have continued until today. Ram Madhav claimed that in 2008, one million people participated in 50,000 *shakhas* throughout the country. This represented an increase of 20,000 *shakhas* since 1991.[32] All the *shakhas* cultivate a powerful commitment to Hindu nationalist ideals but adapt to the interests of different age groups. *Shakhas* provide young boys with recreational after-school activities, assistance with homework, and subsidized school uniforms when they need them. They provide older men with companionship, physical exercise and opportunities to discuss the issues of the day. Through daily rituals and interactions, *shakha* members develop a powerful commitment to Hindu nationalist principles.

Sangh-affiliated activities and organizations are distinctive in some key respects from other civil society groups. They are guided by a single set of ideological principles. The RSS provides directives to affiliated organizations and ensures their loyalty to its dictates. Hindutva organizations, which provided relief after the 2001 earthquake in Gujarat, provided shelter to Hindus but not Christians and Muslims and reconstructed temples but not mosques and churches. Social reform work among tribals seeks to introduce them to upper-caste beliefs and practices. Ekal vidyalaya schools provide students with a revisionist understanding of history that demonizes Muslims and glorifies Hindu rulers. The *shakhas* inculcate militarist identities and propagate anti-Muslim sentiments.

Compared to other civil society organizations, Sangh-affiliated groups have been unusually violent. The VHP and Bajrang Dal have engaged in quotidian acts of violence to propagate Hindutva ideals. They have attacked beauty pageants, ransacked movie theaters showing films they find objectionable, destroyed art they deem anti-Hindu, and threatened and harassed prominent artists and intellectuals. They have damaged shops selling Valentine's cards and harassed women whose attire they consider westernized. One of their major targets has been sexual relations between Hindus and Muslim. The VHP and Hindu Jagran Manch have been publishing and disseminating pamphlets since the late 1990s alleging that Muslim men have abducted Hindu women. Bhabubhai Rajabhai Patel, the head of the Bajrang Dal in Gujarat, described "rescuing" Hindu women who have been "lured" into relationships with Muslim men. He said that the Bajrang Dal sent the girls they had "recovered" back home and taught the boys a lesson: "We beat him in a way that no Muslim man will dare look at Hindu women again." Although he realized that these actions are illegal, he was unfazed by this because he believed his actions are moral . . . "and anyway, the government is ours."[33]

The VHP and its affiliates have drawn on these civil society networks to orchestrate mass violence. One of the VHP's major targets was the Christian community. The VHP has sought to "reconvert" Christian tribals to Hinduism, while branding Christians who did not convert as outsiders. The unprecedentedly large number of Dalits and tribals who participated in the 2002 Gujarat violence is testimony to the VHP's prior success in organizing them. VHP-sponsored anti-Christian violence in Gujarat was a prelude to the massive anti-Muslim violence that followed.

The entire campaign around Ayodhya entailed Hindu nationalists mobilizing civil society around a cause that they deemed ennobling but was founded in violence. From 1989 on, the VHP drew on a rich vocabulary of symbolic politics to link local and national arenas: manufacturing and inscribing bricks with Shri Ram and transporting them to Ayodhya, lighting torches in Ayodhya and lighting other torches along the way, and organizing a "rath yatra" in which Advani traveled in a decorated van from Gujarat to Ayodhya. Each of these campaigns provoked violence. Between September 1 and November 20, 564 people died in one hundred sixteen riots. In UP alone, 224 people were killed in 24 riots. The Sangh organized on a massive scale in Gujarat from 1983–1992. Violence broke out in Ahmedabad in 1985, and again in 1987, amidst the collection of sacred bricks for the temple construction. Advani's 1990 rath yatra provoked riots in 26 different localities, leading to about 100 fatalities between September and November 1990.[34] After the demolition of the mosque, violence in Surat claimed two hundred lives.[35] Moreover, the catalyst for the violence in Gujarat was renewed fervor around temple construction.

Sangh-affiliated civil society organizations are also unusual in the extent to which they have been beneficiaries of foreign funding. Amidst the vast funding that international donors have provided to NGOs in India, most of it has gone to Hindu organizations. No Muslim associations are among the top twenty-five organizations that receive foreign funding.[36] The Sangh has also engaged in extensive fundraising itself through its vast diasporic networks. The most infamous is through an NGO based in the United States, the Indian Development and Relief Fund (IDRF). According to the 2002 report *The Foreign Exchange of Hate,* the IDRF distributed five million dollars to 184 associations, 80 percent of which were affiliated with the Sangh, from 1995 and 2002. Over half of these organizations engaged in religious conversion and Hinduization of poor tribal communities.

The large Gujarati expatriate community has provided lavish support to the IDRF to support the Sangh's Hindu nationalist activities. Even funds earmarked for disaster and relief aid are disbursed in sectarian ways. After the 2001 earthquake in Bhuj, Gujarat, the majority of IDRF and Sewa International UK (SIUK) funds went to Sewa Bharati, an RSS affiliate. The RSS affiliated Vidya Bharati used about a third of the funds for reconstruction and rehabilitation.[37] The IDRF-funded Vanvasi Kalyan Ashram played an extensive role in anti-Christian violence between 1998 and 2000, as well as in anti-Muslim violence in 2002.

The localized, decentralized character of the work that Sangh-affiliated organizations perform can mask their unusually close links to parties and the state. The VHP has campaigned extensively for the BJP when it has expressed the strongest commitment to Hindutva ideals. In return the BJP has nominated many VHP candidates to run for office and appointed them to key positions in its state governments. The RSS has strong links to numerous states bureaucracies in BJP-ruled states. The NDA government at the center and BJP state governments accepted the VHP's authority and accommodated many of its demands.

The fusing of civil society and the state is nowhere more evident than in Gujarat. The BJP governments that occupied office after 1995 provided extensive funding for RSS schools and VHP-supported social work organizations. Modi owed his rise to the RSS networks and remained deeply committed to strengthening them and their relations with the state. The Modi government established strong ties to local government bodies and nongovernmental organizations. For example, it established police cells to monitor interfaith marriages. When Hindus and Muslims registered their marriages, officers would visit the couples and pressure them to break up, threatening their safety if they refused to follow orders.[38] It would send this information to the Bajrang Dal to follow up. It also expanded its global reach by encouraging the growth of foreign-funded Sangh-affiliated NGOs while undermining NGOs that sought to protect Muslims' rights and provide them with relief and rehabilitation.[39] Independent citizen groups created most of the relief camps where Muslims found refuge in 2002.

6. Conclusion

Hindu nationalist discourses are both majoritarian and democratic—they call for the defense of Hindu rights, "real" secularism, regular elections, and state autonomy. Some of the BJP's most significant electoral gains have followed upon the violence it has provoked prior to the elections. Because these elections have largely been free, open, and fair, they have often brought to power anti-Muslim Hindutva activists. Elected officials and heads of BJP state governments have allowed the VHP to organize violent activities around the temple in Ayodhya, particularly in UP in the early 1990s and more dramatically in Gujarat in 2002. Moreover, BJP state governments have pursued a variety of Hindu nationalist goals—sanctioning conversions, banning cow slaughter and saffronizing education—when they have occupied office at the state level.

Parties, states and civil society groups are all to some degree culpable for the spread of antiminority sentiment and violence. Both at the national and the state levels, the Congress party contributed to the growth of Hindu majoritarianism by courting the Hindu vote and failing to provide a real alternative to the BJP. Coalition members were unwilling or unable to force the NDA government to curtail the Gujarat violence and punish its perpetrators. The central government under the leadership of Rajiv Gandhi, V. P. Singh, and Narasimha Rao gave into the VHP's demands and thereby allowed the movement to grow. The most severe violence occurred in two states which the BJP ruled. Hindutva forces have increasingly captured civil society by forging links between private and public domains and politicizing how people dress, marry, eat, shop, study, and worship.

And yet if democratic institutions precipitate violence, they also constrain its spread over time and space. The courts have both prolonged and sometimes conceded to the VHP's claims in Ayodhya, but they also have thwarted them. The Sangh's antiminority violence has alternately attracted and alienated the electorate. The federal system has enabled Hindu majoritarian violence to grow but curtailed ethnic subnationalist violence. The very forces within civil and political society that have produced right-wing, exclusionary parties and movements have also given rise to civil liberties groups and lower-caste parties and movements that have challenged the right-wing parties.

One response to the incessant interweaving of collective violence with non-violent politics, as Charles Tilly suggests, is to identify the causes of violence within the structure of the state or, more broadly, the conditions of modernity.[40] From this perspective, democratic institutions may be the vehicles for violence or peace but are better understood as mechanisms than as causal forces. Although it may well be the case that democracy is neither the ultimate cause of violence or stability, democratic institutions have regulated the timing and severity of violence. Thus my interest is in how the changing contours of democracy may be associated with the growth of certain forms of violence.

Most strikingly, violence has occurred as Indian democracy has engaged in the devolution of power and state governments have gained increased autonomy from the national government. To the extent that the BJP has been constrained from attacking minorities at the national level, it has been freer to pursue antiminority policies and actions at the state level. Violence has been most extreme when the commitments of an ideologically driven party, movement, and state converge, especially when the state and national governments are ruled by the same party. A BJP government occupied office in UP and had close ties to the VHP in 1992 when Hindutva forces destroyed the mosque and precipitated widespread violence. However, the Congress government was in office at the national level and curbed the violence by declaring President's Rule. Violence occurred on a larger scale in Gujarat in 2002 because a BJP government was in power that had close connections with civil society groups and the tacit support of a BJP-dominated national government.

The Sangh Parivar has realized that the key to enacting its broad-based agenda is to simultaneously capture control over the state, the party system, and civil society. It has bridged the chasm between groups that are often deemed non-political and political parties that are uninterested in social and cultural matters. It has effectively linked civil and political society. In this respect, students of Indian politics who identify either the state or civil society or parties as causing and resolving violence have a great deal to learn from the Sangh Parivar's appreciation of their combined strength.

That the Sangh Parivar is unique in tethering an antiminority stance to a strategy for transforming civil and political society might suggest violence is indeed anomalous; it is located in a single set of organizations under unusual conditions. However, this sanguine view ignores the ways in which democratic institutions can precipitate antidemocratic norms without necessarily violating democratic procedures. Congress in the aftermath of Independence provided a real alternative to the Jan Sangh and RSS because of the power and legitimacy it commanded as a party, in both civil society and the state. Although it has recently demonstrated renewed secular commitments, it has yet to reestablish these far-reaching linkages.

While growing dissidence within the Sangh Parivar could weaken its ability to unify around shared ideological goals, neither the RSS nor the BJP are likely to sever their close ties. In the absence of an alternative effective strategy of achieving national strength, the BJP must rely on the RSS and VHP to garner support within civil society. For the RSS to relinquish its ties to the BJP would entail returning to the political wilderness. It is their recognition of their profound interdependence that keeps this "family" together. Gujarat was a product of their best combined efforts. It may be some time before we know whether Gujarat was a precedent or an end run.

Notes

1. I am grateful to Christophe Hébé for research assistance and to Mark Kesselman, Srirupa Roy, and Sayres Rudy for helpful comments.
2. For an earlier version of this argument see Amrita Basu and Srirupa Roy, editors, *Violence and Democracy in India* (Kolkata: Seagull Books, 2007).
3. Paul Brass describes the violence in Gujarat as a pogrom rather than a riot, on the basis of the scale of the violence, its preplanning, the targeting of a large number of mosques, the extent of official complicity, and the spread of the violence from urban to rural areas. See Paul Brass, "The Gujarat Pogrom of 2002," available online at the SSRC website: http://conflcits.ssrc.org/brass.

4. Immanuel Kant, "Perpetual Peace: A Philosophical Sketch," [1795], ed. Hans Reid, *Kant's Political Writing* (Cambridge: Cambridge University Press, 1991), 93–130.

5. Barbara Harff, "No Lessons Learned from the Holocaust? Assessing Risks of Genocide and Political Mass Murder Since 1955," *American Political Science Review*, 97:1 (Feb. 2003), 57–73 and Jack Snyder, *From Voting to Violence: Democratization and Nationalist Conflict* (New York: Norton Books, 2000).

6. Christian Davenport and David A. Armstrong II, "Democracy and the Violation of Human Rights—A Statistical Analysis from 1976 to 1996," *American Journal of Political Science*, 48:3 (2004), 538–54.

7. http://www.freedomhouse.org/country/india#.UxyoN8aYaFE.

8. Yogendra Yadav, "Understanding the Second Democratic Upsurge: Trends of Bahujan Participation in Electoral Politics in the 1990s," in Francine R. Frankel, Zoya Hasan, Rajeev Bhargava, and Balveer Arora, eds., *Transforming India: Social and Political Dynamics of Democracy* (Delhi: Oxford University Press, 2000), 120–45.

9. *Indian Express*, 19 January 1993.

10. Manoj Mitta, "If NHRC Indicts Modi, He Must Be Sacked," *Indian Express*, March 31, 2002, www.indianexpress.com/ie20020331/op1.html.

11. "Gujarat Riots a BJP conspiracy: KR Narayanan," *The Hindu*, March 2, 2005, www.hinduonnet.com/thehindu/holnus/001200503022152.html.

12. Upendra Baxi, "The Second Gujarat Catastrophe," *Economic and Political Weekly, The Hindu* (online edition), August 24, 2002. http://www.epw.in/special-articles/second-gujarat-catastrophe.html.

13. "BJP demands President's Rule in Manipur," *The Hindu* (online edition), September 8, 2009, www.thehindu.com/2009/09/08/stories/2009090860151000.htm.

14. Atul Kohli, "Can Democracies Accommodate Ethnic Nationalism? The Rise and Decline of Self-Determination Movements in India," in Atul Kohli, ed., *Democracy and Development in India: From Socialism to Pro-Business* (Delhi: Oxford University Press, 2009).

15. Amrita Basu, "Reflections on Community Conflicts and the State in India," *Journal of Asian Studies*, 56:2 (May 1997), 391–397.

16. Michael Mann, *The Dark Side of Democracy: Explaining Ethnic Cleansing* (Cambridge: Cambridge University Press, 2004).

17. Malcolm Bull, "Ultimate Choice," *London Review of Books*, 28:3 (February 9, 2006), 3–6.

18. Aijaz Ahmad, "Indian Politics at Crossroads: Towards Elections 2004," in Mushirul Hasan, ed., *Will Secular India Survive?* (New Delhi: Imprint One, 2004), 212.

19. Interview with Gulab Singh Parhar, VHP president for UP, Lucknow, January 4, 1992.

20. K. S. Subramanian, *Political Violence and the Police in India* (New Delhi: Sage Publications, 2007).

21. BBC Online, "Gujarat Riot Muslims 'Eliminated,'" April 14, 2005, http://news.bbc.co.uk/2/hi/south_asia/4445107.stm.

22. Darshan Desai, "Dark Descent," *Outlook,* September 23, 2002.

23. Teesta Setalvad, "Godhra: Crime Against Humanity," in Steven I. Wilkinson, ed., *Religious Politics and Communal Violence* (New Delhi: Oxford University Press, 2005).

24. www.tribuneindia.com/2002/20020916/nation.htm#4.

25. The most influential among these is Robert Putnam, *Bowling Alone: The Collapse and Revival of American Community* (New York: Simon and Schuster, 2000).

26. Larry Diamond and Marc F. Plattner, eds., *Nationalism, Ethnic Conflict, and Democracy* (Baltimore: Johns Hopkins University Press, 1994), 5.

27. Jean L. Cohen and Andrew Arato, *Civil Society and Political Theory* (Cambridge: The MIT Press, 1992), 17.

28. Pralay Kanungo, "Myth of the Monolith: The RSS Wrestles to Discipline Its Political Progeny," *Social Scientist*, 34:11–12 (Nov–Dec 2006), 51–70; 53–4.

29. *The Foreign Exchange of Hatred* (Mumbai: Sabrang Communications and Publishing, Mumbai, and the South Asian Citizens Web, 2002).

30. See Raj Goyal, *Rashtriya Swayamsevak Sangh* (New Delhi: Radha Krishna Prakashan, 1979), Thomas Blom Hansen, *The Saffron Wave: Democracy and Hindu Nationalism in Modern India* (New Delhi: Oxford University Press, 1999), Christophe Jaffrelot, *The Hindu Nationalist Movement and Indian Politics* (New Delhi: Penguin Books, 1996), and Arvind Rajagopal, *Politics After Television: Hindu Nationalism and the Reshaping of the Public in India* (Cambridge: Cambridge University Press, 2001).

31. www.letindiadevelop.org/thereport/chapter5.html#A.

32. Interviwith Ram Madhav, Delhi, November 17, 2009.

33. Prashan Jha, "Gujarat as Another Country: The Making and Reality of a Fascist Realm," Himal South Asia, October 2006 (on-line edition) http://old.himalmag.com/component/content/article/1566-Gujarat-as-another-country-the-making-and-reality-of-a-fascist-realm.html.

34. Gyanashyam Shah, "Tenth Lok Sabha Elections: BJP's Victory in Gujarat," *Economic and Political Weekly*, December 21, 1991, 2921–2924; p. 2924.

35. Ghanshyam Shah, "The BJP's Riddle in Gujarat: Caste, Factionalism, and Hindutva," in Thomas Hansen and Christophe Jaffrelot, eds., *The BJP and the Compulsion of Politics in Gujarat* (Delhi: Oxford University Press, 1998), 243–66.

36. Rita Jalali, "International Funding of NGOs in India: Bringing the State Back In," paper presented at the annual meeting of the American Sociological Association, Montreal Convention Center, Montreal, Quebec, Canada, Aug 11, 2006. www.allacademic.com/meta/p104784_index.html, 6.

37. www.awaazsaw.org/ibf/section2.htm.

38. Tavleen Singh, "Is This Normal, Mr Modi?" *Indian Express*, September 22, 2002.

39. Harish Khare, "Gujarat: the Hindutva Laboratory," *The Hindu*, January 3, 1999.

40. The phrase is from Charles Tilly, "Violence, Terror and Politics as Usual," *Boston Review* 27:3–4 (2002): 21–24. For broader accounts of the links between violence and modernity see Hannah Arendt, *The Origins of Totalitarianism* (New York: Harcourt Brace Jovanovich 1951), Zygmunt Baumann, *Modernity and the Holocaust* (Cambridge: Polity Press, 1991), and Ashis Nandy, *Traditions, Tyrannies, and Utopias: Essays in the Politics of Awareness* (Delhi: Oxford University Press, 1987).

9 TOKENISM OR EMPOWERMENT? POLICIES AND INSTITUTIONS FOR DISADVANTAGED COMMUNITIES

Zoya Hasan

From the 1992 destruction of the Babri Masjid, the issue of discrimination and exclusion has received considerable attention, but most studies so far have focused on issues relating to political mobilization and the construction of identity. Until recently, the Scheduled Castes (SCs) have had the larger share of this attention. Even within this group, the Dalit movement and Dalit assertion has been the focal point of interest, with very little attention being directed at specific institutions relating to the disadvantaged communities and even less attention to policies and institutions for other communities. The Indian state created a web of institutions for the implementation of policies with regard to disadvantaged groups. The creation of these institutions was a distinctive feature of Indian democracy. It marked, on the one hand, the institutionalized commitment to the protection and welfare of the marginalized and the disadvantaged and, on the other, the creation of an organized mechanism for the representation of their concerns.

This essay examines two such public institutions: the National Commission for the Scheduled Castes (NCSC) and the National Commission for Minorities (NCM). The rationale for comparing these institutions is simple: numerous studies have acknowledged the central role of public polices in promoting positive outcomes for disadvantaged groups, but there have been few studies that compare the divergent trajectories of policies and institutions and the politics associated with the varied disadvantaged groups. The essay is partly focused on the Commissions and partly on the general issues pertaining to the state's differential approach to disadvantage and the consequences of this. This comparative study does not include an evaluation of the institutional capacity or efficacy of either or both of the commissions. Beginning with an overview of the policy framework, it seeks to assess the differential approach of the Indian state to the disadvantaged communities and how this might impact the working of institutions that aim directly or indirectly to address social inequality. Apart from the policy approach and institutional context, it is important to note that political processes have the greatest influence on the performance of institutions and impact on the nature and effectiveness of implementation of pluralism. In short, the strengths and limitations of existing institutions cannot be judged only on the basis of institutional logic and design, but these depend critically on the linkages between public policy and institutions and also between political mobilization and ideological contestation.

Through a comparative analysis of the two commissions, this essay aims to understand the government policy for dealing with different types of discrimination crafted around a differential notion of backwardness. For the purpose of comparative analysis, it asks the following three questions: (1) How does the state deal with the problems of different disadvantaged groups? (2) What has been the impact of polices and institutions on improving outcomes for the disadvantaged communities? and (3) How do we account for differences from the point of view of their role in the protection and promotion of the interests of the deprived and disadvantaged?

The argument developed here is that the NCSC has had some beneficial impact on the lives of the SCs, and this has largely arisen from the slew of policies and measures for the protection and political empowerment of lower castes. There is a widely shared consensus and readiness to implement the constitutional mandate to empower and enhance the protection of the Scheduled Castes and Scheduled Tribes. However, deprivation and disadvantage are not confined to a single group in India. Yet official discourse continues to revolve essentially around caste-based discrimination, paying little attention to the deprivation of religious minorities. Hence, the large number of programs and policies are targeted at particular groups seen as historically disadvantaged. While acknowledging the need for giving due recognition to historical dimensions, I argue that in view of the comparative evidence on deprivation of various deprived groups, we cannot avoid the issues and problems arising out of disadvantage and discrimination in the present day. Apart from clear differences in the policy approach, political processes also have a strong influence with regard to the effectiveness of policies and approach toward the disadvantaged. The strengths and limitations of existing institutions cannot be judged only on the basis of institutional logic and design, but these depend critically on the linkages between public policy and institutions and also ideological contestation and opposition.

1. Institutional Frameworks

India was among the first major democracies in the world to recognize and provide for the right of cultural collectivities—diverse religious, linguistic communities, castes and tribes living in the country. This represents a significant and creditable initiative on the part of democratic India's early political leadership because at the time the Indian state framed these policies, most of the western and third world states had not consciously acknowledged in their policy frameworks the internal diversities in their societies. The democratic framework of the Indian Constitution gave recognition to diversity and accepted that the political community consisted of several different communities. Placing the principles of diversity and pluralism in the context of choice rather than tradition, the Indian approach provides large space for the development of a broad-based democracy by arguing that people have the right to linguistic and religious identities and that the adoption of policies that recognize and protect these identities is the only sustainable approach to development and democracy in diverse societies. The secular-democratic-federal design enabled the state to recognize rights of linguistic groups, minority communities, and the socially and economically weaker sections and promoted their political and cultural integration.

Recognizing that equal treatment would be insufficient to ameliorate historic discrimination suffered by the lowest social groups, the Constitution provided legislative reservations for the SCs and STs. In granting rights to various groups, however, a basic distinction was thus made between the rights of groups, which were socially discriminated through untouchability or physical isolation, and the rights of religious minorities, which were viewed as part of the larger concepts of pluralism and diversity. The minorities were given the freedom to observe and preserve their language, culture, and religious practices; establish and administer educational institutions of their choice; and retain separate personal laws for different communities. The state, by earmarking religious minorities for special attention in the cultural sphere and denying them crucial state support in the area of social welfare, placed them at a relative disadvantage.[1] These rights were supposed to safeguard against the possibility of unequal treatment and restrain the hegemony of any community or the state; however, such policies do not guarantee equal status to groups and communities in the social and economic life of the country. The problems arising out of the failure to reconcile the demands of identity and well-being in relation to minorities are obvious from the institutional deficit that they have suffered. Cultural rights are not enough for the protection of minority interests, particularly for those minorities that are disadvantaged.[2]

Initially, the term "minorities" encompassed not only the religious minorities, but the SCs and STs as well. It was only in the process of the drafting of the Constitution that the term itself came to be renegotiated and redefined. Following Partition of India in 1947, the earlier proposal of instituting a special minority officer was now recast as a special officer for the Scheduled Castes and Scheduled Tribes.[3] The existence of a commission for the Scheduled Castes and Scheduled Tribes and their protection was very much due to the earlier Assembly resolution that had implicitly declared them Hindus, and this meant an erasure of religious minorities from a formerly inclusive category. When the Assembly dropped protections for minorities, it did not do the same for the SCs and STs. A conscious distinction was made between the religious minorities and the lower castes, with the latter being declared part of the Hindu community and therefore different from the religious minorities. In other words, the SCs were neither a racial minority nor a linguistic minority, certainly not a religious minority, but they were disadvantaged Hindus who needed protections earlier enjoyed by non-Hindu minorities. Social backwardness of a group in the Hindu caste system was thus the only legitimate ground for group-preference provisions.

Public policies for the lower castes fall broadly into two types: (1) antidiscriminatory or protective measures, and (2) developmental and empowering measures for lower castes. Antidiscriminatory measures includes the provision of legal safeguards against discrimination, proactive measures in the form of reservation policies for the public sector and state-supported sectors, and measures for economic and political empowerment to overcome the past economic and social handicaps. Based on the principles of nondiscrimination and equal treatment, the Constitution envisaged a three-pronged strategy to remove the social disabilities suffered by Dalits, provide for punitive action against violence inflicted on them, and protect their economic interests through legal and legislative measures. It contains explicit provisions spelling out state obligations toward protecting and promoting the rights and welfare of SCs and STs.[4] It provided a good number of social, educational, economic, and political safeguards as a set of social policies and measures for the amelioration of their conditions. It also undertook development initiatives to bridge the gulf between the SCs and the rest of society in respect of economic conditions and social status based on specific programs that were a supplement to the general development schemes to benefit the SCs as well. The 1980s marked a shift in approach toward a greater focus on special schemes and targeted programs for the disadvantaged groups. This period witnessed the introduction of a new strategy for the development of SCs and STs. This took the form of special plans, such as the Special Component Plan (SCP) for the STs and later the same for the SCs.[5]

The SCP's prime objective was to ensure allocation of adequate funds to implement schemes that would benefit SCs, reduce the gap between them and the rest of the society, and speed up the process of integrating them with the mainstream. Although it was clearly a landmark provision for Dalits, it has not been implemented effectively. Out of the 27 states that have formulated SCSP, many of them have not made financial provisions for them in proportion to the SC population in the state.[6] At least 18 states had not reported the flow of funds from their annual state plan outlays to the SCSP in 2007–2008.[7] Many states apportion outlays under the state plan and classify them as SCP without taking into consideration whether implementation of such programs has any bearing on the development of the SCs.[8] In addition, the states did not allocate funds in proportion to Dalits' share in the population because the bulk of the allotments went to nondivisible sectors such as roads, power, communication, and irrigation, leaving little for the divisible sectors from which funds for the SCSP were to be drawn. Overall, it would appear that a "lack of political will, the lethargy of the bureaucracy and the deep-rooted prejudice against Dalits among large sections of civil society, which gets reflected in the attitude of those in the administration, are among the reasons cited for the failure of many a development initiative."[9]

By contrast, in the case of minorities there was a tendency to overemphasize identity, which resulted in a situation where inequalities and deprivation were not adequately recognized and thus not frontally addressed.[10] The state, by earmarking religious minorities for special attention in the cultural sphere and denying them crucial state support in the area of social welfare, placed them at a relative disadvantage.[11] Hence, there was a clear reluctance to be similarly proactive with regard to the special treatment of minorities, despite evidence of minority deprivation and disadvantage.[12] For a long time the state avoided the subject of development of minorities, and this was one factor responsible for keeping them backward. This was responsible for the exclusion of minorities from the category of the governed.

In a landmark decision signaling a major shift in policy toward Muslims, Prime Minister Manmohan Singh in 2005 constituted the High-Level Committee on the Social, Economic and Educational Status of the Muslim Community of India, charged with investigating the socioeconomic status of Muslims. The committee, headed by Justice Rajinder Sachar, submitted its report in November 2006 and demonstrated that the educational, social, and economic development of Muslims has fallen far behind that of other groups in our society and that the Muslim community is barely distinguishable from Dalits on most indices of social, economic, and educational deprivation. The report confirms that Muslims face economic deprivation, social exclusion, and political underrepresentation. The prime minister's new 15-point program for the welfare of minorities was recast to focus action sharply on issues linked with the social, educational, and economic uplift of minorities and provide for earmarking of outlays in certain schemes so that the progress can be monitored.[13] These shifts were partly in response to the pressures from minorities who were not satisfied with cultural autonomy and demanded substantive equality like other deprived groups. These initiatives mark a conceptual shift in favor of socioeconomic development against the past preoccupation with identity politics and the secular–communal divide. It represented a long overdue recognition that the concept of minority rights needed an approach of substantive equality rather than formal equality.

Against this background, the Eleventh Five-Year Plan offered an important opportunity to correct the deficits in empowering of minorities bearing in mind the acknowledgment that "the previous five-year plans have attempted to focus on weaker sections; they have failed to include many groups, especially Muslims, in the development process."[14] Even though there is greater concern for the socioeconomic development of minorities, there are hardly any substantive measures to achieve this. This was apparent from the reluctance to introduce a special plan for minorities on the lines of the tribal subplan or the SCCP in the Eleventh Plan.[15] The planning commission did not approve a minority subplan because of fears of political fallout. The fear of political backlash was real given the BJP's constant attack whenever an issue of affirmative action for minorities came to the fore. Indicating the importance of the idea of Muslim appeasement in its thinking, the BJP had earlier assailed the prime minister's call for a fair share in jobs for minorities, fiscal priority for minorities, and the 15-point program.[16] As in the past, the BJP objected to the incorporation of any special measures or budgetary allocations for minorities and disparaged the latter as communal budgeting.

2. National Commission for Scheduled Castes and National Commission for Minorities

India established an array of institutions to cater exclusively to social justice and the protection of the disadvantaged sections of society. In each case, to monitor the progress of public policies for disadvantaged groups and to provide an institutional forum where communities could present their demands, the Constitution and subsequent legislations created specific institutions for this purpose. Among the most significant such institutions are the National Human Rights Commission (NHRC), National Commission for Scheduled Castes and Scheduled Tribes (NCSCST), NCM, and the National Commission for Women (NCW). These institutions have had a dissimilar history, self-image, popular perception of their worth and effectiveness, and so on.

The establishment of the NCSC is one of the principal features of the constitutional provision for these two groups.[17] The National Commission for Scheduled Castes and Scheduled Tribes was established in 1992 with constitutional status. Its basic purpose is to protect and promote the welfare of the SCs and STs. A separate NCSC came into existence in 2002, when the government took the decision to bifurcate and create two separate commissions for the SCs and the STs. The reports of the commission are supposed to be placed before parliament. However, the First Report of the NCSC (2004–2005) was not placed in parliament until 2008.

Embedded in a complex constellation of laws, policies, and institutions, it is an institution designed to address social inequality.[18] The commission investigates and monitors the implementation of five categories of safeguards: social, economic, educational, cultural, political, and service safeguards provided to the SCs. It covers a wide range of activities that include implementation of laws; provisions relating to reservations in recruitment, promotion, and admission to educational institutions; and economic development, including educational development. It inquires into specific complaints pertaining to the deprivation of rights and safeguards to these sections, advises in the planning process and evaluate the development of these communities, and submits reports annually on the working of the safeguards with appropriate and specific recommendations.

Overall, it is organized to monitor the working and implementation of safeguards, on the one hand, and redress violations of safeguards, on the other. As a result of its concerted efforts, significant gains have been registered in the implementation of reservations and in giving representation to the SCs in public employment. The attention paid to ensuring the participation of the SCs in public employment is sometimes at the expense of more substantive concerns, such as the implementation of social welfare schemes for Dalits. The second major area of intervention is monitoring the progress of scheduled castes in education at all levels. The third issue concerns atrocities, and here the main focus is on the monitoring of the legal provisions with regard to such incidents. It is least effective in dealing with atrocities largely because the commission refers the complaints to the very institutions that are either complicit or implicated in the perpetuation of violence.

Initially set up as a nonstatutory body through a Home Ministry Resolution in January 1978, the creation of the NCM was a response to the frequent appeals from Muslim organizations that the government set up a Minority Commission to check the increasing incidents of violence and discrimination against them. With the enactment of the National Commission of Minorities Act (1992), it became a statutory body. The first statutory commission was set up in 1993. Since 1992, 15 states have set up state-level minorities commissions.

At its apex the NCM consists of a chairman, vice chairman, and five members appointed by the central government. The NCM usually includes representatives from all the minorities, but unlike the NCSCST there is no requirement that at least one member be a woman. Despite a strong demand for autonomy, the NCM lacks both financial and political autonomy necessary for independent and effective functioning. The executive-driven process of appointment for both commissions is such that they have become a sinecure for unemployed politicians and retired bureaucrats, which the ruling parties and their allies find convenient to accommodate in such commissions.

The NCM was established as an institutional mechanism to monitor the working of constitutional safeguards provided for minorities in the Constitution and in laws enacted by parliament and state legislatures. Its mandate was to (1) evaluate the progress of the development of minorities under the union and states; (2) monitor the working of the safeguards provided in the Constitution and in laws enacted by parliament and the state legislatures; (3) look into specific complaints regarding deprivation of rights and safeguards of the minorities and take up such matters with the appropriate authorities; (4) study problems arising out of any discrimination against minorities and recommend measures for their removal; (5) conduct studies, research, and analysis on the issues relating to socioeconomic and educational development of minorities; (6) suggest appropriate measures in respect of any minority to be undertaken by the central government or the state governments; and (7) make periodical or special reports to the central government on any matter pertaining to minorities and in particular the difficulties confronted by them. For the past few years, a system of holding meetings in state capitals to review cases of pending complaints with respective state governments has been helpful in settling these complaints.

The listing of responsibilities of the NCM is more or less on the same lines as the other statutory commissions for all the disadvantaged communities or the NCSC. However, the NCSC monitors very specific and substantial safeguards, which include the abolition of untouchability, child labor, traffic in human beings, and temple entry; educational safeguards (reservations in educational institutions); political safeguards (reservations in legislatures); and service safeguards (reservations in public employment and for purposes of promotion). While the mandate is to monitor progress of minorities, which provides the commission a wide-ranging remit, it is the implementation of constitutional safeguards that has been its central concern.

The NCM works under the Ministry of Minority Affairs, and before the formation of this ministry it came under the Ministry of Social Justice and Empowerment. Theoretically, all the commissions are autonomous from government, but practically they lack effective autonomy from the government. The lack of effective autonomy is most evident in the operations of state minority commissions, which function roughly as government departments and are dependent on the state government. Besides the lack of autonomy, in the case of the NCM there is no machinery or powers for proper investigation of complaints. The NCM's functioning is contingent on the goodwill of state governments. Another issue that has the potential of further reducing the effectiveness of the NCM has been the growing number of commissions that overlap with the mandate of this commission and thereby reducing the remit of this commission. In 1988, the formation of the new Commission on Linguistic Minorities cut into the work of NCM, which was restricted to only religious minorities. This was not just a dilution of the mandate, but also a restriction of the concept of minorities to religious minorities. Then in 1992, on the recommendation of the NCM, the central government established the National Minorities Finance and Development Corporation (NMFDC). In 2004, the United Progressive Alliance (UPA) government established the National Commission for Minority Educational Institutions (NCMEI), for the regulation and recognition of minority educational institutions. By establishing a separate commission for minority educational institutions, the NCM was stripped of yet another major responsibility in its mandate. The problem obviously is not the creation of new commissions, but the lack of coordination between institutions involved in the protection of the interests of minorities.

Although the NCM has the powers of a civil court to summon any person, receive evidence on affidavit, or examine any witness, it does not have the machinery to investigate complaints of discrimination and deprivation of rights and safeguards of minorities.[19] In view of this limitation, the UPA government promised to upgrade the status of the NCM to a constitutional body.[20] The Constitution (103rd Amendment) Bill of 2004 seeks to confer constitutional status to the NCM. The proposed legislation granting constitutional was introduced in December 2006, and has not been passed by parliament until 2008. It has been approved by the Parliamentary Standing Committee on Social Justice and Empowerment, which noted that "in the absence of vocal powers of inquiring and investigation the NCM would be a toothless tiger and hampered a great deal in carrying out its mandate."[21] The power to investigate and to advise in the policy process of socioeconomic development of minorities would put the NCM on par with the NCSC and NCST. It would also enhance its watchdog role as also its efficacy. In its absence the NCM functioning is largely dependent on the willingness of the state governments to accept its interventions and suggestions, which they are often not willing to do when it is politically inconvenient for them to do so.

A quick review of the NCM reports show that its energies are largely consumed, investigating complaints ranging from encroachment of land of religious places, neglect of Urdu to denial of holiday on a particular festival of minorities, hindrance in observing religious ceremonies, and hurting religious sentiments. The commission, which should logically be the agency or instrumentality in the larger context of the protection of minority rights or the enhancement of minority well-being, is ironically not filling that critical political space. It has not been entrusted with the task of tracking and assessing the progress and development of minorities or monitoring the progress of education despite the fact that a scrutiny of these areas is essential for an understanding of the relative levels of deprivation and marginalization. As for service safeguards, even though its functions include service-related issues these are limited to cases of harassment by police and other state authorities. It is supposed to monitor the representation of minorities in public employment and has from time to time documented the gross underrepresentation of Muslims in government jobs, but this effort does not amount to much in the absence of reservations for minorities in government jobs. In other words, the commission's functioning and approach appears largely directed toward the preservation of facilities for minorities rather than the long-term objective of increasing their empowerment and protecting their rights in an institutional sense.

In policy terms, the NCSC has managed to secure legitimacy to carry out its tasks because it a part of a comprehensive set of policies and interlocking institutions, laws, and agencies, while the NCM functions more or less as a stand-alone institution. In its advisory role, the NCM is supposed to interact with the central and state governments. But this does not happen on a routine basis or even on major controversies pertaining to minorities that crop up from time to time. The most glaring instance of the NCM's futility was demonstrated under the National Democratic Alliance (NDA) government when, while the NHRC was lambasting Narendra Modi government in Gujarat, Tarlochan Singh, the Chairman of the NCM, was busy giving certificates to Narendra Modi with regard to the state government's role in the Gujarat violence of 2002. As a watchdog body mandated to protect the rights and interests of minorities, it proved to be a mute spectator to the pogrom against minorities.

The annual reports of the NCM and its recommendations have to be laid before each House of Parliament along with a memorandum explaining the action taken or proposed to be taken on the recommendations relating to the Union and the reasons for the nonacceptance, if any, of any of such recommendations.

But in practice, despite the statutory directive to have the reports placed in parliament, these reports do not come to the parliament table although the commission has been regularly preparing and forwarding its reports to the ministry for laying before parliament as required under Section 13 of the Act. When the odd Report does surface in parliament, it is not taken up. In this regard the experiences of the NCM and NCSC are similar. It is not possible to take any effective action on the basis of Reports that for all practical purposes remain in the Ministries of Home Affairs and Social Welfare and on the shelves of the Parliament Library.

Some differences in the functioning of the two commissions are worth noting. These differences relate to their powers and, more significantly, to the very different conception of safeguards for castes and minorities. Envisaged as a proactive organization, the NCSC has power to investigate any matter relating to safeguards for the SCs, inquire into specific complaints regarding deprivation of rights and safeguards, and participate in the planning for socioeconomic development of the SCs. There is a substantial government apparatus (replicated in the states) to cater to the needs and concerns of the SCs.

The NCM does not participate and advise in the process of socioeconomic development of minorities, as there is very little by way of policies for their social and economic development. In comparison, a crucial advantage that the NCSC has over the NCM in this regard is that it works within an established policy framework backed by reservations and encouraged by the social equality constitutional provisions in favor of disadvantaged caste groups.[22] The NCSC is part of an ambitious structure of policies and institutions for the social uplift of the SCs and STs. This distinctive advantage testifies to the consensus on empowering the disadvantaged castes, which helps in the consultations and interface with the Planning Commission and various ministries on matters relating to SCs that can therefore take place on a regular basis.

The most serious handicap that constrains both commissions is that their recommendations are not binding, but advisory.[23] In spite of this limitation, the commissions continue to place emphasis on addressing themselves primarily to the state rather than attempting to engage civil society and with the larger public discourse. Neither of the two institutions has really attempted to embark on a deeper analysis of the larger social realities. Consequently, they have tended to be directionless and deprived of a larger vision of what are essentially historic responsibilities of increasing the empowerment and strengthening the rights of the disadvantaged citizens, the object of their endeavors. The failure to orient the commissions to the larger task of empowerment results in the inability to formulate policies and prescriptions that can usher in fundamental change in the social realities that would help reduce the inequalities between the privileged groups and the disadvantaged. It is clear that these commissions see themselves as limited to merely preserving existing facilities and provisions, and they are not really looking to place their efforts into a larger context of ensuring democracy and a healthy pluralism.

3. Overview

The continued prevalence of widespread discrimination against Dalits and Muslims that operates in addition to other forms of inequality of access is undoubtedly an indication of the incapacity of public institutions and of the measures and policies for the welfare of the disadvantaged. This would suggest that the public institutions established specifically for the promotion of their interests have failed in addressing the broader goals of antidiscrimination.

While the record of both commissions is mixed in this regard, the NCM is by far the weaker of the two.[24] Envisaged as a proactive organization, the NCSC has unlimited power to investigate any matter relating to safeguards for the SCs; while the NCM has limited power to investigate matters relating to minorities, the NCM functions principally as an agency that forwards complaints to concerned authorities with no real powers do anything about it. Judged in terms of its overall constitutional mandate, the NCSC has fallen short and has failed to provide specific protections in the face of socially powerful opposition.

The record of the NCSC has not been satisfactory in bringing about an end to discrimination or atrocities against Dalits. Social discrimination persists, and so does the stigma attached to persons belonging to the Scheduled Castes. Numerous studies show the continuation of the practices of untouchability and discrimination.[25] Nowhere in the country has the SC/ST (POA) Act been vigorously enforced, and hence it has had a negligible impact on the level of atrocities against SCs. The NHRC Report on Prevention of Atrocities against Scheduled Castes (2004) blamed the "lopsided enforcement" of the Scheduled Castes and Scheduled Tribes (Prevention of Atrocities) Act (1989) in several parts of the country for the continuing discrimination against Dalits.[26] The Sixth Report of the NCSC/ST revealed the continuance of social discrimination, and that too without penalty.[27] Most of the complaints are directed against the conduct of police personnel and security agencies.[28] The NHRC report indicts successive governments for their lukewarm attitude to the oppression of Dalits. The frequency and intensity of violence, the report observes, is an offshoot of desperate attempts by the upper-caste groups to protect their entrenched status against the process of disengagement and upward mobility among lower castes resulting from affirmative action of State Policy [enshrined in the Constitution of India].[29]

Quotas in public employment have, however, played an important part in the enhancement of political participation and incorporation of Dalits in the political elite. In sum, its success has most to do with the political empowerment of scheduled castes.[30] Significant progress has been made, though there remains considerable room for improvement with regard to implementation of development and welfare policies. On the other hand, the transformation that has taken place is largely attributable to political empowerment, which has come about through legislative reservations for them.

However, despite reservations, SCs remain worse off compared to almost all other social groups in terms of social and economic conditions. On most human development indices, the SCs fall below the national average.[31] They would have been in an even worse situation without mandatory reservation and affirmative action for them, however. As a consequence of reservations, there has been some improvement in the status of SCs. The success lies in a discernible improvement in literacy, school, higher education enrollment, and placement in government jobs. Student enrollment has increased substantially. Although percentages of SCs are still abysmally low, they have been able to get access to the fields of engineering, medicine, teaching, law, and the civil services. Even though it is difficult to estimate the direct benefits gained from reservations in higher education, the presence of about a third of SC and ST students enrolled in significant program in universities is attributable to reservations.[32]

Of all the policies, the provisions for political representation for the SCs and STs have been the most important, because this has given considerable power to the disadvantaged groups. The elected representatives have the opportunity to influence decisions concerning their group, and through that the social restructuring of society as a whole. Affirmative action policies not only directly benefit lower castes through welfare schemes; they have a larger impact on public policies when individuals from lower castes are given a voice in the decision-making process. The legislative elite has helped to promote the implementation of preferential treatment programs even at a time when the economically powerful groups make demands for greater resources. A recent study has found that reservations in state legislatures do increase influence in policymaking for scheduled castes and tribes.[33] The best effect of electoral reservation has been to provide a guaranteed minimum number of legislators from the scheduled castes, and it also provides political presence for a group that would not otherwise get adequate representation.

4. Conclusion

Six decades after Independence, the project of empowering SCs remains a matter of substantial national consensus which has much to do with the ideology of India's freedom struggle, the social contract it stood for, and the kind of nation it sought to build. Keen to eliminate caste inequality, the framers of our Constitution took an unequivocal view of the nature of the state and public intervention required to reduce social inequities and discrimination, ranging from the abolition of untouchability to giving representation in public services and legislatures. The improvement in the performance of the SCs in certain sectors demonstrates the importance of these policies of reservations in bringing about change, and not because discrimination against them has lessened.

The record has been quite different in the case of policies in relation to the minorities. In contrast to the assertiveness and will to ensure affirmative action for lower castes, the legislature and executive appear disinclined to take on board as a visible public policy issue—the socioeconomic rights of minorities. Afraid of wading into politically contentious waters, politicians are reluctant to be upfront in this regard. The foot-dragging on the part of political leadership in coming to grips with the facts and actual details of the deprivation of minority groups would suggest that the prevailing political context has an inhibiting effect on the willingness of politicians to chart any new course of action in this sensitive arena of minority empowerment. Circumscribed by the dominant political configuration and discourse, few political leaders have had the imagination to create a space to do justice to the diverse needs of the community without succumbing to extremism or a politics of tokenism. Apart from this, an important reason for the ineffectiveness of the NCM is the absence of social/political mobilization by and around minority issues in contrast to caste issues. Not much mobilization of minorities has taken place except with reference to the perceived threats to Muslim personal law and minority identity against the Shah Bano Judgment in the 1980s and the demolition of the Babri mosque by Hindu extremist organizations in December 1992.

In addition, there is the basic issue of dealing with different forms of disparity and disadvantage and where to draw the line in terms of caste versus class or caste versus community. There are clear indications that at different levels of economic and social policy the debilitating role of class and gender inequality as also the disadvantages of belonging to a particular religious minority receives very little attention, and in this neglect the single-minded focus on caste discrimination did play a role. The fact that these aspects of inequality continues to be subsumed and in fact underplayed in public discourse is not just the result of vested interests, but also because of the competing pressure of the politics of identity. Cultural and identity politics has displaced the earlier politics of economic and social inequality, thus group identities are supposedly primary to our sense of self-worth. Even if this is true in part, it does not generate a workable politics of transformation.

By and large, the functioning of the NCM has been constrained by the absence of a substantive conception of rights to promote equal opportunity. The key issue is the contested nature of minority rights and the lack of a national consensus on public policies toward minorities, which tends to undermine the institutional efficacy of the NCM. On balance, the NCM can act as protector of the rights of minorities when there is a strongly articulated policy framework with regard to minorities. This underscores the point made in the beginning of the chapter that the focus on discrimination and disadvantage in official policy in India has been disproportionately on the past discrimination, which has benefited the lower castes but has resulted in the exclusion of minorities from the policy discourse and rendered them outside the development framework. The remedial goals and policy measures that are required for the promotion of equal opportunities must go beyond the caste paradigm of inclusion by giving careful attention to current discrimination. However, from the standpoint of minority protection, the sheer existence of the National Commission for Minorities has helped to signal the importance of a substantive conception of minority rights, which blends the security concerns of minorities with that of social development and welfare.[34] Today there is much greater focus on social sector programs that include access to education (such as scholarship schemes for students from minority backgrounds), enhanced access to credit through priority lending, and infrastructure development in minority concentration districts.

This brief analysis of public policies and the functioning of the two commissions, each intended to address a particular facet of disadvantage in a society and under a state committed to democracy, equality and pluralism, shows that real empowerment and enshrinement of the rights of disadvantaged groups would come only from the state and society unveiling concrete strategies for empowerment, geared to a larger vision of achieving substantive equality. Otherwise, setting up instrumentalities and agencies such as these commissions would prove mere tokenism or symbolic affirmations.

Notes

1. Rajeev Dhavan, "Religious Freedom in India," *American Journal of Comparative Law* Vol. 35, No. 1, Winter 1987, pp. 209–54.
2. Bishnu Mohapatra, "Democratic Citizenship and Minority Rights," in Catarina and Kristina Jonsson (eds.), *Globalization and Democratizations in Asia: The Construction of Identity*, New York: Routledge, 2002, pp. 172–3.
3. I have discussed some of these issues in my book *Politics of Inclusion: Castes, Minorities and Affirmative Action*, Oxford University Press, New Delhi, 2009. See chapter 3, pp. 41–78.
4. For an overview of policies, see S. R. Sankaran, "Welfare of Scheduled Castes and Scheduled Tribes in Independent India—An Overview of State Policies and

Programmes," *Journal of Rural Development* Vol. 19, No. 4, 2000, pp. 507–33; B. N. Srivastava Srivastava, "Working of the Constitutional Safeguards and Protective Measures for the Scheduled Castes and Scheduled Tribes," *Journal of Rural Development* Vol. 19, No. 4, 2000, pp. 573–602.

5. On central initiatives such as the SCP, see Chapter III on Economic Development of the Scheduled Castes, NCSC/ST, *Sixth Report 1999–2000–2000–2001,* New Delhi, 2001: 28–32.

6. NCSC/ST, Sixth Report 1999–2000 & 2000–2001, 2001, p. 29.

7. Twenty Ninth Report, Standing Committee on Social Justice and Empowerment (2007–08) Fourteenth Lok Sabha, Ministry of Social Justice and Empowerment, Lok Sabha Secretariat, New Delhi, 2007.

8. Ibid., p. 31.

9. *Report on Prevention of Atrocities against Scheduled Castes,* NHRC, New Delhi, 2004.

10. According to the National Commission for Minorities Act, 1992, the officially designated minorities are Muslims, Christians, Parsis, Buddhists, and Sikhs.

11. Rajeev Dhavan, "Religious Freedom in India."

12. Bishnu Mohapatra, "Democratic Citizenship and Minority Rights," pp. 172–3.

13. The prime minister's new 15-point program covers (1) enhancing opportunities for education, (2) equitable share in economic activities and employment, (3) improving the conditions of living of minorities, and (4) prevention and control of communal riots. It was also decided that 15 percent of the funds may be earmarked wherever possible in relevant schemes and programs for the nationally declared minorities.

14. Planning Commission, Government of India, *Eleventh Five Year Plan,* "Status of Minorities and Prime Minister's New 15-Point Programme," Chapter on Minorities, Planning Commission, Government of India, 2007.

15. Planning Commission, Government of India, *Report of the Working Group on the Empowerment of Scheduled Castes During Eleventh Five Year Plan (2007–2012),* Planning Commission, Government of India, New Delhi, 2007.

16. Prime Minister Manmohan Singh's speech reported in *The Economic Times,* December 12, 2006.

17. See Niraja Gopal Jayal and Bishnu Mohapatra, "The National Commission for Scheduled Castes and Scheduled Tribes," in Nanda P. Wanasundera (ed.), *Protection of Minority Rights and Diversity,* Colombo: International Centre for Ethnic Studies, 2004; Niraja Gopal Jayal, *Representing India: Ethnic Diversity and the Governance of Public Institutions,* London: Palgrave, 2006; Tahir Mahmood, *National Commission for Minorities: Minor Role in Major Affairs,* Delhi: Pharos Publications, 2001.

18. The nodal Ministry for SCs is the Ministry of Social Justice and Empowerment, while for the minorities it is the newly created Ministry for Minority Affairs. Before the formation of the Ministry of Minority Affairs, the Ministry of Social Justice and Empowerment was dealing with minorities as well.

19. Information on complaints on the NCM Website, http://110.21.151.69/cms/welcome.htm.

20. National Commission for Minorities, Annual Report 2005–06, NCM, Lok Nayak Bhawan, New Delhi, 2006.

21. Standing Committee of the Ministry of Social Justice and Empowerment (2005–2006), Twentieth Report, Ministry of Social Justice and Empowerment Lok Sabha Secretariat, New Delhi, 2005.

22. Oliver Mendelsohn and Marika Vicziani Mendelsohn, *The Untouchables: Subordination, Poverty, the State in Modern India*, Cambridge: Cambridge University Press, 2000, pp. 145–46.

23. Bishnu Mohapatra and Niraja Gopal Jayal, "The National Commission for Scheduled Castes and Scheduled Tribes: A Report," op. cit.

24. See, for example, Tahir Mahmood's assessment in "National Minorities Commission," op. cit.

25. See articles on different aspects of the continuing impact of caste on discrimination in *Economic and Political Weekly* Vol. XLII, No. 41, October 13–19, 2007, especially Sukhdeo Thorat and Katherine S. Newman, "Caste and Economic Discrimination: Causes, Consequences and Remedies," *Economic and Political Weekly* Vol. XLII, No. 41, October 13–19, 2007, pp. 4121–4. This paper highlights the ways in which caste persists as a system of inequality and its continuing influence on the economy and allocation of labor and other critical resources.

26. National Commission for Human Rights, Report on Prevention of Atrocities against Scheduled Castes, NHRC, New Delhi, 2004.

27. NCSC/ST, Sixth Report 1999–2000 and 2000–2001, 2001:29.

28. Oliver Mendelsohn and Marika Vicziani Mendelsohn, *The Untouchables: Subordination, Poverty, the State in Modern India*, Cambridge: Cambridge University Press, 2000, pp. 145–6.

29. National Commission for Human Rights, Report on Prevention of Atrocities Against Scheduled Castes, NHRC, New Delhi, 2004, p. 102.

30. Oliver Mendelsohn and Marika Vicziani Mendelsohn, *The Untouchables: Subordination, Poverty, the State in Modern India*, pp. 145–6.

31. S. K. Thorat, "Oppression and Denial: Dalit Discrimination in 1990s," *Economic and Political Weekly* Vol. 37, No. 6, February 9, 2002, pp. 572–8.

32. Thomas Weisskopf, "The Impact of Reservation on Admissions to Higher Education in India," *Economic and Political Weekly* Vol. 39, No. 39, September 25, 2004, pp. 4339–49.

33. Rohini Pande, "Can Mandated Political Representation Increase Policy Influence for Disadvantaged Minorities? Theory and Evidence from India," *The American Economic Review* Vol. 93. No. 4, November 2003, pp. 1132–51.

34. Ibid., p. 187.

10 NEOLIBERALISM AND THE FOOD CRISIS

Prabhat Patnaik

1. Declining per Capita Foodgrain Absorption

The post-"reform" period starting in 1991–1992, which has been hailed by many as marking India's awakening to prosperity and economic power, has seen a steep fall in per capita foodgrain absorption in the country. The significance of this fall becomes clear if we locate it in a historical context. At the beginning of the twentieth century (over the quinquennium 1897–1902), annual per capita foodgrain absorption (defined as net output plus net imports minus net additions to government stocks) was 199 kilograms in "British India." It declined to an average of 148.5 kilograms during 1939–1944 and further to 136.8 during 1945–1946.[1] That was the legacy left by colonial rule at the time of Independence. With tremendous effort, the now much-reviled *dirigiste* regime in the post-Independence period raised that figure to 177.0 kilograms for the country as a whole for the triennium ending 1991–1992. This was a significant turnaround, but still brought the country nowhere near where it was at the beginning of the twentieth century.

The post-reform period has witnessed a reversal of this increase. Per capita foodgrain absorption declined, gently at first, to 174.3 kilograms for the triennium ending 1994–1995 and 174.2 kilograms for the triennium ending 1997–1998; after the mid-nineties, however, it fell precipitously to reach 155.7 kilograms for the triennium ending 2002–2003, which was lower than the figure for 1933–1938 for British India (159.3 kilograms). Lest it be thought that, 2002–2003 being a drought year, things have improved since then, the figure for the triennium ending 2006–2007 was 159.88 kilograms, about the same as for 1933–1938, and for the triennium ending 2011–2012 (the latest year for which we have official data), 163 kilograms. The inescapable conclusion emerges that the per capita absorption of foodgrains in India as a whole has been lower during the first quinquennium of this century than in "British India" on the eve of World War II, and not much higher thereafter.

The decline in per capita foodgrain absorption was more rapid in the rural compared to the urban areas. This is also borne out by the per capita calorie intake data. The average daily calorie intake from all foods declined over successive rounds of the National Sample Survey (NSS) in rural India, from 2,309 in 1983 to 2,285 in 1987–1988, to 2,157 in 1993–1994, to 2,047 in 2004–2005, to 2020 in 2009–2010. (The 1999–2000 data are not comparable with the others.) This represents a 13 percent drop between 1983 and 2009–2010. By contrast, the average daily calorie intake from all foods in urban India did not show any such marked secular decline: it was 2,010 in 1983, 2,084 in 1987–1988, 1,998 in 1993–1994, and 2,020 in 2004–2005 and 1946 in 2009–2010. This dismal picture of declining calorie intake in rural India is confirmed by another set of statistics: as many as seven major states in the country in 2004–2005 had more than 30 percent of the rural population with a daily calorie intake of less than 1,800 (which the FAO considers to be the bare minimum), compared to only three states in 1983; by 2009–2010 their number had increased to nine. In short, hunger and malnutrition have been stalking rural India in the post-reform period, especially in the early years of this century, as never before since Independence.

Faced with such statistics, those who extol India's post-reform economic performance argue that according to NSS data there is a shift away from foodgrain consumption among all expenditure classes in rural India, which merely suggests that foodgrains are an inferior good (the demand for which declines as income rises). The decline in foodgrain absorption per capita, therefore, far from being an indicator of a worsening condition of the rural population, actually indicates an improvement in people's living standards. (To this is often added the argument that with mechanization and the consequent decline in the magnitude of arduous manual work, the need for calories goes down and people can afford to diversify their consumption pattern, which again is a sign of greater well-being.)

The problem with this argument is that it refers only to NSS data for *direct* consumption of foodgrains. But all cross-section data, whether across countries or across states within India or across expenditure classes, show that per capita foodgrain consumption is positively related to the level of per capita income; that is, the better-off consume more food grains per capita, provided we take both direct and indirect consumption (through animal feed and processed foods) into account. The per capita absorption data for India, which were cited above, since they refer to total absorption in all forms, should not therefore show a decline unless people were becoming worse off.

No doubt the per capita food grain absorption figure fluctuates a great deal from one year to the next. Even in the past, during the *dirigiste* period, there were years when the per capita foodgrain absorption would decline markedly, such as during the mid-sixties. What is striking about the current situation, however, is that we are witnessing a secular decline, not confined to one or two years, but spanning a prolonged period.

2. The Myth of Declining Poverty

How, it may be asked, can this decline in foodgrain absorption be reconciled with official claims of decline in poverty, especially rural poverty? The simple answer is that it cannot, and that the official claims of declining rural poverty are not just wrong but simply outrageous. Poverty in India has always been *defined* with respect to a calorie norm (which for rural areas is 2200 kilocalories per person per day). There are therefore two different ways of estimating poverty: directly from the calorie intake data provided by the NSS; or indirectly, as is done in Indian official estimates, by looking at the level of expenditure at which the calorie norm was fulfilled in the base year and then bringing that base poverty line forward through a price index. As long as the price index is adequate, the indirect method, though obviously inferior to the direct one given the definition of poverty, should nonetheless be quite adequate. Unfortunately, the price index used till recently, namely the Consumer Price Index for Agricultural Labourers, precluded a whole lot of items, such as health care, whose effective prices have gone up sharply in recent years.[2] Not surprisingly, the official poverty line for 2004–2005 was placed at the absurd figure of twelve rupees (Rs.) per day. An amount that would not even have purchased a single cauliflower in the market was supposed to cover all the daily expenditure requirements of a borderline nonpoor person! The much-hyped declining poverty ratio is derived from such absurd estimates of the poverty line. If we make a direct estimate of poverty on the basis of the calorie norm, then 58.5 percent of the rural population in India would come under this category in 1993–1994, 69.5 percent in 2004–2005, and a massive 76 percent in 2009–2010. The 2009–2010 figure represents an *increase* compared not only to 1993–1994, but even to the base year of poverty estimates (1973–1974) when the figure was 56.4 percent.[3] Poverty in India, especially rural poverty, as officially defined, is much higher than is officially recognized; and its incidence, far from declining, is actually increasing, especially in this period of neoliberal reforms.

Another calculation lends credence to this conclusion. Let us ask ourselves the question: how much has the command over a specific bundle of goods, by an average person belonging to the agriculture-dependent population, increased since the mid-nineties, which mark the beginning of the growth upsurge? As our benchmark bundle of goods, we take the one that underlies the Consumer Price Index for Industrial Workers (since there is no such index for the agriculture-dependent population). It turns out that between 1996–1997 and 2006–2007, the per capita command over this bundle of goods by the agriculture-dependent population did not increase at all.[4] In other words, precisely during the period when per capita real income for the country as a whole was supposed to have been growing at a rate well in excess of 4 percent per annum on average, a vast majority of its population, almost 60 percent, was witnessing a virtual stagnation in its per capita real income, as measured by the amount of a specific bundle of goods commanded. And since a small segment *within* this agriculture-dependent population must have improved its lot, the bulk of it must have experienced a worsening of its position over this period. Much the same can be said for several other segments of the rural population: craftsmen, fisherfolk, and general laborers. The conclusion about increasing rural poverty therefore is a robust one.

This talk of increasing rural poverty must not give the impression that in urban areas the incidence of poverty was declining. On the contrary, the incidence of urban poverty too was increasing in the post-reform period. The proportion of urban population that obtained less than 2,100 calories per person per day (which is the official definition of urban poverty), when estimated directly from NSS data, stood at 73 percent in 2009–2010 compared to 64.5 percent in 2004–2005, 57 percent in 1993–1994 and 49 percent in 1973–1974.[5] The figures are consistently lower than the corresponding ones for rural India, since the nutrition norm is also lower; but the trend they show is unmistakable.

Since poverty in both rural and urban India is defined with respect to calorie norms, increasing poverty ipso facto must be associated with increasing insufficiency of food intake, which is in conformity with the story of declining per capita foodgrain absorption that we began with.

3. "Income Deflation"

The income elasticity of demand for foodgrains being positive (if we take both direct and indirect demand into account), the growth upsurge in the Indian economy, especially after the mid-nineties, should have generated *ceteris paribus* an increasing per capita demand for foodgrains. But if per capita absorption actually decreased after the mid-nineties, then one would suppose that the consumers were constrained by insufficient supplies—that there was a situation of excess demand. Excess demand typically gives rise to inflation, where prices rise relative to the purchasing power of the consumers (which depends largely upon the money wage and salary bill in the economy). Such inflation, which means a rise in prices relative to money wages, has the effect of shifting income distribution away from the workers and salary earners to the profit earners; and since, per unit of income, the latter's expenditure on goods whose prices are rising is not as high as that of the former, inflation automatically brings excess demand to an end, through a cut in the demand of the wage and salary earners.

When such excess demand-caused inflation arises in the foodgrains market, it also has the effect of shifting the terms of trade between foodgrains and manufactured goods against the latter. This is because foodgrain prices rise relative to money wages while manufactured goods prices remain unchanged relative to money wages.[6] The decline in per capita absorption of foodgrains in a situation of rapid GDP growth, which India experienced after the mid-nineties, should therefore have caused excess demand in the foodgrains market, resulting in inflation in foodgrain prices that would have shifted the terms of trade between foodgrains and manufactured goods in favor of the former.

Paradoxically, however, over much of the post-reform period, far from there being an excess demand for foodgrains there was deficient demand, resulting in an accumulation of foodgrain stocks with the government, whose level was generally in excess of what was considered normal. The reduction in per capita foodgrain absorption over much of this period in other words was not because of supply shortages. Of course, per capita foodgrain output too was lower in later years than at the beginning of the nineties: indeed the nineties were the first decade since Independence over which per capita foodgrain output actually declined. But the drop in per capita absorption was even sharper, which resulted in the level of foodgrain stocks with the government being well above the norm throughout the decade (barring a couple of early years), and increasing over the decade right until July 2002 when it reached 63 million tonnes, a full 42 million tonnes above the norm. Drought relief expenditure in 2002–2003, and exports at throwaway prices (even below those charged to the BPL population) brought the stocks down subsequently, but it is only after April 2005 that the actual stocks with the government begin to fall below the buffer norm. From 2007 to 2008 however stocks with the government again start rising and remain consistently above buffer "norms" in subsequent years Over much of the post-reform period, therefore, the decline in per capita foodgrain absorption was associated not with supply shortages, but with excessive stock accumulation with the government.

Likewise, the ratio of the wholesale price index for foodgrains to the wholesale price index for manufactured goods declined marginally from 1.11 in 1996–1997 to 1.05 in 2005–2006; only after that did it start increasing to reach 1.29 in 2011–2012. The decline in per capita foodgrain absorption over this period, in other words, was accompanied not by the usual symptoms of excess demand in the foodgrains market, but by burgeoning foodgrain stocks, and by virtually constant terms of trade between foodgrains and manufactured goods for a long period. It is in this sense that the post-reform situation has been quite unprecedented in independent India: for the first time we have experienced over a long period not a shortage of food grains but a plethora of foodgrains, even in the midst of poor foodgrain output performance.

How has this been possible? The process that has made it possible has been called "income deflation."[7] Income deflation has the same effect as an inflation relative to money wages (or what Keynes had called "profit inflation"[8]) in adjusting demand to dwindling supplies: the latter does it through inflation that curtails real purchasing power, while the former does it through curtailing money purchasing power so that prices do not have to rise any faster than in other sectors. And if the income deflation is sufficiently strong, then money purchasing power is so severely curtailed that excess stocks begin to appear even out of dwindling supplies.

An example will make the point clear. Suppose, to start with, the money wage bill is Rs.100, which is spent on 100 units of wage goods output priced at Rs.1 each. Now, if the output of wage goods gets halved for some reason to 50 units, then there are two ways that the reduced supply can be made to adjust to demand: one is a doubling of the price to Rs.2 for the same wage bill (profit inflation); the other is a halving of the wage bill with the same price (income deflation).

While an income deflation plays the same role as profit inflation in adjusting demand to reduced supplies (and can even curtail demand to a level below the reduced supplies), it is preferred by financial interests over profit inflation. This is because while curtailing demand to make it adjust to reduced supplies, it does not lower the real value of financial assets which profit inflation (or any kind of inflation for that matter) does.

At the same time an income deflation has a drawback that a profit inflation does not have: with a profit inflation, since the profitability of producing the good that is in short supply goes up, there is a stimulating effect on output and hence supply; but with an income deflation there is no such effect. True, insofar as the wage rate in the sector whose good is in short supply is cut, then, with a given price, the profitability of producing the good goes up. But in sectors like foodgrains, characterized predominantly by petty production where the producers are also consumers, a reduction in the purchasing power of these producers affects both demand as well as output adversely.

The chief hallmark of neoliberal economic policies pursued in the era of globalization is that they impose an income deflation on large sections of workers, peasants, and agricultural laborers. There are at least three ways in which this happens.

First, since the neoliberal regime opens up the economy to the vortex of global financial flows, including speculative flows, and since financial interests invariably prefer sound finance and are always opposed to fiscal deficits (with spurious arguments, which Joan Robinson had dismissed as the "humbug of finance"[9]), such a regime is constrained to limit its fiscal deficit (and even pass fiscal responsibility legislation for this purpose, as India has done). In addition, since such a regime has to reduce import tariffs and hence is constrained not to raise excise duties too much, and tries to woo direct foreign investment in competition with other such regimes by offering tax concessions, which, for the sake of *inter se* equity, it has to extend to domestic capitalists too, it experiences usually a decline in the tax-GDP ratio compared to the preceding *dirigiste* regime. This decline and the decline in the fiscal deficit relative to GDP entail a decline in the ratio of government expenditure to GDP, and the impact of this expenditure deflation is felt in particular upon development expenditure, especially rural development expenditure. The curtailment of government expenditure in rural areas means in turn lesser injection of purchasing power into such areas and hence an income deflation for the rural population. The impact of such income deflation in rural areas is further heightened insofar as the running down of public health, education, and other facilities forces the rural population to move to more expensive private ones.

A second way that such income deflation is imposed on the countryside is through the destruction of domestic productive activities under the impact of global competition—from which they cannot be protected, as they used to be in the *dirigiste* period, because of trade liberalization that is an essential component of the neoliberal policies. The extent of such destruction gets magnified to the extent that the country becomes a favorite destination for finance, and the inflow of speculative capital pushes up the exchange rate.

When domestic activities do not disappear under the impact of global competition, they survive by cutting into the subsistence of the producers. Either way, whether through the unemployment caused by the destruction of activities or through the destitution of producers who linger on, there is an income deflation which affects adversely the demand for a range of commodities including even foodgrains.

Even when there is no upward movement of the exchange rate nor any destruction of domestic activity through the inflow of imports, the desire on the part of the getting-rich-quick elite for metropolitan goods and lifestyles, which are necessarily less employment-intensive than the locally available traditional goods catering to traditional lifestyles, results in the domestic production of the former at the expense of the latter, and leads to a process of internal deindustrialization, which entails a net-unemployment-engendering structural change. This too acts as a measure of income deflation.

The third way in which income deflation is effected is a secular shift in the terms of trade against the petty producers of primary commodities, and in particular the peasantry. When there is a shift in the terms of trade against the growers of cash crops, this imposes an income deflation on them and affects their demand for foodgrains. But what is being referred to here is the terms of trade movements not just between *sectors* but also between *classes*. Hence even when there is no decline in the terms of trade for the commodities they produce, there may nonetheless be a decline in the terms of trade obtained by the producers of those commodities because of the increasing hold of a few giant corporations in the marketing of those commodities. And even when the producers' terms of trade do not decline, the giant marketing corporations invariably displace a host of traditional traders and thereby cause income deflation in a manner analogous to deindustrialization. The growing stranglehold of giant corporations in marketing a range of commodities has been a common feature during the neoliberal period; it has the effect, whether via a shift in income distribution from the lower-rung petty producers to the higher-rung marketing corporations or via the displacement of numerous small traders, of curtailing consumption demand for foodgrains and hence restricting inflationary pressures on foodgrain prices, even in the face of declining per capita foodgrain output.

The neoliberal regime in other words unleashes massive processes of income deflation, which, while playing exactly the same role as profit-inflation in curbing excess demand pressures, keep commodity prices in check. To say this, however, does not mean that income deflation is necessarily engineered in such a regime with the avowed purpose of checking foodgrain price inflation, or inflation in general. To be sure, avoidance of inflation is a major obsession of finance capital, and hence of the neoliberal regime characterized by its hegemony. But capitalism is not a consciously planned system; it does not call forth the processes outlined above, only at specific times for serving specific needs. These processes occur anyway in such a regime, and their effect is to impose an income deflation on broad sections of the working population, which curtails their demand even for foodgrains and can do so even to the extent where, notwithstanding declining per capita foodgrain output, excess foodgrain stocks can accumulate in the economy for a long stretch of time.

But the neoliberal regime does not affect only the demand side for foodgrains; it has an adverse effect on the supply side too. The very income deflation that curtails demand, also affects, as we have seen, the supply of foodgrains, since the peasant producers of grains also happen to be the victims of income deflation.

Besides, the curtailment in government expenditure mentioned earlier entails cuts in subsidies enjoyed by the peasantry during the *dirigiste* regime, and hence increases in its costs. The cut in rural development expenditure leads to a decay in rural infrastructure, including irrigation and government extension services. The so-called reliance on the market mechanism means a progressive whittling down of the system of grain procurement at assured prices, which had been followed by the *dirigiste* regime, and which had insulated the peasantry both against the depredations of the grain-trading Multinational Corporations (MNCs) and the fluctuations in world prices. Financial liberalization, freeing banks from any obligation to lend to the peasants at cheap rates, pushes up the cost of credit to the peasantry even as banks turn to what appear to be more lucrative avenues of lending, such as stock market speculation and consumer credit. In short in a variety of ways there is a withdrawal of state support from peasant agriculture in a neoliberal regime as the state gets increasingly drawn into promoting the interests of the financial operators, the domestic big capitalists, and the multinational companies. Since peasant agriculture needs state support for its growth and even its viability, such withdrawal, embedded in the class orientation of a neoliberal economy, leads to a progressive atrophy of its productive capacity.

Under neoliberalism, which affects adversely both the demand and supply of foodgrains, there may be some periods when the adverse effects on the demand side swamp those on the supply side, and other periods when the opposite happens. The former will be characterized by the accumulation of excess stocks even in the face of declining per capita foodgrain output; the latter will be characterized by excess demand-led inflation in foodgrain prices relative to money wages, which will be greatly aggravated by speculative pressures that are rampant in such a regime (the opening up of forward trading in foodgrains, generally banned under the *dirigiste* regime, promotes such speculation). Both periods, however, are merely two alternative manifestations of the food crisis whose chief hallmark is an accentuation of hunger and malnutrition.

4. The Constituents of Food Price Inflation

Both manifestations of crisis have been apparent in the Indian economy in the neoliberal era. Barring six years, the entire period from 1991–1992 to 2013–2014 was characterized by excess foodgrain stocks. This period, and in particular the years after 1996–1997 within it, was one where, notwithstanding the decline in foodgrain output per capita, the demand compression on account of the various forms of income deflation mentioned above was sharp enough to leave excess stocks with the government.

Illustrative figures may be given here for one of the avenues of income deflation, namely through government expenditure cuts. The total outlay, both development and nondevelopment, of the Centre, States, and Union Territories taken together, as a proportion of GDP at market prices, which stood at 31 percent in 1990–1991, on the eve of liberalization, came down to 29.3 percent in 2000–2001, and 28.5 percent in 2004–2005 before climbing to 29.2 percent in 2005–2006 and 31.5 percent in 2010–2011 (RE). The decline in development expenditure was even more precipitous, from 18.6 percent in 1990–1991 to 15.1 percent in 2000–2001, 14.4 percent in 2002–2003, and 12.55 percent in 2004–2005. Once more there was a recovery to 15.4 percent in 2005–2006 and 18.5 percent in 2010–2011 (RE). And within it, the decline in rural development expenditure was even more precipitous.

Rural Development Expenditure (meaning actual plan outlays by the Centre, States, and Union Territories, taken together, under five heads: agriculture, rural development, village and small scale industry, irrigation and flood control, and special area program) as a proportion of GDP at market prices went down from an average of 3.1 percent over 1985–1990 to 1.4 percent in 2000–2001; if we include infrastructure (energy, transport, and communication), though only a part of it is spent in rural areas, the figures are 8.9 percent and 4.45 respectively. There was some increase thereafter, but the figure remained below the 1980–1985 average for all subsequent years for which we have data.

Deflation of this order clearly had both demand and supply-side effects. But in addition, the government took all the steps listed earlier as being typical of neoliberal regimes, which constricted the growth potential of peasant agriculture. The withdrawal of the state from its supporting role in the agricultural sector; the entry of MNCs which now have unmediated access to gullible peasants; the winding up of government extension services; the exposure to world market prices, which, apart from imparting vulnerability to peasant agriculture (one of whose consequences has been the mass suicide of peasants), has entailed a shift of acreage to cash crops from foodgrains; the rise in input costs, especially of credit—all have combined to make peasant (and even small capitalist agriculture) unviable, reducing the growth rate of agricultural, especially foodgrain, output.

From 2005 onward, however, some change has taken place in government policy. There is, as we have seen, some revival of government expenditure, which has meant an easing of income deflation; there is the National Rural Employment Guarantee Scheme; the debt waiver for the peasantry; some increase in procurement prices; and the directive to banks to increase lending to agriculture. Many, especially government spokespersons, have argued that there has been a turn-around in foodgrain production in this period. But this is erroneous.

Between 2001–2002 and 2011–2012, both peak agricultural years, per capita foodgrain output remains roughly unchanged. But since per capita foodgrain output had shown a decline in the decade of the nineties, its level today continues to remain lower than what it had been at the beginning of the nineties. In other words, the impression of a turnaround in the growth rate of foodgrain output in the last few years arises only because of an illegitimate comparison of a trough year with a peak year, not when we compare peak to peak. But the declining *trend* in per capita foodgrain output has been arrested.

The combination of a lower per capita foodgrain output and a relaxation of income deflation would have meant some pressure on foodgrain prices. But this pressure has been greatly accentuated by the government's holding excess foodgrain stocks, presumably for fear that releasing stocks through the public distribution system would entail a larger fiscal deficit that would undermine the "confidence" of finance capital (even though it should have no *genuine* adverse effects on the economy). The terms of trade, as we have seen, have tilted in favor of foodgrains vis a vis manufacturing in the period after 2005–2006. This tilt became more pronounced from around July 2008, when the speculative upsurge in world oil prices contributed to a spurt in world foodgrain prices, which also affected India, owing to the diversion of grains to biofuels.

In short, while the period till 2005–2006 was characterized by the use of income deflation as the instrument through which a decline in per capita absorption was effected, in the subsequent period the more conventional instrument of a profit inflation, aggravated by deliberate excessive stock-holding by the government, has been used. But in either case, the food crisis, in the sense of a secular decline in per capita foodgrain absorption, has continued unabated.

5. Wrong View on World Food Prices

When the spurt in foodgrain prices occurred in mid-2008 a view was advanced, notably by President George Bush, that the reason for it lay in the fact that in rapidly growing developing economies like China and India a variation in the dietary pattern was taking place, involving an increased demand for commodities like meat, the production of which required more foodgrains in the form of animal feed. The world food price inflation, in other words, was because countries like India and China were absorbing (both directly and indirectly) more foodgrains per capita than before, because of their growing prosperity. This, however, is a completely untenable explanation.

No doubt the rich in both these countries are diversifying their diet and are absorbing more foodgrains per capita. But if we take the per capita foodgrain absorption *for the population as a whole,* both directly and indirectly (via processed foods and animal feed), then we find, as already discussed, that in India there has been a secular and precipitous decline compared to the late eighties. Even in the case of China, if we take the per capita absorption of cereals for food and feed (the definition of foodgrains is different in China compared to India), then there is a steady and sharp decline between 1996 and 2003, which gets reversed thereafter, but the level in 2009 is still lower than that in 1996.[10] The idea of an overall increase in per capita food absorption in China compared to the mid-nineties is simply wrong.

Since the rate of growth of population in both these economies has been slowing down, the decline in the per capita foodgrain absorption entails a decline in the rate of growth in the overall demand for foodgrains. In the face of such a decline, it follows that if excess demand pressures arise in the world foodgrain economy, then the reason must lie in an even more rapid decline in the rate of growth of the supply of foodgrains. Hence it is not from the side of Indian or Chinese demand, but from the side of foodgrain supply (including the reduction in supply owing to diversion for biofuels) that we have to explain the food price rise in the world economy in the recent period.

As a matter of fact, since the mid-eighties there has been a sharp decline in per capita cereal output in the world economy. The period when food security was being undermined in India also saw a similar undermining of world food security, though the process began for the world economy somewhat earlier. In the world economy too, as in the case of India, this undermining does not reveal itself in the classical form of a food price-led inflation, because the adoption of neoliberal policies over much of the world economy unleashes the phenomenon of income deflation among large segments of the world's population. But this classical form reemerges when we have supply shortfalls, arising inter alia from a crop failure in Australia and aggravated by the diversion of grains to production of biofuels.

The global financial regime, with an inherent tendency toward promoting speculation, which caused the massive increase in oil prices in 2008 and thus a parallel increase in food prices, has now precipitated a recession that has brought oil prices down and kept food price inflation in check. This has not ended the food crisis, but the income deflation inherent in a recession has kept the price in check even as foodgrain absorption continues to languish. The overcoming of this phase of recession, however, is likely once again to cause an upsurge in world oil prices and hence, given the continued pursuit of biofuels, also in world food prices. For countries of the third world, especially India, the food crisis is likely to be aggravated in the wake of a revival of the world economy.

6. Concluding Observations

Let us draw together the threads of the argument. The period of neoliberal economic policy affects the food economy both from the supply and the demand sides. The withdrawal of the state from active protection and promotion of petty production, especially peasant production, manifested in the relative decline in rural development expenditure, in the drying up of institutional credit to peasant agriculture, in the collapse of government extension services, in the reduction of input subsidies, and in the progressive dismantling of the procurement-cum-public distribution system, has had the effect of keeping the growth rate of foodgrain production for the period as a whole at a level even below the population growth rate. On the other hand, the same decline in rural development expenditure, together with the destruction of domestic activities under the impact of import liberalization and the taking over of several stages of activity between production and sale by the MNCs, has had the effect of imposing an income deflation on the working people, especially in the countryside, and hence restricting the demand for food grains. The second of these tendencies dominated over the first in the entire postliberalization period, until 2002–2003 and even 2005–2006, when, despite declining per capita foodgrain output, massive food stocks built up in the economy through a squeeze on absorption due to income deflation. But in the subsequent period, excess demand pressures have begun to manifest themselves, aggravated by government holding of excess foodgrain stocks and, at the international level, the diversion of foodgrains for producing biofuels. In either form, however, the food crisis has continued; it is a fall-out of neoliberalism.

It follows that the way to overcome the food crisis is to revive the role of the state as the protector and promoter of peasant agriculture, as opposed to its role that typically characterizes neoliberalism—namely, of appeasing globalized finance. Therefore, overcoming of the food crisis requires a retreat from the package of policies that constitute neoliberalism. This retreat cannot be merely to the preceding *dirigiste* regime; it will have to initiate an altogether new development strategy of peasant agriculture-led growth.

Notes

1. These figures are based upon Utsa Patnaik's "The Republic of Hunger," republished in her book *The Republic of Hunger and Other Essays*, Three Essays Collective, Delhi, 2007. The entire argument of my present paper, especially of the first three sections, draws heavily on her research work which appears inter

alia in *The Republic of Hunger;* "Neoliberalism and Rural Poverty in India," *Economic and Political Weekly,* Vol. XLII, No. 30, July 28, 2007, pp. 3132–3150; and "Poverty Trends in India 2004–05 to 2009–10", *Economic and Political Weekly,* Vol. XLVIII, No. 40, October 5, 2013, pp. 43–58.

2. The introduction of Health Insurance Schemes for the below poverty line population by central and state governments in recent years, for countering this phenomenon of health care being beyond its reach, has had too minuscule an impact as yet.

3. The figures are from Patnaik, "Neo-liberalism and Rural Poverty in India." The base year figure is from the Planning Commission.

4. The method of calculation is as follows. We take the income of the agricultural sector in current prices, as measured by the net domestic product at factor cost, in 1996–1997 and in 2006–2007. By applying, to the figure for the total rural population, the ratio of the agricultural workforce (Usual Status) to the total rural workforce (Usual Status), as given by the National Sample Survey data for 1993–1994 and 1999–2000, we get an estimate of the agriculture-dependent population for 1993–1994 and 1999–2000. By assuming that the average rate of growth exhibited over this period in the size of the agriculture-dependent population holds uniformly within the period and also afterward, we estimate the agriculture-dependent population for 1996–1997 and 2006–2007. The income of the agricultural sector divided by the agriculture-dependent population gives us the per capita income of the agriculture-dependent population for these two years in current prices. This, when deflated by the consumer price index for industrial workers, gives the picture of absolute stagnation drawn above.

5. The figures are from Patnaik's paper "Poverty Trends in India 2004–05 to 2009–10."

6. The implicit assumption here is that wage relativities are not affected, or at least not sufficiently affected, by the foodgrain price inflation, and that the manufactured goods sector is characterized by mark-up pricing. On mark-up pricing see Michael Kalecki, *The Theory of Economic Dynamics,* Allen and Unwin, London, 1954; and on the terms of trade implications of such pricing see Ashok Mitra, *Terms of Trade and Class Relations,* Frank Cass, London, 1977.

7. See Patnaik's "The Republic of Hunger."

8. The concept of profit inflation was developed by Keynes in *A Treatise on Money,* 2 volumes, Macmillan, London, 1930.

9. Joan Robinson, *Economic Philosophy,* C. A. Watts and Co., London, 1966.

10. I am grateful to Sriram Natarajan for making his research on China's foodgrain absorption figures available to me.

IV CREATING AN INCLUSIVE PUBLIC CULTURE

11 THE DILEMMA OF A LIBERAL HINDU

Gurcharan Das

I am not an academic, and to make up for this disadvantage I thought I would speak from experience and try to offer a personal account, as honestly as I could, of the inner life of a liberal and secular Indian. I shall focus on one theme primarily, and it is my fear of the loss of tradition, and my own feeble attempts to recapture it. I shall wake up Edmund Burke from the eighteenth century to be my worthy companion in the dilemma that I lay before you.

1. "I'm a Hindu, But . . . "

A few years ago, the confident and handsome friend of our son gave a telling reply to a visiting Englishwoman in Khan Market in Delhi.

"I am a Hindu, but . . . " he said.

He hastily added that he was an Indian first, and then he went into a winding reply about his beliefs. It was a perfectly honest answer, and any other person might have given a similar one about Islam or Christianity. But I sensed an unhappy defensiveness—the "but" betrayed that he might be ashamed of being Hindu.

This incident happened soon after I had received a call from one of Delhi's best private schools, asking me to speak to its students.

"Oh good," I said on the phone. "I have been reading the *Mahabharata,* and if you agree, I shall speak about *dharma* and moral dilemmas in the epic."

"Oh don't do that, please!" was the principal's horrified reaction. "There are important secularist persons on our governing board, and I don't want any controversy about teaching religion."

"But surely the *Mahabharata* is a literary epic," I protested, "and *dharma* is about right and wrong." But my protest was to no avail. She was adamant and she was afraid.

As I think about these two incidents, I ask myself, Why should two highly successful, young professionals feel defensive about their heritage? Something seems to have gone wrong. I fear that modern, liberal Indians, especially those at the helm of our private and public enterprises, may not have any use for their past, and they may abdicate it to the narrow, closed minds of fanatical Hindu nationalists.

In part, this is due to ignorance. Our children do not grow up reading our ancient classics in school or college, and certainly not with a critical mind, as works of literature and philosophy, in the same way as young Americans, for example, read the Western classics in their first couple of years of college as a part of their core curriculum. Some are lucky to acquire some acquaintance with them from their grandmothers or older relatives, who tell them stories from the epics and the *Puranas*. They might read the tales in *Amar Chitra Katha* comics or watch them in as serials on Sunday morning television. Meanwhile, the Sangh Parivar steps into the vacuum with its shrunken, defensive, and inaccurate version of history and happily appropriates the empty space. And if this goes on, the richness of tradition may well be lost in urban India in the following generations.

If Italian children can read Dante's *Divine Comedy* in school, or English children can read Milton, and Greek children can read the *Iliad*, why should secularist Indians be ambivalent about the *Mahabharata*? Indeed, English children also read the King James Bible in school as a text—"text" is the operative word, for they are encouraged to read it and interrogate it. So, why then should our epic be untouchable for a sensitive, modern, and liberal school principal? It is true that the *Mahabharata* has lots of gods in it, and in particular that elusive divinity, Krishna, who is up to all manner of devious activity. But so are Dante, Milton, and Homer filled with God or gods, and if the Italians, the English, and the Greeks can read the texts of their heritage, why can't Indians?

With the rise in religious fundamentalism, it seems to me that it is increasingly difficult to talk about one's deepest beliefs. Liberal Hindus are reluctant to admit being Hindu for fear they will be automatically linked to the Rashtriya Swayamsevak Sangh (RSS). They are not alone in this. Liberal Christians and liberal Muslims, I am sure, have experienced the same misgivings. One can easily imagine hearing: "I am Christian, but . . . " or "I am Muslim, but . . . " In India, I blame Hindutva nationalists who have appropriated our culture and tradition and made it a political agenda. But equally, I blame many of our secularists who behave no better than fundamentalists in their callous antipathy to tradition.

We ought to view Hindutva's rise in the context of religious revivalism with a political bent around the world. Laurie Goodstein wrote in the *New York Times* on January 15, 2005: "Almost anywhere you look around the world . . . religion is now a rising force. Former communist countries are crowded with mosque builders, Christian missionaries and freelance spiritual entrepreneurs of every persuasion." Philip Jenkins's insightful book, *The Next Christendom: The Coming of Global Christianity,* describes this in the America of George W. Bush. This growth in fundamentalism around the globe makes one wonder if the secular agenda is threatened everywhere. And is it the project of modernity, as some think, that has contributed to this vicious, political religiosity?

No one reads Edmund Burke these days, but he exercised considerable influence on eighteenth-century minds. He is relevant, I think, to some of our discontents with secularism today. His critique of the French revolution was based primarily on his fear of the loss of tradition; killing off the church and the aristocracy, he felt, would cut off links with the past. He spoke about "custom, community and natural feeling," and he felt that continuity with the past was necessary to realize our full human potential. The challenge before modern, decent Indians today, it seems to me, is essentially the same. It is the one that Ram Mohan Roy faced in the early nineteenth century or Mahatma Gandhi in the early twentieth century: how to grow up mentally healthy, integrated Indians? How do we combine our liberal modernity with our traditions in order to fully realize our potential?

As a liberal and secular Hindu, I oppose the entry of religion into the public domain, and its mingling with government or public school education. I deeply appreciate the "wall" that the founding fathers of both the United States and India have built. For this reason I admire France and Turkey, who seem to have the strongest walls. But what does one do when the great literary classics of one's country are religious or semireligious? Dante practically created the Italian language with his masterpiece, but his great poem is also a deeply religious work—possibly the most religious in all Christianity. I don't know how Italians handle Dante in their schools, and I wonder what the Italian Left feels about it, say in a Leftish city like Bologna.

In India we *do* have a problem, however, and I don't think there are easy answers. Many Indians regard our great Sanskrit classics as religious texts. To the extent that they are religious, we are committed by our wall to keep them out of our schools. I sympathize with the principal of the school in Delhi. At the same time, unless our children are exposed to the Sanskrit classics and unless these are discussed in a secular environment, our children will grow up impoverished in the way Edmund Burke worried about. Clearly, something is terribly wrong with contemporary Indian education when our most influential schools churn out deracinated products who know little about their own culture but a great deal about the West.

There are some in India who think that the answer lies in providing compulsory knowledge of all religions, and this will engender what Emperor Ashoka called a "respect for all creeds." But this is a dangerous path. For how do you teach religion without worrying about some teacher somewhere who will wittingly or unwittingly denigrate or hurt the sensitivities of the some follower of the religion being taught? And before you realize it, you will have a riot on your hands. So, we do have a genuine moral dilemma here, a *dharmasamkata,* as the *Mahabharata* would call it.

2. I Was Born a Hindu

I was born a Hindu, had a normal Hindu upbringing, and like many in the middle class I went to an English medium school that gave me a modern education. Both my grandfathers belonged to the Arya Samaj, a reformist sect of Hinduism that came up in nineteenth-century Punjab. It advocated a return to the Vedas, a diminished role for Brahmins, and vigorous social reform of the caste system among other social evils. My father, however, decided to take a different path. When he was studying to be an engineer, he was drawn to a kindly guru who taught him the power and glory of direct union with God through meditation. The guru would quote from Kabir, Nanak, Rumi, and Mirabai, and was a Radhasoami saint in the syncretic, *bhakti* tradition.

The striking thing about growing up Hindu was a chaotic atmosphere of tolerance in our home in Lyallpur. My grandmother would visit the Sikh *gurdwara* on Mondays and Wednesdays and a Hindu temple on Tuesdays and Thursdays; she saved Saturdays and Sundays for discourses of holy men, including Muslim pirs, who were forever visiting our town. In between, she made time for lots of Arya Samaj ceremonies when anyone was born, married, or died. My grandfather used to jest that she would also have also called in at the Muslim mosque in her busy schedule had they allowed her in. My more practical uncle thought, however, that she was merely taking out enough insurance, in the manner of Pascal, and someone up there might hear her.

I think it must have been difficult for my Hindu ancestors in the Punjab, who did not have the living memory of a political heritage of their own. Having lived under non-Hindu rulers since the thirteenth century, they must have thought of political life as filled with deprivation and fear. After Muslims had come the Sikh kingdom of Ranjit Singh. With its collapse around 1850 came the powerful British, with Christian missionaries in tow. Hence, three powerful, professedly egalitarian and proselytizing religions surrounded them—Islam, Sikhism, and Christianity. No wonder they were eager to receive Dayananda Saraswati when he came to the Punjab in 1877. And not surprisingly, he succeeded beyond his dreams in establishing the Arya Samaj in the Punjab.

Despite this religious background, I grew up agnostic, which is a luxury of being Hindu. I have a liberal attitude that is a mixture of skepticism and sympathy toward my tradition. I have also come to believe that our most cherished ends in life are not political. Religion is one of these, and it gets demeaned when it enters public life. Hence, religion and the state must be kept separate, and to believe this is to be secular. I have a mild distaste for the sort of nationalism that can so quickly become chauvinism. Hence I do not vote for the Bharatiya Janata Party (BJP). At the same time I feel Indian and I value my "Indian-ness," whatever that may be. This means that I value my past and I wish to cultivate it, and like Edmund Burke, I feel my past is important to me for living a flourishing life. This is a past that contains the influence of Buddhism, Jainism, Islam, Sikhism, and even Christianity.

I like to think that my skeptical temper goes back to a questioning streak within the Indian tradition, all the way back to its very first text, the *Rig Veda* (c.1500 B.C.E.). It may well have originated in the charming humility of its *Nasadiya* verse, which meditates on the creation of the universe:

> Who knows and who can say, whence it was born and whence came this creation? The gods are later than this world's creation. Who knows then whence it first came into being? (RV 10.129)

Despite the skepticism, our Vedic ancients believed then and Hindus believe today that the very substance of their universe is divine. Each god has a secondary or illusory status compared to the divine substance, yet each one is a powerful symbol of and a guide to the divine. Many gods coexist comfortably in a nonhierarchic pantheon in which no god can afford to be jealous. And one ought to expect the devotee of many, nonhierarchical gods to more likely see the many sides of truth—and accordingly be more tolerant. When you have millions of gods, it seems to me, you cannot afford to be theologically narcissistic. This is why it is puzzling how our tolerant pluralism turned into the intolerance of Hindutva and the extremist politics of the Hindu Right.

3. "You Haven't Turned Hindutva, Have You?"

In the spring of 2002 I decided to take an academic holiday. My wife thought it a strange resolve. She was familiar with our usual holidays, when we armed ourselves with hats, and blue guides and green guides, and trudged up and down over piles of temple stones in places like Khajuraho or Ankor Wat. But she was puzzled by the concept of an academic holiday. I explained to her that in college I had read Aristotle, Euripides, Dante, Marx, and other classics of western civilization, but I had always yearned to read the Indian classics and had never had the chance. The closest I had come was Professor Ingalls's difficult Sanskrit class at Harvard when I was an undergraduate. So, now forty years later, I wished to read the texts of classical India if not in the original, at least with scholars of Sanskrit nearby. It was my Proustian search for lost time in order to reclaim my tradition, and appropriately in the *vanaprastha ashrama,* the third stage of my life.

My wife gave me a skeptical look, and after a pause she said, "It's a little late in the day for a midlife crisis, isn't it? Why don't we go to the Turkish coast instead?"

Somewhat to my annoyance, my academic holiday became the subject of animated discussion at a dinner party in Delhi the following week. Our hostess was a snob. She was famous in Delhi's society for cultivating the famous and the powerful. She had ignored us for years but this had changed in the past two, and we had become regulars at her brilliant dinners. I thought her friendly, but my wife reminded me that her warmth was in direct proportion to my recent success as a columnist and writer. She always introduced me as "an old friend," but I don't think she had a clue about what that meant.

"So, what is this I hear about you wanting to go away to read Sanskrit texts?" she suddenly turned to me accusingly. "Don't tell me you are going to turn religious on us?"

Two women in exquisite silk sarees, one from Kanchipuram and another from Benares, now came in and joined us. One had a string of pearls around her neck and the other lovely diamonds on her neck and her wrists. Both had heavily mascaraed eyelashes, painted lips, and rouged cheeks, and it was apparent how much their lives consisted in a desperate struggle to keep their faded charms. They began to speak in loud, metallic voices without a moment's pause, as though they were afraid that if they stopped they might not be able to start again. They were accompanied by a diplomat, who had once been a favorite of Indira Gandhi.

"But tell us, what books you are planning to read?" asked the diplomat casually, as though he were referring to the latest features in a Korean dishwasher in Khan Market.

I admitted somewhat reluctantly that I had been thinking of texts like the *Mahabharata,* the *Manusmriti,* and the *Kathopanishad.*

"Good lord, man!" he exclaimed. "You haven't turned Hindutva, have you?"

I think his remark was made in jest, but it upset me. I asked myself, what sort of secularism have we created in our country that has appropriated my claim to my intellectual heritage? I found it disturbing that I had to fear the intolerance of my secular friends, who seemed to identify any association with Hinduism or its culture as a political act. The pain did not go away easily, even though I realized that it was a pain shared by others. I was reminded of a casual remark by a Westernized woman in Chennai during the launch of my book, *The Elephant Paradigm*. She mentioned that she had always visited the Shiva temple near her home, but lately she had begun to hide this from her friends who proclaimed their secular credentials stridently. She feared they might pounce on her, quick to brand her extremist or superstitious.

4. Does the Conservative Temper Offer an Answer?

When I was growing up in post-Independence India in the 1950s and 1960s, the word "conservative" was almost a term of abuse in the vocabulary of many Indian intellectuals (and many English and American ones, I suppose.) We passionately believed in Nehru's dream of a modern and just India. We likened his midnight speech at Independence about our "tryst with destiny" to Wordsworth's famous lines on the French Revolution: "Bliss was it in that dawn to be alive." I tried to capture this mood in my book *India Unbound*. We laughed at Rajaji and Masani, who founded the conservative Swatantra Party in the late 1950s, and even dismissed Sardar Patel, who was the second most powerful man in India at Independence, after Nehru. Charles James Fox had laughed at Edmund Burke in the same way. Like many Englishmen of his day, Fox thought the revolution in France was an immensely liberating step, calling it the greatest event that ever happened in the world. In denouncing the French revolution, Burke was not expressing an opinion popular among thinking Englishmen; he was going against the tide. To be a conservative in Nehru's India was the same. It meant that one was on the side of age against youth, the past against the future, authority against innovation, and spontaneity against life.

How times have changed! Now, sixty years later, it is the old progressives who have become old, who look back nostalgically to a socialist past. They are the ones who oppose the reforms and continue to have a touching faith in rent-seeking statism, even though it has been discredited as a "licence raj." They condemn too hastily the young of today, painting them uniformly in the colors of greed.

Even after we get over the easy polarities of the mind, "conservative" is an unhappy word for what I am seeking. It conjures up in too many minds the image of what the British mathematician, G. H. Hardy, called a "wide bottomed member of the Anglican Church establishment." But there is more to the problem. What I am seeking is a reverence for the past, and that is less a political doctrine than a habit of mind, a way of living and feeling. Like Burke, I think society is not a collection of loosely related individuals, nor a mechanism with interchangeable parts, but a living organism, and anything that affects the well being of one affects the whole. It is for this reason that Burke had cautioned against pulling down edifices that had met society's needs for generations.

We have had too much ideology in the twentieth century and frankly, we are tired of it. We have had too much of what Burke called variously "speculation," or "metaphysics," or "theoretical reasoning," as applied to social and political questions. Some of my ambivalence about India's Leftist secularists is not unlike Burke's fear of the revolutionaries in France who seriously believed that they would construct the world from scratch by the application of general and abstract principles, and who even wanted to introduce a new calendar to mark the beginning of that new world. Part of the reason that the sensible idea of secularism is having so much difficulty in finding a home in India, I think, is that the most vocal and intellectual advocates of secularism were once Marxists. Not only do they not believe in God, they actually hate God. They literally follow Marx's dictum that "criticism of religion is the prelude to all criticism." As rationalists they can only see the dark side of religion—intolerance, murderous wars, and nationalism, and do not empathize with the everyday life of the common Indian to whom religion gives meaning to every moment of life and has done so since civilization's dawn. Because secularists speak a language alien to the vast majority, they are only able to condemn communal violence but not to stop it, as Mahatma Gandhi could, in East Bengal in 1947.

Over the past fifty years we have realized in India that political activity is infinitely complex and difficult. Our caste system is unpredictable, intractable, and incomprehensible. There are many things at work, and the ways they relate to each other is complex. Politicians, unlike academics, have to act in concrete, discrete situations, not in general or abstract terms. Burke also cautioned about this complexity. So when we address religion's place in the Indian polity, Burke would have us take account of the infinite circumstances of one billion believers and not insist always on the rational, secular principle of consistency. There are also unintended consequences because of the interconnectedness of things. Hence, when initiating change we ought to heed Burke's caution about the "lamentable consequences of plausible schemes." We have learned this lesson painfully over the past fifty years as we lived through Jawaharlal Nehru's well-intended socialism that ended in becoming an ugly statism of the License Raj.

In thinking about our secularism project in India, Burke would have us be humble in recognizing the complexity of society and be careful of radical and rapid change. He would ask us to be skeptical about the role of reason in human affairs. Like many contemporary postmodernists, he had reservations about the Enlightenment's view of man as a predominantly rational, logical, and calculating person. His rational side exists, he felt, but it is a small part of his total make-up. He would have us rely more on practical knowledge that is gained through experience rather than through abstract reasoning. He would have us pay attention to people's habits, instincts, customs, and their prejudices. A generation earlier, David Hume, the illustrious Scottish philosopher, had also emphasized the importance of habit and custom.

Another of Burke's lessons, useful especially in a rapidly globalizing world, is to pay attention to the local and the particular. We speak too often about India's diversity, but we act as though only New Delhi matters. Burke would have us think of the Rights of Man not in the abstract, but of existing rights that people actually possess and enjoy, which they have inherited in the context of their particular situations. However, I disagree with Burke in his conception of the state that has to implement these rights. He was an orthodox Christian and he thought of society as the handiwork of God, a "Divine tactick," he called it. He regarded the state as "inherently and inalienably sacred," and although I share his passion for good government, I would worry about his "consecrated" state according "to one Divine plan." I regard the spiritual and the temporal as two distinct orders, and I find his conception too readily lends itself to the dangerous idea that some particular human will or wills should direct the course of social life. This would not only be oppressive, but fatal to human liberty.

Burke's life teaches us that to be conservative is not to become an apologist for the current order. He defended the American Revolution; he raised his voice for the emancipation of Catholics and for removal of trade barriers with Ireland; he spoke loudly for abolishing slavery and the trade in slaves, and even louder against the privileges and excesses of the rule of the East India Company. Many of us in India remember him not only for instigating the impeachment of Warren Hastings, the governor general, but for drafting the East India Bill, which led to the reform of the East India Company. Although Hastings was acquitted, Burke's speeches created new awareness in England of the responsibilities of empire and the injustices perpetrated in India.

Overall, I think, Burke would have approved of the relatively peaceful flow of India's contemporary history. Unlike the violent French Revolution (which he condemned because it was a sharp break with the past) and unlike the violent histories of China, Russia, and so many countries in the twentieth century, India won its freedom from Britain peacefully. This is why Andre Malraux was moved to say that India was created by saints, and this happened in the shadows of Hitler, Stalin, and Mao. Not only did we escape the World Wars, but we gained political freedom without shedding much blood, thanks to Mahatma Gandhi. Yes, half a million died in the Partition riots, but it was not state sponsored violence. After Independence, Nehru built our polity based on many of the good institutions of colonial rule. This represented a Burkeian continuity. Our addiction to peace might be one of the reasons why we may have become the world's largest democracy.

Nehru's socialism, followed by Indira Gandhi's dark decades, did slow down our economy for almost forty years, but it did not wipe out our private economy with its invaluable institutions of banks, corporate laws, and the stock market. So when we broke free from socialist shackles in 1991, we had this advantage over China. Many Indians (and I include myself in this) are impressed with China's dramatic progress today, and feel impatient and even depressed at the slow pace of our economic reforms. We feel frustrated by the missed opportunities from a higher growth rate. But Burke would have consoled us, telling us that even slow reforms add up. He would say that it is better to grow prosperous with continuity and democracy, albeit more slowly.

5. Gandhi Would Have Understood My Dilemma

Burke expressed his understanding of society famously as a partnership between those who are living, those who are dead, and those who are yet to be born. That is to say, the present is not the property of the living, to make of it whatever they will. It is an estate held in trust. Those who hold it have a responsibility to pass it on in good condition. The French revolutionaries were in the process of wounding this trust, and we in India are guilty of this as well. Mahatma Gandhi understood this and cautioned the Congress leaders about overturning in the name of reason, liberty, and equality the many historical continuities and institutions of the past. For this reason his secularism resonated with the people. It was grounded in the belief that the ordinary Indian was religious and traditional. He showed respect for the "other." This is not true, alas, for many of today's champions of secularism, and this is why no one listens to them. This, combined with the way our political class has exploited the word in a naked quest for power, is why the sensible idea of secularism has acquired a bad odor in today's India.

Gandhi, like Burke, has frequently been dubbed a reactionary. Burke did not defend an exclusive aristocratic or monarchic order—he approved of the mixed system that existed in the Britain of his day, which was a combination of aristocratic, commercial, oligarchic, and democratic elements. Just as Burke preferred prudent and incremental reform, so did Gandhi. Ambedkar called him reactionary and too tolerant of the caste system. However, Gandhi was a realist. Much as he abhorred untouchability and caste, he did not think one could merely legislate them away. In the end, Gandhi probably did as much as any human being to make Indians aware of caste's iniquity. What Ambedkar did not appreciate is that Gandhi's respect for the historical process did not mean that he evaded the responsibility for criticizing the past. In fact, he criticized it relentlessly. But he also respected community and continuity. He felt that secularism would only succeed in India if it did not undermine tradition, but reinforced our "custom, community and natural feeling," in Burke's language. He was more successful than Ambedkar or our modern day secularists because he employed the language of the people, the language of dharma to teach modern liberal ideas such as "liberty" and "equality."

I suspect Gandhi would have understood my dilemma about teaching the *Mahabharata* in our schools and he would have agonized over the lack of easy answers. He instinctively grasped the place of the epic in Indian lives, and he would have approved of what V. S. Sukthankar, editor of the Poona Critical Edition of the epic, wrote: "The *Mahabharata* is the content of our collective unconscious . . . We must therefore grasp this great book with both hands and face it squarely. Then we shall recognize that it is our past which has prolonged itself into the present. We are it." If we are *it*, surely it is important to teach *it* to the young so that they may understand and value who we are.

The debate on teaching the *Mahabharata* in our schools is relevant for another reason, which I found upon reading Michael Oakeshott. It is the idea that there are things to be enjoyed, but that enjoyment is heightened by our awareness that what we are enjoying is in danger of being lost. It is the combination of enjoyment and fear that stimulates conservative thoughts. The epic has given me so much enjoyment in the past six years, that I have become a *Mahabharata* addict. I feel deeply sad that many young boys and girls in India are growing up rootless, and they will never have access to these forbidden fruits of pleasure. My dilemma has a personal dimension, you see, and it has led me to tread conservative paths. Conservatism is unlike other ideologies for it does not offer the vision of an ideal society, as Samuel Huntington wrote in an article called "Conservatism as an Ideology," published in 1957. There is no conservative Utopia because it is concerned not with content but with process, with stability, with continuity and prudence. It is the opposite of radicalism, which expresses enthusiasm over the boldness in embracing change. My fears of the loss of tradition may appear exaggerated. Perhaps, they are. Certainly in the villages of India, where the vast majority of Indians live, the *Mahabharata* is well and alive in the oral traditions. But the future of India does not lie in the villages of India but in the cities. It is there, especially with the powerful onslaught of the global culture, we have to be concerned to preserve continuity with the past.

Let me close with a true story, which I think goes to the heart of the secular temper. A few years ago, I visited the Madras Museum in Egmore. While I was admiring a Chola bronze, a middle-aged South Indian woman came behind me, and without self-consciousness, placed a vermilion mark on the Shiva Nataraja. I was appalled. Slowly, however, I realized that we lived in two different worlds. Mine was secular; hers was sacred. Both of us stood before the bronze statue with very different expectations. For me, it was a nine hundred year old object of beauty; for her, it was God. Mine was an aesthetic pleasure; hers was divine *darshana.*

She did not see what I saw, a brilliant work in bronze by an early Chola artist. I admired the weightless joy of the dancer, so skillfully captured by the sculptor. I moved along, passing by other bronzes, and I got irritated that the bronzes were dusty, ill lit, poorly spaced and badly presented. Suddenly, I felt embarrassed by my petty, niggling concerns. I turned around to look for her. She was still there, absorbed by her light-footed, tireless dancing god, whose dance actually brings the universe into being, and without missing a beat, and in the fullness of time, dances it out of existence. I was struck by the contrast of our lives—the fecund richness of her sacred world versus the poverty of my weary, feeble, and skeptical existence.

I felt drawn to her and to her god. For someone who is carrying out such a momentous mission in this universe, I find that her god looks cool, athletic, and even debonair. This is where our empty secularism has gone awry. Modern, liberal, English educated Indians are fast losing the holy dimension in their lives. They will never know the depth and opulence of her life. They are quick to brand her superstitious, illiterate, and casteist. She is, in fact, probably far more tolerant and accepting of diversity because she is capable of seeing God everywhere. It is in her rich world that the BJP and our Hindu nationalists ought to learn the true significance of Hindutva and the Congress Party and our secularists ought to learn the real meaning of secularism.

In my world of museums, concert halls, and bookstores, there is plenty of search for beauty, but there is no place for the holy. We are lost in a desacralized world of petty, middle-class concerns. Our secularism has robbed us of Kant's moral condition. Partly it is the fault of traditional religion, which has over-laid and trivialized the original inspiration. The fundamentalists of the Vishwa Hindu Parishad (VHP) and Islam have alienated us further. The answer for an authentic life, I think, lies with the woman in Madras in whose attitude lies the possibility of a fullness of being.

I return to the main Shiva Nataraja at the entrance. He still looks unper-turbed and absorbed in the serious task of creating and destroying the universe. But there is something new. Under his raised left leg, there is a marigold flower! So the next time the world gets too much for you, do what I do—go visit the Madras museum, and if you do not experience eternity, you might learn a modest lesson in implementing pluralism in a democracy, the driving theme of this collection of essays. It is not only her attitude, but it is the outlook of the narrator, which is one of respect for the "other," for her alien, sacred worldview. Secularism will only find a comfortable home in India if we respect the sensibilities of a deeply traditional and religious people. Just as India needs a secular liberal party that is right of center in its economic thinking, so too could young, modern Indians learn from Edmund Burke about the value of a secular conservative temper that values the continuity of history and tradition.

As we think about sowing the seeds of secularism in India, we have to go beyond the easy polarities of the mind. The question is of the "how," and not of the "what." You cannot just divide Indians between communalists and secularists. That would be too easy. The average person is decent and is caught in the middle. John Rawls, I think, may have offered a way out when he distinguished between "public reason" and "secular reason." Public reason limits itself to political and civic principles while secular reason is broader and concerns itself with a secular person's first philosophy. In the same vein, Martha Nussbaum distinguished between political and comprehensive liberalism. Advocates of secularism must not forget this distinction and they must refrain from introducing "comprehensive liberalism" and "secular reason" into public debate. In a recent lecture in Poland, "Religion in the Public Sphere," Habermas spoke about the commendable idea of toleration, which is the foundation of modern democratic culture. He called it a two-way street. Not only must believers tolerate each others' beliefs, but also the atheism of nonbelievers. Disbelieving secularists, similarly, must value the convictions of religious citizens. And among religions, only those that can suspend the temptation of narcissism—the conviction that my religion alone provides the path to salvation—are truly welcome.

Notes

As this is not an academic paper, I have not cluttered it with footnotes. However, to those who wish to read some more of Edmund Burke, I would recommend the following books, which have given me much pleasure in preparing this paper:

Edmund Burke, *Reflections on the Revolution in France*, ed. J. G. A. Pocock, Indianapolis: Hackett Publishing Company, 1987, 181

Edmund Burke, *Appeal from the New to the Old Whigs in The Works of the Right Honorable Edmund Burke*, 7th ed., Vol. IV (Boston: Little, Brown, and Company, 1881), 143

Peter J. Stanlis, "Edmund Burke in the Twentieth Century," in Peter J. Stanlis, ed. *The Relevance of Edmund Burke*, New York: P. J. Kennedy & Sons, 1964

V. S. Sukhthankar, "On the Meaning of the Mahabharata," republished by Motilalal Banarsidass, 2003, 24.

12 THE ROLE OF POETRY AND LITERATURE IN IMPLEMENTING A PLURALISTIC DEMOCRACY: WRITING AT THE TIME OF SIEGE

Nabaneeta Dev Sen

This Motherland of ours, India, is a conglomeration of so many contradictory forces that its life and times have never been very simple.[1] And today it seems to have gone beyond the danger signal. Each one of us is trying hard to find a suitable identity, trying to understand the reality of the situation we are in. In one of our ancient slokas, Devi Saraswati blesses her son Kavya Purusha as an ideal literary figure whose body would be made of *vak* and *artha* (word and meaning, respectively) but his face would be made of Sanskrit, his arms of Prakrit, his legs of Paishachi and so on, so that the totality of his existence would consist of several different Indian languages. What could describe a multilingual nation better? Language is only one of the multiple facets of Indian culture, along with class, caste, race, gender, religion, and region. All those embarrassing disparities—economic, religious, social, cultural, geographical, and linguistic—seem to overpower our existence and constantly question our basic idea of democracy. We, Indian writers, have been trying to understand and explain these confusing identities and have been writing India in our different ways, from the time of Tagore and Iqbal until today. In this paper I will share some of my own experiences as a writer responding to the challenges that our pluralistic democracy faces today.

1. Najma

Just before the last elections,[2] I got a phone call from a national newspaper in Delhi saying, "Recently in our newspapers a group of writers and other intellectuals from Delhi have signed an ad supporting the

BJP (the Hindu right-wing Bharatiya Janata Party). Do you think it is fair for the creative community and other intellectuals to sign ads like this?"

My response was, "Why not? A group of writers, painters, actors, filmmakers, and academics in West Bengal have signed a public letter requesting people to vote for secular democracy. If we can do our thing why can't they do theirs? We may not share their views, but we can't deny them free speech in a pluralistic democracy." She didn't like my response, but carried it anyway.

However nonaligned or apolitical one may be, there are times when we should all make our beliefs public and try to effect some positive change. And the creative arts can be an important part of this public dialogue so essential for the democratic process.

In West Bengal we have formed a women writers' group, called *Shoi* (in Bangla it means "signature" as well as "girl friend"). We are very often asked, What are your activities? Do you do social work? What are your approaches toward women's problems?

Well, we tell them, we meet as women writers, not as women activists. Writing is our main activity. You can call it activism if you want. Yes, women's issues happen to be our major focus, but every human problem is our problem, not just women's. And all our activism begins at our writing table, though it does not stop there. It is through our pen that we justify our existence and try to improve the quality of life on our planet, never forgetting the fact that we are active members of a pluralistic democracy. Let's take for example Gujarat. Soon after the Gujarat bloodsheds one of our members, poet and novelist Anita Agnihotri, who also happens to be a member of the Indian Administrative Service, read out a personal letter at one of our meetings.[3] It was an urgent note from her deeply concerned friend and colleague from Gujarat, the now famous Harsh Mander.[4] Shocked and alarmed, we immediately sent a memorandum to Gujarat and took every opportunity to write and talk about it wherever we could, in our creative work, on public platforms, in media interviews, both print and audio-visual. Since then we have talked and written a great deal about it. For example, "Najma," a poem about the massacre in Naroda Patiya, published soon after, had a serious impact upon the reading public. People have recorded the poem on CDs and audio cassettes, and it continues to be recited at Bengali cultural events around the world. It has also been translated into several Indian languages.

Here is an English translation.

> Najma
> The girl lives far away, very far away –
> Her husband, a bright young man,
> Vanished on his way to work

They had special plans for the evening
He would take her along to buy their new TV

He hadn't been to work, but
She didn't know, so she had his evening snack ready –
But it was getting late, too late to go.
Let down, the young wife sulked, her lips pouted,
Work, work, must he work so hard even today?

They were to buy their colour TV that evening,
With a loan on easy terms from the office,
The way their red scooter was bought,
Setting up a new home, little by little,
Needs so much care . . .

He was to come home early today
So he had been up at dawn
It's thirty kilometres to the office
A long, long way from home
The journey seems endless
***
Out of nowhere a pack of faceless men
Pounced on him, pulled him off the scooter
Two, ten, twenty? Who were they?
He didn't know them, they were strangers.
Surely, he had no quarrel with them?

What happened? Did anything happen at all?
Quick as thought, petrol from the fuel tank
Sprinkled like a shower of flowers
All over the young man
Who was it that lit the match?

Flesh burned, the young husband burned
A writhing heap of charred flesh
Young and old cheered, laughed out loud:
"Jai Shree Ram! Jai Bajrangbali!"
"Look! A living man burns like fireworks!"
***
She lives far away, very far away
She stood all night at the window

Clutching the grills as she waited alone
The neighbours had told her nothing,
They all knew—all except Najma

The neighbourhood rocked the next morning
As the police came in, the NGOs too
"Najma, look, do you know this man?"
This photograph here? Is this thing a human being?
Najma turns away, "Nah, I don't know him."

"Najma, take a look, then, at this scooter here
Here's the number plate, do you know it?"
In a whirlwind of grief
The girl crashed upon the ground –
The rider of that scooter was no stranger.

Aziz had bought it only the other day
Their baby was due in September
There was a lot of running around to do
From Naroda it was thirty kilometers to his office
He needed a scooter
***
At the relief camp of Daria Khan
The needle puts her to sleep
Before her throbbing eyes blazes a tangled lump
of blood, bones, flesh and scorched skin –
"Najma, look, is this your husband?"

Despite it all, Najma looks after herself
And tries to live, to rise above the horror
Saraswati Ben has told her:
"Don't admit defeat, my girl,
You must be strong!
This world has got to change!"
Najma, that was *not* the last word—
It *cannot* be

We are here right at your side,
Holding you by the hand
This earth, weighed down by our sins,
Has hit the rock bottom.

To live, we must rise upwards,
There is no option left—
There is no room to sink any lower . . .

Rise upwards—that way lies survival
Najma, you can't fall to pieces
Najma, you must be like a tree,
Yes a tree you must be
Stand straight and strong, rooted in love
And reach for the sky
We will be the ground beneath your feet

How can we lift our eyes to yours?
Eyes that have witnessed a *trishul*-torn foetus . . .
Najma, we know your eyes are now dry –
But let your breasts overflow with milk
A new human being is coming to your arms

We will give her a fresh new world
Just steel yourself and wait—
There is another world right here,
Within this world of ours.

We will give her a whole new sky
Najma, even thunder will not tear that sky apart.

This poem is rather different from the kind of poetry I normally write, but it was written soon after seeing the newspaper photograph of a burning scooter with a blazing lump of a human body lying next to it on the road, in Ahmedabad, in 2002.[5]

2. Activism

Around the same time in Delhi, as a result of talking among friends about the impotence and helplessness of the individual against mob violence as in Gujarat, the award winning playwright and cartoonist Manjula Padmanabhan wrote a play in English called *The Hidden Fire*. It was a big hit with students when staged in Kolkata's St. Xavier's College by a group from Bombay. The organizers felt the play would have a wider impact if it could be translated into regional languages and read out in schools. It is a short, powerful play on the problems of a pluralistic society, on the horror of sectarian violence, the shameless hypocrisy of the media, and the helplessness of the individual. They requested one of our younger *Shoi* members, poet and scriptwriter Srabasti Basu, to translate it into Bangla. She was then invited to various Bangla medium high schools to give readings, introducing the idea of secularism and democracy to the students. The original English text too was being read and discussed in the same way at English medium schools. The point was to make the children feel the pain of violence and the shame of communal disharmony, as well as the importance of peace and resistance in a secular democracy at the time of siege. This was one way of making our beliefs public. So Manjula Padmanabhan's effort at writing the play was successful, it reached out to a wide audience, and hopefully contributed toward the strengthening of the democratic principle in the minds of young Indians.

Activism, as it is generally understood, is not for all of us. Not many of us can be a Medha Patekar, Mahashweta Devi, or Arundhati Roy. But we try to do our bit as conscious human beings. Our approaches differ. All activists are not writers, but I believe *all serious writers are activists*. The very act of writing honestly, of speaking out and making public what we believe in, make us activists in our own way. Rabindranath Tagore had written in a colonized India *"Ei sab mook mukhe ditey habey bhasha"* (To provide speech to the voiceless is my job). The very same cry was repeated by another writer, more than a hundred years later, only last month, in Europe, when Turkish novelist Orhan Pamuk received the Peace Prize of the German Book Trade at the Frankfurt Book Fair.[6] "It's a writer's duty to speak out for those whose voices are never heard," he said, echoing Tagore. Clearly, the need continues.

A Harold Pinter or a Mahashweta Devi are activist writers, and for some people like Betty Head, Toni Morrison, or Begum Rokeya, the very act of writing is a form of activism.

3. Myth and Humor

I strongly believe that it is our duty to speak out in whichever way suits us best, in order to make ourselves heard. Anyone writing with a purpose is actively participating in strengthening the democratic process. It need not be a political speech, it need not be a political novel, it need not be a slogan-infested article. All it needs to do is to touch the human heart and to make the reader take a moment to reflect. The truth will reveal itself to the reader.

To achieve this, I use a special genre of storytelling, rewriting myth as a social comment, and presenting it through humor. Humor is a great winner. I try to use popular memory, but from a different and unexpected context, so that what I say seems familiar at first, and lets one's defenses down, which makes acceptance of the fresh idea easier. More often than not when you are saying something new aggressively, the immediate reader response is to resent it. No one likes to be told what they are doing is wrong. My main purpose is *to be read*, to succeed in communicating my idea to as many people as I can. Therefore, instead of essays I like to write belles-lettres about things that matter, and funny stories about not so funny social situations, about religious fundamentalism, about gender fundamentalism, and so on. And from the enormous feedback I get, I know that they serve their purpose.

4. Durgapuja and Diwali

I'll start with two small examples. Small, but invaluable to me. The first happened about ten years ago, in Bangladesh.

I was in Bangladesh, in 1995, during Durgapuja. After the demolition of the Babri Masjid in 1992,[7] there had been repercussions both in Pakistan and in Bangladesh. We had read about some Hindu temples being vandalized in both countries. Even in 1995, the famous Dhakeshwari temple in Dhaka bore marks of that hatred. We went to Gazipur, quite close to Dhaka, in Tangail, to watch the immersion in the river of the idol of goddess Durga. I was told several Durga *pujas* were organized there, and the immersion was beautiful. They carry the goddess balanced on two boats bound together to the middle of the river, where the ropes are unfastened, the boats part and the idol drops gracefully into the water.

We stopped by a beautiful image of Durga and approached the group of young men sitting nearby. "When would the immersion procession start?" we asked. They answered, "Sister, we are here only to guard the goddess, for the immersion details you would have to ask the Hindus. But don't miss the beautiful floats, Apa, there is Harishchandra by the pond and Chand Saudagar to your right."[8]

Well, this is how we live in this subcontinent. This is the soul of the Indian subcontinent as I see it. Freeing ourselves from the religio-political bondages that often defy our basic human bondings, we need to celebrate the richness of our multicultural heritage that naturally flourishes in the pluralistic democracy of India.

The story of this most precious afternoon in Gazipur was published in both the Bengals, in India and in Bangladesh. Pluralism is alive and well among us. We merely have to recognize it, acknowledge it, point it out to our children, and to those who are unaware. As writers we have to underline it whenever we can and in whichever form seems most suitable for the job.

The next story shifts to India, to Kolkata, my city, ten years later. Just a few days ago, we went to watch the gorgeous Deepavali or Diwali lights and fireworks in North Calcutta, at midnight. After visiting a very famous Kali Puja *pandal* at Amherst Street, we were driving down a crowded lane just by its side, lined for the festive occasion with small roadside shops and carts selling fireworks, candles, Diwali lamps, street food, rural handicrafts, and wooden and clay dolls side by side with plastic toys and cheap costume jewelry. *Papadams* and *pakoras* were being fried. A street full of happy men, women, and children in the celebratory mood with the background music of temple drums and brass bells. After driving down a little while I felt that the lane was looking somewhat different, the crowd had not thinned but the women and children had magically disappeared; there were only men in the crowd. And they were dressed differently, in *kurta*, pyjama and waistcoat, with tiny, white skull caps. The nature of the ware in the roadside stores had also changed—instead of toys and dolls it had *lungis*, scarves, handkerchiefs, and *Fez* caps; instead of Diwali lamps and fireworks they were selling *namaz* mats, prayer books, and *tasbi* beads; instead of *pakoras* and *papadams* you could smell kebabs and *parathas*; and the background music of drums and brass bells had transformed into a high pitched haunting Arabic hymn. The culture of the crowd had quietly changed from Diwali to Eid down the very same lane. The stream of festive people continued to flow, only half the crowd was preparing to celebrate Eid while the other half was celebrating Kalipuja. The whole experience was almost too dramatic to be true. But nothing is too dramatic in our shockproof Indian world.

I had to write my column, naturally, about this illuminating midnight revelation. It still gives me goose pimples to think that this is my country, this is India; our pluralism is manifest even in one tiny street in a metro city. The responses I got were just as exciting. It seemed to many like a symbolic show of pluralism in India. Some nonbelievers asked, "Is this a short story you made up, or did it actually happen?" My simple answer was, "Go and see for yourself. Diwalis and Eids come every year."

5. The Aftermath

Now I shall come to a tale, a myth retold with a purpose. Rewritten myths presented in the form of humorous short stories have a pretty large readership. They have reached out not only to Bengali readers around the world—Bangla is the world's fourth most spoken language at the moment—but also to a large Hindi readership. Here is a story that begins with humor but ends in tragedy. It was written after the demolition of the Babri Masjid in Ayodhya. Named *Uttar Kanda*, after the Seventh Book of the *Ramayana*, the story was translated into English as "The Aftermath."[9]

The idea of my story was borrowed from a tribal tale—not just any tale, but a tribal *Ramayana*, sung by the Mech tribes in the North East. Talking of pluralism, in this strangely special Mech tale the Tribal meets the Brahminical and Hinduism holds hands with Islam. What I offer here, however, is my story fashioned from it, not the original Mech tale. The angle of vision is different, so are the details. It begins as a funny tale but does not end as one.

Here is the story in short.

Uttar Kanda (The Aftermath)

After his coronation Ram and his brothers were taking a joyride through Ayodhya in the royal chariot, when they were mesmerized by an unfamiliar aroma floating in the air. "What is this heavenly aroma?" an enchanted Ram asked the charioteer, Sumantra, who shuddered and responded, "Oh no, your highness, not heavenly at all, but exactly the opposite. It's the smell of foreign food, heathen food in fact, as a matter of fact it is forbidden food, my master . . . Even smelling it is sinful, it will condemn you to hell, *ghranena ardha bhojanam*, you know your *shastras*, Sir, half the fun of eating is in smelling the food, so is half the sin." A shocked Ram ordered Sumantra to drive faster, "Away, away from this filthy place, but tell me, how on earth did the smell get in here, in Ayodhya?" On their way back brother Bharat explained it. While Ram was in exile, a great deal of trade and commerce had developed with neighbouring countries and plenty of business had come in, along with new cultural developments like new languages, new cuisine, new music, new architecture and, unavoidably, a new religion as well. They were different in their looks, speech and habits, he said, but that was not a problem, they were civilized, peaceful people. Once home, busy learning how to be king, Ram forgot all about the smell, but the grand aroma stuck to Lakshman's nostrils. He had to have a taste of it. So he went out one day, in the direction of the smell, and knocked on a door. An old man with a flowing white beard, in a foreign costume, opened the door and invited him in. A straightforward man, Lakshman introduced himself and without losing time asked what was being cooked in the kitchen. "Kebabs, sir," the courteous old man said, and offered him some. Lakshman thoroughly enjoyed the hospitality, as he had never tasted anything so delicious before. Thanking the host profusely, he asked what it was.

And was told that the meat was that of a very young calf.

Lakshman wisely commented, "So, this was why in the Vedic times guests were called *Go-ghna*. Because the sages sacrificed the best calf to serve their guest. I wonder why the fine practice stopped!" Then he froze, as he realized that he must have lost his faith by eating beef. His elderly host was aghast, he apologized profusely and said, though losing faith was not that easy, still, it was probably safer to keep this one single experience to himself and not to mention it even to his family. Why cause complications? Everything would be okay if no one knew about it. But Lakshman could not keep it a secret, he was so happy with the taste of kebabs that soon everyone knew. He requested his wife Urmila to go to the Muslim quarters with the charioteer, and learn their art of cooking. So innocent Urmila went to take her mother-in-law's permission, and all hell broke loose. His mother Sumitra disowned Lakshman at once, called the priest with the express desire to become a *sannyasini*. Ram tried to save the situation as best as he could. Hence he decided to let Lakshman convert to Islam along with his wife Urmila, leave *Ramrajya* peacefully, and be crowned the Nawab of the kingdom next door. So the kingdom Karupath was named Lakshmanavati after Lakshman (Lucknow for short) while Ram continued to reign in Ayodhya (Oudh for short).

Thus the brothers lived their separate existences happily. Ram and Sita had two sons Lav and Kush in Ayodhya, and Nawab Lachmanullah and Begum Urmila Umraojaan also had two sons, Hassan and Hussain in Lakshmanavati. The river Sarayu flowed between the two kingdoms, and a thick forest lined both the banks of Sarayu.

Since it was *Ramrajya,* naturally tigers and deer had to drink together at the river.

On their sixteenth birthday Lav and Kush decided to go on a deer hunt in the forest. Sita, though she did not appreciate the idea of a deer hunt any longer, packed them a big picnic basket with all kinds of royal goodies, and the boys rode off on their chestnut steeds, well armed for the *mrigaya*. Meanwhile Hassan and Hussain were sixteen too, and they wanted to go on a tiger hunt. So Urmila Umraojaan filled a lunch basket with yummies, and well armed, they rode off on their fine white horses.

All four boys came to the river and waited. The deer finally came, and so did the tiger. And forgetting *Ramrajya* the lean and hungry tiger shamefully jumped for his kill. Instantly a cloud of arrows flew across the sky, the next moment the tiger lay dead. And the deer too. The brothers emerged to claim their trophies, but there was one problem. The deer had been killed by Hassan–Hussain, and the tiger by Lav–Kush. This was not what they had originally intended. Now if they went back with the wrong animal it would be clear that they had failed to get their catch. The boys introduced themselves, became friends instantly, and decided to swap the animals so that each could bring home the right trophy. Great solution! All four of them were happy, they embraced one another and sat down for a well deserved meal sharing their picnic lunches. Hassan-Hussain enjoyed the *puris* and the *payasam*, the *rajbhogs* and the *shrikhand*, whereas Lav-Kush were freaking out on the *biriyani* and the kebabs. There had never been a happier moment in their lives. The boys promised to meet every full moon night for a shared picnic, and never to tell anyone about it.

But as luck would have it, just then the quarrelsome divine sage Narad was passing by invisibly; he witnessed the whole process from the sky and was determined to intervene. *Everything* the kids did was *so* unethical. Ugh!

First they were planning to get kudos for the animals they had not killed, and cheat both the royalty and the people. Next there was the bigger problem of sharing lunches and eating forbidden food. As a good, solid ethical Brahmin he had to set it right. The people of Ayodhya were celebrating the deer hunt, and the people of Lakshmanavati were celebrating the tiger hunt of the princes, when Narad appeared in Lucknow and told Nawab Lachmanulla that his sons were frauds. The tiger was not killed by them as they were claiming. They must be punished for cheating the king and the people. Lakshman being what he was, just blew his top at this accusation. "What! My sons? Cheats? Out! Get out of my kingdom this minute!" he said to the revered sage, and added that he could not care less about his famous curses as he was not ruled by the Brahminical scriptures any more.

But Ram being Ram, listened patiently to Narad and tried to find out the truth from his sons. The princes truthfully explained it all. Ram was beside himself with joy to know that the cousins had met and had formed a friendship, and instead of scolding them, he embraced them and blessed them with all his heart. Narad was so annoyed to witness this sentimental nuisance that he forgot the important business of the forbidden food and rushed out to incite the people against the king. The public had been badly cheated, Narad announced. The princes had actually killed a *tiger*, as befits them, not that *deer*, but they had exchanged booties with another pair of princes from the neighboring *mleccha* kingdom, who had killed the deer.

In a moment the celebrating mob became violent. "We have been cheated! We want our tiger back! We want our tiger at once!" they shouted as they gushed forth. The palace gates collapsed, the guards rushed out, the crowd surged in. Ram tried to talk to the people. Then he held a closed door meeting with his ministers, with Narad sitting in.

What happened next?

Raja Ramchandra's army met Nawab Lachmanulla's army. A dead deer lay on one side, and a dead tiger lay on the other. A fierce battle ensued. Two pairs of distraught princes, Hassan-Hussain on their white horses and Lav-Kush on their chestnut steeds, madly rushed to the battlefield, their right hands raised in alarm, pleading, screaming, begging, "Stop it, stop it, please stop this bloodshed!"

But no one noticed the boys.

No one heard their cries.

Thousands of arrows whizzed through the air. In an instant four unarmed, peace-craving young princes fell still upon the earth. As the blood of the innocent boys tainted the pure water of the Sarayu, the angry river gushed forth in a fierce surge. Mad with shock and grief, Ramchandra and Lachmanulla both threw themselves into the swirling, raging, bloodied waters of the Sarayu. And the river, unable to bear the pain, turned into a dry bed of sand.

But the carnage continued. The blazing rage and blood turned trees into lifeless blocks of stone; blades of green grass wilted away and became specks of yellow sand. The verdant forest on its banks was now a harsh desert.

A rather depressing tale I'm afraid. But right from the *Mahabharata*, India has a history of fratricide ruling its mythology. And though with a sad ending, this story actually puts forward a few positive points about pluralism.

Well, below is the original Mech tale as I had found it.

One day Lakshman tasted beef and became a Muslim, so he was sent off to rule the kingdom next to Ram's. He had two sons, Hassan and Hussain, and Ram also had two, Lav and Kush. When they grew up the four brothers attacked each other's kingdom, and everyone in both kingdoms was killed. Unable to continue any further, the *Mech Ramayana* stops there.

The frame is the same, but my story is quite different, and stretches to today: Narad still patrols the skies, unseen, inciting destruction and disaster. The world has accepted him as another UFO. Bloodshed among brothers has not stopped. And Hanuman, the deathless son of Pavana, beats his chest, whenever the storm winds blow, and wails for the dead brothers. "Ha Hassan! Ho Hussain!" he sighs, "Hai Lav! Hai Kush!" His sighs shatter the skies and echo through the clouds.

If you put your ear to the storm winds, you can hear his cries.

My story ends here. I was asked by the editors of this book to look into the "role of poetry and literature in implementing a pluralistic democracy." Well, these were just a few examples of one writer's ways of connecting literature with life as a means of raising awareness and changing attitudes to help nurture a pluralistic democracy. Lucky as we writers are, having earned access to the readers' unsuspecting hearts, it is our duty to reach out as far as we can. In the case of awareness-raising, any path would be a good path as long as it takes you where you wish to go.

There is no harm in being subversive. Usually it works.

Notes

1. This essay was written in November 2005, and all the references are of that time.
2. The 14th Indian Parliamentary Elections of 2004.
3. About 2,000 people, mostly Muslims, were killed in the sectarian violence of February–March 2002.
4. Bureaucrat Harsh Mander resigned from the Indian Administrative Service in protest against what he believed was a state-sponsored pogrom against Muslims in Gujarat, and became a civil rights activist.
5. The Bangla poem was translated by Subhranshu Maitra with the poet and the *Little Magazine*, published in the *Little Magazine* (Vol. IV: 2): Via Media; 2003; Delhi.
6. In 2005. In 2006, Orhan Pamuk won the Nobel Prize for literature.
7. The 400-year-old mosque built by Mughal emperor Babar was demolished by Hindu fanatics of the BJP and related parties on December 6, 1992. They claimed the site was sacred to Hindus as the birthplace of Lord Ram, and demanded to build a Ram temple there.
8. Harishchandra and Chand Saudagar are characters from the Hindu folk tradition of Bengal.
9. For the full story see "The Aftermath," translated by Ahitagni Chakraborty and Antara Dev Sen; the *Little Magazine* (Vol. III: 5&6): Bloodsport, 2002, Delhi.

13 THE BABY AND THE BATHWATER: SECULARISM IN THE WORK OF A CONSERVATIVE WRITER

Pratik Kanjilal

The turn of the twentieth century in India was marked by the rise to power of the Hindu Right, which ended the monopoly of the Congress over the centrist vote and the middle-class majority community. The media discourse of the period suggests that there was a sort of glamour contest between a youthful, energetic right and the dowdy old centrists, both vying for the attention of the floating vote of middle India—mainly the middle-class Hindu majority—but the truth is more complicated. Aggressive Hindutva did not play by the rules. It redrew the game board, polarizing the polity and shrinking the middle ground. By depriving Hindu centrists of their natural habitat, it forced them to choose between the Bhartiya Janata Party (BJP), with which they have cultural affinities, and the Left, which despises them as reactionary opportunists.

The choice was obvious, and the BJP came to power with a decisive mandate in 1998. But was this the result of a "wave," as was claimed at the time? The BJP's persistent failure to get reelected thereafter suggests that Hindu India had not swung to the right, as was widely believed. It was just a period of confusing alarms and excursions and we were all ready to believe the worst, even of our own and our selves.

Let me illustrate by personal experience—a funny-peculiar Jekyll and Hyde experience. Had it happened to someone else, I might have found it as entertaining as Stevenson's original, but to be part of the plot was a disturbing experience. What happened was not unusual for the time, of course—friends who had known me for years, and had known me to be moderately left of center, suddenly became convinced that I had turned right-wing. A few became deeply suspicious, even hostile.

Well, I reasoned, it was 2002. The "Gujarat experiment," which I had first heard of in 1996, had just raised the bar in India's national sport of political impunity. The weak-minded and the weak-kneed were reeling with awe at the compelling temerity of Hindutva. Eternally in search of the strong man and forever incapable of distinguishing between strength and savagery, the floating vote was moving to the BJP camp. For a while, it looked liked the experiment had succeeded nationally, whipping up powerful emotions, polarizing the entire electorate and changing the profile of the Right forever. In that charged atmosphere, to be merely misunderstood was a very small matter.

But I am still amazed at the smallness of the provocation for the misunderstanding—not a political column I may have written, nor any regressive slant visible in the journal I publish, but a mere translation of a novel, a completely apolitical novel about growing old. An innocuous thing, you will agree. And yet it was enough to get me banished, though briefly, from the world of reason to that of *tilaks* and *mandirs*.

Out there, I found that some of my new neighbors were in an identity crisis as well. A section of the new BJP voters were just conservative traditionalists who would not have been caught dead packing a *trishul*. Their natural political habitat was the middle ground, but they had been turfed out of there by the steady polarization of India, which began with L. K. Advani's *Rathayatra* in 1990. It had effectively divided the nation between those with faith and those without, and there was only no man's land between the two. When forced to choose, most conservatives gravitated toward the former camp. And anyway, feelings ran so high at the time that if a person had any faith at all, they were suspected to favor mass murder. Hindus were damned if they changed allegiances and damned if they didn't. The faithful from minority religions were in any case looked upon with suspicion—at best wily Christian missionaries, at worst Muslim terrorists.

Polarization was a project of the right, but it was energetically supported by the left. Unfortunately as exclusionist by instinct as any organized religion, the Left has inadvertently helped the Right to secure its aims, at the expense of secularism. With puritanical fastidiousness, it has rejected conservatives who were actually potential allies, as uncomfortable about the violent, fundamentalist excesses of militant Hindutva as they are about the Left's revolutionary projects.

In several parts of the country, especially in central India, the electorate has explicitly rejected the Hindutva project. The turmoil in the BJP after the reelection of the Manmohan Singh government in 2009 owes much to the desperation of several leaders to leave the politics of Ayodhya behind and forge a new future as a secular, multicultural, right-of-center party. They understand that a conservative party which rejects fundamentalism and violence can expect to gather a huge following, but are held back by colleagues who cling to precisely these characteristics, which had originally brought the right to power.

So the politics of polarization is not history yet. The Rashtriya Swayamsevak Sangh (RSS) is back in charge of the Hindu undivided family, determined to steer it back toward identity politics. Something has gone deeply wrong if half a century after Independence, secularism still works so erratically and is so easily ignored or subverted. And this is not a simple result of sectarian forces being more ruthlessly efficient proselytizers than secular forces, which is what we usually like to believe.

But first, my own little story from 2002, in which I became an accidental translator and Jekyll thereby became Hyde. The journal I publish in India, the *Little Magazine*, had carried a section of the popular Hindi novelist Nirmal Verma's last novel, *Antim Aranya*, in English translation. A few days later, Verma called up to say that he wanted us to do the whole book, and publish it. A happy accident, for we had no experience in book publishing at the time. I did the translation myself, because I was the only staffer available with decent Hindi and English and some time to spare—yet another accident. I was pleasantly surprised to see my very first translation, titled *The Last Wilderness*, getting excellent reviews. Later, in 2005, it won the translation prize of the Sahitya Akademi, India's central academy of letters. But I was unpleasantly surprised to find that some old friends were quite upset about it. Accidents, by definition, strike in unexpected ways, but I soldiered on.

"Hello," I would say hopefully when I met clearly upset friends.

"Hello," they would reply bitterly, and fix their gaze on the middle distance and breathe heavily.

After a long, tense silence, they would ask: "Why Nirmal?" in the tone in which Gunter Grass may have been asked, "Why the Hitler Youth?"

True, Nirmal Verma had raised right-wing questions both in public and private and was widely believed to have BJP connections. But equally, he never let right-wing politics color his fiction, I pointed out, so what was the problem with translating his stories?

"Read his essays," they would say darkly, and stalk away. I was surprised that the corpus of a novelist's creative work could be negated by a handful of conservative essays. It seemed a bit extreme.

Nirmal Verma died in September 2005, the year my translation of his last novel won the recognition of the Sahitya Akademi. His funeral and memorial ceremonies drew all sorts of people, with the singular exception of the worthies of the BJP with whom he was said to have been in unholy alliance, and who do not enjoy the reputation of forgetting their friends. The majority of the people present were decidedly left of center and included the very people who had been so upset with me for translating an author of unapproved political leanings.

To try and understand this paradox, I read Nirmal Verma's essays as advised. In what follows, I shall be quoting from this Hindi novelist and short story writer, a card-carrying communist who was disillusioned by Prague Spring, to which he was witness, and turned conservative in later life. And then I shall quote from Kaifi Azmi, vastly popular Urdu poet and lyricist, decidedly left-wing, who died in 2002. I use Azmi as a control experiment, to show that the disquiet, confusion, and sense of unreality expressed by a writer identified as right-wing is not peculiar to one end of the political spectrum.

I should clarify that I refer only to the atypical work of these two writers. I quote only from the novelist's essays and from the poet's satirical newspaper column, which ran through the sixties. Writers are often less circumspect and therefore more likely to be honest when they are working in a form other than the one they are celebrated for. The translations are my own and not published elsewhere.

Let's begin with a short take from Nirmal Verma's diary:

9 DECEMBER, 1992: Three days ago, the mosque at Ayodhya was demolished. Sometimes, I wake up in the middle of the night and think that this is only a nightmare that will pass. And then, so much more horrifying, I realise that I am not asleep. I am awake, and this is reality.

Is this the reality of fear?

The news from India always has an impact on a different scale. Bhopal, Bombay ... When I think of how people were dragged from their homes and murdered, the very act of imagination becomes unbearable. In the face of this terrible reality, religion seems like a mere figment of the imagination.

Not exactly the nocturnal fulminations of a right-wing novelist, are these? I went on to Nirmal's essays. Earlier, I had been assured that decent people did not read them and had dutifully kept away. Now, what I found was some common ground between what the author was saying and what the loudspeakers spout at BJP rallies and RSS meets, but the author's take was informed by a very human logic which is entirely missing from political propaganda, and it tried to secure less suspect ends. In fact, there was very little in there that would disturb a conservative, unaggressive traditionalist of any nationality.

So how had this very harmless-looking writer gotten into so much trouble over so little? If the problem did not primarily lie with the text—and I see nothing wrong in individuals airing traditional views, so long as they don't interfere with other people's freedoms—perhaps it lay with the reader. Perhaps the reader was being as intolerant as he was accusing the writer of being.

If secularism is to work in India, we must reinterpret it more liberally. It needs to be positioned so that people at the middle of the political spectrum are able to relate to it more readily, and it cannot be seen to encourage wholesale rejection of all things premodern, even the harmless jujus of private life. At present, we are perhaps forcing unpleasant choices on people, which is a very efficient way to get them to turn hostile to secularism.

In the period from the rise of the right in the late eighties to the Gujarat experiment in 2002, the Indian political spectrum was steadily polarized. The majority community had become severely bipolar, and there was no middle ground. Everyone was doomed to be either Left, Right, or a middle-class opportunist, and therefore irrelevant. In this world, anyone from the Hindu majority who had any sympathy for faith, tradition or old-world concerns was clearly a right-wing extremist who endorsed the genocide in Gujarat. This was as absurd as accusing Graham Greene, who ventilated a few Catholic issues in his fiction, of complicity in the violence in Ireland. But in our slightly crazy society, the erasure of the middle ground passed without comment.

Unfortunately, the middle ground is the place where most of a nation's people like to make their home. Typically conservative, when they find the very ground pulled away from under their feet, they will usually gravitate to the Right, whose ideas and iconography seem more familiar than those of the Left, and will remain with it until the Right begins to pursue extremist agendas with due diligence—as it did in Gujarat—and frightens them off.

Meanwhile, the state offers little aid to the confused citizen. Though it is founded on the principle of equidistance from all faiths, in its operation, it is merely distant from all faiths—and thereby distant from people whose lives are mediated by religion. Secularism has been imposed top-down and has not really been referred for legislative debate or endorsement in recent times. The Constitution gives the state almost no role in matters of religion. It can intervene only through the instruments and institutions of the law and therefore, it must wait for religious issues to resolve themselves into law and order issues, or human rights or civil liberties issues, before it is called upon to act. In other words, it is tacitly understood that it will stay out of the picture until people start killing, raping and looting each other over matters of faith.

This strategy was appropriate for the years after Independence, the period of nation-building. The composition of society had been drastically altered and groups needed room to redefine themselves and their relations with each

other, and thus reestablish the social fabric. But now, when religion has poi-
soned national politics, it seems inadequate. In fact, it has become a dupli-
tous position. As we have seen repeatedly under Congress and BJP ministries
(most notably in the riots in Delhi in 1984 and Gujarat in 2002), government
is actually at liberty to promote the sectarian violence it is duty-bound to
contain. In fact, it can officiate as master of ceremonies of a riot and get away
with it.

Decades of top-down secularism prepared the ground for the incredible
increase in the popularity of the right and the success of its politics based
on violence through the 1990s. A good theory based on sound principles is
essentially dysfunctional if it cannot be put into practice—or is indeed subverted in practice—and in the interest of practicality, we should recognize
two related truths. The general public, largely traditionalists, find the current version of Indian secularism dry and remote, and the manner in which
secularism is propagated and enforced ignores the concerns of common people and seems rather incredible to them. While we must routinely combat
sectarianism, it has been a mistake to do so in a manner which can be read
as opposition to religion and indeed, to the cultural beliefs of the majority.
One cannot escape the feeling that for the last fifty years, we have been trying
to straitjacket Indian society. I quote from Nirmal Verma's essay "Religion,
Democracy and Sectarianism":

> It is said that once, a hardline Muslim League leader went to meet
> Mahatma Gandhi. When he returned after a long discussion, someone
> asked him about his reaction to the meeting. He said, "I felt somewhat
> strange, talking to Gandhiji. I had thought that he would speak against
> the Muslim League. On the contrary, I think he was telling me how to be
> a good Muslim."

Isn't it extraordinary that Gandhi did not ask this gentleman to quit the
Muslim League, but rather expressed the hope that he would be a good Muslim?
Is the distinction between religion, democracy and sectarianism not expressed
rather clearly in this short, simple sentence? I would like to add a thought
here: Gandhi did not ask him to be a good human being, which would have been
natural to the humanist tradition of Europe, but which carries no special meaning in the cultural milieu of India.

It's a different inflection, a different way of looking at the issue, but it seems
to work and at this point, practicality has its attractions. Let's move on to a few
paragraphs from Verma's essay "A Middle Path":

We have been living in a secular society for the last fifty years. What is the result? There is no place for education about religions in our schools, colleges and institutions of learning. And so Hindu, Muslim, Sikh and Christian students in the same class have neither knowledge nor curiosity about each other's beliefs, rites and festivals. We are very proud of our plurality of faith and thought, but the classical languages—Sanskrit, Farsi, Arabic—through which we can gain some insight into each other's points of view and philosophy of religion, have not only lost out to the dominance of English, but their institutions, libraries and centers of learning are slowly disintegrating. The United States has institutions for the study of the Indian faiths, but India itself has no room for such teaching . . .

I have spoken earlier of the darkness of ignorance. The growing sectarian sentiment in our society is the harvest gathered in this darkness. When people are denied clean water, they must perforce quench their thirst with dirty water. When religion is separated from society, disease spreads. Sectarianism is one symptom of this disease, a means of filling the void of the spirit. Since we have no faith, it beguiles us by masquerading as faith. Just as, once upon a time, in the costumes of equity and egalitarianism, communism had misled our intellectuals.

If these very intellectuals and political analysts are now drawn by the slogan of secularism, it is because they see the fallen form of faith—or, more accurately, the caricature of faith—that is visible in sectarianism, but not the true form of faith, which we have banished from this land.

We've thrown out the baby with the bathwater, as they say in English. Or, worse, we've chucked the baby and kept the soiled water, from which sectarianism is born. Our politics has to do with this filth, not with that larger truth which has been identified as religion and cast out.

I'm afraid Verma is speaking for a very large portion of the Indian population. More pertinently, he is speaking for the floating vote, which went over to the BJP and propelled it to political office, largely traditionalists who were unsure of where they stood. They instinctively vote for politics that assures peace and quiet. But if they feel their identity is threatened, they will side against secular forces.

In his acceptance speech of the Sahitya Akademi Award in 1985, Nirmal Verma elaborated on the role of the writer in a society with many competing versions of reality, where order is only the current state of chaos:

Is there a single image which adequately represents the Indian reality? Or is the very quest for it illusory? In such a situation, it is possible that a disappointed writer may wish to revert to a personal reality, a purely individual world of light in which he can turn away from the meaningless darkness and irrelevant uproar of external reality and concentrate his gaze, with absolute responsibility and faith, upon the lonely flame of his own truth and hope that in its light, he will be able to quench the darkness outside and in his silence, give meaning to the noise out there. Perhaps, in this way, he can keep his creative integrity intact. Or perhaps his vision of reality may become a little clouded over, may not remain as realistic as the vision that people acquire so easily in this media-rich age. The writer will no doubt be harmed by this, but he will be less unfortunate than the writer who, in the hope of being a representative of his times, confines the many-faced diversity of the Indian reality to little, narrow gutters. By binding himself to one form of the truth, this writer is no longer an independent observer of reality. He ignores the call that had summoned him to literature in the first place. Whatever he may be, he is no longer a writer.

Now, is this sense of unreality, this suspicion that all is not well in the world of ideas, restricted to the conservative writer? Here's a fable from Kaifi Azmi's weekly column in Urdu, "Nayi Gulistan" ("The New Garden"), which ran from 1963 to 1973. It's titled "The shepherd who raised wolves and wept for his sheep":

> In a certain nation there was a shepherd who, like shepherds in all nations, raised sheep, took them out to pasture and kept them from wolves. But our shepherd's real occupation was to make development plans and show his sheep the way ahead, and he thought, why don't we start a project to graze sheep and wolves together? If they feed together, if they live and die together, the mountain of enmity will be shaken and the wolves will enter the mainstream of society.
>
> The sheep bleated, take us to the pasture and show the wolves to the paddock—if they come into the pasture, we'll be eating grass and they'll be eating us. But the shepherd smiled and lovingly explained that they mustn't be afraid, mustn't bleat on for no good reason. If I listen to you and take the wolves for your enemy, he said, if I take only you to pasture and keep them out, democracy will be destroyed and the freedoms of the pasture will be as ashes, he said.

The wolves, some of whom were green in color, some saffron, some housebroken, some running wild, danced for joy and freely stalked the pasture. The sheep were reassured. Perhaps life would indeed be easier now. The wolves had changed, utterly changed—their very teeth had fallen out. The shepherd watched and smiled, and composed a slogan— 'The face of enmity is blackened, the fame of democracy is established. Now take one step more, bring socialism to the pasture.'

The wolves went berserk at the name of socialism. In one voice, the green and the saffron cried out, this shepherd will be the end of us. He will make vegetarians of us. And then they began to show the skill of their teeth and made the sheep their quarry, and in the space of a couple of breaths the pasture ran with blood.

The poor shepherd rushed to the pasture, out of breath. He explained to the wolves and barked at the sheep: if you are violent, if you break the peace of the pasture, democracy will be defeated. Let democracy be defeated, said the wolves, let the pasture be damned. Hell, other pastures are damned too, and democracy stands defeated there too. We have no bone to pick with the sheep—they are not strangers to us. But you, who raise sheep and hatch plots on behalf of socialism, all the violence is about you. You make up these slogans about socialism to get on our nerves. We shall listen to you and acknowledge you as our shepherd only when you organize riots everywhere and liberate the other pastures. But the shepherd kept trying to convince them, kept telling them: if you do not know good from evil, if you do not take me for your shepherd, the wheels of progress will grind to a halt and the pasture will be shamed. And the wolves chorused, now who can explain the truth to you? Who can unfold the secret? You want to see precisely the future that you are trying to frighten us with.

The world of the arts, which usually restricts its comments on secularism to powerful depictions of the dehumanizing horror of sectarian violence, knows that we face a deeper problem than a mere face-off between the impersonal forces of fundamentalist bigotry and those of progressive reason. In a democracy, combatants cannot afford to forget that the battle is always for individual hearts and minds. Just thinking about the wolves is not enough—we also have to ensure the safety and comfort of the sheep before secularism can be seen to work. Normal, unaggressive conservatives should be given their space back and allowed to make respectable homes there. The middle ground is integral to a healthy polity, and its neglect by the left and annexation by the right has contributed to the progressive desecularization of the Indian polity.

References

Antim Aranya, Nirmal Verma, Rajkamal Prakashan, New Delhi, 2000.

The Last Wilderness, Nirmal Verma (Pratik Kanjilal, tr.), TLM Books, New Delhi, 2002.

Aadi, Ant aur Aarambh, Nirmal Verma, Rajkamal Prakashan, New Delhi, 2001.

Bharat aur Europe: Pratishruti ke Kshetra, Nirmal Verma, Rajkamal Prakashan, New Delhi, 1991.

Kala ka Jokhim, Nirmal Verma, Rajkamal Prakashan, New Delhi, 1981.

Nai Gulistan, Kaifi Azmi, Rajkamal Prakashan, New Delhi, 2001.

THE BJP'S INTELLECTUAL AGENDA: TEXTBOOKS AND IMAGINED HISTORY

Mushirul Hasan

How could I tell my tale in this strange land?
I speak a tongue they do not understand.[1]

1. The Agenda

Encounter's first issue in 1953 carried an article on India that concluded on the following note: "Between a past reduced to practical impotence but offering a resistance to depth, and a future only skin-deep, India's present seems to lack substance." Today, almost all rank-and-file Indian politicians will disagree, for there is no limit to their imagined triumphs. The stark reality is that the shadows of doubts and uncertainties move among us, almost too many to count and sometimes even hard to name.

In this essay I am concerned with the Bharatiya Janata Party (BJP)'s agenda of rewriting history textbooks.[2] I do so principally because this exercise, conducted under the aegis of official and semi-official bodies, entails the dissolution of history and necessarily jeopardizes historical study as normally understood. Just as the arrival of postmodernist theory in the 1980s led to an extended epistemological crisis in the West, India's current intellectual climate has thrown the historical profession into disarray. Such is the power and influence of the BJP polemicists that a growing number of people, drawn mainly from the urban elites, are abandoning the quest for an objective approach to the past.[3] No wonder so many historians are worried about the future of their discipline.

In one of her witty books, *The Moving Finger*, Agatha Christie introduces a girl fresh from school and lets her run on about what she thinks of it. "Such a lot of things seem to me such rot. History, for instance. Why, it's quite different out of different books!" To this, her sensible elderly confidant replies: "That is its real interest." This seems like a perfect point of entrée for commenting on the uses and abuses of history under the BJP regime.

The knowledge of history has been used—or perhaps misused, as in nineteenth-century Germany—to legitimize chauvinistic national identities, authoritarian regimes, and military dictatorships. As George G. Iggers points out, the task of historical research was to help contribute to the construction of a national identity, and this is exactly what the historians did, even openly in the case of the so-called Prussian school. Historians went into the archives not so much to be guided by the sources as to find support for their arguments.[4]

Likewise, the Holocaust of 1941–1945 and the Arab-Israeli war in 1948–1949 coalesced with invented myths or "official truths" to determine the Jewish people's collective identity. Several Israeli historians, having subjected their reconstruction of the past to the interests of the state, the party and nation, hammered home Zionist myths and served up to a great extent apologetic or propagandistic versions. But at least on the matter of the 1948 war, the new historians introduced a discordant note: the desire for territorial expansion, they argued, was just as prominent as the desire for peace among many Israeli leaders. They pointed out that most Palestinians fled as a result of acts of war; in some cases Palestinians were deported by Israeli forces, and there were also massacres. It was, commented the historian Lars Hoff, far from being David's battle against Goliath: the Israeli forces were in the majority throughout the war and, with the exception of the first few weeks, they also had superior weapons. When the historians presented their findings in the 1990s they were fiercely attacked, as it was feared that the Israeli/Zionist identity would unravel.[5]

British historians writing on India during the colonial period regularly invoked aspects of medieval rule to prove that Britain had done more for the substantial benefit of the people than the despotic medieval sultans. Henry Elliot referred to "the few glimpses we have, even among this single volume, of Hindus slain for disputing with Muhammadans, of general prohibitions against processions, worship and ablution, of other intolerant measures, of idols mutilated, of temples razed, of forcible conversions and marriages." With its despotism and anarchy, "Muslim India" had only a negative value: "to foster in us a love and admiration of our country and its venerable institutions." In British India itself, "we have already, within the half century of our dominion, done more for the substantial benefit of the people, than our predecessors, in the country of their own adoption, were able to accomplish in more than ten times that period."[6] Elliot candidly conceded that his purpose was to make "our native subjects more sensitive of the immense advantages" of British rule.

The representation of the past has been central to the concerns of publicists, reformers, and scholars in South Asia. Thanks to James Mill's well-known periodization of Indian history, the vast corpus of historical literature in the last quarter of the nineteenth century touched upon issues of identity and, in the process, invented a Hindu and Muslim past. Each of the contesting groups—more numerous in regions affected by religious and social reforms—constructed fresh images of itself, reformulated history to suit its ideological predilections, and projected images of the "other" as different and dangerous. The evangelical fervor of the missionaries heightened religious and cultural anxieties, leading to the search—one that continues even in this millennium—of the Hindu past, its philosophical underpinning, and its metaphysical dimensions. Thus the Arya Samaj, drawing upon aspects of popular culture in Punjab, especially in its southeast region (now Haryana), sought to equip the Hindus to face the cultural and religious assault of the West by acquainting them with their great religious traditions.[7] It gave birth to a resurgent Hinduism, free of Islamic and Christian accretions.

There were striking parallels with earlier and contemporary Muslim revivalist movements, but the Indian nationalists appropriated the Hindu reformist currents, keeping similar trends among Muslims from their agenda. Instead of any degree of convergence—and that is what the nationalists should have tried to achieve—the Hindu and Muslim reform movements ran a parallel course. In fact, serious efforts were underway, especially in the Punjab, Bengal, and western India, to homogenize the segmented Hindu population and to create what the historian Romila Thapar characterizes as "syndicated, semitised Hinduism." The Muslim initiatives were, by contrast, feeble and largely unsuccessful. Whereas the *tabligh* (propagation) and *tanzim* (consolidation) movements born after the Khilafat movement collapsed in 1922–1923 failed to get off the ground, *shuddhi* (purification) and *sangathan* (consolidation) campaigns gathered momentum because of their patronage by certain key leaders and their merger into the larger stream of Hindu nationalism.

In the second half of the nineteenth century, textbook transmission formed but one facet of the wider significance of print culture. A marked shift in the approach to history took place in school textbooks in Bengali.[8] At another level, contestations over history reveal the part played by school textbooks as ideological tools in the Raj's projection of itself through critical representations of the precolonial past.[9] The British government carefully monitored, with the aid of an extensive bureaucratic network, what was to be included in or left out from the school or college curriculum. Thus the Director of Public Instruction recommended an elementary treatise on the art of writing the Persian character as "original and scholarly, and will be of use in schools." In another case, Munshi Zakaullah, the headmaster of a school in Delhi, was rewarded "for the industry displayed in the preparation of this excellent series of scientific works, and for his public spirit in publishing them." Another work by Mohammad Nazir Ahmad, a Settlement Officer in Jaloun, was approved for an award on the grounds that "there is no pandering to the passions or appeal to the marvelous, which appear to be the ordinary passports to popularity among Oriental writers."[10]

Professional historians sought autonomy in compiling and transmitting to schoolchildren their understandings of the precolonial Indian past. Some mounted a trenchant defense of the belief that history is a search for the objective truth about the past. Iswari Prasad, writing in Allahabad, a city that produced some of the finest liberal historians (among them Banarsi Prasad Saxena, Shafaat Ahmad Khan, Tara Chand, and R. P. Tripathi), endeavored "to correct the common errors of history and to make the presentation of the subject [*History of Medieval India*] as attractive as possible." Pointing out that a historian was neither a party politician nor a political propagandist, he defined her function simply—to state and interpret the facts without allowing his own prejudices to influence the discussion of his theme or warp his judgment.[11] In June 1935, Shafaat Ahmad Khan, another Allahabad-based historian, stated what became the credo of nationalist historiography. Addressing the All India Modern History Congress (later the Indian History Congress), he stated:

> We must keep vividly before us the conception of Indian history as a whole. We must not divide ourselves into watertight compartment of Marathas, Sikh, Muslim, and Bengali historians. . . . Every Indian historian should aim at a conception of united India. . . . We are not only Marathas and Muslims, we are also part of a larger whole, and it is our duty as historians to emphasise this point, and bring home to the young the spiritual energy and intellectual force which impelled many of our national heroes to work . . . for the general progress and improvement of our motherland. . . . [Our historical research] must be inspired by the new sentiments which animate India today. It is the spirit of a common Indian nationality, basing itself on the fundamental unity of the Indian people, and having its origin in the numerous forces, spiritual, intellectual and economic, which have fused various communities and classes, provinces and States, into an organic whole.[12]

In theory, strict standards of objectivity were laid down. In practice, though, Hindu polemic against Islam was constructed, especially with Dayanand Saraswati and his Arya Samaj followers, on the notion of a standardized and canonical view of Islam. They treated the Muslim intrusion as an aberration or a break in the continuity of Brahmanical traditions; Indian culture was equated with Vedic culture; Indian philosophy with Vedanta, Puranas, and the Upanishads; and Indian religions with Hinduism. A government report from the United Provinces on Arya Samaj educational publications concluded that there "was no appreciable diminution ... in the rancour of their polemical literature."[13]

In Bengal, Bankim Chandra Chatterjee saw in Islam a quest for power and glory, devoid of spiritual and ethical qualities, irrational, bigoted, devious, sensual, and immoral, and a complete antithesis of his "ideal" religion. He saw medieval India as a period of bondage, and interpreted a Hindu chieftain's resistance to the Mughals as a form of national resistance. Thus, for the Bengali intelligentsia of Nirad C. Chaudhuri's generation, "nothing was more natural ... than to feel about the Muslims in the way they did." They were told, even before they could read, that the Muslims had ruled and oppressed the Hindus, spread their religion with the Koran in one hand and the sword in the other, abducted Hindu women, destroyed temples, and polluted sacred places: "As we grew older we read about the wars of the Rajputs, the Marathas, and the Sikhs against the Muslims, and of the intolerance and oppressions of Aurangzeb."[14]

Suffice it to say that such images and representations led to the creation of opposite camps, each trying to create its own icons and golden epochs and constructing the past accordingly. The smoldering fire of bigotry blazed up in the romances of Indian chivalry, of which several were published in early twentieth century. Whereas "Hindu" writers depicted the Turkish conquerors in very lurid colors and praised as heroes those who had offered resistance to the medieval rulers, the "Muslim" historians spiritedly described the inferiority of Rajput courage and strategy. They invoked, moreover, the exploits of Mahmud of Ghazni and Aurangzeb, and idealized the medieval Indian past. The facts of history mattered little, if at all, to such writers. This is reflected in the following comment:

> When the scrutinising gaze of research penetrates the dust-clouds raised by trampling armies and fighting hordes, a vision of the real sultanate is granted to the student which reveals a pageantry of patient administrators, of earnest philosophers and teachers, of artists and master-builders, of religious thinkers and saintly reformers.[15]

Independence led to a vigorous articulation of divergent points of view. Indeed, pasts were articulated in constant dialogue with one another—dialogues animated by the differing claims of rival groups and political agendas.[16] Thus K. M. Munshi and R. C. Majumdar, editors of the Bharatiya Vidya Bhavan series, echoed the rhetoric of Hindu extremist politics, tracing the misfortunes of *Bharat* to centuries of tyrannical Muslim rule. Instead of studying and interpreting other cultures by the same standards and criteria as their own, without prejudice or condescension, their scholarship was designed or even trimmed to serve some nonscholarly purpose, whether religious, regional, ideological, or other. In their writings, Islam is represented as a hostile and aggressive force and Muslim societies are caricatured as rigid, authoritarian, and uncreative. Still, they wielded influence, enjoyed a fair degree of government patronage, and found support for their activism (for example, over the reconstruction of the Somnath temple) in the upper echelons of the Congress hierarchy.

Although Marxist historiography had taken firm roots in India in the 1930s and 1940s, it began dominating the intellectual landscape only after Independence. With D. D. Kosambi as their model, Marxist historians studied—without a strong narrative of political events and without recognizing religion as a marker of social and economic identity—class formations, social structures, and agrarian economies. Leaving aside for the moment the merits or defects of their arguments, what they achieved in broad terms was to challenge, on the strength of rigorous principles of source-criticism, many of the colonial and nationalist shibboleths that had robbed historical studies of their depth and vibrancy.

The significance of the Marxian enterprise lies in the context of the euphoria generated by the rapid pace of decolonization and the Indian project of social transformation. Notwithstanding the bloody partition of India and reservations on the Left over the Congress' commitment to a socialist polity, Independence ushered in an era of hope and optimism. Watching the Republic Day Parade in 1955, the country's first Prime Minister found a sense of fulfillment "in the air and of confidence in our future destiny."[17] The scholarly community, though divided across the board and critical of the Congress government's policies, shared Nehru's optimism. It was more self-assured than the previous generation tutored in a colonial milieu, more sensitive to the anticolonial struggles in Asia and Africa, and more respectful of the people's nationalist aspirations. Again, this community, though dispersed across regions, was greatly influenced by a wide variety of socialist and Marxist ideas. Although the country's partition divided its constituency and the Congress' hegemony weakened some of its initiatives, the Progressive Writers' Movement and Indian People's Theatre Association were still alive and kicking. Memories of the Tebagha and Telengana uprisings were, equally, still part of the popular memory.

The first generation of free India's historians was largely drawn from this small but influential community. With hopes of a socialist revolution fading, they nonetheless became an integral part of the great debates on nation-building. For several historians—mostly based in Calcutta, Allahabad, Lucknow, and Delhi—the task at hand was not simply the rejection and repudiation of the colonial interpretations but the legitimization of a secular polity and society. They defended, for this reason, the composite tradition to prove the hollowness of the "two-nation" theory as against the idea of a Hindu Rashtra.[18]

In this way, nationalist historiography, with a strong imprint of Marxism, was entwined with the nation's agenda and with issues of development and underdevelopment.[19] There was nothing wrong in this. Indian historians, having inherited the rich and vibrant legacy of the nationalist movement, were uniquely placed among the postcolonial states to so powerfully articulate, despite the ruptures, the amazing unity and continuity of their historical traditions.

Soon after the partition massacres there emerged a nationwide consensus on promoting rationality, independent thinking (somewhat skeptical and wholly scientific), and preserving the composite values of this society. This, wrote Nehru, was the task of modern liberal education. In 1950 he told Nagpur University students that "men who talk of Hindu culture miss the basic human culture and show a narrow, barren and limited outlook on life. They are completely against the assimilating and absorbing nature of India's ancient and glorious culture." Nehru told the same audience, "keep your windows and doors of your mind always open. Let all winds from the four corners of the earth blow in to refresh your mind, to give you ideas, to strengthen you."

Right-wing Hindu ideologues, however, contested the Nehruvian vision. R. C. Majumdar, general editor of the Bharatiya Vidya Bhavan volume *Struggle For Freedom*, referred to the "additional difficulties" created by the fact that Gandhi and Nehru were "looked upon by a large section of Indians with veneration, incompatible with dispassionate judgement."[20] He added: "A regular propaganda has been kept up to preserve untarnished the halo of glory which the contemporaries, in the first flush of enthusiasm, put round their heads."[21] This was just a small part of an orchestrated campaign against Nehru's sledgehammer efforts to change the fabric of Hindu society, his lenient policy toward Pakistan, and his undue tenderness for the Muslims.

Yet the liberal-Left combine pursued its scholarly agenda, exemplified in, for example, Tara Chand's three-volume history of the freedom movement. It held its ground until the Janata government decided, in 1977, to withdraw the history textbooks written by R. S. Sharma, Romila Thapar, Bipan Chandra, and others.[22] The past, it appeared then, would become a casualty in the ideological battle of the present. However, the storm blew over owing to the fragile nature of the Janata coalition. With the establishment of the BJP-led government in October 1999, the BJP-RSS combination began its veritable *cultural counterrevolution*[23]—its subversion of academia through its time-tested method of infiltration and rewriting of textbooks and fine-tuning of curricula.

The intervention in 1977 was feeble; the one starting in 1999 represents a strong body of opinion in the country that subscribes to the view that the Hindus have been wronged, and that their histories have been distorted at the hands of the secular fundamentalists. Exponents of this view say in effect: "You have invaded and pillaged our past. You, the inheritors of the Nehruvian legacy, have robbed us of our present. And you have endangered and perhaps compromised our future." This kind of criticism is often accompanied by very harsh, even coarse, language, and has given rise to a new term of abuse—"intellectual terrorists." Earlier, the common expression "pseudosecularists" denoted the liberal and Marxist writers; now the same term has been salvaged, reconditioned, and turned to a new purpose.

The critical assault comes principally from political activists, polemicists, propagandists, and some journalists and, in recent years, from the unwarranted intrusion of expatriates. Secular historians, they point out, fail to highlight the achievements of Hindus during the Vedic period and ignore instances of Muslim oppression—for instance that Muslim rulers deliberately kept Hindu farmers at subsistence level, forcing them to migrate as indentured labor to Mauritius and the West Indies. And the same historians are said to overlook the fact that the Ayodhya problem existed during Wajid Ali Shah's time.[24] These charges are unfounded. If Professor K. S. Lal, the author of such views, had read the German historian Leopold von Ranke, a profoundly conservative figure, he would have judged, from his own conservative standpoint, that the past should not be judged by the standards of the present. It has to be seen in its own terms.

What Professor Lal is saying is that the critical approach is forbidden to us, and that we should accept what is selected, prepared, processed, and presented for our instruction. So that even to mention—let alone to discuss or explore—beef-eating in ancient India, the destruction of Buddhist stupas and Jain temples, or the role of a Sikh guru is denounced as evidence of unpatriotism and of Christian-Muslim designs. The same applies to other delicate topics, such as the fate of the Indus Valley civilization, the antecedents of the Aryans, the mythical Saraswati River, and the caste system. The range of taboos is very wide.

Today, the unfinished Hindu agenda—to provide a corrective to the distorted secular perspective—is being promoted at the Sarawati Shishu Mandirs and Vidya Bharati primary and secondary schools. The first Vidya Bharati School was founded in 1952; today, they number 19,741 with 70,000 teachers.[25] Students at these schools are told that Qutub Minar was constructed by Samudragupta; that Alauddin Khalji imposed fifty percent land revenue on the Hindus; that women adopted *jauhar* to defend their religion and chastity; and that child marriage, *jauhar*, sati, and various superstitions were all due to fear of the Muslims.[26] "When you are teaching a child to distinguish between good and bad," says the principal of a Shrin Sanatan Dharma Saraswati Bal Mandir, "you tell them that Shivaji was good . . . then how do you tell them that Aurangzeb was good?"[27] At the RSS Vidya Bharati schools in the BJP-ruled state of Gujarat, students are told:

- The Varna system was a precious gift of the Aryans to mankind;
- The Catholic priests accumulated wealth through unjust taxes, and spent the money on worldly pleasures and immoral behavior;
- Islam teaches only atrocities: "Have not Islamic invaders perpetrated this wherever they have gone: be it India, Africa or Europe?"; and
- Between 1528 and 1914, three lakh fifty thousand devotees of Rama laid down their lives to liberate the Rama temple.

2. Saffronization

In short, we live in a time when efforts are underway to falsify the record of the past and to make history a tool of propaganda. We live in a time when the government and its allies of every kind control the exchange of historical knowledge through official and nonofficial bodies. This explains why the Indian Council for Historical Research (ICHR), a government body, has withheld publication of the two volumes compiled for the "Towards Freedom" project by Sumit Sarkar and K. N. Panikkar, two leading Marxist historians. The arguments in defense of such an administrative decision are untenable; the real reason behind this intellectual censorship is that the RSS and the Hindu Mahasabha are portrayed in a poor light in this documentary record.

India is a multicultural and multireligious society, and yet a single definition of Indian culture and society is projected through educational channels.[28] No wonder the changes announced by the NCERT (National Council of Educational Research and Training) in the school curricula in January 2002 woefully neglect the study of the medieval period. The relative importance of *our* history and *their* history can be seen in the apportionment of space and attention to ancient and medieval India. While the former has as many as fifteen rubrics, the latter has only one.[29] In addition, the one unit of the social science syllabus that looks at the features, spread, and basic values of major religions leaves out Islam. The motivation is clearly political and ideological. Sometimes there are other variants: although the "advent of Islam" has been included in the social science syllabus for the next class, it is put in a unit alongside West Asia. That is because, says Murli Manohar Joshi, the Minister of Human Resources and Development (HRD), Islam "grew out of that area—its history is linked with the history of the Arab civilisation, its spread and emergence."[30]

The late Girilal Jain, editor of the influential *Times of India*, had opined that "while the emerging Hindu elite linked itself with dominant Western civilisation and adopted the road to modernity and progress, Muslims turned their gaze toward a past incapable of being restored."[31] Arun Shourie, a former journalist and currently a Central Minister in the BJP-led government, had this to say: "For centuries wherever Islam actually ruled it had been sacrilegious and traitorous to study, develop or propagate what had been the very essence of the life of our people."[32]

Not only have such distorted and ill-informed views gained wider acceptance in recent years, but they are echoed, much to the delight of the Sangh Parivar, by several writers of Indian origin. For example V. S. Naipaul, the Trinidad-born writer, talks of India's fractured past solely in terms of the Muslim invasions and the grinding down of the Hindu-Buddhist culture of the past. In rejecting the possibility of Islam working out reconciliation with other religions on the subcontinent, he notes that Islam is a religion of fixed laws—something, he points out, goes contrary to everything in modern India. Here in a few crispy sentences is the clash of civilization theory applied to the subcontinent.

The question that opponents of the study of medieval Indian history usually put is: Why should *we* study *their* history? The NCERT seems to be saying that it is not their business or that it is not relevant—a word with new and sometimes menacing implications—to their needs or concerns or purposes. Islam is, after all, alien to the Indian environment, even though almost simultaneously with political conquests in the seventh-century Islam began to find lodgments in India's western coast. Muslims and Christians, wrote Guru Golwalkar, the high priest of the RSS,

> are born in this land, no doubt. But are they true to its salt? Are they grateful towards this land which has brought them up? Do they feel that they are the children of this land, its traditions and to serve it as their great good fortune? Do they feel it a duty to serve it? No. Together with the change in their faith, gone are the spirit of love and devotion for their nation.[33]

Likewise, the Bharatiya Itihas Sankalan Samiti, an RSS outfit with four hundred branches, is out to cleanse Christian influence on historical chronology. The *kalgana* or the scientific way of calculating time does away with the B.C.E./C.E. system and works according to the traditional Hindu system of periodization.[34] The Vidya Bharati Akhil Bharatiya Shiksha Sansthan, the education wing of the Sangh Parivar, claims to run 17,396 schools with 93,261 teachers and 2,252,848 students.[35] In July 1992, a Congress report stated:

> The BJP has introduced the Vidya Bharati School system with syllabi that include the Hinduised version of history. They have issued instructions to the RSS to open more and more schools all over India.

Excepting the Hill States of the NE region, Vidya Bharati schools function in all the states of India. The four states they are in power, this is being practised in full swing and the influence is bound to spread over. This is nothing but a systematic attempt to indoctrinate the youths to Hindu fundamentalism.[36]

Doubtless these institutions play a major part in communalizing Indian society, but the HRD Ministry, now headed by an avowed swayamsevak, plays a pivotal role in formulating the saffron agenda. Despite the fact that his blueprint on education was rejected at the State Education Ministers' Conference on October 22, 1998, M. M. Joshi has pursued his goal relentlessly, ruthlessly exploiting the vulnerability of the NDA partners and the weakness of the Congress party. Hence Joshi's "second war for the country's cultural freedom," and the establishment of a new "forum of doctorates" to promote and package Hindutva in universities.[37]

The introduction of moral education, Vedic mathematics, and Vedic astrology into the college/university curriculum reiterates in essence the nineteenth-century Orientalist construction of the Indian past, which saw history in terms of a precocious flowering of Indian science and civilization, followed by a long period of degeneration caused by the advent of Muslim rule in the thirteenth century.[38] Although leading scientists, along with parliamentarians cutting across party lines, have criticized the introduction of Vedic sciences and objected to the revival of antiquated notions, the minister insists on changing the prevailing "Eurocentric mindset." He wants to develop confidence and pride among Indians in their past and also their future. According to him, Aryabhatt had preceded Isaac Newton by several centuries in propounding the theory of gravity; the people in ancient India knew that the earth was round and revolved around the sun;[39] and, finally, computers were invented on the strength of the Indian binary system of zero and one.

Saffronization, the new mantra of the HRD ministry, is the antithesis of what constitutes liberal education, for it seeks to instill a set of beliefs into the minds of the young before they are capable of thinking and exercising independent judgement. And when two opposite groups are taught in this fashion, they produce two armies that clash, not two parties that can discuss. Saffronization breeds fanaticism, heightens caste and communal consciousness, and stifles the natural inclination of a student to cultivate a balanced and cautious judgement. This is bad news for the country. As Anjali Modi, the journalist, points out:

> Historians who continue to argue that this battle of books is about the discipline of history are refusing to grasp the nettle. They must, if there

is to be a debate, rather than a dialogue of the deaf, accept that what is at stake is not the discipline of history but a larger and more profound idea—that of the Indian nation.[40]

The idea of an inclusive Indian nation was precious to the liberal-Left historians. Under the BJP dispensation, this very idea is assailed. What has changed from the previous decades is that under the present dispensation, the historian is not expected to raise embarrassing questions, confront orthodoxy and dogma, or represent all those people and issues that are routinely forgotten or swept under the rug. What we have, in other words, is indeed a dialogue of the deaf, with no genuine debate. The minister's diktat runs through a lazy bureaucracy.

Marxists or pseudosecularists historians, whose "intellectual terrorism" Joshi and his friends attack,[41] have been excluded from academic bodies and replaced, without any consideration for merit, with a fresh breed of intellectual managers-cum-BJP-RSS ideologues. With the nodal agency for sponsoring research passing into the hands of right-wing historians, the politics of exclusion has been directed against the "opponents of Bharitakaran, the human progeny of the threefold family of Macaulay, Marx and Madrasa, who do not want that the contradictions of history be resolved."[42] The patronage extended to like-minded intellectuals corresponds with, on the other hand, the larger Hindutva project of enlarging its intellectual constituency. The Forum for Hindutva in Indian Scenario, formed recently, is designed to further this objective.

Rewriting history textbooks is, in any context or time frame, a desirable exercise. History for young children must be simplified, and this means that as they grow up not only must their history be retaught and relearned, but also unlearned. Everything is continually not quite what they thought it was. This process, trying but necessary, can be helped through discussions with students, parents, and teachers. And yet the recent enterprise lacks transparency; hence the pointed criticism, leveled by the two former directors of the NCERT, that "never before in its history was NCERT viewed with mistrust by a large section of the academic opinion." They add that the books brought out by their organization, "written by some of the country's outstanding historians, have added to the prestige of the NCERT as an academic body."[43]

From the indications available, the rewriting involves no more than an imaginary construction of the past: that is, the claim that the Rig Veda is seven thousand years old (although according to all scientific chronologies the Rig Veda cannot be dated beyond 1500 B.C.E.); that the Aryans had gone from India and colonized the world and that they had all the possible knowledge and sciences; and that Buddhism and Jainism were just trends within Hinduism (with Ashoka, who became a Buddhist after renouncing Hinduism, bearing the brunt of their criticism).

Historical imagination has its place, but somebody must also insist on the strict limits within which that imagination is bound. The exercise that is being undertaken now does not force historians to rethink the categories and assumptions with which they work, or to justify the manner in which they practise their discipline. That is because, as the educationist Krishna Kumar points out, professional ethics and standards have become irrelevant for a dispensation concerned only with the instrumentality of education as a means of social and ideological propagation.

Attempts to Talibanise India's history are exemplified in the deletion of certain passages from school textbooks of the Central Board of Secondary Education: for example, references to beef-eating practices, the martyrdom of the Sikh guru, and the ransacking of Delhi by the Jats. "There is no denying the fact," commented the *Times of India* editorial, "that the deletions amount to an unprecedented violation of academic freedom. In a country where the lines between history and mythology are increasingly blurred, the dangers of such revisionism may not be immediately apparent. But we can ignore the old adage—those who forget their history are condemned to repeat it—only at our own peril."[44] Indeed, the issue is between prejudice and propaganda on the one hand, and rational argument and scholarship on the other.

Those unwilling to confront the past will be unable to confront the present and unfit to face the future. As the radical currents have been swept aside by the winds of Right-wing discourse, at least momentarily, it is pertinent to recall the Saidian dictum that "nothing disfigures the intellectuals' public performance as much as trimming, careful silence, patriotic bluster, and retrospective and self-dramatizing prophecy."

Defending the freedom of information and expression is central to our profession. The reason for this priority is clear: without these freedoms, historians cannot discharge their first professional obligation—the pursuit of historical truth—nor their other social responsibilities toward past, present, and future society.[45] The artist and the scholar operating outside party structures and the political establishment can at best sensitize the intelligentsia to the values that are dear to them and lay down the parameters of a healthy and creative debate. They cannot be expected to strictly define the thought processes of young and impressionable minds. In the last quarter of the nineteenth century, the greatest Urdu poet Mirza Ghalib left the following message for future historians:

> I filled the bloodstained pages with the story of my love
> And went on writing, even though my hands were smitten off.

"Useful" uses of history for a nation can include the promotion of conciliation, or the opposite, the promotion of hate or antagonism. The former is precisely what took place in South Africa under the aegis of the Reconciliation Commission. The aims of the Commission were to help the country achieve reconciliation and to engage in a corporate nationwide process of healing through contrition, confession, and forgiveness. That is why the truth is so central to the exercise. I believe we, too, need a Reconciliation Commission to help us build up a shared national identity by interpreting the past independently of state-sponsored ideologies.

At a time when some of "the intellectual barbarians at the disciplinary gates are loitering there with distinctly hostile intent,"[46] it is hard to establish historical truths or to defend the cult of objective historical inquiry. What the professional historian can strive to achieve is to live up to the ideals of intellectual honesty and not allow himself to be controlled or manipulated by various agencies. At a time when knowledge is so highly politicized, the past should not be instrumentalized and distorted for political and other purposes. Liberal and secular-minded professional historians must dictate the ground—the rules for public debates—not ministers and bureaucrats, who raise themselves to the position of irrefutable prophets.

History seeks to discover causal laws connecting different facts, in the same way in which physical sciences discover interconnections between facts. In doing history we hope to derive an enhanced understanding of the past, "ever devouring the transient offspring of the present," in the words of Bertrand Russell. Indeed, history has been a desirable part of everybody's mental furniture because it makes visible and living the growth and greatness of nations, enabling us to extend our hopes beyond the span of our lives. In all these ways, added Russell, knowledge of history is capable of giving rise to statesmanship, and lending our daily thoughts a breadth and scope unattainable by those whose view is limited to the present.

I do not wish to exaggerate the power of a historical education in mitigating the impact of caste or communal prejudices. Yet such training does encourage independence, intellectual integrity, and clear thinking. Therefore those who think these virtues necessary should find it worth teaching.

Is there a breath of fresh air drifting through the pollution that we have been accustomed to take from our normal atmosphere? In 1953 the *Encounter*'s editor sounded the right note: "After the apocalypse come another day. Just another day. But our own." I wish I could share the *Encounter*'s optimism—but recent events, notably in Gujarat, make it hard to do so.

Appendix

TEXT OF DELETIONS MADE FROM NCERT BOOKS

Deleted portions are italicized.

Ancient India, by R. S. Sharma, for Class XI

(a) **Page 7**

A band of scholars took upon themselves not only the mission to reform Indian society but also to reconstruct ancient Indian history in such a manner as to make case for social reforms and, more importantly, for self-government. In doing so most historians were guided by the nationalist ideas of Hindu revivalism, but there was no dearth of scholars who adopted a rationalist and objective approach. *To the second category belongs Rajendra Lal Mitra (1822–1891), who published some Vedic texts and wrote a book entitled Indo-Aryans. A great lover of ancient heritage, he took a rational view of ancient society and produced a forceful tract to show that in ancient times people took beef. Others tried to prove that in spite of its peculiarities the caste system was not basically different from the class system based on division of labor found in preindustrial and ancient societies of Europe.*

(b) **Pages 20–21**

Archaeological evidence should be considered far more important than long family trees given in Puranas. The Puranic tradition could be used to date Rama of Ayodhya around 2000 B.C., but diggings and extensive explorations in Ayodhya do not show any settlement around that date. Similarly, although Krishna plays an important part in the Mahabharata, the earliest inscriptions and sculptural pieces found in Mathura between 200 B.C. and A.D. 300 do not attest his presence. Because of such difficulties the ideas of an epic age based on the Ramayana and Mahabharata has to be discarded, although in the past it formed a chapter in most survey books on ancient India. Of course several stages of social evolution in both the Ramayana and Mahabharata can be detected. This is so because the epics do not belong to a single phase of social evolution; they have undergone several editions, as has been shown earlier in the present chapter.

(c) Page 45

The people living in the chalcolithic age in southeastern Rajasthan, western Madhya Pradesh, western Maharashtra and elsewhere domesticated animals and practised agriculture. They kept cows, sheep, goats, pigs and buffaloes, and hunted deer. Remains of the camel have also been found. But generally they were not acquainted with the horse. Some animal remains are identified as belonging either to the horse or donkey or wild ass. People certainly ate beef, but they did not take pork on any considerable scale. What is remarkable is that these people produced wheat and rice. In addition to these staple crops, they also cultivated bajra. They produced several pulses such as the lentil (masur), black gram, green gram, and grass pea. Almost all these foodgrains have been found at Navdatoli situated on the bank of the Narmada in Maharashtra. Perhaps at no other place in India so many cereals have been discovered as a result of digging. The people of Navdatoli also produced ber and linseed. Cotton was produced in the black cotton soil of the Deccan, and ragi, bajra and several millets were cultivated in the lower Deccan. In eastern India, fish hooks have been found in Bihar and west Bengal, where we also find rice. This suggests that the chalcolithic people in the eastern regions lived on fish and rice, which is still a popular diet in that part of the country. Most settlements in the Banas valley in Rajasthan are small but Ahar and Gilund spread over an area of nearly four hectares.

(d) Page 90

The agricultural economy based on the iron ploughshare required the use of bullocks, and it could not flourish without animal husbandry. But the Vedic practice of killing cattle indiscriminately in sacrifices stood in the way of the progress of new agriculture. The cattle wealth slowly decimated because the cows and bullocks were killed in numerous Vedic sacrifices. The tribal people living on the southern and eastern fringes of Magadha also killed cattle for food. But if the new agrarian economy had to be stable, this killing had to be stopped.

(e) Pages 91–92

According to the Jainas, the origin of Jainism goes back to very ancient times. They believe in twenty-four tirthankaras or great teachers or leaders of their religion. The first tirthankara is believed to be Rishabhadev who was born in Ayodhya. He is said to have laid the foundations for orderly human society. The last, twenty-fourth, tirthankara, was Vardhamana Mahavira who was a contemporary of Gautama Buddha. According to the Jaina tradition, most of the early tirthankaras were born in the middle Ganga basin and attained nirvana in Bihar. The twenty-third tirthankara was Parshvanath who was born in Varanasi. He gave up royal life and became an ascetic. Many teachings of Jainism are attributed to him. According to Jaina tradition, he lived two hundred years before Mahavira. Mahavir is said to be the twenty-fourth.

It is difficult to fix the exact dates of birth and death of Vardhamana Mahavira and Gautama Buddha. According to one tradition, Vardhamana Mahavira was born in 540 B.C. in a village called Kundagrama near Vaishali, which is identical with Basarh in the district of Vaishali, in north Bihar. His father Siddhartha was the head of a famous kshatriya clan called Jnatrika and the ruler of his own area. Mahavira's mother was name Trishala, sister of the Lichchhavi chief Chetaka, whose daughter was wedded to Bimbisara. Thus Mahavira's family was connected with the royal family of Magadha.

In the beginning, Mahavira led the life of a householder, but in the search for truth he abandoned the world at the age of 30 and became an ascetic. He would not stay for more than a day in a village and for more than five days in a town. During next twelve years he meditated, practised austerities of various kinds and endured many hardships. In the thirteenth year, when he had reached the age of 42, he attained Kaivalya (Juan). Through Kaivalya he conquered misery and happiness. Because of this conquest he is known as Mahavira or the great hero or jina, i.e. the conqueror, and his followers are known as Jainas. He propagated his religion for 30 years, and his mission took him to Koshala, Magadha, Mithila, Champa, etc. He passed away at the age of 72 in 468 B.C. at a place called Pavapuri near modern Rajgir. According to another tradition, he was born in 599 B.C. and passed away in 527 B.C.

(f) Pages 137–138

Causes of the Fall of the Maurya Empire

The Magadhan empire, which had been reared by successive wars culminating in the conquest of Kalinga, began to disintegrate after the exit of Ashoka in 232 B.C. Several causes seem to have brought about the decline and fall of the Maurya empire.

Brahmanical Reaction

The brahmanical reaction began as a result of the policy of Ashoka. There is no doubt that Ashoka adopted a tolerant policy and asked the people to respect even the brahmanas. But he prohibited killing of animals and birds, and derided superfluous rituals performed by women. This naturally affected the income of the brahmanas. The antisacrifice attitude of Buddhism and of Ashoka naturally brought loss to the brahmanas, who lived on the gifts made to them in various kinds of sacrifices. Hence in spite of the tolerant policy of Ashoka, the brahmanas developed some kind of antipathy to him. Obviously they were not satisfied with his tolerant policy. They really wanted a policy that would favor them and uphold the existing interests and privileges. Some of the new kingdoms that arose on the ruins of the Maurya empire, were ruled by the brahmanas. The Shungas and the Kanvas, who ruled in Madhya Pradesh and further east on the remnants of the Maurya empire, were brahmanas. Similarly the Satavahanas, who founded a lasting kingdom in the western Deccan and Andhra, claimed to be brahmanas. These brahmana dynasties performed Vedic sacrifices, which were neglected by Ashoka.

(g) Pages 240–241

The Varna System

Religion influenced the formation of social classes in India in a peculiar way. In other ancient societies the duties and functions of social classes were fixed by law which was largely enforced by the state. But in India varna laws enjoyed the sanction of both the state and religion. The functions of priests, warriors, peasants and laborers were defined in law and supposed to have been laid down by divine agencies. Those who departed from their functions and were found guilty of offences were subjected to secular punishments. They had also to perform rituals and penances, all differing according to the varna. Each varna was given not only a social but also a ritualistic recognition. In course of time varnas or social classes and jatis or castes were made hereditary by law and religion. All this was done to ensure that vaishyas produce and pay taxes and shudras serve as laborers so that brahmanas act as priests and kshatriyas as rulers. Based on the division of labor and specialization of occupations, the peculiar institution of the caste system certainly helped the growth of society and economy at the initial stage. The varna system contributed to the development of the state. The producing and laboring classes were disarmed, and gradually each caste was pitted against the other in such a manner that the oppressed ones could not combine against the privileged classes.

The need of carrying out their respective functions was so strongly ingrained in the minds of the various classes that ordinarily they would never think of deviating from their dharma. The Bhagavadgita taught that people should lay down their lives in defense of their own dharma rather than adopt the dharma of others, which would prove danger-ous. The lower orders worked hard in the firm belief that they would deserve a better life in the next world or birth. This belief lessened the intensity and frequency of tensions and conflicts between those who actually produced and those who lived off these producers as princes, priests, officials, soldiers and big merchants. Hence the necessity for exercising coercion against the lower orders was not so strong in ancient India. What was done by slaves and other producing sections in Greece and Rome under the threat of whip was done by the vaishyas and shudras out of conviction formed through brahmanical indoctrina-tion and the varna system.

Ancient India, by Romila Thapar for Class VI

Pages 40–41

Hunting was another common occupation, with elephants, buffaloes, antelopes and boars being the objects of the hunt. Bulls and oxen were used for plowing. The cow held pride of place among the animals because people were dependent on the produce of the cow. *In fact, for special guests beef was served as a mark of honor (although in later centuries brahmans were forbidden to eat beef). A man's life was valued as equal to that of a hundred cows. If a man killed another man, he had to give a hundred cows to the family of the dead man as a punishment.*

Medieval India, by Satish Chandra for Class XI
Pages 237–238

The Sikhs

Although there had been some clashes between the Sikh Guru and the Mughals under Shah Jahan, there was no clash between the Sikhs and Aurangzeb till 1675. In fact, conscious of the growing importance of the Sikhs, Aurangzeb had tried to engage the Guru, and a son of Guru Har Kishan remained at the Court. After his succession as Guru in 1664, Guru Tegh Bahadur journeyed to Bihar, and served with Raja Ram Singh of Amber in Assam. However, in 1675, Guru Tegh Bahadur was arrested with five of his followers, brought to Delhi and executed. The official explanation for this as given in some later Persian sources is that after his return from Assam, the Guru, in association with one Hafiz Adam, a follower of Shaikh Ahmad Sirhindi, had resorted to plunder and rapine, laying waste the whole province of the Punjab. According to Sikh tradition, the execution was due to the intrigues of some members of his family who disputed his succession, and by others who had joined them. But we are also told that Aurangzeb was annoyed because the Guru had converted a few Muslims to Sikhism. There is also the tradition that the Guru was punished because he had raised a protest against the religious persecution of the Hindus in Kashmir by the local governor. However, the persecution of Hindus is not mentioned in any of the histories of Kashmir, including the one written by Narayan Kaul in 1710. Saif Khan, the Mughal governor of Kashmir, is famous as a builder of bridges. He was a humane and broad-minded person who had appointed a Hindu to advise him in administrative matters. His successor after 1671, Iftekhar Khan, was anti-Shia but there are no references to his persecuting the Hindus.

It is not easy to sift the truth from these conflicting accounts. Sikhism had spread to many Jats and Artisans including some from the low castes who were attracted by its simple, egalitarian approach and the prestige of the Guru. Thus, the Guru, while being a religious leader, had also begun to be a rallying point for all those fighting against injustice and oppression. The action of Aurangzeb in breaking even some temples of old standing must have been a new cause of discontent and disaffection to which the Guru gave expression.

While Aurangzeb was out of Delhi at the time of the Guru's execution, acting against rebel Afghans, the Guru's execution could not have been taken without his knowledge or approval. For Aurangzeb, the execution of the Guru was only a law and order question, for the Sikhs the Guru gave up his life in defence of cherished principles.

Whatever the reasons, Aurangzeb's action was unjustified from any point of view and betrayed a narrow approach. The execution of Guru Tegh Bahadur forced the Sikhs to go back to the Punjab hills. It also led to the Sikh movement gradually turning into a military brotherhood. A major contribution in this sphere was made by Guru Govind Singh. He showed considerable organizational ability and founded the military brotherhood or the Khalsa in 1699. Before this, Guru Govind Singh had made his headquarters at Makhowal or Anandpur in the foothills of the Punjab. At first, the local Hindu hill rajas had tried to use the Guru and his followers in their internecine quarrels. But soon the Guru became too powerful and a series of clashes took place between the hill rajas and the Guru, who generally triumphed. The organization of the Khalsa further strengthened the hands of the Guru in this conflict. However, an open breach between the Guru and the hill rajas took place only in 1704, when the combined forces of a number of hill rajas attacked the Guru at Anandpur. The rajas had again to retreat and they pressed the Mughal government to intervene against the Guru on their behalf.

The struggle which followed was thus not a religious struggle. It was partly an offshoot of local rivalries among the Hindu hill rajas and the Sikhs and partly an outcome of the Sikh movement as it had developed. Aurangzeb was concerned with the growing power of the Guru and had asked the Mughal faujdar earlier "to admonish the Guru." He now wrote to the governor of Lahore and the faujdar of Sirhind, Wazir Khan, to aid the hill rajas in their conflict with Guru Govind Singh. The Mughals forces assaulted Anandpur but the Sikhs fought bravely and beat off all assaults. The Mughals and their allies now invested the fort closely. When starvation began inside the fort, the Guru was forced to open the gate apparently on a promise of safe conduct by Wazir Khan. But when the forces of the Guru were crossing a swollen stream, Wazir Khan's forces suddenly attacked. Two of the Guru's sons were captured, and on their refusal to embrace Islam, were beheaded at Sirhind. The Guru lost two of his remaining sons in another battle. After this, the Guru retired to Talwandi and was generally not disturbed.

It is doubtful whether the dastardly action of Wazir Khan against the sons of the Guru was carried out at the instance of Aurangzeb. Aurangzeb, it seems, was not keen to destroy the Guru and wrote to the governor of Lahore "to conciliate the Guru." When the Guru wrote to Aurangzeb in the Deccan, apprising him of the events, Aurangzeb invited him to meet him. Towards the end of 1706, the Guru set out for the Deccan and was on the way when Aurangzeb died. According to some, he had hoped to persuade Aurangzeb to restore Ananadpur to him.

Although Guru Govind Singh was not able to withstand Mughal might for long, or to establish a separate Sikh state, he created a tradition and also forged a weapon for its realization later on. It also showed how an egalitarian religious movement could, under certain circumstances, turn into a political and militaristic movement, and subtly move towards regional independence.

Modern India by Arjun Dev and Indira Arjun Dev for Class VIII
Page 21

Punjab

North of Delhi, the territories of Lahore and Multan were ruled by the Mughal governor. However, as a result of Nadir Shah's and later, Ahmed Shah Abdali's invasions, their power was destroyed and the Sikhs began to emerge as the supreme political power in the area.

Another power that arose in this period in the region around Delhi, Agra and Mathura was that of the Jats. They founded their State at Bharatpur wherefrom they conducted plundering raids in the regions around and participated in the court intrigues at Delhi.

Notes

1. *Mir Taqi Mir.*
2. Love of power (as opposed to lust), in various limited forms, is almost universal. There is, however, a great difference between power desired as a means and power desired as an end in itself. The BJP's crisis of political and moral legitimacy is partly the result of opportunist politics, but mainly the consequence of its own failure to provide good governance; hence the widening chasm between the posturing of leaders and their short-term goals. Gujarat 1998–2000 is live testimony to the utter contempt that the Indian Constitution and the rule of law have been reduced to by the BJP's elected representatives and their VHP and RSS allies. In Uttar Pradesh, the land of Aryavarta, poor governance, combined with the movement for constructing the Ram temple, has exacerbated caste and communal antipathies. What had contributed to the BJP's electoral success was its ability to convince the electorate that it stood for certain principles. Even if one does not scan those principles skeptically, the fact is that they have been willy-nilly consigned to the dustbin of history.
3. See for example Coomi Kapoor, "At the Altar of Tokenism," in the *Indian Express* (January 30, 2002).
4. George G. Iggers, "The Uses and Misuses of History," *Apollon*, Oslo (2000). Available online: http://www.apollon.uio.no/2000_english/focus/misuses.shtml.
5. Lars Hoff, "History For and Against Reconciliation," ibid., pp. 6–7.
6. J. S. Grewal, *Muslim Rule in India: The Assessment of British Historians* (New Delhi: 1970), pp. 171–2.
7. Nonica Datta, *Forming an Identity: A Social History of the Jats* (New Delhi: Oxford University Press, 1999).
8. Partha Chatterjee, "History and the Nationalization of Hinduism," in Vasudha Dalmia and H. von Stietencron (eds.), *Representing Hinduism: The Construction of Religious Traditions and National Identity* (New Delhi: Sage Publications, 1995).
9. Avril A. Powell, "History Textbooks and the Transmission of the Pre-colonial Past in North-western India in the 1860s and 1870s," in Daud Ali (ed.), *Invoking the Past: The Uses Of History in South Asia* (New Delhi: Oxford University Press, 1999).
10. Statistical Abstract of British India, Vol. 23 (London, 1929).
11. Iswari Prasad, Preface to the first edition, 1925, of *History of Medieval India* (Allahabad, 1927), p. ii.

12. All India Modern History Congress, First Session, Poone, June 1935 (Poona, 1938).

13. Report on the Administration of the United Provinces of Agra and Oudh, 1914–1916 (Allahabad, 1916), p. 72.

14. Nirad C. Chaudhuri, *The Autobiography of an Unknown Indian* (New York: Macmillan, 1951), p. 227.

15. Ishtiaq Husain Qureshi, *The Administration of the Sultanate of Delhi* (Lahore: Muhammad Ashraf, 1942), p. 229. The impact of all this is easily seen. Not so long ago, Karnataka was the site of an acrimonious debate with strong communal overtones that centered on Tipu Sultan, one of the key figures in the mythological and historiographical constructions of the subcontinent. In 1990, when the BJP sought a court injunction to prevent the screening of a television serial entitled "The Sword of Tipu," the complainants argued that the series presented Tipu sympathetically, as a secular ruler rather than the fanatical Muslim persecutor of Hindus they imagined him to be. VHP and Bajrang Dal activists have aired the same arguments to decry the state-sponsored celebrations to mark two hundred years of Tipu's martyrdom. The battle lines were drawn between those who insist that the "Tiger of Mysore" was a martyr to the cause of independence, and those who regard him as a tyrant and a Muslim bigot. The fear, then and now, is that the southern states, so far untouched by the great communal debates that have raged in the Indo-Gangetic belt, will soon be embroiled in a protracted controversy.

16. "Introduction," in Ali, *Invoking the Past*, p. 4.

17. Cited in S. Gopal, *Jawaharlal Nehru, A Biography 1946–1956*, Vol. 2 (Delhi, 1999), p. 317.

18. K. M. Munshi contested this view. According to him, "another problem that we have to consider is the persistent demand for the rewriting of history to foster communal unity. To my mind, nothing can be a greater mistake. History, in order to generate faith in it, must be written as the available records testify, without any effort to exaggerate or minimize the actual facts." "Foreword," in R. C. Majumdar (ed.) *Struggle for Freedom* (Bombay, 1969), p. viii.

19. Krishna Kumar's recent book *Prejudice and Pride: School Histories of the Freedom Struggle in India and Pakistan* (New Delhi: Viking, 2002), points to the poor quality of history teaching in schools, its indifference to childhood intellectual development and interest in the past, and its use as a means of ideological indoctrination. Both in India and Pakistan he argues, history is pressed into service to promote the project of nation-building. Consequently, the rival ideologies of nationalism are underlined not to heighten the critical faculties of students but to create a sense of pride in Indian or Pakistani citizenship.

20. It is not intended to equate R. C. Majumdar, a leading historian with astonishing skills, with present-day Hindu polemicists.

21. "Preface," in R.C. Majumdar (ed.), *Struggle For Freedom* (Bombay, 1969), p. xxx.

22. For a powerful refutation of the arguments against their textbooks, see V.C.P. Chaudhary, *Secularism Versus Communalism* (Patna: Navdhara Samiti, 1977).

23. The expression is Praful Bidwai's, and appears in his "Nationalism Gone Berserk," in *Frontline* (February 15, 2002).

24. *The Hindustan Times* (December 19, 1999).

25. Anjali Modi, "Manufacturing Believers," in *The Hindu* (February 10, 2002).

26. Nalini Taneja, *BJP's Assault on Education and Educational Institutions* (New Delhi: A CPI (M) Publication, n.d.), pp. 14–15.

27. Modi, "Manufacturing Believers."

28. Romila Thapar, "Secular Education and the Federal Polity," in *Biblio*, Vol. xxvi, no. 1 (Jan. 2002), pp. 8–9.

29. Irfan Habib points out that by clubbing Medieval India into three units, the NCERT used an age-old trick to sideline a particular topic. While the Delhi Sultanate was classified as "the Rise of the Ghaznavis," the Mughal period was perfunctorily mentioned under the rubric "the Political Conditions." Habib insists that the syllabus is not only anti-Muslim, but also reflects the regional and religious prejudices of the Sangh Parivar. *The Hindu* (February 1, 2002). See also Krishna Kumar, "Curriculum as Politics," in *The Hindustan Times* (February 21, 2002); Krishna Kumar, "Education Reforms: Inspired Incompetence," in *Economic and Political Weekly* (March 2, 2002); and T. K. Rajalakshmi, "Imparting Prejudice," in *Frontline* (February 5, 2002).

30. Interview with Murli Manohar Joshi in *The Indian Express* (January 29, 2002).

31. *The Times of India* (March 16, 1993).

32. Arun Shourie, *A Secular Agenda* (New Delhi: ASA Publications, 1993), p. 19.

33. Madhav Sadashiv Golwalkar, *Bunch of Thoughts* (Bangalore: Jagran Prakashan, 1966), pp. 127–8.

34. Taneja, *BJP's Assault on Education and Educational Institutions*, p. 3.

35. *The Hindu* (December 16, 2001).

36. "Extracts From the Report Of the General Secretaries of the Congress (I) to the Seventh General Conference of the North-East Coordination Committee, Guwahati, 3 July 1992," in Shourie, *Secular Agenda*, p. 302.

37. *Indian Express* (January 31, 2002).

38. David Arnold, "A Time for Science: Past and Present in the Reconstruction of Hindu Science, 1860–1920," in Ali, *Invoking the Past*, p. 156.

39. *The Times of India* (January 10, 2002).

40. *The Hindu* (December 16, 2001).

41. See Saradindu Mukherjee, "Beware of the Academic Fascists," in *The Hindustan Times* (January 23, 2000); and Bhpendra Yadav, "History of the Undoing of History," in *Economic and Political Weekly* (January 19, 2002), for additional references.

42. *The Indian Express* (November 25, 2001).
43. P.L. Malhotra (director, NCERT, 1984–90) and A.K. Sharma (director, 1993–99), "Mutations on the Sky," in *The Hindustan Times* (January 24, 2002).
44. *The Times of India* (November 28, 2001).
45. Antooon De Baets.
46. Richard J. Evans, *In Defence of History* (London: Granta, 1997), p. 8.

V GENDER AND DEMOCRACY

15 "SHED NO MORE BLOOD": WOMEN'S PEACE WORK IN INDIA

Ritu Menon

On July 11, 2004, at 3:30 p.m., Havildar Suresh Kumar in Imphal (Manipur) signed a memo stating that he was arresting Thangjam Manorama Devi, thirty-two years old, a suspected insurgent, explosives expert and hard core member of the banned People's Liberation Army (PLA), according to the arrest warrant. Three hours later she was found dead, having been raped and shot in her vagina.

Nearly six kilometers from where Manorama's body was found lies Irom Sharmila, who has been on an indefinite fast, refusing to eat a morsel since November 2000 in protest against the Armed Forces (Special Powers) Act (AFSPA), in force in Manipur since 1980. The original anti-AFSPA heroine, she is being kept alive by force-feeding.[1]

On July 15, four days after Manorama was killed, the entire country was stunned to see photographs in the national press of a most extraordinary protest by women—fifteen middle-aged women demonstrated naked in front of the gates of Kangla Fort, HQ of the seventeen Assam Rifles, shouting "Indian Army, Rape Us!" "Our anger made us shed us our inhibitions that day," said seventy-five-year-old Thockchom Ramani, secretary of the Women's Social Reformation and Development Samaj. "If necessary, we will die—commit self-immolation to save our innocent sons and daughters."[2]

For over three months the state of Manipur was in turmoil with frequent strikes, bandhs, protests, and demonstrations, demanding that the AFSPA be revoked. Reacting to a spate of custodial and encounter killings, anger and resentment flared across the state at the central government's perceived indifference to their demand for punishing the guilty and revoking the AFSPA by August 15, 2004. Strikes and work stoppage were widespread as protesters took to the streets. Activists of the women's group Meira Paibis (meaning torch-bearers) marched in a candlelight procession through Imphal, and Apunba Lup, an umbrella group of thirty-two civil and human rights organizations, called for civil disobedience against the AFSPA.[3] Manorama's home became a virtual shrine, uniting activists and ordinary people against the act.

The all-women's group Meira Paibis has been one of the most important social organizations in Manipur to resist a wide range of social ills. It was formed initially to mobilize women against alcoholism and rowdyism among Manipuri men, but it has extended its activities to take in other social issues as well, especially the increasing militarization of the state. Among other things, the Meira Paibis have consistently opposed the AFSPA; they have demonstrated, fasted, held protest meetings, and systematically brought abuses by the armed forces to public notice. They have taken up rape cases and volunteered legal help. They have even mediated with the army on occasion, and organized public meetings with them, and they have intervened between civil society and underground groups.[4] These are ordinary women, by no means radical or even subversive, yet they remain undeterred in their demand for the withdrawal of the AFSPA from Manipur. Notwithstanding this history of resistance, the naked protest by fifteen women at the gates of Kangla Fort on July 15 was unprecedented, both as a statement of outrage and for what it signified.

Twenty-five years ago, in February 1984, the Naga Mothers' Association (NMA) was founded in Kohima, the capital of Nagaland, as a voluntary organization open to all Naga women. It was formed in response to more than three decades of violence, armed conflict, and social upheaval in Nagaland, intended to be a forum where issues of concern to Naga women in particular and Naga society in general could be raised. Although its core group consists of elected members, the organization itself has no rules or conditions for membership: all the district tribal women's organizations are its members, and through them it reaches the grass-roots; it also supports local women's organizations in their efforts to stop violence.

Like many other women's organizations in the country, the NMA too started out as a group of mothers dealing with social problems—in particular alcohol abuse, drug addiction, and AIDS. Through these, the mothers were able to mobilize women on a large scale and achieve considerable mass awareness in rural and urban areas. The NMA has set up a drug rehabilitation center and an AIDS care hospice, among other charities. As an organization of mothers, the NMA has consistently highlighted its mothering and healing character; its language of mobilization also revolves around motherhood, to the extent that it eschews formal political representation. Neidonuo Angama, immediate past president of NMA, says, "We have our role to play as mothers, they [the men] have theirs."[5] When the NMA spoke out against "the simply intolerable way" that society was being run both by the Underground (UG) militants and the overground government, it said, "Mothers have the right to speak out and tell them (the leaders) what we want to say, whether they listen or not."[6] When inter-racial warfare between factions in Nagaland escalated alarmingly, the women's groups worked tirelessly to keep the channels of communication open between them. "All of them are our children, we care for them equally, though we do not support their differences," says a village woman elder in Jotsoma. And when the NMA rushed to stem fratricidal violence in Phek district, Neidonuo Angama pleaded, "Before you kill your brother, listen to your mother."[7]

As with all other protracted armed conflict in South Asia, the long years of violence in Nagaland have thoroughly militarized and brutalized Naga society. State violence has been particularly relentless, with whole villages being razed to the ground; torture and encounter killings are commonplace, rape and sexual assault routine, and there are numerous civilian killings and desecration of places of worship.

The whole of Nagaland is under the Armed Forces (Special Powers) Act of 1958, the only state in the Union to have been continuously subjected to it for the last ten years, since 1995. Elsewhere in this study I have elaborated on widespread sexual violence against women by the armed forces in Nagaland; here we wish to focus on the protest against and subsequent intervention by the NMA on *all* violence in the state, in clear recognition of the fact that violence against women will not stop unless all other forms of violence also cease. And so, ten years after it was formed, and departing from its earlier work of mobilizing on drugs, alcohol and AIDS, in August 1994 the NMA launched its "Shed No More Blood" campaign at its Fifth General Body Meeting in Zunheboto. The immediate cause for this plea was the growing number of unclaimed dead bodies lying in the bazaars and streets of towns and cities across the state. The NMA came forward to honor the Naga tradition of giving every unclaimed body a dignified funeral, the deceased draped in the shawl of the tribe to which she or he belonged. August 4, 1994 was designated Mourning Day by the NMA, and more than 3,000 mothers from various tribes attended this memorial meeting.[8] "Can we mothers remain silent, merely waiting to see who is the next victim?" they asked. The mothers, unmindful of their own safety, have prevented local boys from being taken into custody where they would certainly be tortured or killed. On occasion they have negotiated with local commanding officers for their release, going so far as to stand surety for them. They have campaigned for the removal of army posts in towns and army camps in villages targeted by the underground for spreading generalized fear and insecurity, especially among young girls.[9]

It would be fair to say that it was women's groups—all groups, including local organizations, the Naga Women's Union of Manipur (NWUM), and the

NMA—who first protested large-scale human rights violations in the whole Naga territory, by both militants and armed forces, especially cases of sexual assault and abuse. In the Ukhrul district in 1974, for instance, when the army and paramilitary forces were accused of sexual violence against women, local village women got in touch with the district tribal women's organization and organized a mass mobilization for justice. In a case of rape by two NSCN (National Socialist Council of Nagalim) cadres near the Jotsoma bypass in Kohima, the NMA coordinated a meeting between the victim's tribe and NSCN Isak-Muivah (I-M) leaders, following which action was taken against the offenders.

Violence against women aside, the NMA and other women's organizations have continued to highlight the escalation of all kinds of violence in the state, and to negotiate—between the UG and the armed forces, between warring factions of the militants, between tribes, between the Kuki and Meiteis in Manipur, between women's groups—and keep up a sustained dialogue on peace. In a public demonstration of this work, the NMA organized a Peace Rally in Kohima in November 1995 on "Human Integrity and the Consequences of Killing." Ten members from each tribe participated, and representations were made to the governor, the chief minister, and the commandant of Assam Rifles for the withdrawal of the Disturbed Areas Act. In particular, they expressed their disappointment at the lack of action on accusations of rape against the security forces.[10]

The tradition of Pukrelia among the Tangkhul tribe of Nagaland entailed the marriage of a woman from one tribe to a man from another, and goes back to the tribes' head-hunting days. The marriage signified a truce of sorts between them; the woman would intervene by stepping between the two tribes, stretching out her arms and declaring, "Stop, stop fighting. You on my brother's side, and you on my husband's side, stop fighting and let peace prevail for my sake." Rita Manchanda recounts how, in another version of Pukrelia, "if two villages are at war and the death toll is rising, a wise woman has the prerogative to step forward and shake or whip open her *mekhala* (sarong), and by this shaming intervention stop the violence."[11]

The NMA may not be the only association of mothers to have intervened or protested against violence by invoking the power and moral authority of the mother, but they were probably the first to do so in South Asia and certainly the first in India. Curiously enough, they are still the only mothers' front to explicitly protest sexual violence against women. Admittedly, there is no shortage of women in the women's movement who protest violence against women who are also mothers—but motherhood itself is neither the organizing principle underlying their campaigns, nor their primary identity. The Association of the Parents of Disappeared Persons in Kashmir, for instance, set up by Parveena Ahangar, whose son has been missing for the last seventeen years, came into being many years after the NMA; even though its membership is largely female, it has the single-point agenda of locating all those missing persons, often in the hundreds or thousands, so that their families can either get them back or put a dignified closure to their lives, much like the Mothers' Front in Jaffna, Sri Lanka.

The trajectory of the NMA's activism, however, is interesting and unusual for two important reasons: one, it rapidly gained social acceptance and commanded respect in a society where, traditionally, women have been excluded from public activity; and two, its role evolved from that of social worker (attacking alcoholism, drug abuse, and AIDS) to becoming social conscience—that is, demanding accountability *on behalf of society*, as mothers of the Naga community, from the state, from the armed forces, and from the militants. In short, they moved from protest to active intervention, very much in the public sphere, claiming that it was their right and their duty to stop the violence, to see that no more blood was shed. Because they speak as mothers, Neidonuo Angami claims, they are trusted by everyone. Moreover, as Rita Manchanda has elaborated, their political language is an extension of their everyday life—they talk "kitchen politics," providing "a natural, nonthreatening environment for facilitating dialogue in their kitchens, the heart of the Naga home."[12]

The singular and startling contribution of the NMA lies in their assertion that the whole of society is a victim of violence in Nagaland; that as mothers, their concern is with everyone, and they cannot be partisan in their condemnation. Though they can't be called feminist by any means, their stand on violence has been unequivocal. Their campaign has been the longest running and, I would argue, because of this and because it embraces society as a whole, their transition from protest to intervention has been far more clearly articulated and realized. It has also allowed them to enter the political arena through the peace process, another advance on their earlier reluctance to be political.

Like myth, the powerful charge of motherhood has been used by the NMA to mobilize women across the state-rural, urban, tribal, Christian, and non-Christian in their mission to end violence: "We appeal to them as mothers, that we should all work for peace because if a child dies, it touches us, it grieves us. Because for a mother anybody's child is our child."[13] But these mothers, unlike many others in the region, have reached the negotiating table primarily because they did not hesitate to intervene on behalf of everyone—women, militants, the government. As one mother said, "When the Indian army came, it was the women who stepped forward between the villagers and the soldiers, it is only women who can intervene. We constantly had to talk to the army. We mothers would go to the Warring factions, walk to their camps and plead with them not to kill each other and not to harass the villagers. We mothers can't stay quiet."[14] Through their action and their mobilizing the NMA has not only validated a completely alternative and domestic kitchen politics; they have signaled an alternative way of doing politics *and* peace, one that is nonviolent, democratic, and consensual.

The distinguishing feature of conflicts in South Asia over the last fifty years (barring peasant and other struggles for social and economic justice) is that they have been (a) predominantly ethnic or communal, and (b) protracted, and increasingly violent. The most persistent of these have been the armed struggles for self-determination by the Liberation Tigers of Tamil Eelam (LTTE) in Sri Lanka and by separatist groups in Kashmir; others like the Chakma uprising in Bangladesh, the hostilities between the Bodos and recent immigrants in Assam, the Nagas and Kukis in Nagaland, the *muhajirs* in Sind, the Nepalis and "Bhutanese" refugees in Nepal, and the earlier Baloch and Khalsa "nationalisms" in Pakistan and India have more or less established identity politics as an undeniable lingering reality in the region.

The ethnic or communal dimension of South Asian conflicts has had all the well-known, and relatively more closely observed and analyzed, consequences on society and polity. Rada Ivekovic and other political philosophers, speaking of the "majority-minority syndrome," have posited that the very categories are dictated by a communalist principle. Ivekovic says, "Different from *society* which presupposes, among other things, the *social* link between individuals and a shared public space, communities do not themselves recognize either social link or public space in their constitution."[15] Each community, thus, is organized around a paternal pattern. Religious or ethnic communities are, almost by definition, paternalistic and patriarchal; they are therefore rarely emancipatory for women, because they are rarely democratic. And they are not democratic, because the basic requirement of democracy, the individual, is generally subordinated in such collectivities.

Women are the first Other within a community because, as Ivekovic says, they embody the very principle of mixture which is the basis of life in biological terms.[16] They thus represent a dangerous potential for a dilution of the "pure"— ethnic purity is an article of faith for the communalist—which is why both their appropriation by the Other and their control by their own community are a particular characteristic of interethnic violence. In her analysis of recent conflicts, especially in Ireland and Bosnia-Herzegovina, Cynthia Cockburn has developed a succinct and useful classification of gendered power relations in what she calls four moments of armed conflict. They are:

1. The period before armed conflict breaks out, which is often characterized by economic stress and impoverishment; militarization and the presence of increased arms dealing—the marketisation of violence; and identity politics.

2. The period of war and repression itself; the entry of armed forces; the escalation of communal conflict; the disruption of everyday life, and the brutalization of the body, male and female.
3. The period of peacemaking or refusing the logic of violence.
4. The postwar or postconflict period, in which displacement and return, rehabilitation and sometimes reconstruction and reconciliation take place.[17]

I shall attempt a brief examination of three of these moments—namely two, three, and four—and suggest that far from being distinct periods with defined before and after chronologies, in South Asia, at least, they have tended to overlap. One reason for this may well be that armed conflict in the region has usually been very protracted, thus blurring the lines between phases; the other that we are never really in a decisive "postconflict" or conflict-free situation for very long. A gendered analysis of the long duration of such conflicts, then, may enable some fresh insights to emerge.

The protracted nature of contemporary South Asian conflicts has had significant and far-reaching repercussions for all our countries—most evident in sharply escalating military activity and a crackdown by national governments on civilians as well as "terrorists"—but also on everyday life and work, which have experienced a kind of disruption that has not yet been adequately understood or analyzed. "War and terror have the effect, sometimes deliberate, sometimes incidental," says Cockburn, "of rending the fine fabric of everyday life, its interlaced economies, its material systems of support and care, its social networks, the roofs that shelter it."[18] Existing scattered studies note their specific impact on women: the high number of civilian casualties and the very large numbers of refugees and female-headed households; a serious dislocation of social and economic life and a much higher incidence of daily violence. According to preliminary findings in the northeast of India, for instance, the long period of violence has had an adverse impact on the sex ratio not in favor of women (as one might expect), but against them. Paula Banerjee, working on Manipur, reports a decline from 1,015 women to 1,000 men in 1961, to 961 in the 1990s, and in Nagaland, it is down from 933: 1,000 to 890.[19]

The general failure of states across our region to reach politically negotiated, peaceful resolutions of the conflicts in their countries has had one unexpected outcome. It has propelled nongovernmental organizations (NGOs), civil society groups (including businessmen and industrialists), professionals, academics, women's organizations, and sundry peace activists into being more proactive on peace. Together, they have initiated a range of activities both within their countries and across borders, which include everything from research and dialogue to track-two diplomacy and actual relief work.

Men make war and women make peace—this has the kind of clichéd associations that are difficult to shake off, perhaps because there is a kernel of truth in the statement. Women are generally supposed to be nurturing and caring, naturally maternal, and therefore predisposed toward peace, just as men are supposed to be the opposite. Women are more open to mediation, to negotiation and compromise because, it has been suggested, they are obliged to carry on the business of survival and sustenance when all social and economic supports have broken down, and they are often obliged to do so in the absence of their menfolk. And so they are more likely to be found caring for the sick or wounded, in relief and rehabilitation and in rebuilding communities, than carrying guns and going into combat. Because they are also among the worst sufferers in any situation of conflict, armed or otherwise, they are believed to be more inclined toward peace.

Feminist analysis has tried to move away from biological, essentialist, and culturalist arguments in favor of women's tolerance and nonviolence, and suggested instead that "if women have a distinctive angle in peace it is not due to their being 'nurturing' but more to do perhaps, with knowing oppression."[20] Their historical exclusion from structures of power both in the private and public domains, as well as their experience of subjugation, gives them a stake in working for peace and justice—or a just peace—as well as in keeping democracy alive, for it is only through social justice and democracy that they will be able to realize their right to equality. According to this logic, a feminist culture of peace fundamentally critiques unequal structures of domination and is built on learning to live with difference, without aggression.[21]

I would like to suggest an additional factor that may be at work in women's peace activism, and this is their particular, gendered experience of violence in war as well as in supposed peace. As recent empirical work the world over has shown, for women, weapons of war are much the same as weapons of peace; those who wield them in the battlefield or on the front often return home and turn the violence inward. Women have first-hand knowledge of the connected forms of domestic, communal, and political violence that stretches from the home to the street and into the battlefield.[22]

It is the combined experience of oppression and violence, plus the responsibility for survival and sustenance during and in the aftermath of conflict, that I believe provides the strongest impetus to women's peacemaking. Parveena Ahangar's search for her missing son in Kashmir eventually led to the formation of the Association of the Parents of Disappeared Persons (APDP) and to a cry for collective justice. The refusal of the women of Kunan-Poshpora to remain silent about their rapes by the Indian security forces led to the highlighting of military atrocities; the public cursing of the Mothers' Front in Sri Lanka forced the government into acknowledging its role in the disappearance of thousands of young JVPers; the Women in Black, the Madres of the Plaza de Mayo, and the Jaffna Mothers' Front take their private sorrow and make it public, thus not only radicalizing the personal, radicalizing even motherhood, but shaming the institutional and authoritarian. As Rita Manchanda says, "Women's construction of the legitimacy or illegitimacy of conflict is a critical factor in women turning their backs on it. In Kashmir, a turning point in the armed struggle came when Kashmiri women began to shut the door on militants."[23] Elizabeth Jelin, speaking of women's protest against violence and for peace in the Southern Cone of South America, says: "Mothers, relatives, grandmothers and widows erupted in the public arena as the bearers of the social memory of human rights violations."[24]

But is there such a thing as women's practice of peace activism? Do we "do peace" differently from other peace activists, and if so, are these alternative practices effective in the long run? Can they, for instance, work across borders, national as well as regional?

As with economic activity in South Asia, in peace work too, women belong in the informal sector, the informal spaces of politics, which by its very nature affects our practice. The ritualized cursing of the Mothers' Front or the sustained protest by the Mothers of the Plaza de Mayo, indeed the public mobilization of motherhood in the cause of peace and as a direct challenge to the state, are quintessentially "womanist" forms of peace activism. Bearing witness, as happens in the World Courts on Violence Against Women and in various tribunals on violence or other crimes, is not womanist in the same way, but it has radicalized the hitherto marginal and powerless and forced public and institutional notice outside the traditional arenas of such activity—the court, the police station, the executive, and the bureaucracy.

Dialogue and networking have been among the most effective strategies used by the global women's movement, in working for social change as well as in raising awareness. Dialogue that bridges difference and is predicated on respecting that difference is at the other end of the spectrum from what Ranabir Samaddar calls "maximalist friendship."[25] Such a friendship, he says, "like cold war friendship depends on maximum enmity, and then, maximum hostility." Far from being conducive to peace, it kills understanding; the alternative to this is accommodating difference, which, more than solidarity, requires a *politics of understanding*. And it is this politics of understanding, I believe, that women in the region are trying to forge.

Cynthia Cockburn, describing a few notable examples of cross-border peace initiatives by women in Ireland, Israel, and Bosnia-Herzegovina, identifies six characteristics that she believes made the difference between the women's efforts, and others.[26] They are: (i) affirming difference, (ii) nonclosure of identity, (iii) reducing polarization by emphasizing other differences, (iv) an acknowledgement of injustice, (v) defining the agenda, and (vi) group process. Again, these may not be essentially womanist ways of doing peace, but they have been worked at successfully by the three groups she studied, and they are clearly different from conventional Confidence Building Measures (CBMs), two-tracks, and other people-to-people dialogues. Cockburn also draws attention to the importance of recognizing what she calls "the space between us" in peace work—that social and political space in which we separately live and work—in order to craft a politics of understanding.

It is not easy to do.

In Sri Lanka, for example, the Jaffna Mothers' Front and the Sinhala Mothers' Front were unable to cross the ethnic divide; nor could the Naga Mothers Association make common cause with the Watsu Mongdung in north-eastern India. Occasionally groups may come together on specific issues, as national women's groups did in Bangladesh with the Hill Women's Federation, but they part company on issues of national identity. One instance of successful bridge-building, however, is that of the Mohajir Qaumi Mahaz (MQM) and the Women's Action Forum in Karachi.

But the crucial point is that women's fledgling attempts at making peace have highlighted the necessity of transparency and democratic process in any peace accord or negotiation *that will endure*. The inclusion of "marginal" and hitherto unheard voices in this process, painstaking and protracted though it may be, may actually have a better chance of succeeding than that reached through force or subjugation. It may be, as Rita Manchanda says, what "makes the difference between the survival or collapse of otherwise binary and closeted peace processes between armed groups and the state."[27]

Notes

1. *Indian Express,* August 1, 2004.
2. *Tehelka,* August 7, 2004.
3. *Indian Express,* August 10, 2004.
4. Anuradha Chenoy, *Militarism and Women in South Asia* (Delhi: Kali for Women, 2001).
5. Rita Manchanda, *We do More Because We Can: Naga Women in the Peace Process* (Kathmandu: South Asia Forum for Human Rights, 2004), p. 28.
6. Ibid., p. 27.
7. Ibid., p. 43.
8. Ibid., p. 45.
9. Ibid., p. 38.
10. Ibid., p. 45.

11. Ibid., p. 23.
12. Ibid., p. xii.
13. Ibid., p. 62.
14. Ibid., pp. 37–8.
15. Rada Ivekovic, "The Bosnian Paradigm," *Dialogue*, international edition, 9/10, 1998, pp. 61–86.
16. Ibid.
17. Cynthia Cockburn, "The Gendered Dynamics of Armed Conflict and Political Violence," in Caroline O. N. Moser & Fiona C. Clark, *Victims, Perpetrators or Actors? Gender, Armed Conflict and Political Violence* (Delhi: Kali for Women, 2001), pp. 13–28.
18. Cynthia Cockburn, op.cit.
19. Quoted in Rita Manchanda, "Gendering Peace Processes," paper presented at the WISCOMP summer symposium on "Human Security in the New Millennium," Delhi, August 2000.
20. Cynthia Cockburn, *The Space Between Us: Negotiating Gender and National Identities in Conflict* (London: Zed Books, 1998), Introduction.
21. Ibid.
22. Indai Lourdes Sajor (ed.), *Common Grounds: Violence Against Women in War and Armed Conflict Situations* (Philippines: ASCENT, 1998).
23. Rita Manchanda, op.cit.
24. Elizabeth Jelin, *State Repression and the Labours of Memory* (Minneapolis: University of Minnesota Press, 2003), p. xvi.
25. Ranabir Samaddar, "Friends, Foes and Understanding," n.d., unpublished paper.
26. Cynthia Cockburn, *The Space Between Us*, op.cit., pp. 222–30.
27. Rita Manchanda, "Gendering Peace Processes," op.cit.

16 VIOLENT AND VIOLATED WOMEN IN HINDU EXTREMIST POLITICS

Tanika Sarkar

1. Violence Against Women and the Hindu Right

This essay seeks to clarify two sets of activities among Hindu militants in contemporary India, generally known as the Hindutva combine. One relates to the mobilization of a violent female will; the other, to the pattern of male violence against Muslim women during ethnic pogroms. There has been a great deal of violence against Christian women as well, especially against teachers and nuns. That, however, has a logic of its own and merits a separate study.

Let me begin with a few caveats and point out where my representation of these themes departs from, and may even offend, certain categories of secular feminist writings which otherwise form the broad framework of my own understanding. In the first place, the figure of the violent woman of the Hindu Right is an uncomfortable, even unnatural one for Indian feminists who, very understandably, choose to focus on the woman-as-victim-of-patriarchy. The woman who victimizes is incorporated into this form of writing only with a strenuous strategy. She gets translated as a dupe of masculine violence, so imbued with male messages that she has become a clone of her teachers: she is, therefore, desexed, defeminized. In being violent, she acts like a man.

It is true enough that, historically, organized violence has been a male preserve. Male socialization norms, therefore, almost invariably prepare boys for violent or aggressive activities. Nonetheless, there are a few problems that a far-too-quick identification between maleness and violence involves. In the first place, violence and nonviolence are thereby essentialized and biologized as male and female natures. If a woman is violent, she is seen to lose her true identity. This presupposes that violence belongs to the male identity naturally, and not as a result of socialization. That, in turn, hides the vital mediation of an entire ideological apparatus that instills aggressive drives in men and which can, in a new historical context, attempt to do so in women as well. When an extension of the original habitat occurs, we need to attend to the changed conjuncture where violent women are required for a new politics, and to the ways in which women respond to a call for female violence. That investigation is short circuited before it has begun, if we classify violence as irretrievably and naturally male.

Sometimes, the biologized essentialism is refined by calling violence patriarchal rather than male: the specific violence against Muslim women is then derived from the "normal" structures of patriarchal norms that routinely violate women in domestic and public spaces. An undifferentiated and over generalized notion of patriarchy, however, blurs over the dividing line between what is actually normative and open in a patriarchal world and what is shamefaced and happens under cover. No patriarchal norm ever recommends rape, even if conservative social systems tend to minimize or deny male guilt in various ways, sometimes punishing the rape victim rather than the rapist. At the same time, in their formal injunctions, rape is invariably a crime.

When the surreptitious becomes open, when the forbidden becomes the prescribed norm, a critical boundary has been breached, even within patriarchy. This is what happened in Gujarat in 2002, and, to a lesser extent, in the pogroms that followed in the wake of the demolition of the Babri Mosque. In the second half of the essay, I will try and show how a powerful Hindutva ideologue argued that rape of the enemy woman is a historical necessity. To reabsorb this momentous break within the familiar parameters of patriarchy is to deny the radical discontinuity, the new beginning, a different history. It domesticates the extraordinary, and, to that extent, it dims its particular distinctions, even its special horrors. We need new names for it—not patriarchy, nor even fundamentalism.

Sometimes, when we separate out violations of women from other aspects of pogroms, we eschew the ethnic violence that happens against men. Violations of women, then, appear as the chief purpose and function of communalism. I am sorry that my theme allows me to focus on women alone, for Muslim men have suffered equally horribly in pogroms, as have Muslim children. Muslim people, as a whole, are objects of Hindutva hate and aggression, not their women alone. At the same time, there is a distinctive symbolic logic in the pattern of attacks against Muslim female bodies, which, in its turn, derives from the larger Hindutva discourses on history and nationhood.

The gender norms that structure the woman's location in Hindutva political organizations and in Hindu extremist households partly explain why the women of Hindutva become active agents in the hate campaigns. There is a hidden relationship between how Hindutva men and women are taught to live and to relate to each other, and how they are taught to hate Muslim women.

2. Violence and Nationalism

Violence committed by Hindutva militants in India may appear rather feeble by the standards of global violence against Muslims. Nonetheless, it has a few distinctive characteristics that are instructive for an understanding of processes of hegemony formation. In the first place, it unfolds within a democratic form of parliamentary politics. The extent of Hindu consent to ethnic violence and the techniques for its mobilization are, therefore, of critical importance. At the same time, such mobilization happens without an overwhelming electoral victory of the Hindu Right. The Bharatiya Janata Party (BJP), the electoral wing of the Rashtriya Swayamsevak Sangh (RSS), was, indeed, the dominant partner in a coalition that formed the government at the center between 1998 and 2004. But it could be so only with tactical alliances with a host of other parties, not all of them necessarily committed to its policy of ethnic violence. Except for Gujarat, the BJP has rarely held power in any of the states for more than an electoral term.

This thrusts a paradox upon us. On the one hand, Hindutva forces have instigated episodes of violence in many parts of the country in the last two decades, with the complicity of very large and heterogeneous groups of Hindus. On the other hand, that impressive mobilization for violence does not stem from a massive or universal or enduring popular mandate for its governance. We have to conclude, then, that its violent ideology has a certain hegemonic pull, which does not extend to its other activities. Their success in violence thus depends on the forceful language of their rhetoric and imagery, the modes of disseminating the message of hate and the techniques of organizing combatants. In this project, their women have been important agents—in ways that have changed over the years and along with their political circumstances.

We need to elaborate some of the peculiarities of the organizational apparatus in order to understand their remarkable techniques of mobilization.[1] The Hindu Right is a cluster of intricately calibrated, overlapping mass fronts, each with affiliates and subaffiliates of its own. Media reports, which focus on their electoral fortunes, often miss out on the connections that integrate the subaffiliates with the total combine. The Bajrang Dal, the youth wing of the Vishwa Hindu Parishad, for instance, is named as the perpetrators of some of the most spectacular campaigns of violence: against Christians in Orissa, and in the demolition of the Babri Mosque, for example. Media reports do not mention their structural links with the Sangh combine as a whole, nor the intermixing of their members with those from other fronts. As a consequence of the media blindness and ignorance, the more prominent bodies—the Bharatiya Janta Party and the RSS—can escape some of the stigma of lawlessness and ruthlessness that attach to the Bajrang Dal alone. The ceaseless proliferation of different fronts conceals the true scope of Sangh activities.

The combine is self-multiplying, acquiring different names and bodies for different functions. This allows for a delicate and flexible doublespeak to mobilize disparate, even mutually opposed constituencies. A good example would be the BJP's close embrace of neo liberal policies and of foreign multinationals during its term at the Centre. This was counterpointed by the rhetoric of the Sangh's Swadeshi Jagaran Manch, which campaigned for self-sufficiency in indigenous production and for a boycott of foreign goods.

The entire structure is trained by the RSS, which was founded in 1925 and which provides leaders for all the affiliates of the combine. It runs daily training schedules or *shakhas* for combat and ideological training. Its electoral wing is the BJP and its ecclesiastical wing is the Vishwa Hindu Parishad (VHP), which is also very active among Non Resident Indians in the West. The womens' auxiliary of the RSS, the Rashtrasevika Samiti, was founded in 1936.[2] Both Sangh and Samiti have full-time, celibate teachers, the *pracharaks* and the *pracharikas*. They train lay members in the *shakhas* and conduct other pedagogical programs. Through its different fronts, the Sangh combine controls and organizes schools, temples, congregations of priests and religious ascetics, Hindu missionary propaganda, charity, and some minimal welfare work, especially in the tribal belts. It has its own trade union—one of the largest in the country—its students' and teachers' associations. Its bands of cohorts systematically infiltrate into and influence newspapers, TV channels, film and video companies, chambers of businessmen, and army officers. Its sprawl straddles governance, faith, leisure, entertainment, education, and politics. Its organizational structure, consequently, is enormously complex and widespread, biting into most aspects of everyday life, aspiring to very thoroughly make over individuals and collectivities, religion, and political belief.

What is very remarkable about Sangh activities is that not all of them are institutionalized and formal. Much of the significant work happens at everyday levels, through informal conversations, interactions, relationships. At the same time, they are not casual, undirected, or purposeless. The Sangh's genius lies in suffusing quotidian activities with political intent. Women are an important part of its formal organizational structures. But their real and continuous contribution is, perhaps, greater at the level of the ordinary, the everyday.

The Sangh combine has lived through and grown amidst volatile and changing political situations. As a result, the original aims and forms have also changed significantly. If we look at the last two decades—the years when the combine became a decisive force in national politics—we can identify three distinct phases. The period between the late eighties and mid-nineties was the time of growth and expansion, both among the organizations and in their broad influence. This happened through the Ramjanambhoomi movement for the demolition of the Babri Mosque, a mass movement largely of the urban upper-caste, middle-, and lower-middle classes. They achieved, apart from the actual demolition itself, a trail of bloody pogroms in areas where the organizations had, so far, little presence. Riots emerged as the primary mode of short and long-term recruitment, and of expansion.

The gains sharpened their electoral ambitions and the appetite for political power. Between 1998 and 2004, the BJP was the dominant partner in the coalition that controlled the central government. It also ruled over various states. Power sharing meant a certain public caution. Open solicitation for violence had to be reined in and the phase of mass movement was tempered. At the same time, its power ensured that when vicious assassinations or mass genocides did happen—in Orissa against Christians, in Gujarat, against Muslims—central lawkeeping forces did not intervene to stop the actions, and the sheltering of the guilty was managed very effectively.

After it lost power at the center, it seemed to lose a clear sense of direction. The BJP remains the main opposition party and the mass fronts continue to operate and proliferate. At the same time, its dormant mass movements cannot be easily revitalized nor new bases gained without them. The program of mosque demolition and the construction of the Ramjanmbhoomi Temple in its place had powered the earlier phase of agitations. It cannot be switched on again without running the risk of repetitiveness. The relative lack of focus in the present phase carries a dangerous lesson: excess and not moderation in violence may be its most effective weapon, after all. Gujarat remains the only state, which it has held for three terms in succession. At the same time, its earlier violent mass movements had carried the promise of a more disciplined, effective, and cleaner governance, inspired by religious purposes and figures. Its term in power exposed that pretense quite thoroughly, making future movements difficult.

There may, perhaps, be a sharper fault line running now between the people who are primarily concerned with the electoral front and those who work entirely with the RSS: the pursuit of state power has necessitated alliances and compromises that mitigate the totalitarian project of producing a new Hindu subject. Of late, the number of *shakhas* has declined and hardliners complain of a dilution of the earlier discipline among the trained cadres. At the same time, the work of the various mass fronts remains intact, even acquiring some new forms: Hindu bomb factories and terror attacks on mosques masterminded, allegedly, by a female ascetic and an army officer.[3]

What remains constant is the complex organizational multifariousness with multiple and seemingly autonomous fronts working within the capillaries and small veins of civil society.[4] This enables a pattern of protean and creeping growth, corresponding to what Gramsci has termed molecular hegemony, a unit-by-unit expansion in ideological influence. The multifariousness is saved from incoherence or formlessness only by the unity and stability that is conferred upon all constituents of the combine by an invariant agenda of communal hatred, the vision of Hindu nationism or an Indian nation for, by, and of Hindus alone—an agenda of primary importance for all its fronts. Its organizational complexity and thickness, then, contrast with its ideology which is as thin and as monotonous as its organizational forms are diverse.

As early as 1923, V. D. Savarkar, the most creative writer of Hindutva texts, defined the nationism very precisely. All those whose places of worship lie outside the boundaries of India are not Indians, he said, fusing nation and faith together, and branding Indian Muslims and Christians as non- and anti-Indian: hence, less than citizens and, indeed, more of enemy aliens.[5] Golwalkar, the second supreme leader or *sarsanghchalak* of the Sangh, was a great admirer of the Nazi treatment of Jews.[6]

The Hindu Right justifies their nationism with what they call Indian history. A (largely manufactured) history of wars constitutes the central axis for their narrative: wars where Hindus in the past fought, often without success, against foreign invaders, largely Muslims. Wars were allegedly accompanied with temple wrecking, abductions of Hindu women, forced conversions by Muslim rulers, and, finally, with the partition of the subcontinent and the foundation of Pakistan.[7] So wars that led to defeats and losses are as important to the historical narrative as are highly colored accounts of the glories of ancient Hindus when gods, Brahmans, and warrior-kings built magnificent Hindu empires. As with Nazism, a brooding over the hurt of defeats and losses in the past has been the way to ensure and stabilize a Hindu urge for redemptive revenge and violent victories in the present, for internal colonization. Memories of past defeats are a narrative necessity, the condition of vengeful nationhood, of masculinity, and of female virtue. Defeats are always depicted as a source of loss especially of and for Hindu women—during conquests by Muslim dynasties in medieval times, during the civil war that accompanied partition. So, an intimate and persistent connection is built up between Sangh histories and Hindu women. In 1990, when I was one of a group of activists who went to interview the VHP leader of Delhi, B. L. Sharma Prem, we were struck by the meticulousness with which he laid out the connection. Rape of Hindu women was absolutely central to the historical narrative and very skillfully the message of necessary counterrapes of Muslim women was inferred persistently as the condition of the survival of Hindus and of the nation.

Vengefulness extends beyond foreign victorious powers and Indians suspected of being their stooges. It encompasses Muslim and Christian cultural sites and signs as well as western values: discourses of equality, social justice and libertarianism which are ascribed to western influence. The distinction between cultural signs and social-political values is important. But, sometimes, they fuse into one. The VHP attacks the exchange of Valentine Day cards among courting couples as an alien celebration. It also attacks courting couples in public places. With an identical mission, in 2009 a new outfit calling itself, significantly, Ram Sene, savaged some women inside a pub in Mangalore. What is attacked is a commodity or an activity—cards, visibility as a couple, female presence in a place of drinking—supposedly a sign of foreign cultural intrusion. But the real issue is the right to love and to friendship between men and women, the right to exert individual choices in public. In an identical manner, in 1998, the representation of lesbian love in the film *Fire* was attacked by the VHP as foreign, anti-Indian, and theatres screening the film–which had been passed uncut by the Central Board of Film Certification–were attacked and vandalized.

I would suggest that the offensive against "alien" values carries a hidden transcript. By stigmatizing individual rights and social justice as alien, the Hindu Right reinforces existing social hierarchies of caste, class, and gender. To compensate for real equality, the underclasses as well as women are promised an equality in ethnic violence, which will lead them toward Sanskritization or absorption into the culture of dominant powers. At the same time, they have no project for equality or social or gender justice, for poverty alleviation or a minimal safety net, except through charity. So the material bases of domination and subordination remain intact. In this way—insidiously and implicitly, since any explicit statement would jeopardize their electoral status in conditions of universal suffrage—upper-caste and class and male dominance are strengthened and yet transvalued: as authentic Hindu/Indian culture.

3. Women in the Samiti

Much of the regular work of the RSS is quiet, subterranean, informal, and everyday. It depends on personal networks of local exchanges, relationships, and influence, all of which create a thick and dense ideological transmission belt of concepts and convictions. The Rashtrasevika Samiti was formed primarily to train women in RSS households in these functions. They were to take forward the Sangh lessons, morals, and messages into familial, kin group, neighborhood, and workplace sites. Through the continuous, informal, almost casual inputs, the mobilization of children, relatives, neighbors, and colleagues is ensured with a maximum economy of formal effort. Once that is accomplished, these spheres of personal contact can be, from time to time, effortlessly pulled into effective action during moments of violence, elections, and movements. I have heard Samiti members describe how, over the years, they spoke about the Babri Mosque demolition project to all the people they met and knew well, and how their work paid good dividends at last during the actual demolition in 1992. The Samiti trains the wives from non-RSS families who marry into RSS households, just as they train RSS daughters who marry into non-RSS families: about how to influence and remold their new environment.[8]

The Samiti was formed at the behest of female relatives of Nagpur RSS members who actually wanted to join the Sangh and who eventually managed to procure a compromise solution: they would have a women's organization while the Sangh would—as it still does—remain an all male body. At the same time, the training schedule was identical for RSS and Samiti members, involving combat training and antiminorities messages. Combat training for women indicates a paradox of sorts. The Samiti, like the Sangh, had stayed away from all anticolonial movements and movements for gender rights. Its history, till recently, has been nonconfrontational, nonagitational. Why, then, women require martial training? Samiti symbols, moreover, are suffused with invocations of violence and aggression: from combat training to a devout contemplation of the weapons in the arms of their divine icon, to the daily chants which offer the death of the self in the cause of the nation. It appears that if militant political agitations were not made available to the women for a long time, their martial training was meant to impart other immediate, practical advantages. Samiti members explain that martial skills strengthen their physique. This develops self-confidence among their middle-class women who generally come from conservative families in small towns and who have just entered the public domains of education and jobs. Above all, *shakhas* aspire to produce strong, healthy maternal bodies that would produce, in their turn, strong and fierce Hindu extremists.

There was a significant moment of departure from this pattern. In the early 1990s, the Samiti did train some young women to become a part of the demolition squad that destroyed the Babri Mosque in 1992. Apart from this, for most of its life, it has led a low-key, moderate existence in small towns and some big cities of the North and the South West, among middle-class and upper-caste women. It has always desperately lagged behind in strength in relation to radical and Left women's organizations, even at the height of the RSS mass movement over the mosque demolition issue. The Sangh combine, until the early nineties, did not display prominent female politicians among its public figures.

Even after the Samiti was formed, Golwalkar continued to ignore it. His speeches addressed mothers at home who should train preschool children the Sangh values and dispositions—the correct *sanskaras*.[9] The Samiti, for him, was a supplementary effort, to teach mothers what to teach their children. For him, the woman was a domestic and not a political animal as yet. The Samiti does little to disturb the domestic priorities. It does not offer legal counseling even to battered wives; it maintains that domestic discord is the wife's responsibility. It does not join any of the large women's campaigns against dowry, sexual harassment, or domestic violence. It teaches its girls to obey parental discipline and not to assert self-choice in education, work, or marriage.

On the other hand, there are hidden forms of political work that is has always undertaken. Its women tell and retell stories about miracles of Hindu female chastity and submission in ancient times, which allegedly filled women with a sacred energy against enemies of their faith and nation. There is a valorization of strong female warrior queens and goddesses, mythological and historical, who led in battles against demons and enemies. There was, then, an inculcation of transgressive female roles, of female anger and defiance. But that anger is to be directed at non-Hindu Others and not against the social order within which they themselves had been disciplined. In the founding narratives of the Samiti, both possibilities are intertwined. The founder, Mrs. Kelkar, was supposedly moved to great anger when she saw a Hindu woman being molested by criminals, her husband unable to help her. The story gestures at the need for female self-strengthening and at Hindu male culpability. At the same time, she also supposedly wanted to save Hindu women from the allure of "equal rights and economic freedom" which she found to be "unnatural."[10] It is the latter strand that dominates later self-images.

Things changed quite significantly in some respects during the phase of Sangh mass movements. Affiliates spawned female subaffiliates: Durga Vahini and Matri Mandal of the VHP, for instance.[11] The VHP began to publish a women's journal called *Matrishakti*. The BJP sported its women members as its prominent public face: Sushma Swaraj, Vijayraje Scindia, Uma Bharati. Saddhvi Rithambhara's audio casseteted hate speeches were the most effective resource for the Ramjanambhoomi campaign: the intertwining of her ascetic and female identities becoming a sign of the all pervasiveness of the Sangh message of violence.[12]

At this point, in the early 1990s, I did some Delhi-based fieldwork among Samiti women. I found them in an upbeat mood. They were an active part of a phase of violent mass movement that the Sangh had generated all over North

India. Women cadres had participated in the actual demolition job at Ayodhya and that had taken a certain degree of struggle inside the combine. They rejoiced at their doubled victory: the Babri Mosque was destroyed and their men had conceded them a place in the campaign. Their violent commitments had given them a slightly improved bargaining power at home, and earned them the respect of their RSS minded fathers, husbands, and sons. The new freedom and violent commitments went hand in hand; they were interdependent. They were confident enough to express some impatience about familial expectations, especially about early marriage which disrupted their political work. Their journal criticized sexual discrimination in workplaces and in public spaces, if not at home. It taught them how to negotiate these problems.

In the late 1990s, after the BJP had grasped the government at the center, I found them changed.[13] The public role had dwindled, *shakhas* were declining in numbers and recruitment was primarily from middle-aged housewives or the elderly. They had called their journal *Jagriti* earlier. The name signified awakening and the picture on the cover page showed a woman striding away confidently. Now it had been renamed *Sevika,* or the Woman Who Serves. Installed as the ruling power, the combine had distanced itself from mass movements and women now retreated to a more domestic role that they used to play earlier. Some of the tentative self-assertion and questioning that I had noticed earlier was gone, and conservatism about social issues had become far more pronounced. I heard strong denunciations of the concepts of equality and rights, about their foreign origins and their disruptive influence at home. That particular accent had been relatively absent in the earlier phase. Their organizational activities had declined as well. Daily *shakhas* had largely disappeared, they had come biweekly or even once a week affairs, and the members were now overwhelmingly older women and housewives, not young working girls or students.

Two aspects were, nonetheless, carried over from the earlier phase. At no point of time, could they think of anything meaningful to say about problems of Indian poverty or about caste. When in 1999, I asked a senior Samiti member what she would identify as the greatest problem for India, she could not come up with an answer for a long time. Finally, she said, rape of Hindu women by Muslims, adding, in answer to my question, that domestic sexual abuse or Hindu rapists were not a real problem. They were equally silent about caste. Their young women had been very active in 1990 in the protests against the extension of caste reservations to Other Backward Castes. In fact, their newfound public status in education and jobs stitched them more closely with the caste/class interests of their men, in ways that older housewives would not have been.[14]

In the late 1990s, they fulminated against lesbian love and its representation in films: sliding easily from censorship of emotions to censoring freedom of expression. Both were destructive foreign values, they said. At the same time, they explicitly said that their women were free to wear western clothes and use foreign cosmetics, to visit beauty parlors. Young women should look attractive to their husbands, they said. There was, then, a trade off between foreign commodities, which were permissible and foreign values which were proscribed. A consumerist individualism was encouraged whereas individual freedoms in love, self-expression, and life choices were not.

On the whole, then, there was a pronounced conservatism in gender thinking rather than a definite fundamentalism. What still ensured female loyalties to the Sangh agenda if the public profiling of their activism had declined along with spaces for political work and if the Sangh combine steadfastly refused to address gender inequities on their own terms?

If the disavowal of the politics of equal rights has become more explicit than before, it is important to point out that this did not, as yet, involve an annulment of the existing basket of opportunities for women from these conservative families who had entered the public domain only recently. They were still allowed education and jobs,[15] and they were directed toward fashion products, albeit within well-laid-out domestic constraints. Their political life was, indeed, encouraged and if much of it was conducted in domestic exchanges, they were still inspired by the dazzling female political figures that the BJP flaunts in Parliament and in state politics. What it involved, rather, was a closure of the horizon of future possibilities: of freedom, self-determination, equality. Above all, they were integrated with the men of the Sangh because they had a certain equality in generating violent compulsions and intentions, though in their own and different ways. The tenor of their hate speech remained constant, violently abusive, and aggressive, full of misinformation and manipulativeness.

I concluded, from very extensive conversations, that there still operated a women's politics that remained crucial to Sangh functioning. Women had once more been restored to the more conventional roles of domesticated mothers and wives, but these roles and functions have become profoundly political and purposeful. It is not a decline as such, but a shift in the register of activism. Women retreat into the immediate and the familiar circles to introduce and consolidate Sangh messages through intimate exchanges, personal networks, and informal conversations. They proudly told us that in the course of these they would reinterpret daily news because newspapers, especially the English ones, were prejudiced. They also would provide information that the media did not provide. They became counselors and leaders within kin groups, workplaces, neighborhood associations, temple complexes, sessions of *bhajans* or congregational devotional music, and local yoga centers. A steady drip-drip-drip of the Sangh intentions and commands would thus percolate through everyday interactions, creating a potential support base, electoral as well as violent and confrontational, ready for future harvesting. Mass mobilization was accomplished on intimate terms, through gossip channels in female sociabilities and kin group or workplace contacts.[16] The pattern strongly recalls what Kathleen. M. Blee described as "a poison squad of whispering women" of the Ku Klux Klan in the southern states of the United States in the 1920s.

4. Violence Against Muslims

The third round of fieldwork that I did was in 2002, when I visited the riot-torn areas of Ahmedabad as a part of the Concerned Citizen's Tribunal: this time, to listen to devastated Muslim survivors in the shelters. There had been public, open, unhidden sexual torture and rapes of Muslim women in Gujarat: prolonged flogging of female bodies, followed by gang rapes, mutilation of sexual organs, dismemberment of body parts, insertion of weapons into the vagina, tearing apart of pregnant wombs, and cutting up of fetuses. Women of the Hindu Right had been present on such occasions, they cheered and enjoyed the spectacles and the reports.[17] This requires of us an explanation of why the Muslim woman's body proved to be such an irresistible site of prolonged, varied, and public torture and destruction, providing an excess beyond rape and killing. I will refer to an elaborate structure of arguments, which are heard in the daily *shakhas*, in daily conversations, in temple discourses, and in RSS texts. They circulate so massively and in so constant a manner that, over the years, they have formed a part of a popular Hindu commonsense.

A part of this comes from the demographic myth that the Sangh combine spreads so diligently: about excessive breeding by Muslims that will make Hindu India a Muslim-dominated country in no time. I have attended a Delhi meeting organized by the prestigious Presidency College alumni, which included several senior civil servants.[18] They played methodological havoc with census data to reach strange conclusions about this dangerous overabundance. Several assumptions structure this myth, which is now a part of a wide commonsense, going beyond committed Sangh constituencies. It is supposedly a combination of over fecund Muslim female bodies and of overactive Muslim male lust, which makes them take four wives. The Muslim growth rate is, therefore, four times as much as the Hindu one. Not only do Muslims breed more, Muslim births are construed as acts of aggression, infiltration, occupation, and expansion—all of which diminish Hindus in India. The Muslim woman's sexual and reproductive organs, even the baby in her womb, thus appear as powerful political enemies, engaged in a war against the Hindu numerical majority. This calls out for counterattacks against the woman and the child, against her sexual reproductive organs and against her womb, more specifically. It also calls out for counterrapes of Muslim women for Hindus lost out to Muslims because they were not ready to rape: Muslims, therefore, had little to fear from them. The Muslim woman's body is thus invested with a dual evil: in its contrast with the bodies of Hindu women who were violated by Muslim men while her body is intact, and in its function as the source of endless Muslim growth. Its destruction is, therefore, a condition of Hindu survival, it is a legitimate symbolic site of Hindu revenge, it should pay for the humiliation and violation of Hindu women. The dividing line between the symbolic and the real, the imagined past and the lived present is very thin. Abduction, rape, and impregnation of Hindu women by Muslims continued in the same way, it is said, in the partition violence. It must, therefore, be regarded as a present danger as well, potential or actual.

So intense is the conviction in Muslim rapes and so absolute the desire for revenge that when I interviewed a senior Samiti leader in 1999 about the rapes of Muslim women, she did not even bother to deny that these had happened. She justified it: "They have raped so many of us, we must now rape some of them." Her own self doubled up as both the rapist and the rape victim; she appropriated both genders.

V. D. Savarkar, the creator of the Sangh ideology and their sense of history, elaborated this narrative and its logic and message at great length in his book on the relationship between the Hindu Maratha rulers and the imperial Mughals.[19] Rape was a political weapon for Muslims, he argued, and because great Hindu warriors like Shivaji would not use that against captive Muslim women, Hindus lost the most important deterrent in their wars: the only fear that could have kept the Muslims away from Hindu land and women. India was lost for want of Hindu rapes. The lesson is amply clear. Rape is necessary and just, as revenge and as self-defense. It is an act of faith, of patriotism.

Not only is rape justified, but also the killing of little babies, because they are the children of enemies: something that happened on rather a grand scale in Gujarat in the anti-Muslim riots of February 2002. Once again, Savarkar naturalized the idea in his book about the great popular uprising against British rule in 1857. He dwelt compulsively on images of massacre—of women and children in particular. He spoke of how babies were torn out of British wombs by Indian patriots, how women were killed in such numbers that Indian soldiers had to wade through a sea of blood, how children clinging to their mothers were beheaded as mothers watched, how children trying to escape were dragged back and thrown into wells. Patriotism must learn to be ruthless, he said, and "one does not spare the litter of poisonous snakes."[20]

What enables the positive reception of such messages? Partly their constancy and the weight of endless repetition through numerous and diverse channels of communication: lessons in RSS schools, popular literature and media products, *shakhas*. The medium of instruction is predominantly storytelling—an occasion that so enraptures the listener that she forgets to ask about the source and to evaluate the authenticity of the event it depicts. Stories compel complicity; they avoid critical enquiries and queries for authentication. Lalit Vachani's documentary film underlines the importance of storytelling as a pedagogical tool in the *shakhas*.[21]

But who can be a better storyteller than the mother: the first person to captivate the infant mind with marvelous tales that remain indelible early memories, received in total belief? M. Golwalkar had urged mothers of RSS families to initiate the child's first education at home by telling him stories of Hindu warrior heroes, of patriotic wars.[22] If he did not see the woman as a worthy member of organizations, he certainly gave her a crucial role at home: he made motherhood a political act. And a political act of a very precise kind: one that implants in impressionable, innocent mind, images of violence and revenge. Stories are not any more modes of emotional bonding, a shared universe of tender imagination, something that will stay in the child's mind as a place of wonder and deep affect. The Hindutva mother creates tales for her child not with love, not to teach love, but to train him in hatred. Through such tellings, the child is transfigured: from a child to a Sangh worker.

Saddhvi Rithambhara, a female ascetic of the VHP, produced a famous audiocassette in 1990 that was broadcast in public places continuously in the riot-torn days in the early 1990s. She describes the ideal Hindu mother as one who teaches the child how to hate and kill for revenge. She first calls her a mother but, later, changes the word to *konkh* or womb. The meaning is contracted. The woman becomes literally an organ to breed hate: she gives birth in anger, and she gives birth *to* anger.

Once again, however, it was Savarkar who first rewrote motherhood. For him, the woman is beautiful only when she is a mother, when she feeds the child at her breast: a conventional enough image of maternal nurture. But, abruptly, there is a shift in meaning. The human mother is transfigured as a lioness who sits at the site of the kill, blood-smeared, and suckles her cub in the middle of the gory remains of the prey—giving her cubs the first lesson in the absolute necessity for violence. Thus alone, the cubs grow up as lions. What is remarkable about the transfiguration of motherhood is not merely the positivity of hate. More important is the deliberate evacuation of gentleness and peace from situations where they most properly belong: the mother with the baby at her breast.

Savarkar effected a major transvaluation of values with a powerful language and with his personal reputation for heroic patriotism that made his words all the more memorable: rape and the killing of innocents as necessary and just, mothers as teachers of violence in their most tender moments. The Sangh combine developed many and varied modes of retelling the messages. The transvaluation involves women as motifs and as active agents. Women have complied admirably, exercising rightwing agency to reshape domestic and maternal functions.

Notes

1. On this see Tapan Basu et al., *Khaki Shorts and Saffron Flags: A Critique of the Hindu Right*, Delhi: Orient Longman, 1993.

2. On the Samiti, see Tanika Sarkar, "Heroic Women, Mother Goddesses: Family and Organisation in Hindutva Politics," in Sarkar and Butalia, eds., *Women and the Hindu Right*, Delhi: Kali for Women, 1995; Paula Bachhetta, "Hindu Nationalist Women as Ideologues: The Sangh, the Samiti and Their Differential Concepts of the Hindu Nation," in Christophe Jaffrelot, ed., *The Sangh Parivar: A Reader*, Delhi: Oxford University Press, 2005. See also Bachhetta, "Communal Property/Sexual Property: On Representations of Muslim Women in a Hindu Nationalist Discourse," in Zoya Hasan, ed., *Forging Identities: Gender, Communities and the State*, Delhi: Kali for Women, 1994.

3. On recent investigations into Hindu bomb factories, see Rana Ayyub, "Counter Terror" and "The Fiery and Fanatical Saddvi," in *Tehelka*, November 15, 2008.

4. For a discussion of some of these fronts, see Shubh Mathur, *The Everyday Life of Hindu Nationalism: An Ethnographic Account*, Delhi: Three Essays Collective, 2008.

5. V. D. Savarkar, *Hindutva*, Bombay: Swatantrya Veer Savarkar Rashtriya Smarak, 1999, Seventh Edition.

6. M. S. Golwalkar, *We, Or Our Nationhood Defined*, Nagpur: Bharat Prakashan, 1938, p. 27.

7. On the rhetoric and myths about conquests which masquerade as history, see Purushottam Agarwal, "Surat, Savarkar and Draupadi: Legitimising Rape as A Political Weapon" in Sarkar and Butalia, *Women and the Hindu Right*.

8. Tanika Sarkar, "The Woman as Communal Subject: Rashtrasevika Samiti and Ramjanambhoomi Movement," *Economic and Political Weekly*, November 10, 1990.

9. M. S. Golwalkar, *Bunch of Thoughts*, Bangalore: Jagarana, 1980.

10. Sarkar, "The Woman as Communal Subject."

11. On the VHP organizations, see Manjari Katju, *Visva Hindu Parishad and Indian Politics*, Delhi: Orient BlackSwan, 2003.

12. Amrita Basu, "Feminism Inverted: The Gendered Imagery and Real Women of Hindu Nationalism," in Sarkar and Butalia, *Women and the Hindu Right*. Also Tanika Sarkar, "Aspects of Contemporary Hindutva Theology: The Voice of Saddhvi Rithambhara," in *Hindu Wife, Hindu Nation: Community, Religion and Cultural Nationalism*, Delhi, 2001.

13. Tanika Sarkar, "The Gender Predicament of the Hindu Right," in K. N. Panikkar, ed, *The Concerned Indian's Guide to Communalism*, New Delhi: Viking, 1999.

14. V. Geetha and T. V. Jayanthi, "Women, Hindutva and the Politics of Caste in Tamil Nadu," in Sarkar and Butalia, *Women and the Hindu Right*.

15. In this the situation is strikingly different from that in Nazi Germany, where a legal abolition of many of the freedoms and rights that had expanded in Weimar times occurred. See Claudia Koonz, *Mothers in the Fatherland: Women, the Family and Nazi Politics*, London: Methuen, 1988.

16. Blee, *Women of the Klan: Racism and Gender in the 1920s*, Berkeley: University of California Press, 1991, pp. 123–53.

17. See Rakesh Sharma's documentary film on this, *The Final Solution*, 1993.

18. On the dimensions of this myth and about its refutation, see Patricia and Roger Jeffrey, *Contesting Hindutva Demography*, Delhi, 2006.

19. V. D. Savarkar, *The Six Glorious Epochs of Indian History*, Delhi: Bal Savarkar, 1971, p. 124.

20. Cited from Savarkar's *First War of Independence*, in Jyotirmaya Sharma, *Hindutva: Exploring the Idea of Hindu Nationalism*, Delhi: Penguin, 2003, pp. 146–8.

21. *The Boy in the Branch*, documentary film made for Channel 4, 1990.

22. Golwalkar, *Bunch of Thoughts*.

VI INDIA'S POLITICS ON THE US STAGE

17 SPEAKING ABOUT, FOR, TO, AGAINST, AND WITH HINDUS: SCHOLARS AND PRACTITIONERS IN THE DIASPORIC POSTCOLONIAL MOMENT

Paul B. Courtright

There is a well-known story that Hindus have told for centuries. It goes like this. Once, long ago, there was only a great ocean, and it was without form and void. All the gods and demons gathered there. They took a huge pole and wrapped around the middle of it a great serpent. Then the gods and the demons each taking one end of the serpent began to churn the ocean. Slowly, as they churned, all the good things of life began to appear, especially milk, the elixir of life and immortality. Then, as they continued churning, the milk began to turn to poison and contaminate everything it touched. The story presents the opposing forces, gods and demons, competing for the prize of immortality, power, *dharma*, and truth; and offers a cautionary note about the limits of desire, even for the good things of life. It's not so much that the gods are good and the demons are evil (each group has its virtues and vices); it's that both groups want the same things, but pull in opposite directions to get them. According to one telling of the story, the universe is saved only when the great god Shiva, who is immortal—he was never born and cannot die—drinks the poison and rescues the gods, constrains the demons, and preserves the world order.

I offer this story as an allegorical frame within which to describe a recent moment of contest in the academic arena between India studies, the study of religion, and Hindu nationalism in the context of American higher education. My comments will focus briefly on three locales of this churning: an overview of the study of religion as an academic discipline, my own experience as a scholar of Hinduism being churned by various voices that describe themselves as speaking for all Hindus, and some of what I hope are constructive reflections on where scholars and practitioners might churn forward toward less toxic and more nurturing results. There is much by way of background that could be explored regarding the emergence of a militant Hindu nationalism in India in recent decades and its relation to the middle-class professional Indian diaspora in the United States and its anxieties and concerns about how India is presented within American education, media, and popular culture. My purpose here is to explore a particular case that resides within this larger framework, a case with which I have some personal familiarity.

1. The Academic Study of Religion

Within many contemporary colleges and universities there are departments within the general area of the humanities that engage in the academic study of religion or religious studies. These programs are relative newcomers into the liberal arts tradition and are largely unique to the United States and Canada, along with a few programs in the United Kingdom, Australia, and New Zealand. They emerged from two sources: from the study of Christian theology in nineteenth-century Europe in the context of learning about the variety of religious traditions that were becoming increasingly familiar in the encounters of colonial domination, and from the development of area studies as interdisciplinary approaches to various culturally distinctive parts of the world.

The emergence of the modern university as a center for rational inquiry and the disenchantment of the world brought by rationality left religion aside as an artifact of an earlier mindset that was embedded in magic and superstition. Alongside this inclination toward disenchanted knowledge, however, came a certain disenchantment with this disenchantment. Religious studies' own genealogy is to be found within this process of a disenchanting discourse venturing into the not-yet or not-ever disenchanted worlds of religion. In other words, the secular turn away from religion as a normative world created a vacuum into which the study of religion could venture as a discourse allied with scientific or historical inquiries of the nineteenth-century university in what was called a "science of religion." The core question religious studies has been asking is whether or how human beings may be generically religious, or whether or how in some moments or under some conditions, some human beings, may be religious. The corollary question follows: What is the distinctive content of religion? This question itself only came into view as the development of the academy shifted out from the hegemony of Christian tradition and into something called secular culture. Once a nontheological space was established, religion came into focus in a new way. At the same time the expansion of the West into the larger world through colonial domination provided a vast new repertoire of texts, practices, and cultures—data—to think about human beings as having something that may be called "religion."[1]

Looking at various religious communities and traditions comparatively in historical and ethnographic frameworks, foregrounding rituals, practices, narratives, architectures, iconographies, and cosmologies (notions of a general order of existence), gave religious studies much of its subject matter. Drawing upon a repertoire of approaches—historical, anthropological, philosophical, psychological, and psychoanalytic, and categories and approaches religious communities themselves use in interpreting their own practices—religious studies has been attempting to render a critical appreciation of human capacities in their specific settings and comparatively across various cultural landscapes. As a child (or perhaps grandchild) of the Western Enlightenment tradition of the pursuit of objective knowledge—however fragile that quest may seem today—it is also important to note what religious studies does *not* do. It does not promote a particular religious perspective as normative; that is the work of theology. It does not attempt to speak for or against a particular religious tradition. It does not attempt to invent a meta-religion that is imagined to lie somewhere beneath historical religious traditions. By following these basic intellectual practices, religious studies is able to provide a hospitable locale where believers and nonbelievers can engage in shared inquiry about what religion does, how it shapes and is shaped by its historical contexts, and what insights it may offer to what we might call the general human condition. Religious studies takes up its residence in the university, not in religious institutions. In the American context, where many colleges and universities maintain affiliation with religious traditions, religious studies programs are often hypervigilant about their intellectual autonomy.

Religious studies' conversation partners are other disciplines in the arts and sciences, and the public. As a comparative, pluralistic, and multimethodological activity, religious studies as I have described it does not therefore claim to be totally objective. Like the fields of literary studies, history, and the arts, religious studies has what Amartya Sen calls "positionality," or positional objectivity. Every discourse has a history, and religious studies continues to work through category formations that were drawn from Christian theology toward more comprehensive conceptual frameworks for understanding religion. For example, thirty years ago scholars described the group of Hindu rituals called *samskara* as "sacrament," a term drawn from the Christian tradition. Contemporary studies and textbooks are more likely to translate *samskara* as "life-cycle ritual"—a category drawn from the social sciences—or, closer to its indigenous meaning, "perfection." Indeed, we are closer to a discourse in which basic categories of other religions need not be translated at all, but become part of the vocabulary of the field. For example, how might one think differently about Christian rituals if one spoke of the *samskara* of baptism in addition to understanding it as the sacrament of baptism?

This process of developing a more generic set of categories is ongoing. I have argued in my work on Hinduism that categories of religious practice that emerge historically from that tradition such as *darshan, pratishtha*, and *bhakti*, when applied to other religious contexts such as Christian eucharist, illuminate their meanings in important and sometimes surprising ways.[2] Like other disciplines, religious studies has its own set of rules, practices, and expectations for those who participate in it. These include the study of languages and primary texts, ethnographic fieldwork, and acquaintance with a variety of approaches and theories, many developed in other disciplines, which require critique and adaptation to religious studies' own subject matter. There is a dialectic between identifying the positionality of who and what is being interpreted and the who that is doing the interpreting. Neither is totally fixed, but reciprocal, interactive, and provisional.

2. Religious Studies and the Study of Hinduism

Turning now to the study of Hinduism as a world religion, it is important to remind ourselves of the history of Western interpretations of Hinduism and India more generally. From ancient Greco-Roman writers through early modern travelers to colonial administrators to the Beatles, India has functioned often as the West's exotic "other." This other came onto the screen of Euro-American imagination in ambivalent images: as bizarre, depraved, inspiring, sublime, and in need of supervision in its own landscape by colonial management and reform. The academic study of India's religions has had to navigate its way through these multiple sets of representations as it goes about its research and publication. From this general profile of the academic study of religion and Hinduism, let me now turn to my own experience of churning.

As one who grew up in the early years of the academic study of religion, I directed my own research toward the Hindu god Ganesha, in two major settings: the narrative traditions of the *puranas*, and the practices of Hindu devotees in Maharashtra as I learned about them in the early 1970s.[3] I was guided by the principles outlined above and attempted to identify major themes in the narratives in relation to the interpretations of Ganesha I had gathered while in India, and I also explored potential meanings they might have that emerged from applying various interpretive frameworks that were part of religious studies itself: principally, structural analysis and psychoanalysis, both of which were approaches widely used at the time. The bulk of the book was actually an attempt at a description of what people in Maharashtra did in their homes, communities, and public festivities. The book came out in 1985 and had, like most monographs, slowly migrated into obscurity, or so I thought. In the years since the completion of that book I have turned to other topics.

Then, in 2001, Motilal Banarsidass Publishers, a press that specializes in scholarly books on Indological topics, brought out an Indian edition, along with a new preface, and with a cover selected by the publishers. In September of 2002, events took a surreal and menacing turn on the semireal landscape of the World Wide Web. There, on that flat-world terrain, appeared one Mr. Rajiv Malhotra, a self-described "Indian American public intellectual and philanthropist," who wrote on his blog:

> The India Studies industry consists of the development of knowledge about India, as well as its distribution and retailing. It includes India-related academic research, school and college education about India and its culture, media portrayals of India, independent think tanks work on India, government policymaking on India and corporate strategic planning of India. The impact of India Studies also includes the diffusion of ideas about India to Indians, many of whom are ignorant and/or even suffer from cultural shame.[4]

In order to exert supervision over the fields of India studies, Malhotra recommends that "a knowledgeable Diaspora evaluation and monitoring committee [should be appointed] to oversee what goes on in each program, and don't just leave it to the university scholars to send you status reports. The committee should attend classes, read the publications of the department and participate in the events organized."[5]

Such a proposal implies a privileged ownership by the Indian diaspora in the United States of knowledge about India. It also presupposes that scholars should, in effect, work for the diaspora and submit their research to the discipline of the diaspora's interests in presenting India as a commodity to the American public. Malhotra also published a much-read blog entitled "Wendy's Child Syndrome," a lengthy polemic against several scholars: Wendy Doniger, Jeffrey Kripal, Sarah Caldwell, and me, arguing that we had engaged in interpretations of Hinduism that drew upon psychoanalytic theory (an approach which, he claimed, had been long discredited in the field of psychology), and that our books emphasized sexuality in ways that denigrated the Hindu tradition. What he did not explain, and to my knowledge has not yet addressed, is the question of why the category of sexuality "denigrates" Hinduism. One way or another all religious traditions address issues of sexuality as part of the human—and divine—experience. Why should Hinduism be exempted from such an inquiry?

Turning to the mechanisms of knowledge production about Hinduism, Malhotra alleged that there exists what he calls a "cartel" that controls what knowledge is transmitted. This imagined gathering of scholars, academic institutions, publishing companies, and funding agencies, he claims, present Hinduism in a negative light. He argues that the children of the Hindu diaspora are encountering such denigrations in their courses in colleges, a negativity that reinforced a corrosive sense of humiliation and embarrassment among young Hindus growing up in America. He offers no evidence beyond one anecdotal response from a young Hindu American woman commenting on her experience in high school. He calls on his readers to become more proactive in scrutinizing the academic study of religion and sounds an alarm that Hindu culture in the American diaspora is being poorly served by such negative representations. He noted that barely one fifth of the scholars and teachers of courses on Hinduism in American colleges and universities are themselves Hindu.

This point, implicitly, puts forth the "insider/outsider" dichotomy: only those who are themselves existentially formed by Hinduism have the sufficient experience, authority, and perspective to teach the religion appropriately. He continues, "This concentration of power is exacerbated by the fact that humanities scholars within a given discipline typically have an inner circle or cabal that closes ranks, vitiating the policy of peer reviews. Ideologies and political agendas often drive the direction and interpretation of research, producing vastly distorted images of the subject." With respect to religious studies specifically, he continues, "Religious Studies is based on the use of mainly non-Indian categories. This discipline is witnessing a recent trend to interpret Indian culture using Freudian theories to eroticize, denigrate and trivialize Indian spirituality."[6] Malhotra links psychoanalysis, eroticism, denigration, and trivialization in a string that leads from a descriptive statement to an evaluative and polemical conclusion. It's not clear what he means by a "trend"; in any given year there are perhaps fifty to a hundred academic books on Hinduism published, and perhaps one in a hundred draws upon Freud in any significant way.

3. A Personal Narrative

Regarding my own book on Ganesha specifically, Malhotra gathered up a dozen or so quotations in which I suggested that one reading of the stories of his creation by Parvati, beheading, and adoption by Shiva may be read, from a psychoanalytic perspective, as an exploration of the primal dynamics of mother-son-father/

husband relationships. I made two analogies to which Malhotra took particular umbrage: that Ganesha's trunk might be read as a caricature of Shiva's *linga*, and that Ganesha's doorway location as the guardian of his mother's private chambers was structurally parallel to the role played by eunuchs in protecting the harem. Malhotra cherry-picked a few sentences out of a 280 page book, disregarding the core argument of the book as an appreciative reading of the depth and profundity of a tradition that might, to Western readers—to whom the book was originally directed—seem exotic or incomprehensible. The irony here, of course, is that Malhotra is adopting the very stereotyping and caricaturing he accuses India studies of doing about India.

Within a few months, the idea that a western scholar had represented Ganesha's trunk as symbolizing a limp phallus and argued that he resembled a eunuch seized the imaginations of some of Malhotra's readers both in India and America. Web blogs flourished denouncing my book, alleging that I was "anti-Hindu" and that my intent was to malign the great Hindu religion. The attack shifted from the content of the book to my motives and integrity as a person. To my knowledge, few if any of those engaging in the denunciations actually read the book. In response to a number of hostile e-mails I replied that I would be willing to have a discussion about the book on the condition that my attackers actually read it. That hardly seemed to me to be an inappropriate or burdensome condition. I got no takers to my offer.

The president of one chapter of the Hindu Student Council, an undergraduate affiliate organization of the Vishva Hindu Parishad in America, presumably with the approval of his faculty advisor, posted a Web petition calling for the withdrawal of the book, an apology from me, and some disciplinary activity to be taken by my university such that I no longer be permitted to teach courses on Hinduism. Within a few days about 5,000 signatures and comments were posted, some calling for my death. In Atlanta, where my university is located, a group calling itself "the Concerned Citizens" wrote a similar petition to the president of my university. My department chair received phone calls demanding to know why I had not been fired, or why she had not publicly denounced me. The Concerned Citizens, including some who flew in from elsewhere, asked to meet with my dean, which he agreed to do at my encouragement. They presented their perspective, including the recommendation that Emory should set up some kind of oversight committee including community members to discipline the teaching of Hinduism and India studies so that "negative" representations could be corrected. The dean subsequently notified the Concerned Citizens that he found no evidence in my scholarship or teaching of any attempt to denigrate Hinduism, and that my application of psychoanalytic interpretations were consistent with its use in a number of fields from history, literary studies, cultural studies, and religion.

This period of several months was, for me personally—and for my family—disturbing. I went to India in December of 2003 to a New Delhi conference on the study of Hinduism supported in part by the Infinity Foundation, whose president was Mr. Malhotra. I'm happy to say that there were no incidents of harassment or aggression. Indeed, most of the scholars I met in India were not aware of the controversy. Many expressed regret and embarrassment that such bullying tactics were being used in the United States. The situation with the Indian publisher was not so benign, however. The editor recounted to me that regrettably he was obliged to withdraw the book from their list. In addition to allegations of the offensiveness of the contents of the book—at least those parts dealing with the "limp phallus"—the cover was denounced as being pornographic. The cover depicted an elephant faced toddler, crawling, with appropriate anatomical specificity. No explanation was offered by the offended parties as to why the body of a toddler constituted pornography, at least in their minds. A few months later, I found an almost identical image of the child Ganesha in a local Indian supermarket in the section selling images and ritual supplies.

One of the questions this whole episode raised for me (as it might have for Freud) includes, as I wrote to Malhotra at the time, "What is it about the phallus?" Most of the denunciations of scholars' work on Hinduism that have been circulating around the Web focus on masculinity, particularly some notion of alleged compromised masculinity: limp phallus, eunuchs, and homoerotic mysticism (in the case of Jeffrey Kripal's study of Ramakrishna). So far as I can tell, the vast majority of the blogs and petitions attacking my book have come mainly from diaspora males. I don't have an adequate explanation for this, nor am I attempting any psychoanalysis of the Hindu diaspora. But I do think it is noteworthy that the frequent use of terms of "denigration, disgust, pornographic, perverse" that have been used gather around the notion of masculinity and emerge around the same time that the issues of Rama as the ideal male warrior and Hindutva appeals to heroic displays of manhood were central to the discourse around the destruction of the Babri mosque at Ayodhya in 1992. Martha Nussbaum's study of the dynamics of shame, the categories of disgust, and aggression in the context of violence in Gujarat in 2002 speaks to many of these multilayered issues. I found a similar, though much less lethal, version of that in my own experience. Here the violence has to do with rhetoric of humiliation from scholars and the academic study of religion, with occasional eruptions of cyber-hooliganism.

From the perspective of Hindu nationalist voices in the United States, scholarly interpretations of Hinduism, when they attempt to interpret sub-textual levels of stories, rituals, and symbols—especially when conducted by non-Hindu, non-Indian interpreters—become instances of predatory misrepresentation. Aggression against such interpretations is warranted and justified in order to protect the purity of the tradition from the contaminating influence of "outsider" representations.

4. A Global Blessing

One of the features of the emerging global culture is that, like people, ideas, and commodities, stories migrate across national boundaries. Myths, like religions, have no owners. They don't come with brand names, trademarks, or copyrights. Stories invite interpretations from anyone who reads them or hears them. In the case of the Ganesha story, no doubt Hindus bring a vast reservoir of knowledge, memories, and associations that give it life and meaning. But for those outside the tradition within which the story maintains its primary home, the call to interpret within another context is also compelling.

The well-known American poet and cultural critic, Robert Bly, wrote a chapter on Ganesha in his book *The Sibling Society*. He learned about Ganesha from a conversation we had once at a conference several years ago. I sent him a copy of the book, and he made the following observations about the relevance of the Ganesha story for understanding contemporary American culture:

> People are noticing that the Oedipus story is becoming less and less applicable to our present society. It doesn't describe current father-son relations. Not only do men not want to kill their father; many have never even met him. Father-longing is beginning to replace father-anger. The longing is palpable in maximum security prisons, as well as kindergartens, where small boys tend to hold onto the legs of any man who enters the room and don't want to let him go.[7]

This is an extraordinary claim coming from a poet and writer, that a Hindu story brings more prescient insights about contemporary American culture than Oedipus—the foundational myth of the modern family! In discussing the story of Ganesha guarding the door to his mother's private chamber, Bly notes,

> I think the Ganesha story is a blessing. It fits our current society more closely than the Oedipus story, which we're all tired of anyway. Women in the United States are resecuring some of their sovereignty; and that is very good. Sons often feel more weight now in their relationships with their mothers than with their fathers . . . Through the details of the Ganesha story we can sense the complicated feelings that some sons of single mothers and absent fathers have, feelings we rarely pictured in paternalistic

literature and art . . . The story brings in fresh viewpoints, and it may model new father-son and mother-son relationships that allow continuity and "proximity."[8]

So here is an example of a non-Hindu, attempting to speak to areas of cultural and social longing in an American context, who finds a Hindu story offering significant interpretive power in a situation quite far, geographically and historically, from its origins. This is an example of Hinduism's gift to the world. As for the "psychoanalytic" reading of Ganesha's story, the interpretation that brought down a hail of abuse from my critics, I don't know whether the story would have come into view for a writer like Robert Bly, a non-Hindu and non-Indologist but one who resonates to mythic themes from Freudian and Jungian perspectives. Through Bly's voice the story of Ganesha made its healing way into an important insight about American culture and its discontents. It is precisely the public domain dimension of the migration of stories that extends their reach and recontextualizes their meanings.

While scholars working within the field of religious studies are taught to strive toward the vanishing horizon of objectivity, the subject matter of religion itself draws one into the life-worlds being studied. In light of my own experience noted above, the question comes back: What about my own relationship with Ganesha? In the process of researching the stories, ceremonies, and meanings of Ganesha I developed my own connection to this deity. While not a Hindu in the sense of being born into the tradition, or a convert to it, I do keep an image of Ganesha over the door to my home. It is there not as a trophy or a souvenir but as an ever-present reminder of the thresholds of life, of beginnings and obstacles and the ways in which the ordinary comings and goings through the doorways of life are moments to reflect on the larger significance of what do we in the world. I do not claim to speak for Hindus, but about them, and sometimes to them. I speak against Hindus only when they accuse me of mendacity in my motivation. Like everyone else, I don't like being bullied or lied about. At the end of the day I think a fair reading of my own work and that of my colleagues in the study of Hinduism, and the work produced by the field of religious studies more broadly, were it to be undertaken by those in the Hindu diaspora with open minds, will disclose a critical appreciation for an extraordinarily rich and various display of human achievement.

Scholarly writing on religion is a different genre than devotional writing. Each has a different purpose. As India's visibility rises in American society, there has never been a more urgent time for Hindus in America and American scholars who study their religion to arrive at a mutually respectful relationship. Broadside, uninformed, and ad hominem attacks on scholars reveal a weak and defensive self-image on the part of the attackers. These bullies who claim to speak for them have poorly served Hindus in the United States. Hindus, in India or the United States, have nothing to apologize for, or be embarrassed about. Every religion has its virtues and vices. The highest form of respect scholars can offer is to take their subject matter seriously, engage it critically, and acknowledge the incompleteness of their interpretations. This environment of freedom and mutual understanding offers the best hope for everyone concerned. As more Indian Americans enter the field of religious studies it will be further enriched. Hindu American parents can make a critical contribution in supporting their own children's aspirations to become scholars of their heritage, confident that critical engagement in that heritage will make an important difference in bringing Hinduism's particular perspectives to enlarge the humanity we all share.

Notes

1. See Walter Capps, *Religious Studies: The Making of a Discipline*. Minneapolis: Fortress Press, 1995; Mark C. Taylor, ed., *Critical Terms in Religious Studies*. Chicago: University of Chicago Press, 1998.

2. "Looking at Eucharist through the Lens of *Puja*: An Experiment in the Comparative Study of Religion." *International Journal of Hindu Studies*, 2/3, 1998, pp. 423–440.

3. Paul B. Courtright, *Ganesha: Lord of Obstacles, Lord of Beginnings*. New York: Oxford University Press, 1985; Delhi: Motilal Banarsidass, 2001.

4. www.sulekha.comiblogs/blogdisplay.aspOcid.4715. Accessed Feb. 22, 2006.

5. Rajiv Malhotra, "Does South Asian Studies Undermine India," htip://rediii.comllnews/2003/dec/08rajiv.htm. Accessed Nov. 7, 2005.

6. www.sulekha.com/blogs/blogdisplay.aspx?cid.4715. Accessed Feb. 22, 2006.

7. Robert Bly, *The Sibling Society*. Reading, MA: Addison-Wesley, 1996, p. 67.

8. Ibid., p. 72.

18 THE FIGHT FOR THE HISTORY OF HINDUISM IN THE ACADEMY

Wendy Doniger

1. Introduction

One of the many reasons why I took up the study of ancient Hinduism and Sanskrit as a freshman at Radcliffe in 1958 was to escape from my red diaper childhood, to avoid politics. In retrospect my reasoning seems to resemble that of the man who, in the 1930s, realized that a great war was gathering in Europe and decided to escape it by moving to a far-off place no one had heard of or cared about—Iwo Jima (smack in the middle of the South Pacific theatre of war).[1] For writing about the ancient history of Hinduism has now become highly politicized.

2. Hindutva

The problem arises with Hindutva ("Hindu-ness"), a territorial and racial conception of Hinduism and a form of fundamentalism. There are many ways to define fundamentalism, but, as US Justice Potter Stewart remarked of pornography, I know it when I see it, and in this context I would define fundamentalism as a fanatical disapproval of people, both inside one's own religion and outside, who deviate from a narrowly defined essence of that religion. The three primary advocates of Hindutva ideologies are the Rashtriya Swayamsevak Sangh (RSS, National Volunteers' Organization), the Vishva Hindu Parishad (VHP, World Hindu Council), and the Bharatiya Janata Party (BJP, Peoples' Party of India), often known collectively as the Sangha (with perhaps unfortunate, perhaps intended, resonances with the Sangha as the ancient term for Buddhism), and sometimes called the Hindutvavadis ("Those who speak for Hindutva").

In many ways, Hindu fundamentalism, while protesting that it is a reaction against European pressures, actually apes Protestant evangelical strategies, with its emphasis on the priority of personal experience (conversion and reaffiliation) justifying a new definition of "Hindu" that has to do with an experience of Hindu-ness ("If you do not meditate, you cannot understand the Upanishads," someone objected after one of my lectures). As fundamentalism raised its ugly head in the twentieth century among the major monotheisms (Judaism, Christianity, and Islam), Hinduism, too, caught the virus, and used the Western weapons of mass cultural destruction—television, the blogosphere—to broadcast its message of repression (of the wrong sort of Hindus) and hatred (of Muslims and Christians). Hindus of this persuasion have attempted, as Amartya Sen eloquently expressed it, "to miniaturize the broad idea of a large India—proud of its heterodox past and its pluralist present—and to replace it by the stamp of a small India, bundled around a drastically down-sized version of Hinduism."[2] Their hatred is directed not only against Hindus of the more diverse traditions but also, ironically, against the very monotheisms that started the rot (including the insistence that Hinduism is monotheistic[3]) in Hinduism: Islam and Christianity. The good news is that the other sort of Hinduism, the full screen, pluralist, creative sort, remains in the majority, and it, too, can call up mass media to rally its forces. There is an irony in the observation that the Hindutvavadis learned much of their anti-Western identity politics from the West, but they also have older, more culturally particular and relevant beefs (if I may use that word), many of them stemming from the still gaping wound left in India by the centuries of the British occupation.

Protestant missionaries within the British Raj in the nineteenth century tried to recast Hinduism as a monotheism, with a Bible (sometimes the Gita, sometimes the Laws of Manu, neither of which had ever before had anything remotely approaching canonical status) and a newly central, quasi-universalist ideology (often called Sanatana Dharma, or Eternal Dharma). In lifting up this monolithic form of Hinduism, the British (and the many Hindus who followed them) trampled down and largely wrote off the dominant strain of Hinduism that celebrated the multiplicity of the divine, the plurality of forms of worship. But they could not kill it; indeed, most Hindus of this type didn't even know that they were regarded as either beneath contempt or entirely nonexistent. They went on worshipping their gods, singing their songs, telling their stories.

3. Hindu History in India

In an article titled "India: The War Over History,"[4] the historian William Dalrymple reviewed a number of recent books about Indian history whose authors have been attacked—through words, threats, occasionally blows—by reactionary forces in India. He listed some of the most egregious examples of the rewriting of school history books in India and general misrepresentations of the history of Hinduism, a list to which, alas, many new examples have been added, or resurrected, since he wrote, in 2005. One of my favorites is P. N. Oak's argument (in *Tajmahal: The True Story*, first published in 1989) that the Taj Mahal is not a Islamic mausoleum but an ancient Shiva Temple, which the Mughal emperor Shah Jahan commandeered from the then Maharaja of Jaipur, that the term Taj Mahal is not a Persian (from Arabic) phrase meaning "crown of palaces," but a corrupt form of the Sanskrit term Tejo Mahalaya signifying a Shiva Temple, and that persons connected with the repair and the maintenance of the Taj have seen the Shiva Linga and other idols sealed in the thick walls and in chambers in the secret, sealed red stone stories below the marble basement.

To take another example: the only shocking thing about Dwijendra Narayan Jha's book *The Myth of the Holy Cow* is the news that anyone has been shocked by the argument that people used to eat beef in ancient India.[5] (Whether they ate castrated steers, as most beef-eaters do, or cows in the particular sense of the female of the species, is the only ambiguous point, and Jha marshals Vedic texts that suggest that they sometimes ate cows, though generally just steers.) Yet the cover of the book proudly proclaims "A Book the Government of India Demands be Ritually Burned," and the flyleaf assures us that the book has been "banned by the Hyderabad Civil Court and the author's life has been threatened." The *Observer* likened the book's reception to that of Salman Rushdie's *Satanic Verses*, and even the more-PC-than-thou (and now defunct) *Lingua Franca* felt that the case was sexy/trendy enough to justify a notice that the book "was pulled from the country's shelves." Jha was so violently attacked, physically as well as in the press, that he had to have a police escort 24 hours a day for several years after his book was published in India. The shocked resistance to the idea that Hindus ever ate beef inheres, for some, in the fact that it contradicts the party line of the Hindutvavadis, who argue that We Hindus have always been here in India, and have Never Eaten Cows; Those Muslims have come in, and Kill and Eat Cows, and therefore must be banished or destroyed.

In 2010, six elderly gentlemen brought a criminal suit against Penguin, India, and me, demanding that my book, *The Hindus: An Alternative History*,[6] be withdrawn from publication and all extant issues destroyed. They argued that the book had offended them, thus violating an Indian law that makes it a criminal offense to offend any religious group. In February, 2014, Penguin, India, decided not to go on defending the suit, and agreed to withdraw the book from publication and to pulp all remaining copies. In fact, not a single book was destroyed; Penguin had only a few copies in stock in house, and all the copies in the bookstores were quickly bought up. Outside of India, sales of the book soared astronomically; in India, many PDF's were downloaded from several Indian websites established for that purpose. Penguin Indian sold the New York edition on its website, and booksellers sold that edition in the Delhi airport and Khan Market. More important, there was an astonishing volume of international protest against Penguin's actions and against the censoring law; a number of academic institutions issued protests, and thousands of individuals signed petitions. There was terrific media coverage. The storm is still raging as I write this, on March 11, 2014, and I am hopeful that much good will come of it all in the long run. But it certainly was a low-water mark in the history of censorship in India. And it may well serve to make Indian publishers increasingly wary of publishing books that challenge Hindutva ideologies.

4. Textbooks on Hinduism in America

We have seen that same process at work in the United States, too. Hindutvavadis first attempted to revise school textbooks in India (literally cutting out the pages dealing with Islam among world religions, and making other, equally radical changes), but more recently the field of battle has shifted to attempts to revise American textbooks.

The March 6, 2000, *San Francisco Chronicle* printed an article, "A Different Agenda," by Romila Thapar and Michael Witzel, about the attempts of the Hindu Sangha to alter school textbooks. They wrote: "Initially, the goals of these pressure groups seem benign, and even righteous. They aim to rectify culturally biased and insensitive depictions of India and Hinduism, and they would like Hinduism to be treated with the same respect as Christianity, Judaism, and Islam." These goals are entirely justified. Time and again, when I give a public lecture in the United States, no matter what I talk about, the first question from the American audience is, "What about the caste system?" Most textbooks, too, dwell upon, and exaggerate, the human abuses in the caste system and pay insufficient attention to the rest of Hinduism. But some of the Hindu interest groups have demanded that the textbooks not mention the caste system at all, which is as bad a distortion as the overemphasis on it. And this is not all that is at stake, as Thapar and Witzel went on to point out:

> If such reasonable changes comprised the full extent of the desired amendments, there would be no controversy. There are, however, other agendas being pushed that are oddly familiar: the first Indian civilization is 1,900 million years old, the Ramayana and Mahabharata are historical texts to be understood literally, and ancient Hindu scriptures contain

precise calculations of the speed of light and exact distances between planets in the solar system. . . . By spelling God with a capital letter they are trying to position Hinduism as monotheistic, making it look more "modern."

In October 2005, the Vedic Foundation and the Hindu Education Foundation met with an ad-hoc committee that included a consortium of California Department of Education staff and persuaded them to approve a number of changes in the way that school textbooks presented Hinduism. The changes involved such matters as pushing back the dates of major milestones in Indian history. (This is an old, old fight that began early in the European encounter with India: many Hindus today regard Hinduism as timeless, but they tend to date this timelessness at 10,000 B.C.E. or earlier, while the British generally used to put it much later.) It also involved erasing or minimizing features of Hinduism that could be perceived as negative, such as the social category of untouchables (Dalits), and the status of women. A host of prominent historians and scholars of South Asia, including many Hindus, protested against this,[7] urging the Board not to allow a religious chauvinism of India to become the policy of the State of California. Eventually, the scholars won; most of the proposed changes were not made. In February 2009, the Federal District Court of California ruled resoundingly against the Hindu interest groups that had brought a subsequent suit.

But the damage had been done. Charles Burress, writing in the March 10, 2006, *San Francisco Chronicle* commented:

> Even though the board refused many of the changes sought by activist groups this time, the conflict could still impact future textbooks with publishers being tempted to soften the content on their own initiative, said Stanford University professor of education Sam Wineburg. "Publishers will tread on this territory ever more lightly," Wineburg said. . . "The result," said Gilbert Sewall, director of the American Textbook Council, "is textbook editors censor themselves. They fall all over themselves to try to cater to one pressure group."

Self-censorship has indeed caused many scholars, especially young scholars still without the armor of tenure, not only to bite their tongues and hold back their true judgments on many sensitive issues, but even to refrain from tackling such topics at all—until, they tell themselves, they get tenure. But the sad truth is that generally by the time they do get tenure they have forgotten what it was that they wanted to say.

It is important to note that there is as much variation in the attitudes of the Hindu diaspora as there is among Hindus in India. Many American Hindus, both inside and outside the academic community, objected to the more extreme textbook changes. But it is also true that extremists in the American Hindu diaspora have fueled Hindutva in India, and elsewhere in the world, with both financial support and ideological fury.

5. Hindutva and History

What is the relevance of history to this conflict? Sumit Sarkar has pointed out, in his excellent essay "Hindutva and History,"[8] several reasons why control over the writing of history is so central to Hindu nationalism, including the fact that the Hindutvavadis need the historical myths to rally their own quite diverse people, to establish their own identity as a unique and uniform group. The situation is well summarized by Amanda Huffer Lucia:

> They have much to lose from the accurate historical account. The accurate historical account would illustrate the Sangha's complacency with British rule in the years leading up to Partition. It would admit to Savarkar's initial agreement with Jinnah's two-nation theory on Nov 15, 1943 and the cover-up thereafter. It would implicate the RSS in the assassination of Mahatma Gandhi. It would reveal the complexities of the Sangha's ambivalent position on the caste system. With regard to ancient Indian history, it would refute the equation of Hindu with Aryan and subsequently deny the ethnic theory of Hindus as a superior race. It would bring to light institutionalized discrimination along the lines of caste and gender in the Hindu tradition. Ultimately, it would undermine the Sangha's claims to eternal righteousness and legitimacy based on an antiquated timeline of Hindu civilization. Certainly, the Sangha has enormous incentive to create a new and more complimentary version of history.[9]

That is why they care about history, and why good historical study does indeed hit the Sangha where it hurts.

There are also lessons to be learned from the academic discipline of the history of religions. If we could prove, for instance, that human sacrifice was attested in the ancient Sanskrit texts (and humans were, at least theoretically, included in the list of sacrificial victims or *pashus*, in the *Brahmanas*, c. 800 B.C.E., along with horses, cows, goats, and sheep), would that justify human sacrifice today? Not logically or legally, but to a certain type of reactionary religious mind it would indeed; the past is a very important template for the present; we must do in the present what our ancestors did *in illo tempore*, as the historian of religions Mircea Eliade taught us to call the paradigmatic past. And for many centuries, people in India have supported their arguments for particular religious ideas by insisting that those ideas come from the Vedas, and that the Vedas date from the dawn of time. The word "Veda," that once, for me, meant a beautiful, mysterious, and wise ancient text, now often signals a rallying call for fundamentalism, jingoism, and chauvinism.

6. Myth and History

Hinduism is as rich in history as it is in myth, but they are not the same thing, and we have to be careful how we use history and myth to understand each other. In this context I would define a myth as a story that a group of people believe for a long time despite massive evidence that it is not actually true; the spirit of myth is the spirit of Oz: pay no attention to the man behind the curtain. Myths reveal to us the history of sentiments rather than events, motivations rather than movements. When we read a text that says that a Hindu king impaled eight thousand Jains,[10] we need to use history to understand myth—that is, we need to know a bit of history to understand why such a text was composed and retold many times: that means knowing the reasons for the tensions between Hindus and Jains at that time (such as the competition for royal patronage). But we cannot use the myth to reconstruct the actual history behind the text; we cannot say that the text is evidence that a Hindu king actually did impale Jains. To take another example, when the *Ramayana* speaks of ogres (Rakshasas), it may be simultaneously constructing an imaginary world in which evil forces take forms that can destroy us and using ogres as a metaphor for particular types of human beings. But it does not record an actual event, a moment when people from Ayodhya overcame real people in India (tribals, or Dravidians, or anyone else), nor does the story of the building of a causeway to an island that the text calls Lanka mean that Rama and a bunch of monkeys actually built a causeway from India to present-day (Sri)Lanka. Yet this mythical causeway was real enough, in September of 2007, to put an end to a major Indian Government project to build a canal through the area where Rama's bridge was said to be.[11]

But stories, and the ideas in stories, do influence history in the other direction, into the future. People who heard or read that story about the impaled Jains may well have acted differently toward Jains and/or Hindus (better or worse) as a result. More often than not, we do not know precisely what happened in history, but we often know the stories that people tell about it. In some ways, the stories are not only all that we have access to, but all that people at the time, and later, had access to and hence all that drove the events that followed. Real events and sentiments produce symbols, symbols produce real events and sentiments, and real and symbolic levels may be simultaneously present in a single text. Myth has been called "the smoke of history,"[12] and we must constantly strive to separate the smoke of myth from the fire of historical events, as well as to demonstrate how myths too become fires when they do not merely respond to historical events (as smoke arises from fire) but drive them (as fire gives rise to smoke). Ideas are facts too; the belief, whether true or false, that the British were greasing cartridges with animal fat, started a revolution in India in 1857.[13] For we are what we imagine, as much as what we do.

To say (as I do) that the *Ramayana* tells us a great deal about attitudes toward various social groups (including women and the lower castes) in the early centuries C.E. is a far cry from saying that someone named Rama actually lived in the city now known as Ayodhya and fought a battle on the island now known as Sri Lanka with a bunch of talking monkeys on his side and a ten-headed demon on the other—or with a bunch of tribal peoples (represented as monkeys) on his side and a proto-Muslim monster on the other— as some contemporary Hindus have asserted. Rama left no archeological or inscriptional record. There is no evidence that anyone named Rama did or did not live in Ayodhya; other places, too, claim him, in South India as well as North India, for the *Ramayana* was retold many times, in many different Indian languages, with significant variations. There is no second Troy here for a Schliemann to come along and discover. Or, rather, there is a second, and a third, and a nineteenth Troy for anyone to discover.

Placing the *Ramayana* in its historical contexts demonstrates that it is a work of fiction, created by human authors who lived at various times, and shows how the human imagination transformed the actual circumstance of the historical period into something far more beautiful, terrible, challenging, and elevating than the circumstances themselves. Texts reveal histories, but we need to find out about those histories and ground them in solid evidence to read against, not into, the texts' narratives. Reconstructing the ways in which human authors constructed the fictional works, in reaction to earlier texts as well as to historical circumstances, reveals their texts as works of art rather than records of actual events.[14]

Though I would characterize myth in general, and Hindu myth in particular, as "the positive connotation of something culturally richer and psychologically more revealing than history alone, a portal into civilization's inner self,"[15] to borrow David Arnold's words, myth also has, like the supernatural creatures it portrays, its dark side, as Arnold continues:

> Myth-making can be the deliberate, self-interested falsification of history. The myths surrounding the eleventh-century sack of the temple of Somnath are a case in point, but increasingly in America and across the globalized world [there is] a new kind of Hindu mythologizing, in which moral conformity is being imposed on a religion that once had reason to rejoice in its decentred plurality, and where myths, which once survived because of their ability to speak to the human condition, can now be exploited by the power of the internet. The televised *Ramayana* shown in India has, for many ideologues, become the only acceptable form of what were once, and still should be, the many *Ramayanas*. The . . . textual tradition [is] threatened by those who claim to be its guardians, and who would make of something as rich as myth something as routine as religion.[16]

7. Is Writing Well the Best Defense?

What, if anything, can we as historians do to combat the positioning of false myths, in particular politically driven false myths, as true history? Dalrymple lamented the absence of "accessible, well-written, and balanced histories of India," and concluded that "this as much as anything else has allowed myths to replace history among the members of India's middle class . . . Here perhaps lies one of the central causes of the current impasse. It is not just up to the politicians to improve the fairness and quality of India's history. Unless Indian historians learn to make their work intelligible and attractive to a wider audience, and especially to their own voraciously literate middle class, unhistorical myths will continue to flourish."[17] Michel Foucault and Edward Said, among others, have taught us that scholarship is often deeply implicated in creating the political mess in the first place, but scholarship has demonstrated far less power to clean the mess up; like the sorcerer's apprentice, or Frankenstein, or the scientists on the Manhattan Project in Chicago, scholars create imperialist monsters that they cannot control but merely watch, aghast, from the sidelines, crying, "No, no, put it *down*!!!" The trouble with the strategy of out-writing the opposition is that the Hindutva rank and file by and large do not read scholarly writings, but merely parrot what their leaders (who may or may not read) say, generally on the Internet. When I received a furious e-mail from a Hindu who objected to what I had said about Hinduism, and I replied and asked him to tell me which of my books, and precisely what statements in them, had offended him, he replied, "I would never read any of your books."

Salman Rushdie, in *Midnight's Children*, imagined a private version of radio, a magic ether by which the children born at midnight on the day of India's Independence communicated, and now we have that in reality, the website, the chatroom, the listserve, the blog from outer space. Unfortunately, a self-selecting, small, but vociferous group of disaffected Hindus have used this Indian ether to communicate with one another within what is perceived as a community. This accounts in large part for the proliferation of these groups and for the magnitude of the reaction to any incident, within just a few hours; it's more fun than video games, and a lot more dangerous, too. Another radio metaphor comes to mind, from two American films in which a bomber pilot is instructed to *turn off his radio* as soon as he gets the command to bomb, so that he will not listen to false counterinstructions.[18] It is this tendency to tune out all other messages that characterizes the blog mentality of the Hindu Right.

8. Non-Hindus Writing About Hindu History

William Dalrymple was in the chair at the London lecture on November 12, 2003, where someone lobbed an egg at me, missing me in more ways than one; in his article on Indian history he described the incident and continued: "Other lectures on India have since been broken up in similar circumstances. Within India, mobs mobilized by the Hindu Right have occasionally attacked art exhibitions, libraries, publishers, and movie houses for their alleged unpatriotic and anti-Hindu bias; but for the first time the campaign now seemed to be spreading onto campuses worldwide."[19] American scholars are the small fry in the larger global community at risk; we have relatively little to complain about; we are relatively safe. But we too have our troubles here below, and there is a powerful and direct connection between the rise of Hindutva and the rise of Internet Hindutva, or Hindu Blog. When books published by American scholars— Jeffrey Kripal, Paul Courtright, Jim Laine—were attacked in India, the Indian editions were suppressed, and although the books remained in print in America, the offending American scholars received death threats here.

In what I have now come to think of, wistfully, as the (good) old days, *in illo tempore*, whenever I gave a lecture on Hinduism, afterward, in the question period, an elderly Hindu gentleman (always a man) would rise, pay me an elaborate compliment, and proceed to give a mini-lecture of his own, often learned and sometimes relevant, as if to say, I know things that this American woman does not know. There was no malice in it, just, perhaps, an understandable desire to have the upper hand, the last word, or even, perhaps, to reclaim Hinduism for himself, a Hindu and a man. Usually he added something of value and of interest, and we would often continue the conversation after the lecture, at the reception. Sometimes it was just a ritual gesture, in which the content was largely irrelevant; it was the act of standing up, of claiming the space, that was important. That ritual gesture remains at the heart of the more recent interventions, but now there is certainly malice, and the people on the Internet are not nearly so learned as those old gentlemen used to be. I never thought I would miss those guys, but I would be greatly relieved to have some of them in my audiences now.

The Hindus who object to the books about Hinduism by non-Hindus are primarily concerned with three problems:

1. Non-Hindus rather than Hindus are writing about Hinduism;
2. Some non-Hindus (and indeed some Hindus, too) are writing about the "wrong sort" of Hinduism; and
3. Prominent authors, non-Hindu or Hindu, are writing from an academic rather than a faith stance.

These three issues are often wrongly conflated, exacerbating the problem and further muddying the muddy waters. Let us consider them one by one.

1. Non-Hindus rather than Hindus are writing about Hinduism. Dalrymple, after recounting the incident that I think of as "the egg and I," continued: "During the questions that followed the lecture, Doniger faced a barrage of insults from a group who had come with the egg-thrower, and who maintained that as a non-Hindu she was unqualified to comment on their religion."[20] There is an understandable move to have Hindus be the ones who tell about Hinduism, just as, it is alleged, Christians and Jews control the teaching and writing about Christianity and Judaism. (This latter assertion is not exactly true; for centuries, many Hindus, perhaps most prominently Ram Mohan Roy and Swami Dayananda, have written penetrating critiques of Christianity. But it is largely true). And one has to have sympathy for this concern, as a political concern.

There remains the shadow of the bad days of the so-called pillow dictionaries (or "long-haired" dictionaries, in Chinese studies) in the academic study of Hinduism: white men talked about Hinduism, and ideas, while women of color (often the wives of the men with the ideas) merely taught the languages, a much undervalued skill in academic departments to this day. Now the stereotype returns in a new avatar, no longer gendered but still racist: white men (or women) teach men and women of color their own tradition, as if to recast the old racist dictum that "we understand them better than they understand themselves."

Answer to objection 1: It is simply not true that non-Hindus *rather than* Hindus write about Hinduism. Both groups are engaged in this enterprise. There are obvious advantages to books about Hinduism by Hindus, things that only a Hindu can know about Hinduism. And those non-Hindus who, like myself, do teach and write about Hinduism, if they are any good at all, always base their teachings on both the ancient sources, written by Hindus, and the many excellent contemporary books written by Hindus, as well as those by non-Hindus. Some Hindus in answer to this would object that books by non-Hindu scholars have a kind of power, are part of a club, a closed group that publishers and teachers favor and that Hindu scholars cannot break into. There was some truth to this in the past, but it is less and less true nowadays, as more and more excellent books by Hindu scholars have become available and are widely read and widely used in classes all over the country.

There are also some people who were born Hindus in India and have been educated both there and in America or Europe, in both non-Indian and Indian methodologies. Such people have a double vision; they are the hyphen in "Indo-American," as A. K. Ramanujan used to joke about himself; they live amphibiously in both Indian and non-Indian intellectual worlds and produce works that none of us one-world types can rival. Nothing could bring into more vivid focus the threat to freedom of speech in contemporary India than the fact that a serious political attempt was made to remove a pivotal essay (about the *Ramayana*) by A. K. Ramanujan from the reading list of a course at the University of Delhi and from the in-print list of Oxford University Press, India; and nothing gives more hope for the survival of democracy in India than the power and success of the protest against that attempt.[21]

But our appreciation of scholars who are both Hindu and non-Hindu should never be taken to mean that *only* Hindus (or even only Hindus with a two-culture education) should write about Hinduism. I certainly would not deny the validity of the insider view, but I would insist that it needs to be supplemented. To acknowledge the right of Hindus to express their opinion about their religion is obviously an essential principle; to insist that their view must be accepted as the only view because they are Hindus would damage basic principles of the academic study of religion. Comparative religion—such as the study of Hinduism by someone who is not a Hindu, always an implicitly comparative enterprise—is not the same thing as interreligious dialogue, which would limit the discussion of Hinduism to Hindus alone. (The interreligious dialogue school of comparison, sometimes satirized as the "take a Hindu to dinner" approach or "the zoo," was for many years the specialty of Harvard University's Center for the Prevention of World Religions [as it, too, is sometimes satirically known], especially under the inspiration of Wilfred Cantwell Smith.) Both approaches, comparative religion and interreligious dialogue, are valuable, but they have very different goals and limitations.

For there are also advantages to a book about Hinduism by a non-Hindu. Non-Hindu scholars of Hinduism are doing something different from what Hindu scholars are doing, something also worth doing, viewing Hinduism through nontraditional eyes formed by non-Hindu ways of looking at religion, from Marx and Freud to Derrida and Edward Said. This approach brings a useful distance, asking questions that some non-Hindus might want to ask but that may not be interesting to all Hindus. More important, no single Hindu can know all of the Hinduisms, let alone represent them, nor can any non-Hindu. Non-Hindu scholars can open out to the faith community a different range of knowledge and interpretation of their own religion.[22] Always there is bias, and the hope is that the biases of Hindus and non-Hindus will cancel one another out in a well-designed study of any aspect of Hinduism.

But the contributions of non-Hindu scholars of Hinduism are challenged by a second objection: **2. Some Non-Hindus (and indeed some Hindus, too) are writing about the "wrong sort" of Hinduism.**

The Hindutvavadis do not merely want to speak, to be heard: they want to silence other people who are saying what they do not want to hear about Hinduism. They want to exclude what they regard as defamatory accounts of their religion that Americans (including some American Hindus) are perpetrating. And, again, one can see some justice in their objection to, for instance, the ways that Hinduism has been cheapened and misrepresented by a number of American cults that call themselves Hindu, mostly but not all "Tantric." Many Hindus object rightly to the casual appropriation of Hindu ideas, or Hindu images, by people who make no attempt to understand what Hindus raised in the tradition believe these ideas and images to be. Americans have, in David Gordon White's words, "cobbled together the pathetic hybrid of New Age 'Tantric sex,'" "eclectically blending together Indian erotics, erotic art, techniques of massage, Ayurveda, and yoga into a single invented tradition." Thus, "New Age Tantra is to medieval Tantra what finger painting is to fine art." White rails against "the funhouse mirror world of modern-day Tantra, in which Indian practitioners and gurus take their ideas from Western scholars and sell them to Western disciples thirsting for initiation into the mysteries of the East."[23] One can certainly see why Hindus would object to this sort of distortion.

There is irony in the realization that, through a kind of double-back pizza effect, India is the source of much of the Western misappropriation of India. Hindutvavadis adhere to a de-eroticized line of Hinduism that can be traced back in history to the *Sannyasa Upanishads*, to Abhinavagupta's eleventh-century interpretation of Tantrism, and then, eventually, to the British Victorian imprint upon nineteenth-century Hinduism. Hindutvavadis object to sex, to Freud (whom they mistake for sex), to the erotic aspects of their own tradition (such as the *Kamasutra*), and to scholars (like myself) who have written—not only, I hasten to say, but also—about the erotic, sensual aspect of Hinduism.[24] Complex psychological and historical factors have bred in certain contemporary Hindu men and women a sense of shame for the eroticism of their own religion. It has also robbed them of their sense of humor: scholars who celebrate the humor and satire in many Sanskrit texts are sometimes criticized as laughing at, rather than with, Hinduism. But part of the greatness of Hinduism is its ability to laugh at its own gods, and it would be a shame to lose that.

Answer to objection 2: To limit the study of Hinduism to a single, narrow form of it (in this case, the de-eroticized form) would be equivalent to writing a book about Christianity and saying that all Christians believe that Darwin was wrong and that god created the world in seven days, instead of saying that *some* Christians think that, but others do not. A book about the things that some Hindus do not know about Hinduism, by contrast, has somewhat the same relationship to the Hinduism lived by most Hindus today as the relationship between lived Christianity and Elaine Pagels's book about the Gnostic Gospels: most Christians don't know about Gnosticism, but, though rejected by the mainstream, it has left its traces. And the understanding of Gnosticism that Pagels has given us is part of our broader understanding of Christianity today.

A person can be an insider in any of several senses, from racist to ideological. The ideological bias against the wrong kind of Hinduism is actually more destructive than the racist bias against non-Hindus, if not as ugly, since the ideological criterion demands not necessarily that the scholar in question be a member of the ethnic group but that she share the opinions of the one particular group within the group that is making the truth claims. (Hence the Hindutvavadis accuse certain Hindu scholars, who may be deeply pious but play by the rules of the academy, of being Uncle Toms.)

But the main target of the Hindutva attack is not necessarily someone of another religion (say, Protestantism), or even a wrong-thinking member of the Hindu community (what my Stalinist mother would have called a Trotskyite), but someone (Hindu or non-Hindu) who uses academic rather than faith criteria. This brings us to objection **3: Prominent American authors, non-Hindu or Hindu, are writing from an academic rather than a faith stance.**

Answer to objection 3:

Yes they are, and a good thing it is, too. This third objection is based on a misunderstanding that is not historical or scholarly but religious and political. To *require* first-hand experience of a religion that one writes about would be a violation of the basic and essential pillar of the enlightenment project—as would be any move that, on the other hand, *excluded* from writing about any religion someone who, in her private faith life, happened to have first-hand experience of that religion. We should not, therefore, write about Hinduism from a Protestant standpoint, as has been done for several centuries now, and has rightly spurred some of the anger on the Internet; nor should we write about Hinduism from a Hindu standpoint. We should do it from an academic standpoint. Many forms of Hinduism are alive and well and living both in India and throughout the world, some of them known only to scholars, others known only to a few devotees—and, of course, these two groups often overlap. But the scholar who is also a devotee must wear only one hat when she writes, and that is the hat of the scholar.

Notes

1. There is a famous Orientalist parable on this theme, based on an ancient Arabic tale (though one not included in the *Arabian Nights*) that Somerset Maugham told in his play *Sheppey* (1933) and that John O'Hara cited, a year later, as the epigraph for a novel to which he gave the title *Appointment in Samarra*:

   [Death speaks:] There was a merchant in Baghdad who sent his servant to market to buy provisions and in a little while the servant came back, white and trembling, and said, Master, just now when I was in the marketplace I was jostled by a woman in the crowd and when I turned I saw it was Death that jostled me. She looked at me and made a threatening gesture. Now, lend me your horse, and I will ride away from this city and avoid my fate. I will go to Samarra and there Death will not find me. The merchant lent him his horse, and the servant mounted it, and he dug his spurs in its flanks and as fast as the horse could gallop he went. Then the merchant went down to the marketplace and he saw me standing in the crowd and he came to me and said, Why did you make a threatening gesture to my servant when you saw him this morning? That was not a threatening gesture, I said, it was only a start of surprise. I was astonished to see him in Baghdad, for I had an appointment with him tonight in Samarra.

2. Amartya Sen, *The Argumentative Indian: Writings on Indian History, Culture and Identity* (Gordonsville: FSG, 2005), 72.
3. See Wendy Doniger, "Are Hindus Monotheists or Polytheists?" in Wendy Doniger, *On Hinduism*. Delhi: Aleph Book Company, 2013; 2nd edition, 2014; New York: Oxford University Press, 2014, 10–20.
4. William Dalrymple, "India: The War Over History," *The New York Review of Books* (52: 6), April 7, 2005.

5. D. N. Jha, *The Myth of the Holy Cow* (London: Verso, 2001). Review by Wendy Doniger, "A Burnt Offering," in the *Times Literary Supplement* 5183 (August 2, 2002), 9.

6. Wendy Doniger, *The Hindus: An Alternative History*. New York: Penguin Press, 2009; Delhi, Penguin Books, 2010.

7. They included Michael Witzel, Homi Bhabha, Madhav Deshpande, Steve Farmer, Robert Goldman, Sally Goldman, Richard Meadow, Patrick Olivelle, Sheldon Pollock, Romila Thapar, and Stanley Wolpert.

8. Sumit Sarkar, *Beyond Nationalist Frames: Postmodernism, Hindu Fundamentalism, History* (Indiana University Press: Bloomington, 2002).

9. Amanda Huffer, "The Religious Believer versus the Historian of Religions: The California Textbook Debate." Unpublished essay, February 12, 2006.

10. Doniger, *The Hindus: An Alternative History*, 364–5.

11. BBC News, September 12, 2007, and Doniger, *The Hindus*, 665–6.

12. John Keay, *India, a History* (New York: Grove Press, 2000), 2.

13. The Great Rebellion, formerly known as the Sepoy Mutiny, was triggered when Indian troops serving under the British feared that the British were greasing cartridges—which the troops had to bite—with pig fat (anathema to Muslims) or cow fat (anathema to Hindus) or both. See Doniger, *The Hindus*, 585–7.

14. I owe this concern, and much of its wording, to Arshia Sattar, personal communication, August 13, 2006. I also used some of the ideas in this section of this essay in my book, *The Hindus: An Alternative Narrative*.

15. David Arnold, "Beheading Hindus, and Other Alternative Aspects of Wendy Doniger's History of a Mythology," *Times Literary Supplement*, July 29, 2009.

16. Ibid.

17. Dalrymple, "India: The War Over History."

18. Two films made on the same topic in the same year (1964), *Dr. Strangelove* and *Failsafe*, imagined a doomsday plan (think: Kali Yuga) for American planes to drop atomic bombs on Russia.

19. Dalrymple, "India: The War Over History."

20. Dalrymple, "India: The War Over History."

21. See, among many articles, Soutik Biswas, "Ramayana: An 'Epic' Controversy," BBC News, South Asia, October 19, 2011; Scott Jaschik, "Scholarly 'Self-Abasemet,'" *Inside Higher Ed*, November 29, 2011; and Ramachandra Guha, "Read the Fine Print," *Hindustan Times*, December 5, 2011.

22. See Wendy Doniger, *The Implied Spider: Politics and Theology in Myth* (New York: Columbia University Press, 1998), pp. 154–6.

23. David Gordon White, *Kiss of the Yogini: "Tantric Sex" in its South Asian Contexts* (Chicago: University of Chicago Press, 2003). See also Wendy Doniger, "Going with the Flow: Why Sex Has To Be Put Back into Tantra," review of David

Gordon White, *Kiss of the Yogini* (*Times Literary Supplement* May 21, 2004), 3–4.

24. See Wendy Doniger, "From Kama to Karma: The Resurgence of Puritanism in Contemporary India," in *Social Research, India's World* (78: 1, Spring 2011, pp. 49–74); and "God's Body, Or, The *Lingam* Made Flesh: Conflicts over the Representation of the Sexual Body of the Hindu God Shiva," in *Social Research, The Body and the State* (78: 2: Summer 2011, pp. 485–508). Reprinted in Wendy Doniger, *On Hinduism* (Delhi: Aleph Book Company, 2014), pp. 396–408 and 192–206.

19 PARTISAN DREAMS, FRACTURED HOMELAND: GUJARATI DIASPORA POLITICS IN AMERICA

Mona G. Mehta

Gujarat aspires to be the 51st state of the United States of America.

—GIRISH PATEL, *lawyer, Gujarat*[1]

The above statement captures the well known global orientation of the Indian state of Gujarat. Despite its hyperbolic quality, it rightly notes the high status of the United States as the land of desired destination for Gujaratis. Unofficial figures claim that about 40 percent of Indian Americans trace their origin to Gujarat.[2] The Asian American Hotel Owner's Association (AAHOA)—an influential body that controls 40 percent of the US hotel industry worth more than $60 billion—is dominated by people of Gujarati descent. The determination of many Gujaratis to migrate to America is accompanied by their desire to maintain active political ties with the homeland. This essay explores the political mobilization by the Gujarati diaspora in the United States to shore up partisan politics in Gujarat, especially since 2002. How and why does the Gujarati diaspora actively endorse an exclusionary political vision in the homeland? What are the implications of diaspora politics for democracy and pluralism in India?

The diaspora can sometimes become a powerful site from where political visions of the homeland are articulated, celebrated, and actively realized.[3] Gujarati diaspora politics is a product of the complex interplay of twenty-first-century processes of globalization and the emergent dynamics of Indian democracy. Seen from this framework, we can better appreciate the transnational dimensions of homeland politics and the ways in which politics in India is constituted by local and supranational loyalties. This essay shows how the Gujarati diaspora has helped foster a consensus in favor of exclusionary politics in Gujarat and India at large through a combination of claims about Gujarati victimhood, economic prosperity, and representative democracy. The evidence for this study is based on fieldwork in Gujarat and the United States between 2004 and 2009, which includes ethnographies of diaspora community events, personal interviews and content analysis of newspapers, magazines, and material on the Internet.

The term "diaspora" means dispersion and was initially used to describe the dispersed Jewish population in the world. With the advent of Paul Gilroy's influential work *Black Atlantic* in 1993, it became widely associated with African diasporic cultures. As many authors have noted, a problem with the more recent capacious literature on diaspora is the elastic and slippery usage of the concept.[4] For instance, diaspora has been used descriptively to refer to a wide range of groups including immigrants, expatriates, refugees, guest workers, exile communities, overseas communities, and ethnic communities.[5] In addition, the term has also stood in to connote complex processes such as "travel, creolization, transculturation and hybridity."[6] I use the term diaspora in two related senses: first, as a descriptive category to refer to the network of displaced people settled in the United States that identifies as Gujarati and maintains direct or indirect links with Gujarat through a variety of activities[7]; second, as a sociocultural formation and a political community that identifies with a set of ideological positions about the homeland. In this latter sense, diaspora is an analytic category similar to Brian Axel's notion of the "diasporic imaginary," which refers to a process of identification that is simultaneously generative of the homeland and diasporic subjects.[8]

Benedict Anderson was among the earliest scholars to formulate the now widely deployed term "long-distance nationalism."[9] Nina Glick Schiller defines long-distance nationalism as a "set of identity claims and practices that connect people living in various geographical locations to a specific territory that they see as their ancestral home."[10] Unlike the classical concept of nationalism, "long-distance nationalism" is not tied to physical or legal membership in the putative homeland. Moreover, long-distance nationalists may seek to endorse or undermine the dominant political regimes in their respective homelands. Long-distance nationalists have often, but not always, tended to support violent, extremist and secessionist movements in the homeland. Jewish-American right-wing extremists, Irish-American supporters of the Irish Republican Army, the Tamil Tigers settled in England and Norway, and Kurds throughout Europe are some examples of long-distance nationalists who have supported violent conflicts from afar.[11] Seen in this light, the protagonists of the Gujarati diaspora in my research can be called "long-distance nationalists" whose support for exclusionary politics in their homeland is not without historical precedent. However, the case of the Gujarati diaspora illuminates important aspects about the contradictory relationship between transnational diaspora politics and democracy.

Gujarat possesses a fourth of India's coastline that has historically helped facilitate overseas trade and commerce in the region for over four millennia,[12] giving rise to a substantial diaspora. However, the Gujarati diaspora is not a monolithic category but has a varied history of dispersion to different parts of the world. In the modern era, the spread of Gujaratis overseas is broadly associated with three waves of migration since the late nineteenth century. The first wave led Gujaratis, predominantly Gujarati Muslim traders, to travel to east Africa for trade in the late nineteenth and early twentieth centuries. The second wave entailed their migration from Africa to England following persecution from authoritarian regimes in the late 1970s. The third wave of migration brought Gujaratis to the United States due to favorable US immigration policies in the 1960s—at first as educated professionals and later as small business and blue-collar workers.

Overseas Gujaratis, also known as Non Resident Gujaratis (NRGs), occupy an important space in the official and popular consciousness of Gujarat. This is partly because the diaspora maintains active links with the homeland in the form of remittances, business, or visits to extended families. Noting the substantial and economically successful diaspora across the world, the Gujarat government set up a bureaucratic cell to encourage investments from NRGs in 1970. Tracking the flows of capital from the diaspora to the homeland in the form of investment and remittances is a common approach in understanding the diaspora's influence on the homeland. For instance, the following newspaper report emphasizes the contribution of NRGs to the development of rural Gujarat:

> Talk to a rustic Gujju and chances are he'll give the credit for development of his village to the benevolence of some non-resident Gujarati businessman who left the village years ago for foreign shores. And when he did strike millions, he didn't forget his roots; instead, he routinely pumps in dollars to fund roads, schools and other developmental projects in his village ... it's thanks to the evident love that NRGs have for their homeland that vast parts of rural Gujarat are so much better off than their country cousins elsewhere.[13]

Despite these investment flows and links, this report notes that the contribution of NRGs to Gujarat's Foreign Direct Investment (FDI) is no more than 4 percent. Although monetary contributions from overseas Gujaratis have altered the physical landscape of parts of Gujarat, the diaspora's noneconomic activities can often be more fruitful sites for investigating its influence in the homeland. In fact, the production of diasporic authority in Gujarat is a complex phenomenon in which financial flows are inextricably linked with sociopolitical factors.

According to Siddharth Patel, the President of the Congress Party in Gujarat in 2009, an NRG is an influential person who is looked upon with great respect and admiration in the small towns and villages of Gujarat. The opinions of NRGs carry weight far beyond their monetary might because of their status as well informed people who have traveled the world and achieved success. The ability and willingness of the Gujarati diaspora to wield political influence in the homeland by leveraging their social standing as opinion makers is one of the central concerns of this essay. Planeloads of overseas Gujaratis visit Gujarat during every election to campaign for their preferred political party and candidates.[14] The Gujarati diaspora's political ties with the homeland are not a unique phenomenon. Aihwa Ong notes a similar trend among the global Chinese diaspora who she says "may be living and working in the United States, but their hearts and politics are tied to the interests of the Chinese nation."[15] However, the Gujarati diaspora's intervention in homeland politics is not simply marked by the creation of Internet-based transnational cyberpublics or through campaign funding that produces top-down influence on local political affairs. NRGs may not vote to elect local leaders in Gujarat but they participate in homeland politics through affective public events and political demonstrations in their adopted land.

The Hindu nationalist Bharatiya Janata Party (BJP) appointed Narendra Modi as the chief minister of Gujarat in 2001 in the midst of the party's dwindling political fortunes in the state. On February 27, 2002, a train carrying activists of the Hindu Nationalist group VHP (Vishwa Hindu Parishad) was burned at the Godhra station, killing fifty-seven activists. They were returning from a controversial political agitation at the town of Ayodhya in Uttar Pradesh to demand the building of a Ram temple at the site where a four hundred year old mosque was illegally demolished by Hindu extremists in 1992. Interpreting this event as a Muslim provocation, Hindus in Gujarat engaged in a three-day retaliatory killing of Muslims in the state. The evidence gathered by independent investigative agencies and India's National Human Rights Commission attests to the then chief minister Narendra Modi's complicity in the anti-Muslim violence. The state's law enforcement agencies were ordered to turn a blind eye to anti-Muslim attacks and allow Hindus to express their anger. Narendra Modi's controversial role during the violence increased his popularity in Gujarat. He was hailed as a "savior of Hindus" and won a resounding electoral victory in the state months after the violence in December 2002. Beyond Gujarat, Modi's complicity in the violence was widely condemned and he became a political pariah at the national and international level. The English media criticized him as the "Hero of Hatred"[16] and likened him to Milosevic.[17]

1. Exiled in the Homeland: Politics of Victimhood

Gujaratis in the diaspora began to increasingly express their support for the leadership of Narendra Modi in private gatherings and public community events. Just as Gujaratis in the homeland did not buy the scathing criticism of Modi made in the rest of India and abroad, diaspora Gujaratis also chose to stand by the Gujarati chief minister. In 2005, the Asian American Hotel Owner's Association (AAHOA) announced its intention to invite Modi as the chief guest at their annual convention in Ft. Lauderdale, Florida. The financially powerful AAHOA consists mainly of the politically dominant caste group of Patels from Gujarat.[18] Another group of Indian Americans formed the Coalition against Genocide (CAG) to oppose AAHOA's invitation. CAG consisted of a range of secular and religious Indian American organizations and demanded that Modi's invitation be withdrawn on the basis of his alleged role in the violence of 2002. Members of CAG prepared petitions, wrote letters, and made phone calls to senators and the US State Department to register their protest and provide evidence collected by human rights groups about the role of Modi's regime in the violence of 2002. In addition, CAG mobilized a petition signed by scholars of South Asia at US universities, which explained the history of attacks by Hindu Right wing groups on religious minorities and other marginalized groups in India.[19] Extensive media campaigns and public opinion pressure ultimately prompted the US administration under George W. Bush to revoke Modi's visa on March 18, 2005. This was done under Section 212(a)(2)(G) of the US Immigration and Nationality Act which prohibits the admission to the United States of any foreign government official believed to have responsibility for serious violations of religious freedom.[20]

The reactions of Gujaratis in the homeland and America towards the US administration's ban on Modi's entry into the United States were remarkably aligned with each other. The fact that no Gujarati diaspora organization joined CAG revealed the Gujarati/non-Gujarati polarization within Indian American diaspora around the issue of Modi's controversial invitation to the United States during these early years after 2002. The pro- and anti-Modi mobilization in the United States was quickly interpreted by the Gujarati media as a sharp divide between Americans of Gujarati descent and other Indian Americans.[21] Mainstream Gujarati newspapers, intellectuals, and religious gurus criticized Modi's visa ban as unjust and an insult to the people of Gujarat.[22] American flags were burnt and warehouses of Pepsi and Coke—the ultimate symbols of American consumerism and soft power—were attacked.[23] Some cars carried stickers that read "America has denied a visa to Narendra Modi, Throw out all American goods and Americans from Gujarat."[24] Modi played up the discourse of "Gujarati victimhood and offense" by organizing a *Swabhiman Yatra* or "Self-Respect Rally" in Gujarat to protest against America's decision.[25]

The Gujarati diaspora organized its own mobilizations to oppose CAG's campaign to block Modi's visit to the United States. A group of prominent Gujarati Americans formed the Association of Indian Americans in North America (AIANA).[26] On March 20, 2005, two days after Modi's visa was revoked, AIANA was scheduled to organize an extravagant event in honor of his visit. Undeterred by the last minute visa revocation, AIANA refused to cancel the event. Instead, it decided to turn its show of support for Modi into a public spectacle of protest against the US administration's visa denial. The event's venue was the famous Madison Square Garden Theater in New York City. The organizers decided to screen Modi's speech live via satellite from Gujarat to the heart of Manhattan. About five thousand Indian Americans, mostly Gujaratis, from the tri-state area had gathered at this famous theater to listen to the popular leader from their home state.

Through this much publicized protest, the diaspora endorsed Modi as the legitimate leader of Gujaratis and endorsed the dominant political sentiment in the homeland. Inside the Madison Square Garden Theater, the stage was lined with chairs that seated AIANA organizers, Democratic Congressman Frank Pallone from New Jersey's Sixth District, the founder of the Vishwa Hindu Parishad of North America (VHPA, World Council of Hindus in North America), and officials of the Overseas Friends of the BJP (OFBJP). Each of them wore a bright yellow scarf around their necks with "Jai Shri Krishna" or "Hail Lord Krishna" printed in red in both English and Gujarati.[27] The explicit allegiance to Hindu deities and the line-up of dignitaries affiliated to the BJP and Hindu right-wing groups revealed the politically partisan nature and religious bias of the event. The function resembled a political rally of the BJP rather than an occasion to honor an elected representative of Gujarat.

Prominently placed in the middle of the stage was an empty chair that towered above all others. The audience soon learned that the chair was meant to resemble a king's throne. An AIANA functionary and a hotel owner explained the symbolic significance of this empty throne. He noted that it was only the second time in history that a throne or *gaadi* had been kept vacant for a great Indian leader. The first instance was five thousand years ago when the Hindu lord king Ram had gone into exile, and the second time this was done at the Madison Square Gardens in America for the sake of Gujarat's popular leader Narendra Modi.

The narration of the events leading to Modi's visa denial was suffused with emotional references from the Indian epic of *Ramayana*, complete with its tropes of divine kingship, palace intrigue, betrayal, sacrifice, and loyalty. In this diasporic recitation of the twenty-first century version of the *Ramayana*, Modi was likened to the epic's hero *Ram* and the US administration was equated with King *Dashratha*, the father of *Ram*. Just as *Dashratha* was hoodwinked into banishing his son from his kingdom, so was the United States duped into framing false charges against Modi. The role played by the scheming and wily palace servant *Manthra* who instigated *Dashratha's* unjust decision was ascribed to CAG, whose campaign prompted the United States to revoke Modi's visa. By displaying an empty seat on the stage the Gujarati diaspora appropriated for itself the noble character of *Bharata*, the loyal half brother of *Ram*, who patiently waits over the vacant throne for *Ram's* return from exile.

Through the enactment of an episode from the *Ramayana* with diasporic characters, NRGs provide a revisionist reading of the political reality in the homeland. In this narrative, Modi's Gujarat is depicted as *Ram rajya* or the ideal polity, thereby rejecting any criticism of a politics of violence in the homeland. The symbolic empty throne in Madison Square Garden transposes Ayodhya, the site of *Ram's* kingdom, from the homeland to America. This imaginary disloca-tion of Ayodhya is accompanied by another twist in the epic's script in which *Ram's* return from exile turns into an anxious yearning for Modi's arrival from the homeland. Contrary to most narrations in which the diaspora experiences a feeling of exile in its host country, Modi's inability to leave Gujarat renders the homeland rather than America as the site of exile. By waiting for the arrival of their leader in Manhattan, Gujarati Americans identify themselves as the trans-national loyal subjects of the putative kingdom of Modi's Gujarat.

In his absence, Modi emerged larger than life. Through his live satellite speech, Modi thanked his fellow Gujaratis for their support. He praised the diaspora for their achievements and reminded them that their success in for-eign lands was due to the universalistic value of *Vasudhaiva Kutumbakam* (the world is one united family), which he claimed underpinned Gujarati culture. Questions about the visa denial dominated the teleconference between the Gujarati leader and his overseas compatriots. Modi responded by stating that the campaign of falsehood against him and Gujarat by a handful of people that had led to the American visa decision could not harm him. He compared himself to the world's most famous Gujarati, M. K. Gandhi, who was thrown out of a train in Durban for being a colored man. Just as Gandhi later drove British colonial rule out of India, Modi promised to restore Gujarati pride by making Gujarat the most desired international destination to which the world would queue up for entry.[28]

In declaring this event as the biggest protest by any diaspora in the United States,[29] the protagonists of this self-conscious political spectacle challenged the reasoning behind Modi's visa denial. It projected Modi, and by extension the people he represented, as the objects of prejudice and injustice. Diaspora Gujaratis offered not so much a counter-reading of the violence of 2002 as a reassignment of moral culpability about it. This account concurred with and reiterated another dimension of the corrosive consensus that Hindus rather than Muslims are the victims of long standing injustice. Through this narrative of victimhood, NRGs identified themselves with homeland Gujaratis as one "imagined community"[30] that happened to exist in physically separate places but was unified through its common victimhood.

2. Producing a Vibrant Homeland

Modi's visa denial episode exemplified how his image as an aggressive anti-minority leader had become a hindrance in securing his political legitimacy outside Gujarat. In the backdrop of this image crisis, Modi launched the Vibrant Gujarat campaign in 2003. Organized around a biennial Global Investors Summit, the campaign projects Gujarat as India's top investment destination. Modi evolved from the "hero of hatred" to a builder of modern Gujarat by hosting Global Investment Summits, lowering government controls over business, and advertising Gujarat's minimal labor regulations.[31] Riding on the global popularity of the neoliberal paradigm of economic growth, the Vibrant Gujarat campaign sought the support of those who were otherwise critical of Modi's hardline identity politics. The campaign used the global appeal of neoliberal economic efficiency and development to shore up popular support for authoritarian and exclusionary politics.

At the discursive level, the Vibrant Gujarat campaign generates an assemblage of signs and symbols aimed at shifting Gujarat's association from violence to development. The discursive shift from victimhood to vibrancy facilitated by the Vibrant Gujarat campaign was picked up and reiterated by the diaspora. At community events, NRGs began to celebrate Modi's avatar as the harbinger of economic prosperity and moved away from protesting the continued denial of his visa. AIANA, the group that organized the Madison Square Garden protest, now arranged the biannual World Gujarati Conference in Edison, New Jersey. Each year, the conference gathered around 35,000 Gujaratis from all over the world. Titled "Chalo Gujarat" or "Let's go to Gujarat," the event was meant to serve as a platform for NRGs to show solidarity, and define their identity, shared values and dreams.[32] Over three days, the conference showcased music, dance, theater, cuisine, discourses of Hindu gurus, and films about Gujarat. The event's advertisement described it as a "mini-Gujarat coming alive in New Jersey!" Stalls of businesses, social organizations, religious sects, and government agencies from Gujarat promoted products and services before a captive diasporic audience. In contrast to their earlier stance of protest, the AIANA organizers adopted the theme of progress and festivity to identify the homeland. The Gujarat government's promotional films and literature for the Vibrant Gujarat campaign were prominently showcased at "Chalo Gujarat." The live telecast of Gujarat Chief Minister Narendra Modi's speech became a common feature of all major Gujarati diaspora events after the 2005 protest in Madison Square Garden.

In spring 2008, Gujarati American organizations hosted "Gujarat Day" celebrations in the prosperous Chicago suburb of Bartlett. The event aimed to commemorate May 1st as the forty-eighth anniversary of the creation of Gujarat as a separate linguistic state within the Indian Union in 1960. The venue was a Jain temple built on 15.4 acres of sprawling suburban lawns. Modi's speech—the event's central attraction—was to be transmitted across North America where similar celebrations had been organized in Atlanta, Houston, Los Angeles, and Toronto.[33] The temple's auditorium was packed with more than 1,500 people facing two large TV screens. The evening's program began with the singing of the American and Indian national anthems. With greetings of *Jai Jai Garvi Gujarat*! (Long Live the Glory of Gujarat!), the event's host posed a question to the audience: Why was Chicago the chosen location for this celebration? As if to elucidate an answer, a short audio-visual film was screened. It showed the Art Institute of Chicago and a room in the museum where the Indian spiritual figure, Swami Vivekananda, had given his historic "Chicago Address" before the World Parliament of Religions in 1893.[34] Swami Vivekananda's speech had famously enamored American audiences and single handedly made Hinduism known to the West at the turn of the twentieth century. The film showed how America has memorialized this historical event by officially naming the part of Chicago's famous Michigan Avenue in front of the Art Institute as "Swami Vivekananda Way" in 1995.[35]

Gradually, the host revealed exactly how this event featuring a speech by the chief minister of Gujarat was linked with Swami Vivekananda's visit to Chicago more than a century ago. Both Modi and Vivekananda shared the first name, Narendra.[36] But more importantly, just as Vivekananda had addressed the world from Chicago in 1893, Modi would address the Gujarati diaspora via Chicago that day. Finally, it was declared that the Gujarat Day celebration symbolized a historic journey from Narendranath (Swami Vivekananda) to Narendra Modi. The audience applauded.

Swami Vivekananda was a prominent Hindu revivalist in British India who actively championed Hinduism based on his conviction in the spiritual superiority of India. Like other Hindu revivalists of his time, he sought to reinterpret the essence of Hinduism as a rational and scientific set of doctrines and purge Hindu society of its many unjust practices. His religious goal was coupled with a patriotic fervor and a strong nationalist sentiment to fight colonial injustices, alleviate poverty and rejuvenate Indians.[37] He translated Hinduism and Yoga for a Western audience and spread his message of spirituality with an activist's zeal that was proud and aggressive in style. The incredible reception of his "Chicago Address" at the World Parliament of Religions in 1893 made him famous in India and abroad.

Through an event intended to fabricate a "Second Chicago Address," the organizers of Gujarat Day put Swami Vivekananda and Narendra Modi on the same pedestal and projected their lives as part of a single historical trajectory of strong Hindu leadership and glory. The official flier of Gujarat Day referred to Modi as "Gujarat Kesari," which means the Lion of Gujarat (it can also be read as the Pride of Gujarat.) The flier's graphic layout superimposed the leader's head-shot on a map of Gujarat, thereby depicting him as the face of the state, both literally and metaphorically. I suggest that the comparison of Modi and Vivekananda captures an important moment of diasporic reflexivity that illuminates its vision for the homeland. By celebrating Modi as a crusader for Hindu interests and a new age *Sanyasi* (holy or spiritual person without family attachments), the diaspora aligned itself with the dominant political mood back home. The Gujarat Day celebration was as much about venerating and endorsing Modi as the popular leader of Gujarat as it was a commemoration of the state's inception.

Modi's speech focused entirely on the success of Gujarat's neoliberal model of economic growth. With the poise of a seasoned technocrat, he provided statistics and highlighted development schemes. Playing to the audiences' fetish for technology, he declared that every village in Gujarat had broadband Internet connectivity. He talked about Gujarat's booming economy, new projects for universities, ports, and tech-financial cities, and invited NRGs to participate in building modern Gujarat. After the speech, Gujaratis across North America posed questions to the chief minister. The inquiries ranged from investment opportunities for NRGs in the homeland, the problem of mosquitoes and stray cattle in Gujarat, and the scope for medical tourism to his strategies for tackling terrorism. Modi assured his listeners about his commitment to fight terror based on his preferred strategy of "an eye for an eye." The audience cheered and applauded his stern position. In the political language of Hindutva (political doctrine of Hindu supremacy over other religious minorities and political viewpoints) the term "fighting terror" is widely understood to be a signifier for "Islamic extremism" and suppressing Muslims at large. This language especially resonated in post-9/11 United States, where terrorism is often associated with the followers of Islam. Every spokesperson of the Gujarati diaspora congratulated the chief minister for his performance and raised no other issues of contention or concerns about Gujarat.

The issue of the visa denial found no mention in the celebrations of "Chalo Gujarat" and "Gujarat Day" which focused on Modi as the architect of modern Gujarat. The idioms of economic and cultural vitality used to portray their homeland replaced the diaspora's earlier rhetoric of Gujarat's victimhood. This shift in the narrative about the homeland was a way to erase the stigma associated with the violence of 2002, which necessarily lingered behind the claims of victimhood. By adopting this new language, the diaspora seemed to be acting as the overseas agents of Modi's campaign of "Vibrant Gujarat." According to an AIANA member, the organization's events "are meant to be a platform for what is happening in Gujarat and showcase it before the diaspora and rest of the world."[38] However, the very projection of Gujarat on diasporic platforms was an act of "producing" a certain idea of the "Gujarat model" as an economic success story that must be emulated. Modi's endorsement as the cherished leader of Gujarat by diaspora Gujaratis render the claims of "Vibrant Gujarat" even more powerful back in the homeland.

3. Contradictions of Democracy and Cosmopolitanism

Gujaratis often think of themselves as cosmopolitans who are at home everywhere without forgetting their cultural roots. An article in a diaspora publication titled "The Motto of Today's Gujaratis: I am a Gujarati World Citizen"[39] details the cosmopolitan traits of Gujaratis. It notes that Gujaratis easily mingle with their host populations and gladly learn new languages while continuing to proudly speak their mother tongue. A popular Gujarati poem of the late nineteenth century asks and answers the question: "Whom does Gujarat belong to?" In his answer, the poet Narmad suggests that anyone who cares about the well being of Gujarat and speaks Gujarati—irrespective of ethnicity and religion—is after all a Gujarati.

The organizers of the "Gujarat Day" celebrations in Chicago had placed posters displaying the popular lines of a Gujarati poem which may be translated as: "Wherever settles a Gujarati, Gujarat will forever flourish there" (*Jya jya vasey Gujarati, tya sada kaal Gujarat*).[40] These lines, which are routinely invoked at diaspora events and publications, demonstrate the prevailing self-understanding of Gujaratis as a cosmopolitan people. The ability of Gujaratis to assiduously adapt to a variety of milieus in different corners of the world also figures in jokes Gujaratis make about themselves. For instance, the host of Gujarat Day jokingly announced that if a motel is ever built on the moon, it would likely be at the behest of some Mike or Sam Patel from America! The audience broke out in peels of laughter and clapped approvingly. The joke referred to the renowned business skills of the Patels and implied that the scope of Gujarati entrepreneur-ship and zeal to travel to new locations was not bound to this planet. The whole universe was its potential entrepreneurial canvas.

Gujarati long-distance nationalism brings to light the deep contradictions in diaspora groups as cosmopolitan communities and invites us to think about the challenges this poses to democratic pluralism. Cosmopolitanism is broadly understood both as an "inspirational ethic and a mode of practice" that is char-acterized by "empathy, toleration and respect for other cultures and values."[41] It entails reaching out across cultural differences through dialogue and living together with diversity.[42] Cosmopolitanism is seen by its advocates as a liberat-ing alternative to ethnic nationalist chauvinism. Diasporic existence compresses time and space such that the experiences of many places appear to occur at one moment.[43] Moreover, diasporic subjects are said to experience dual and often multiple identifications that preclude essentialized and nativist identities associ-ated with notions of the homeland.[44] Such subjectivity is often presumed to be cosmopolitan primarily because its existence is marked by heterogeneity and a decentering of the nation as a fixed location called home.[45]

Many scholars question the tendency to trace the genealogy of cosmopoli-tanism to Western and enlightenment thought. Instead, they seek to identify the cosmopolitan ethic by looking at "the world across time and space and see how people have thought and acted beyond the local."[46] They believe that a con-ception of "cosmopolitanisms" instead of a singular cosmopolitanism can allow us to account for its plural and exclusionary manifestations. Others argue that cosmopolitanism's universal and plural claims are nothing but a trope of colo-nial modernity and nationalism.[47] More central to my discussion is the observa-tion by Ong that "the frequent claims that diasporas and cosmopolitanisms are liberatory forces against oppressive nationalism, repressive state structures, and capitalism . . ." are hasty and inaccurate readings of the specific histories and geopolitical situations on the ground.[48]

The Gujarati diaspora is simultaneously characterized by multiple national identifications, narratives of cosmopolitanism, and ethnocentric political posi-tions. Even as the diaspora's transnational location enables it to claim a cos-mopolitan identity, its endorsement of exclusionary politics is subversive of cosmopolitanism's inclusive ethic and claims. Through the spectacles of Gujarat Day, the World Gujarati Conference, and the Madison Square Garden pro-tests, the diaspora celebrated an ethno-centric vision of Gujarat as an exclusively Hindu polity in which Muslims were seen as the "Other." These activities belie the contradictions in Gujarati claims of cosmopolitanism, riddled as they are with exclusionary and chauvinist visions of the homeland.

Seen in this light, the observations of James Clifford that diaspora articulations of purity and racial exclusivism are exceptions and instances of subaltern diasporic discourses that have almost never actually founded nation-states seem too sanguine. This is because he assumes that only those long-distance nationalisms that succeed in creating new states can undermine the stability and diversity of otherwise pluralistic homelands. In contrast to Clifford's claim that the cosmopolitanisms expressed by diaspora discourses are in "constitutive tension with nation-state/assimilationist ideologies,"[49] the example of the Gujarati diaspora suggests that a diaspora's vision of the homeland may facilitate rather than challenge the dominant ethno-centric nation-state project in the homeland. These contradictions show that an inclusive worldview does not necessarily emerge from experiences of displacement and multiple national identifications. If that was the case, all diasporas would automatically endorse inclusive political visions by the virtue of their diasporic experiences.

Non Resident Gujaratis adopted the language of representative democracy in their appeal to the US administration at the Madison Square Garden protest. One AIANA leader insisted that Modi was a legitimate representative of Gujaratis despite the violence under his regime because he was freely elected.[50] A member of the hotel owner's association, Dilipkumar Patel, argued that the ban also infringed on his own personal freedoms as a private citizen. Condemning the efforts to prevent Modi's entry to the United States, Patel said "It means they are controlling me. They are telling me what to do. They are trying to control my freedom of speech."[51]

The diaspora pointed out that the ban on Modi's visa was a serious lapse in America's democratic judgment. The invocation of democracy in the diaspora's appeals builds on a recognition that a dialogue between the world's two great democracies—India and the United States of America—is best carried out in their shared language of democracy. In his speech, NJ Congressman Pallone agreed with this argument of electoral representation made by Gujarati Americans. Pallone deplored the violence but simultaneously criticized the US visa decision. He observed that Modi was, after all, a democratically elected official and therefore ought to deserve a visa.[52]

At Madison Square Garden, the diaspora launched a democratic protest to plead recognition for an elected leader accused of disregarding the democratic rule of law in their homeland. The desire to endorse an illiberal political project through extensive appeals to liberal democracy, electoral representation, the rule of law, personal freedoms, and rights betray a crucial contradiction in Gujarati diaspora politics. In each of these instances, democracy became an instrument for its own subversion.

In the first decade of the twenty-first century, Gujaratis in America have supported the political project of *Hindutva*. Sometimes they have expressed this support through openly partisan declarations. For instance, a coalition of Gujarati diaspora organizations under the banner of "Gujarati Samuday (community) of North America" placed a prominent half page advertisement in a mainstream Gujarati daily.[53] The advertisement declared the unequivocal support of diasporic Gujaratis for Narendra Modi's leadership and exhorted Gujaratis in the homeland to vote for him (the BJP party) in the then Gujarat assembly elections in December 2007. In 2014, influential Indian Americans led by doctors and businessmen of Gujarati descent have actively campaigned for the BJP's staunchly Hindu nationalist Narendra Modi for the post of prime minister of India. At other times, the diaspora have resorted to more symbolic forms of performative politics and demonstrations.

It is not unusual for diaspora groups to maintain transnational linkages with the homeland to lobby for certain causes, even exclusionary and violent ones. Expatriates sometimes endorse the suspension of democracy in the homeland even as they enjoy the fruits of democracy in their adopted lands. Benedict Anderson has long been concerned with the unaccountable and non-democratic potentialities of long-distance nationalism. He worries that long-distance nationalists are able to intervene in the politics of their home country without paying taxes, are not answerable to its judicial system, do not cast absentee ballots in elections due to their citizenship elsewhere, and have no need to fear prison, torture, or death as they are safely positioned in first world countries.[54] Scholars offer different explanations for the motivations of diaspora groups to intervene in homeland politics. According to Ong, the imbalance between Asian diasporas' professional economic power and political-cultural weakness in their adopted lands creates conditions ripe for the emergence of what Stuart Hall calls "ethnic absolutism."[55] In their study of long-distance nationalism in the Haitian context, Nina Glick Schiller and Georges Fouron explain that many Haitian Americans may choose to be benefactors of their extended kin networks in Haiti as a way of restoring their social status as they struggle to maintain their self-esteem in America's adverse racial climate.[56] These comparative insights of other diaspora groups are certainly relevant in understanding the dynamics of Gujarati transnational politics, but they still leave many puzzles of the Gujarati case unanswered. They do not explain, for instance, the Gujarati diasporic consensus about partisan *Hindutva* politics, despite the diaspora's demographic (caste, class, regional) diversity. Why do Gujarati Americans act like spokespersons of a particular ruling political party in Gujarat? Why are overseas Gujaratis willing to take on other Indian Americans and the US administration at the risk of undermining their own political equation in their adopted land in order to uphold this partisan politics?

Although, there are no clear answers to these questions, it is possible that Gujarati long-distance nationalism is not so much attempting to undermine democracy in the homeland as it is using the procedures and rhetoric of liberal democracy for realizing an illiberal political project in the homeland. Unlike some diaspora groups such as Tamils from Sri Lanka, Jews after WWII and Catholics from Northern Ireland, migration from Gujarat was not triggered by a history of political persecution, economic desperation, or violence. The physical homeland of the modern Gujarati diaspora was not under existential threat from political instability. As Sandhya Shukla notes, the Indian diaspora was created largely "out of a sentiment of progress and modernity."[57] As a result, its history is distinct from other groups whose diasporic imaginary was "very much premised on a rehearsal of originary forms of suffering and persecution that have created dispersals, and that construct a compensatory nation."[58] A majority of Gujaratis left Gujarat for better economic prospects and not due to political turmoil. Moreover, many of them had personal finances to acquire a professional or technical education at the graduate level in the United States. Before emigrating, India's post-independent diaspora experienced a stable and functioning democracy in a multicultural polity.

The complex transnational linkages between the Gujarati diaspora and Gujarat are best understood in terms of the diaspora's political and economic aspirations in the homeland. India's economic rise and its perceived benefits for the diaspora have played an important role in the diaspora's willingness to forge political alliances with homeland elites. First generation NRGs use their sojourn to and nexus with America to enhance their project of political and social ascendancy in an economically ascendant Gujarat and India. Their increased financial and political clout in America is a way to leverage their stakes in a homeland that is now on the path of economic ascendance. The politics of *Hindutva* is therefore not just a vehicle for upwardly mobile Hindu caste groups residing in Gujarat to secure their political dominance. These caste groups settled overseas, particularly Patels, are increasingly able to directly or indirectly benefit from *Hindutva* politics through their overseas endorsements. The diaspora's interests in India's economic boom and the Gujarat government's need for transnational political allies have aligned around the consensus about *Hindutva* at this particular historical moment.

Ironically, even as these diasporic aspirations are a function of the success of India's democracy, their political ambitions for the homeland threaten to undermine India's pluralism. It is from the intersections of these transnationally and locally produced visions of the ideal polity that politics in Gujarat and America get constituted. This argument raises further questions that have implications for Indian democracy and the future of diaspora groups more generally.

To what extent will the desire of first generation immigrants in America to be stakeholders in the homeland reflect in the political preferences of subsequent generations of the diaspora remains to be seen. Whether the political ambitions of the Gujarati diaspora signify a larger trend among diaspora groups in certain historical and political contexts is a question that invites further exploration.

Notes

1. Girish Patel, *Law, Society and Girishbhai: Letters to the Editor*, Ahmedabad: Girishbhai Patel Sanman Samiti, 2009.
2. Raymond Williams, *Williams* on South Asian Religions and Immigration: Collected Works, Ashgate, 2004; Steve Fox, "Patel Motels," *Span*, July/August, 2009, New Delhi.
3. Jeganathan Pradeep, "Eelam.com: Place, Nation, and Imagi-Nation in Cyberspace," *Public Culture* vol. 10 (1998): 515–28.
4. James Clifford, "Diaspora," *Cultural Anthropology* vol. 9, no. 3 (1994): 302–38; Brent Edwards, "The Uses of Diaspora," *Social Text* vol. 19, no. 1 (2001); Sandhya Shukla, "Locations for South Asian Diaspora," *Annual Review of Anthropology* 30 (2001): 551–72.
5. Khachig Tölölian, "The Nation State and its Others: In Lieu of a Preface," *Diaspora*, vol. 1, no. 1 (1991): 4–5.
6. Clifford, "Diaspora," 303.
7. Ibid.
8. Brian Axel, "The Diasporic Imaginary," *Public Culture* vol. 14, no. 2 (2002): 412.
9. Anderson, Benedict. "The New World Disorder," *The New Left Review*, May–June, 193, 1993.
10. Melvin Ember, Carol R. Ember, Ian Skoggard, *Encyclopedia of Diasporas: Immigrant and Refugee Cultures Around the World*, New York: Springer, 2005, 570.
11. Ibid., 579.
12. Yagnik 2005, 20.
13. "Gujarat: Getting NRGs to Invest," *Financial Express*, January 16, 2006.
14. Siddharth Patel personal interview, Ahmedabad, July 26, 2009.
15. Aihwa Ong, *Neoliberalism as Exception*, Durham: Duke University Press, 2006, 63.
16. Cover page, *India Today*, March 2002.
17. *India Today*, March 2002; "Modi, India's Milosevic," Gulam K Noon, *Hindustan Times*, May 23, 2002.
18. The Patel caste makes up 20 percent of Gujarat's population. Patel is an intermediate landowning catch-all category of caste groups that have prospered in the past century due to several factors including land and social reform. Most Patel families in Gujarat have at least one family member abroad as the others manage the ancestral land in their home state.

19. *Faculty Letter to AAHOA*, CAG, February 24, 2005, http://www.coalitionagai nstgenocide.org/press/support/faculty.aahoa.php.

20. "Decision taken at the highest levels" by Aziz Haniffa, *Rediff News*, March 19, 2005, http://in.rediff.com/news/2005/mar/19modi9.htm, See also, another report for a more detailed account of the visa revocation. "A Slap in Mr. Modi's Face," *The Hindu*, March 19, 2005, http://www.hindu.com/2005/03/19/stories/2005031901081000.htm.

21. "Two Factions Among Indian-Americans on the Issue of Modi's Visa," *Jai Hind*, March 3, 2005.

22. "America's Efforts to Insult Gujarat by Declining the Indian Government's Request on Modi's Visa Issue," *Loksatta-Jansatta*, March 22, 2005; "Why is the World's Bully America Jealous of India?" *Gujarat Samachar*, March 23, 2005; "The Insult of the Chief Minister is an Insult of the People of Gujarat," *Sandesh*, March 19, 2005; "It is Easy to Find Faults with Modi, Difficult to Defend America: Says Thinker Gunwant Shah," *Divya Bhaskar*, March 20, 2005; "Such an Insult can Never be Tolerated: Morari Bapu," *Jai Hind*, March 20, 2005.

23. "Australian Flags Burnt instead of American Flags," *Gujarat Samachar*, March 25, 2005; "The Violent Fallout of Modi's Visa Episode," *Divya Bhaskar*, March 20, 2005.

24. A photograph of such a sticker appeared in *Jai Hind*, March 19, 2005.

25. "Going along the Swabhiman Rally," *Divya Bhaskar*, March 21, 2005.

26. AIANA describes itself and its goal as follows: "AIANA is an organization that represents the point of view of the majority of Indian-Americans in the United States. It's an organization which helps Gujaratis worldwide to express themselves in many different ways. AIANA offers the opportunity to find and connect with the regenerating impulse in their life, toward their roots. To make them feel proud of their roots and to introduce the young Gujaratis, born abroad, to their rich culture and progressive heritage and bring them all at one point. To establish unity among the community people and make them stand for their roots. This is the first step in what we hope will become a powerful bridge between the Diaspora and Gujarat. This is what AIANA has endeavored to achieve and has had a phenomenal success in what it has tried to achieve." www.wgc08.org/html/html/aiana.html.

27. Jai Shri Krishna is a popular salutation among many Gujarati Hindus who are followers of the Vaishnava sect (Krishna devotees).

28. "Modi's Call to Gujaratis to make India a Super Power," *Fulchab*, March 22, 2005.

29. AIANA describes this event as a protest of historic proportions in the following way: "In March 2005, when Honorable Chief Minister Shri Narendra Modi was denied the visa to USA, AIANA organized an event to protest the action taken

by the US govt. Shri Modi addressed the event through Video Conferencing. The event was hosted at Madison Square Garden which is one the most prestigious arenas of USA. The event created history in many ways. It was the biggest ever political protest done by any Diaspora in the history of USA. It was the biggest crowd ever addressed via video conferencing in the history of USA. It was the first time a protest program was done at such a prestigious place. The event was attended by Indian and American Senators, Assembly Men and was supported by all the major Indian organizations," *World Gujarati Conference, Chaalo Gujarat* 2008, brochure.

30. Benedict Anderson. *Imagined Communities: Reflections on the Origin and Spread of Nationalism*, Verso, 1983.

31. "Gujarat Now India's SEZ: Modi," *Indian Express*, September 6, 2007; "Foreigners Flock to Vibrant Gujarat," Harit Mehta, *Times of India*, January 3, 2009; "Moditva to Modinomics," Harit Mehta, *Times of India*, January 18, 2009.

32. "Chalo Gujarat" World Gujarati Conference 2008, *Little India*, www.littleindia.com/news/174/ARTICLE/3283/2008-08-01.html.

33. Official Gujarat Day flier.

34. The World Parliament of Religions was part of the World Columbian Exposition, also known as the Chicago World's Fair, held in Chicago in 1893 to celebrate 400 years of Columbus's discovery of the New World.

35. On July 12, 1998, a 10'2" bronze statue of Swami Vivekanand, the largest public statue of Vivekananda in America, was installed at the Hindu Temple of Greater Chicago, from the website of the Vivekananda Vedanta Society: www.vedantasociety-chicago.org/chi_history.htm.

36. Swami Vivekanada's birth name was Narendranath Dutta (1863–1901).

37. Tapan Raychaudhuri, *Europe Reconsidered: Perceptions of the West on Nineteenth Century Bengal* (Delhi: Oxford University Press, 1988).

38. Interview with Ashish Mehta, member of AIANA, at the Chalo Gujarat Conference, NJ, August 28, 2008.

39. "Aajna Gujarati nu sutra: Hun Gurjar Vishwaniwasi," an excerpt from the Gujarati Encyclopedia, Gujarat Vishwakosh Trust publication, *Gujarat Times*, August 29, 2008.

40. The poem is written by a Parsi poet who went by the pen name "Khabardar."

41. Pnina Werbner, ed., *Anthropology and the New Cosmopolitanism: Rooted, Feminist and Vernacular Perspectives*, Oxford, New York: Berg, 2008, 2.

42. Ulf Hannerz, *Transnational Connections: Culture, People, Places*, New York: Routledge, 1996; Pnina Werbner, ed., *Anthropology and the New Cosmopolitanism: Rooted, Feminist and Vernacular Perspectives*, Oxford, New York: Berg, 2008.

43. Sandhya Shukla, "Locations for South Asian Diaspora," *Annual Review of Anthropology* vol. 30 (2001): 551.

44. Janna Brazeil, and Anita Mannur, *Theorizing Diaspora*, Oxford: Blackwell, 2003, 5.
45. James Clifford, "Diaspora," *Cultural Anthropology* vol. 9, no. 3 (1994): 302–338.
46. Carol A. Breckenridge and Sheldon I. Pollock, *Cosmopolitanism*, Durham: Duke University Press, 2002.
47. Ibid.
48. Aihwa Ong, 1999, 15–16.
49. James Clifford, "Diaspora," *Cultural Anthropology* vol. 9, no. 3 (1994): 307–308.
50. "Matthews of 'Hardball' Retreats from Speech After Muslim Protest," Josh Gerstein, *The New York Sun*, March 10, 2005, http://www.nysun.com/national/matthews-of-hardball-retreats-from-speech-after/10338/.
51. Ibid.
52. Modi: "Live" at Madison Square Garden, *Rediff News*, http://www.rediff.com/news/2005/mar/21sld5.htm.
53. Political advertisement, *Sandesh*, December 9, 2007.
54. Benedict Anderson, "Exodus," *Critical Inquiry* vol. 20, no. 2 (Winter, 1994): 327.
55. Aihwa Ong, *Neoliberalism as Exception*, Durham: Duke University Press, 2006, 66.
56. Schiller Glick Nina and Fouron Eugene Georges, *Georges Woke Up Laughing: Long-Distance Nationalism and the Search for Home*, Durham: Duke University Press, 2001.
57. Sandhya Shukla, *India Abroad: Diasporic Cultures of Postwar America and England*, Princeton: Princeton University Press, 2003, 13.
58. Ibid.

20 THE HINDU DIASPORA IN THE UNITED STATES

Ved P. Nanda

1. Introduction

The Hindu population of Indian origin in the United States stands at approximately two million people.[1] In addition, there are perhaps a million Hindus who are not Indian in the United States.[2] Hindus are not a monolithic entity, due to strong Indian regional affiliations (Punjabi, Gujarati, Marathi, Bengali, Tamil, Telugu, etc.) and worship and sectarian preferences (such as between those worshiping Shiva, Vishnu, Rama, Krishna, Durga, or Kali, or those belonging to organizations such as Arya Samaj, Swaminarayan, Swadhyaya, and Ramakrishna and Vedanta centers). This population also includes approximately 200,000 Hindus primarily from the Caribbean and in smaller numbers from Nepal, Sri Lanka, Fiji, and several other countries. Then there are nonresident Indians (NRIs), Indian nationals who are in the country temporarily or intend to immigrate. Contrasted with NRIs, people of Indian origin (PIOs) are those who have settled in the United States as their adoptive land. However, these differences do not impinge on the religious and spiritual activities of these groups, which remain mostly common.

Indian Americans, of whom a vast majority are Hindus, are often described as an "ideal minority" because of their business, professional, and educational success, social status, and integration into the US mainstream.[3] Their numbers have substantially risen since the 1980s, and while the first generation was primarily occupied with the realization of the American dream and moving up the career ladder, this no longer remains their preoccupation. They have begun to actively engage in economic and political life of this country, holding responsible positions.

On the economic front, several Hindus serve or have served in prominent positions, such as Vinod Khosla, cofounder of Sun Microsystems creator of Pentium chips Vinod Dham; founder and creator of Hotmail Sabeer Bhatia; Arun Netravalli, President of AT&T Bell Labs; General Manager of Hewlett Packard Rajiv Gupta; President of United Airlines Rono Dutta and President and CEO of US Airways Rakesh Gangwal; Vikram Pandit, CEO of Citigroup; and President and CEO of Pepsico, Indra Nooyi.

A disproportionately large percentage of the owners of motels and hotels in the hospitality sector in the United States are Indian-origin Hindus, hence the adage "Patel, Patel, & Patel." They own more than a million hotel rooms, which comprise 50 percent of the economic lodging sector and 30 percent of all hotels.[4] Similarly, a large percentage of physicians in the United States are also of Indian origin. In February 2006, Dr. Prabhakar Tripurneni, President of the American Society for Therapeutic Radiology and Oncology (ASTRO), organized the organization's 47th annual meeting in Denver, Colorado, attended by 11,000 people.[5]

In the political arena, Hindus have also occupied a number of high profile positions. These include in former President George W. Bush's administration Deputy US Trade Representative Karan Bhatia, and Preeta Bansal on the US Commission on International Religious Freedom, who has also chaired the organization. Sonal Shah, former head of Global Development Initiative at Google, is head of President Barack Obama's administration Office of Social Innovation and Civic Participation, promoting government efforts to help nonprofit groups and social entrepreneurs tackling pressing social problems. In June 2009, President Obama nominated Vinai A. Thummalapally to be US Ambassador to Belize.[6] During his second term, the President has appointed many Hindu Americans to prominent positions.

In Virginia, Aneesh Chopra was appointed as the state's Secretary of Technology, and Vivek Kundra as Assistant Secretary of Trade and Commerce.[7] Even in states in which the Hindu population is rather small, they have started playing important roles. For instance, Swati Dandekar is Iowa's first Indian American legislator, and in the same state Anuradha Vaiteshwaran serves as a judge on the Court of Appeals.[8] In Utah, Dinesh Patel, founding partner and managing director of Spring Capital, a venture capital firm, who was also responsible for hosting the first Hindu Diwali celebration in the governor's mansion, served as cochair of Governor Jon Huntsman's transition team and helped the governor put together his administration.[9] It should be noted that Diwali has also been celebrated at the White House since 2004.

On the educational front, more than 5,000 Indian Americans serve on faculties of institutions of higher education in the United States. These include provosts, deans, and chaired professors. Indian American students have excelled, receiving numerous awards and fellowships. Six out of the eleven finalists in the 2009 National Spelling Bee, including the champion, were from Hindu American families.[10] Since then, several champions have been Hindu Americans. Om Lala, a student at Harvard University, founded Dharma, Harvard's Hindu Association, and started the Harvard Interfaith Council.[11]

The economic and political clout of the Hindu diaspora notwithstanding, my discussion here will highlight selected religious and spiritual activities of the Hindu diaspora. The next section will focus on such activities of a few selected organizations for illustrative purposes. Next, I will relate activities of the Hindu diaspora in the cultural, educational, charitable, and human rights spheres. The section following that will highlight the struggle of several organizations to correct the perceived distorted image and negative stereotyping of Hinduism in the United States. The final section will provide an appraisal with a few recommendations.

2. Religious and Spiritual Activities of the Hindu Diaspora

Recently there has been a surge in temple building in or near major metropolitan areas in the United States. There are more than 400 Hindu temples and hundreds of Sikh Gurudwaras and Jain temples in the United States.[12] In addition, thousands of yoga centers and yoga studios are operating in the country. Although some of these centers and studios are run not by Hindus but by those of other faiths, most promote some aspect of Hindu philosophy and way of life. Similarly, there has been a steady increase of consultants who bring in the holistic view of health and well-being embodied in the Ayurveda system of medicine that originated in ancient Vedic traditions. Meditation, in various forms such as Transcendental Meditation, Kriya Yoga (the Self-Realization Fellowship, for example), and others has become extremely popular, with meditation centers in virtually every major city. Many ashrams (in ancient times, the dwelling of a Hindu sage, where disciples were instructed, and now also a religious retreat) and gurukulas (schools where Hindu traditions and Sanskrit language are taught) have been established.

A selected list of these various entities includes Shri Aurobindo's Centers;[13] Bochasanwasi Shree Akshar Purushottam Swaminarayan Sanstha (BAPS);[14] Chinmaya Mission;[15] Integral Yoga International;[16] International Society for Krishna Consciousness;[17] International Society of Divine Love;[18] Kriya Yoga Institute;[19] Mata Amritanandamayi Center;[20] Self-Realization Fellowship;[21] Sri Sri Ravi Shankar's Art of Living;[22] Swadhyaya Movement;[23] Vedanta Society of New York;[24] and Vedanta Society of Southern California.[25]

These temples, ashrams, and religious and spiritual movements maintain Hindu religious traditions and celebrate Hindu cultural heritage. To illustrate, a typical small Hindu temple, of which I am the founding President, the Hindu Temple and Cultural Center of the Rockies in the Denver, Colorado, area, serves the religious and spiritual needs of Hindus in the community. It has two priests, one from the North and one from the South of India. The temple provides daily worship and deity service, and Sunday congregational pooja, usually drawing more than 100 people; it celebrates all the major Hindu festivals and religious observances, often attended by many hundreds of devotees. The priests visit homes and offer special poojas and the temple has a Sunday school (Bala Mandir), in which children are taught. As a 501(c)(3) institution, the temple manages its affairs through a Board of Trustees.[26] Plans are underway to build a larger facility for the Temple and Cultural Center. Colorado has around 10,000 Hindus. Larger temples, in areas such as New York/New Jersey, Washington, DC, Chicago, Atlanta, Houston, Pittsburgh, the San Francisco Bay Area, and Los Angeles undertake these activities on a much grander scale.

3. Cultural, Educational, Charitable, and Human Rights Activities

Several organizations are engaged in these activities. I will, however, select a few organizations for discussion here.

3.1. Cultural and Educational Activities

Activities of four organizations—Vishwa Hindu Parishad of America (World Hindu Council of America) (VHPA), Hindu Swayamsevak Sangh (HSS), Hindu Students Council (HSC), and Ekal Vidyalaya—will be briefly described here.

3.1.1. Vishwa Hindu Parishad of America

VHPA was established in 1970 with the purpose of bringing the "Hindu migrant community together" and "cultivat[ing] a spirit of self-respect in Hindu way of life and respect for the people of all colors, creeds, races and religions."[27] It does so through conferences, seminars, publications, and media. The objective, according to VHP, is to act as the voice of Hindus and to represent Hindu organizations and institutions on matters of Hindu interests. The organization's goal is

> to create a dynamic, vibrant, visible and effective Hindu society based on and inspired by the eternal values of Dharma, and the lofty idea of Vasudhaiva Katumbakam, "the entire creation is one family." VHPA works to preserve, protect, and promote the Hindu way of life. The

Parishad is of the view that Hindus are those who believe, practice and respect the spiritual and religious principles and practices having roots in India. Thus, Hindus include Jaina, Baudhha, Sikha, and people of different sects and traditions within the Hindu ethos.[28]

VHPA's activities include providing "community service to people in distress, without consideration of race, religion and nationality," and creating opportunities for instilling "Hindu values based on Hindu scriptures and heritage through Bala Vihars [children's programs], camps . . . family retreats and educational institutions."[29]

Through Bala Vihars, youth camps, and youth conferences VHPA imparts training in yoga, Hindu heritage, and Indian languages. Young people discuss the issues created in their lives by the mix of cultures in which they live, study Hindu scriptures, learn meditation, and familiarize themselves with various aspects of Hindu culture. VHPA held major conferences in the 1980s and 1990s in New York and Washington, DC, respectively, drawing more than 5,000 participants in New York and 10,000 in Washington. In 2000 VHPA organized a Dharma Ganga in conjunction with the United Nations Millennium Peace Summit, with 108 eminent monks from India participating in spiritual discussions at the UN and later around the country.

In the twenty-first century, VHPA has intensified its work with temples, ashrams, and Hindu institutions to create awareness regarding issues relating to the concerns of Hindu society, as well as American society. Among many initiatives it has recently undertaken are the following:

establishing of the Hindu University of America in Orlando, Florida;
holding Hindu temple executives' and priests' conferences, where more than 100 temple executives and a similar number of priests gather to discuss temple management, activities, impact on Hindus and American society and work with other likeminded organizations;
founding the Hindu Students Council, aimed at educating Hindu values through programs and projects;
creating Ekal Vidyalaya Foundation (one-teacher village schools) in India; and conducting seva (service) activities to benefit all segments of American society.

In sum, through its programs and activities, VHPA strives to enable all sections of the Hindu diaspora to address their concerns regarding their heritage and dharma.

3.1.2. Hindu Swayamsevak Sangh

Established in the 1989, HSS envisages that as inheritors of a rich Hindu tradition, including yoga, meditation, Ayurveda, and the vision of seeing divinity in everyone and everything, which are some of the gifts of Hindus to the world, it is HSS's mission to make these gifts available to the humanity for the sake of harmony among all.[30]

HSS's aim is to

> organize the Hindu community in order to preserve, practice and promote Hindu ideals and values. HSS conducts structured programs of regular athletic and academic activities to develop strong character and leadership skills in its members (known as swayamsevaks for men and sevikas for women), emphasizing values such as self-discipline, self-confidence and a spirit of selfless service (seva) for humanity. [It encourages] maintaining Hindu cultural identity in harmony with the larger community. Sangh is inspired by the idea that the whole world is one family and conducts activities across the United States in order to spread this message widely.

Each chapter of HSS is called a "*shakha*," and meets weekly for an hour and a half with all the family members coming together to participate in its activities. These activities focus on personal development—through games and exercises for physical health, discussions and lectures on historical, cultural, social, and current topics for intellectual development, and yoga, seva (community service), and discourses for spiritual upliftment. The children's program in *shakha* is known as Bala Gokulam. *Balagokulam* Magazine provides a forum for children to express their talents, including articles, poems, paintings, crossword puzzles, stories, and contests.[31] There are presently more than 140 *shakhas* in the United States.

As an independent not-for-profit organization registered in the United States, HSS has its own constitution, its own officers, and manages its own finances. However, it derives its inspiration to work for Hindu society in particular and humanity in general from the unique model of *Shakha* from Rashtriya Swayamsevak Sangh (RSS) in India. HSS believes in the peaceful settlement of disputes and denounces violence. Thus, it has condemned communal violence in India as and when it occurs, such as the tragic events in Gujarat, including Godhara, in 2002. HSS activities in the United States include celebration of many Hindu festivals such as Makar Sankranti, Yugadi, Raksha Bandhan, Guru Purnima, and Vijaya Dashmi. Other activities include Hindu heritage camps and a forum for teenagers to enhance their understanding of Hindu culture with activities such as yoga, discussions and debates, lectures, and cultural programs.

In July 2001, Hindus in the San Francisco Bay Area, with the impetus of HSS organized a historic event, a grand cultural festival attended by more than 10,000 Hindus and community members. More than 30 organizations made the Sangam possible. During the Sangam conferences were held on yoga and Ayurveda, spirituality, and Sanskrit language and literature, as well as special programs for children and youth. Guests included local mayors and other elected officials. HSS continues to organize such activities throughout the country.

In 2013, HSS celebrated the 150th birth anniversary of the Hindu monk, Swami Vivekanand, who introduced Vedanta to the West with his addresses at the World Parliament of Religions in Chicago in 1893. Audiences in more than 30 cities during this anniversary year ranged from 1,000 in Denver to between 12,000 and 14,000 in the San Francisco Bay Area. The special focus of the celebration was on Swami Vivekanand's teachings of the Hindu precept of universal brotherhood.

Among many other initiatives undertaken by HSS are Hindu women's conferences in various cities; two exciting nationwide contests for schoolchildren, "Kaun Banega [Who will become] Ramayan Expert?" and "Dharma Bee"; Hindu Education Foundation (HEF), which strives to remove misconceptions and project accurate understanding about Hinduism; sponsorship of seminars on Hindu Dharma for teachers and students; work with education committees in various states to improve school curricula regarding Hinduism; and traveling exhibitions on Hindu culture and Dharmic traditions of India. HSS also conducts intensive leadership camps in locations around the country to impart to young people the confidence and skills required to take active roles in Sangh activities and the broader Hindu community.

3.1.3. Hindu Students Council

With its motto "Dharma, unity, knowledge and progress," HSC's vision emerges from fundamental Hindu principles such as *Vasudhaiva Kutumbakam* ("the entire creation is one family"); *Ekam Sat Viprah Bahudha Vadanti* ("truth is one, sages call it by different names"); and *Sarve Bhavantu Sukhinah Sarve Santu Niramayah* ("let everyone be happy, healthy, and blessed"). As HSC describes it, its mission is

to develop a bond of extended Hindu family relationship and awareness about the universal Hindu System. It aims to achieve this through education and through the promotion of various activities and projects on and off campuses. HSC also strives to raise awareness about social, political, and religious issues affecting Hindus.[32]

HSC's goals are to provide its members and nonmembers alike with opportunities to learn about Hindu heritage and culture, to foster awareness of issues affecting Hindus, and to provide service to the community. It was started in 1990 and has more than 70 chapters. To celebrate the anniversary of Swami Vivekanand's address in Chicago, HSC organized the Global Vision 2000 Global Youth Conference, attended by more than 2,000 people. In 2003, HSC was the main organizer of Global Dharma Conference in New Jersey, in which more than 2,000 people participated. It was a unique conference of its type, organized solely by second-generation Hindu American youth. In addition, the organization annually holds a national summer camp as well as regional seminars, conferences, and retreats aimed at bringing together its members from various chapters.

As HSC focuses on maintaining Hindu culture among students and youth, especially college students and young professionals, its campus activities include group discussions and lectures on the lives of great people and epics such as the Ramayana and the Mahabharata. It also holds discourses and discussions on Bhagavad Gita, Hindu customs and traditions, the status of Hindu women, Hindu history, and science and spirituality. It provides student assistance in the form of hospitality to new students.[33] Cultural events include celebration of festivals such as Diwali, Dussehra, Shri Krishna Janmashtami, Holi, and Durga Puja.

3.2. Charitable Activities

The Indian diaspora is very active in charitable work, both in India and in the United States. Several organizations and individuals, too numerous to mention here, are keen to adopt entire villages and educational institutions in India, assist children, provide medical assistance, and do all sorts of relief and rehabilitation work. For example, Sewa International USA assisted in reconstruction of villages in Tamil Nadu, India, and in Sri Lanka after the tsunami of 2004.[34]

After the Hurricane Katrina disaster in the southern United States it provided donations and voluntary work, for which the then-governor of Louisiana Kathleen Blanco recognized its efforts. It worked with the American Red Cross, the Federal Emergency Management Agency, and other nongovernmental organizations (NGOs), and partnered with many Hindu Temples throughout the United States.[35] In concert with the HSS, Sewa International USA coordinated with temples and other Indian American organizations in Houston, San Antonio, and Atlanta; organized hundreds of volunteers; and raised more than $100,000 for relief in less than one week. More than 240 Sewa workers from all over the country assisted in shelters, fed people, and assembled hygiene packets for evacuees at the Houston Astrodome, and found alternative accommodations for those staying in hotels and motels.[36] Their assistance was provided to all in need, regardless of faith. More recently, in many cities, the organization has been helping Bhutanese Hindu refugee families to find accommodation and jobs and to resettle in their new American home.

On December 8, 2005, the Mata Amritanandamayi Center in the United States handed over $1 million to the Bush-Clinton Katrina Fund to aid hurricane recovery efforts in the Gulf Coast.[37]

Another active service organization, the India Development and Relief Fund (IDRF), has supported charitable activities for several years, primarily in India, through fundraising in the United States.[38] Its development efforts are focused on five key areas: education, health care, child care, women, and tribal welfare, while their relief and rehabilitation support is offered to address natural or man-made calamities such as the Orissa super-cyclone, Gujarat earthquake, or the Kargil (Kashmir) war.[39] IDRF was severely criticized in a 2002 report titled "The Foreign Exchange of Hate: IDRF and the American Funding of Hindutva,"[40] alleging that some of the funds were used in India for inciting violence. Shortly thereafter, a group of supporters of disparate professional, personal, and academic backgrounds came together to form a team called "Friends of India," and in February 2003 released a report, "A Factual Response to the Hate Attack on India Development and Relief Fund (IDRF),"[41] refuting the incitement charges and providing a transparent accounting of the money disbursed by IDRF on development and rehabilitation projects.

As a charitable trust that initiates, supports, and runs one-teacher village schools in India (popularly known as *ekal vidyalayas*), the Ekal Vidyalaya Foundation has emerged as the premier nongovernmental educational movement in India.[42] In the United States, the organization is active in raising funds, especially in lump sums of $365 per donor to fund one school for one year.

Among other organizations, HSS, VHPA, and HSC also provide charitable work. For example, in the San Francisco Bay area, HSS has participated in visiting senior citizen convalescent hospitals, undertaken bone marrow donor registration drives, and served the local community, not just Hindus, through various seva projects.[43] VHPA has contributed millions of dollars to various charitable causes, working with numerous aid agencies, including the American Red Cross and Vivekanand Vedanta Society. Approximately half of its total annual budget is earmarked for seva activities.[44] HSC participates in soup kitchens and disaster relief funds, among other charitable activities.[45] One unique feature of these organizations' efforts is that the overhead expenses are almost negligible. They claim that more than 90 to 95 percent of the donations for seva causes reach the people for whom they are intended.

3.3. Human Rights

The Global Organization of People of Indian Origin (GOPIO) was the first America-based organization to work on civil and political rights of people of Indian origin around the world.[46] It has presented petitions on behalf of PIO victims of human rights violations in Fiji and Sri Lanka, and has addressed such violations in other countries, as well, including the Caribbean. Recently, two other organizations, the Hindu American Foundation (HAF) and Hindu International Council Against Defamation (HICAD), were formed on the model of the Anti-Defamation League of B'nai B'rith to promote and protect human rights of Hindus.[47]

3.3.1. Hindu American Foundation

The Hindu American Foundation, which was established in 2003 as an advocacy group, has as its purpose to provide

> a progressive voice for over two million Hindu Americans. The Foundation interacts with and educates leaders in public policy, academia, media and the public at large about Hinduism and global issues concerning Hindus, such as religious liberty, the portrayal of Hinduism, hate speech, hate crimes and human rights. By promoting the Hindu and American ideals of understanding, tolerance and pluralism, HAF stands firmly against hate, discrimination, defamation and terror.[48]

HAF has worked with several NGOs, such as the American Jewish Committee and Amnesty International, to present Hindu issues to mainstream America. In pursuance of its goal to educate governments and the media about Hinduism and issues of concern to Hindus locally and globally, it has issued policy briefings on discrimination against Hindus in various countries.[49] HAF has published major studies on Hindus in Bangladesh, Pakistan, Malaysia, and Kashmir.[50]

HAF annually releases a report on the status of human rights of Hindus in various countries. For example, its 2008 report is titled *Hindus in South Asia and the Diaspora: A Survey of Human Rights 2008*. Its briefings on Capitol Hill have included those on Kashmir, Malaysia, and Fiji, among others. It celebrated its tenth anniversary with a briefing on Capitol Hill, attended by several hundred people, a dozen US Senators and House members.

In the spring of 2009 HAF led interfaith efforts to shut down offensive Facebook groups. And in a rare meeting in June 2009, senior Hindu spiritual and religious leaders from India met with Jewish leaders met in Washington, DC, in sessions convened by a group of NGOs, including HAF.[51] The Foundation was awarded *Hinduism* Today magazine's "Hindu Renaissance Award" in March 2009.[52]

Earlier, in a newsletter of March 3, 2006, HAF condemned blasphemous anti-Muslim cartoons but stated that violence is not an acceptable solution. Its president, Mehir Meghani, said, "Though as Americans we are committed to freedom of speech and expression, cartoonists and their editors demonstrated a monumental lapse of judgment at best, and outright bigotry at worst." He added, "As a Hindu, having experienced painful depictions of my faith in this country, I can relate to the protests by the Muslim world, but violence is simply not an acceptable solution."[53] Subsequently, on February 11, 2006, HAF empathized with the congregations of nine Baptist churches which were burned in Alabama, expressing the outrage of the Hindu American community.[54] HAF has several times challenged the use of inflammatory and vulgar depictions of Hindu symbols and sacred beliefs in the United States and Europe. It was also actively involved in the California textbook controversy discussed below.

4. Correcting Misinformation and Distortion about Hindu Dharma and India

Several Hindu organizations have recently taken action to correct what they perceive as misinformation and distortion of Hinduism and India prevalent in the media, schools, and institutions of higher learning in the United States. As an example, the French fashion group Minelli manufactured and sold shoes decorated with the image of Lord Rama. After persistent efforts by Hindu human rights groups, Minelli finally apologized and removed the shoes from store shelves.[55]

In 2003, a fourteen-year-old middle school student, Trisha Pasricha of Houston, Texas, wrote a letter lamenting her embarrassment and shame at what was being taught in her social studies classes about India and Hinduism.[56] Dr. Rakesh Bahadur, whose children were in a northern Virginia school, told the magazine *Hinduism Today*, "One day my daughter came home and said, 'Daddy, what you teach us about Hinduism is wrong, since the description of Hinduism in my textbook is different.'"[57] For example, it was said that the Mahabharata was "made up"; there were clichés and oversimplifications often lacking context with overemphasis on the exotic, not adequately representing the fundamental belief systems of Hindus. At the urging of Hindu parents who brought these distortions to the attention of the Fairfax County (Virginia) School Board, a scholarly committee reviewed the books and proposed several changes, most of which were accepted by the Board.[58] According to the *Washington Post*,

> Balaji Hebbar, a George Washington University religion professor who was one of three scholars hired by Fairfax County to review the books cited by the group of Indian parents, said he and his colleagues found few factual errors. But he said the lessons boiled down a complex culture to "karma, cows and caste" and largely glossed over the morality and ethics at the core of one of the world's oldest religions. . . . Based on the concerns of Fairfax educators, five publishers made modest changes in the texts, and the professors recommended that the county purchase eight revised books, reject one and supplement the curriculum with other materials. The school system has begun a series of seminars on India and Hinduism for world history teachers and created a team that will work over the summer to gather other resources.[59]

In 2005, California Hindu parents and community leaders, in conjunction with the Hindu Education Foundation (HEF) and the Vedic Foundation, suggested that the California State Board of Education make changes in sixth grade history books to be used for the next six years. The suggestions, 160 edits in all, were to correct what the group considered to be a derogatory and inaccurate depiction of Hinduism. At a February 27, 2006 meeting of the State Board of Education subcommittee considering the recommendations, several parents and students requested that changes suggested by the practicing Hindus be accepted.[60] A tenth-grader said, "Hindu kids are embarrassed about their religion because their classmates make fun of them. How many California students know that there is more to Hinduism than just the caste system?"[61] Another wondered why the scriptures of Hinduism are referred to as myths and legends, while those of all other religions are said to come from God. They demanded that equal treatment be provided to Hinduism as is given to other religions.[62]

The controversy accelerated after Dr. Michael Witzel, professor of Sanskrit at Harvard University, along with several other scholars, charged in a letter to the California Department of Education that the changes were motivated by

"Hindutva" forces. Several organizations joined in opposing these changes, such as Friends of South Asia, an activist group, the Ambedkar Center for Peace and Justice, and the Coalition Against Communalism. Supporting the changes was Dr. Shiva Bajpai, a renowned Indologist from California State University at Northridge.

The Board of Education subcommittee ultimately accepted several of the proposed changes but rejected others pertaining to the Aryan Invasion theory, the status of women, and the status of untouchables. Both sides claimed victory as the staff reviewers appeared to have chosen a middle path. The president of the State Board of Education, Glee Johnson, told *India-West*, an Indian community newsweekly, that the panel had considered 126 pages of edits and corrections, nine proposed textbook submissions, and 1,500 to 2,000 pages of letters and e-mails.[63] Khanderao Kand, coordinator for the Hindu Education Foundation, said, "On behalf of the Hindu community, we have done significant progress to correct the biases and distortions in the textbooks. . . . We need to work further. There are gross inaccuracies."[64]

However, that was not the end. The case dragged on until finally in June 2009 the State of California acknowledged Hindus' concerns and agreed to pay $175,000 to California Parents for the Equalization of Educational Materials (CAPEEM) in exchange for a voluntary dismissal of the lawsuit.[65]

I note these instances to underscore the perception widely shared among Hindus that Hinduism suffers from a distorted image and negative stereotyping in this country. Seemingly insensitive depictions and treatment of Hinduism and Hindu history, particularly Hindu deities and saints, by commercial interests, the media, and occasionally even by scholars, have long been a sore point.[66] A recent essay discussing biases in Hinduism studies aptly makes the point regarding academia:

> The purpose of this essay is to highlight the growing dissatisfaction on the part of the Indian American Hindu Diaspora with the way Hinduism, Hindus, and India have been depicted and mis-portrayed in the American education system, and about the urgency to engage the system along the same as is already being done by other American minorities, such as the Native Americans, African-Americans, Hispanics, Jews, Muslims, Chinese, Japanese, and Koreans. This article also explores how Hinduism and India studies directly or indirectly form American perceptions of India and its culture, its products and services, and of the Indian American minority, and the need to bring objectivity and balance to these studies.[67]

I do not speak for the whole Hindu diaspora, but if devout Hindus feel hurt and take affront at what they consider to be misrepresentation of symbols of their devotion, these are voices of dissent and should not be dismissed as voices of fanaticism. Would such writings and depictions about Islam or the Prophet Muhammad, or Christianity and Jesus, or any others, be acceptable? Thus the need is to portray Hinduism as other religions are portrayed, with respect.

5. Outreach Efforts

This brief and rather partial sketch of the Hindu diaspora in the United States indicates that several Hindu organizations, including Hindu Temples and NGOs, have been active in this country for quite some time. However, it is only since the 1980s that many of them have systematically started their outreach efforts. After the tragic events of 9/11 and the inflammatory rhetoric by many that followed, several Hindu organizations, including some temples, have actively begun to present their worldview, especially on interreligious and interracial issues, trying to reach the media and decision-makers. A constant theme has been interreligious harmony.

One special initiative by several organizations of the diaspora has been to participate more actively in community interfaith groups; in some instances they themselves have established such groups. One such example is a "Gathering of National Religious Leaders."[68] Organized by Religions for Peace USA, a coalition of leaders from more than 50 religious communities, it aims to achieve social development, justice, and peace through cooperation. The World Sikh Council–America Region, Federation of Jain Associations in North America, Buddha's Light International Association, and the Hindu Temple Society of North America are among participating members. The Sikh Religious Society of Chicago hosted the gathering in January 2006. I myself participate in a broadly constituted interfaith group in Denver, known as the Interfaith Council, which also serves as a religious advisory group to the University of Denver.[69] I also serve as Vice-President of the Interfaith Alliance of Colorado, which is part of a national interfaith organization.

Among recent efforts to create awareness of the Indic traditions—Hinduism, Buddhism, Jainism, and Sikhism—in the United States is the establishment of the Uberoi Foundation for Religious Studies. An academician, Dr. Mahinder Uberoi, bequeathed his entire estate to this cause. The foundation, with assets of $8.5 million, is aimed at enhancing scholarly activities in US universities about these traditions, in addition to undertaking outreach activities through conferences, colloquia, and grants. I serve as the chair of the Board of Trustees of the foundation.

The Foundation's first meeting of a few selected scholars from these traditions, held in Orlando in October 2009 featured discussion of Monotheism/the Ultimate Reality and the Doctrine of Karma, among other topics. Since then, it has held experts' meetings annually in different cities, with the September 2014 meeting being hosted by Naropa University in Boulder, Colorado, on the theme of Compassion from the Perspective of the four Dharmic traditions. The Foundation's priorities are training American classroom teachers in the authentic depiction of these traditions and correcting distortions in school textbooks. Since its inception it has given grants amounting to more than $1 million to scholars at several North American universities.

Another recent arrival on the American scene is the Los Angeles-based Dharma Civilizational Foundation (DCF). DCF's current focus is to fund professorships and endowed chairs on Hinduism in a number of American universities, the first being the University of Southern California.

6. Appraisal and Recommendations

In response to the perceived negative stereotypes of Hinduism, some proponents of Hinduism have perhaps reacted rather harshly. Not being media-savvy, as they tend to be untutored and unsophisticated in media relations, they vent their emotions. To remedy the situation, as I have noted earlier, some Hindu organizations have now established human rights education, media watchdog, and advocacy groups to provide a more accurate portrayal of Hinduism. A few human rights groups have also been formed with similar objectives.

In a pluralistic society, the role of religious identity has to be clarified. We do need a nuanced understanding of secularism and especially Indian secularism as it has come to be known. Several assertive Hindu groups and individuals have suffered from accusations and allegations of being militant and have been demonized by critics under the characterization of Hindutva. The Hindutva label is used pejoratively to connote Hindu nationalism that is exclusive and intolerant. This is in fact a misuse of the word, for Hindutva, an adjective, simply means "being Hindu," and there is nothing pejorative about it.

Communal violence in Gujarat was a flashpoint for such characterization, as was the mistaken allegation that IDRF had disbursed funds in India to organizations involved in the violence. For the record, after these tragic events in Gujarat, I frequently spoke out both in private conversations and public gatherings denouncing the use of violence on the part of both Muslims and Hindus. HSS, too, has always deplored communal violence. A few years ago the Prophet

Muhammad cartoon controversy in Europe sparked violent global protests and demonstrations, the burning of embassies, destruction of property, and loss of life.[70] There was a lot of soul searching on all sides as a result. Free speech and freedom of expression, whether in the media or in academia, is undoubtedly a fundamental right, not to be curtailed. And there was no justification for violence on the part of those protesting the publication of the cartoons. However, respecting the beliefs and tenets of all religions is also essential.

As the United Nations, the European Union, and the Organization of the Islamic Conference said in a joint appeal of February 8, 2006, calling for an end to the violence around the Muslim world: "The anguish in the Muslim world at the publication of the offensive caricatures is shared by all individuals and communities who recognize the sensitivity of deeply-held religious belief."[71] The statement asserted that while free speech is a right, it is one that entails "responsibility and discretion," respecting the beliefs of all religions.[72] Then-President Jacques Chirac of France declared that freedom of expression was "one of the foundations of the Republic," but added a plea for "respect and moderation" in its application.[73] Indeed there is a need for responsibility and discretion in exercising free speech.

I am deeply grateful to my colleagues who engage in scholarly work and teach Hinduism in colleges and universities. I would like to consider such colleagues as great friends of Hinduism and India, for they have expertise and capability to present Hinduism not only to their students, but through their writing and scholarship to the American public as well. I very much hope that they present it with sensitivity and respect. Do they have a right to criticize Hinduism? Absolutely. They have every right to present their interpretation of a sloka or a scriptural text, for example. However, the difficulty is that unlike the study of other religions with various and divergent scholarly voices, the study of Hinduism in the United States lacks diversity of those voices. Thus, when there is a criticism of, say, Jesus Christ or an inappropriate rendering of a Christian text by some scholars, there are likely other voices to counter the criticism and provide a balance. Hinduism lacks such representation in Western academia, because there are today few voices of actual practicing Hindus among academics to balance the criticism of Hinduism by some, and hence disrespectful portrayals go unanswered.

What is the solution? The need is for scholars of Hinduism to engage in an ongoing dialogue with the Hindu community to learn from and give consideration to their grievances. It is extremely important for the benefit of Hinduism outside India that young practicing Hindus pursue Hinduism studies to expand the base of scholarly knowledge. Also, it is essential that Hindu organizations engage in rigorous scholarly activities. As other religions have their think-tanks,

Hindus must do the same. The Hindu diaspora needs to take the initiative to enter into a respectful dialogue with scholars to exchange ideas, present views, and find common ground based on mutual understanding.

Notes

1. I gratefully acknowledge the research assistance of the late Devang Vyas, Esq., and the help of my wife, Katharine Nanda, Esq. I wish to express my deep gratitude to my distinguished colleagues Professors Martha Nussbaum and Wendy Doniger for their kind invitation to participate in the conference and for their gracious hospitality and equally gracious reception of my opinions. This essay is an expanded and adapted version of my presentation at the conference.

2. The Hindu American Foundation puts the number at approximately 2 million, available at www.hinduamericanfoundation.org/hintro_rising_numbers.htm (the organization compiled these statistics based upon the following sources: Pew Research Center for the People and the Press, www.people-press.org/reports/display.php3?PageID=385; American Religious Identification Survey, www.gc.cuny.edu/studies/aris.pdf; Bharatiya Pravasi Divas, www.india-day.org/aboutus.htm; US-India Friendship Net, www.usindiafriendship.net/; Asian Nation: The Landscape of Asian American, www.usindiafriendship.net/; Harvard Pluralism Project, www.pluralism.org/about/index.php; Adherents.com, www.adherents.com/Na/Na_298.html#1868; Return of the Overseas Indian, www.straitstimes.asia1.com.sg; www.hindustantimes.com/news/5967_651401,001600060001.htm; www.aapiusa.net/membership.htm).

3. USINPAC, a national bipartisan political action/education committee of the Indian American community, which represents the community's concerns on a broad: range of issues and provides a voice for the Indian American community in Washington, provides the following information:

   1. According to the 2007 census, the Indian American population stands at 2.5 million people. The community is multireligious and multiethnic.
   2. 10.5 percent—average annual growth rate of the Indian American community. This makes Americans from India and their descendants the fastest-growing ethnic group in the United States.
   3. $69,470—the median income of Indian American families, nearly double the median income of all American families.
   4. 200,000—the number of Indian American millionaires.
   5. 64.4 percent—percentage of Indian Americans over the age of 25 who have a college degree (BA or higher).
   6. 57.7 percent—percentage of Indian Americans in the workforce employed as managers or professionals.

7. 38,000—the number of Indian American physicians. There are also a disproportionate number of Indian Americans employed as lawyers, engineers, academics, financiers, and business-owners.
8. 12,000—the number of Indian American medical school students and interns.
9. 300,000—the number of Indian Americans working in the high-tech industry.
10. 15 percent—percentage of Silicon Valley start-up firms owned by Indian Americans.
11. 5,000—number of Indian Americans on the faculties of institutions of higher learning.
12. 80,000—number of foreign exchange students from India studying in United States. This represents 13 percent of total foreign enrollment in US colleges and universities—the second highest number from any one country.

Sources: US Census Bureau (Census 2007); American Association of Physicians of Indian Origin; Asian American Hotel Owners Association; Merrill Lynch; Indian Embassy. Available at www.usinpac.com.
4. Asian American Hotel Owners Association, www.aahoa.com.
5. *India Abroad,* February 17, 2006, C7.
6. *Times of India*, June 13, 2009, 11.
7. *India Abroad,* February 10, 2006, A4; id., February 10, 2006, A8.
8. *India Abroad,* February 17, 2006, A24.
9. *India Abroad*, February 17, 2006, A10.
10. "Kansas Gal Kavya Shivshankar Bee-Comes Spelling Princess," *Times of India*, May 28, 2009, www.timesofindia.indiatimes.com.
11. J. Pais, "Harvard Student Om Lala Wins Prestigious Fellowship to Cambridge," *India Abroad*, February 17, 2006, C1.
12. For the number of Hindu temples in different states see www.indians-abroad.com. See generally Mahalingum Kolapen, *Hindu Temples in North America—A Celebration of Life* (Orlando, FL: Hindu University of America, 2002), presenting detailed depictions of 30 selected temple structures, their histories, and the tradition of Indian temple architecture and iconography); Ved Chaudhary, Dharma Summit 2005, "Introduction," www.hicad.us/Dharma_Summit_2005.htm. For the number of Sikh Gurudwaras in different states, see www.gurdwara.us. For the number of Jain temples in different states see www.adherents.com.
13. Several centers in the United States, available at www.Matagiri.org.
14. A sociospiritual religious community with its roots in the Vedas, having a large number of temples and centers around the country, available at www.swamina-rayan.org/globalnetwork/america/index.htm.

15. A worldwide Vedanta movement founded by Swami Chinmayanand, which has several missions in the United States, available at www.chinmaya.org/centers/cmw.

16. An international yoga community based in the United States at Swami Satchidanand's Yogaville Ashram, available at www.yogaville.org.

17. The Hare Krishna movement, launched in the United States by Swami AC Bhaktivedanta, available at www.iskcon.org.

18. Swami Prakshanand's international community based at Barsanadham, Austin, Texas, available at www.ISDL.org.

19. Several centers in the United States.

20. American based worldwide humanitarian and religious organization, available at www.ammachi.org.

21. Dedicated to self-realization through the practice of Kriya Yoga, available at www.yogananda/srf.org.

22. Several centers in the United States, available at www.artofliving.org.

23. Worldwide sociospiritual movement with a large number of study centers in the United States. The movement has strong youth and children focus for spiritual and cultural education. Available at www.swadhyaya.org.

24. The first Vedanta Society in the United States, founded by Swami Vivekananda in 1894, available at www.vedanta/newyork.org.

25. It includes Vedanta temples, monasteries, retreat centers, and a bookstore, available at www.vedanta.org.

26. Available at www.hindutempleofcolorado.org. The author is founding president and now a trustee of the temple.

27. Available at www.vhp-america.org.

28. Id.

29. Id.

30. Available at www.hssus.org.

31. www.balgokulam.org.

32. www.hscnet.org.

33. For information, contact or e-mail hsc@hindunet.org.

34. www.sewausa.org. Sewa International was first organized in the United Kingdom in 1991 and now in fifteen countries.

35. Id.

36. "Katrina Relief by Hindus," *Hinduism Today*, January–February–March 2006, 8.

37. "Hindus Help Katrina Relief," *Hinduism Today*, April–May–June 2006, 6.

38. www.idrf.org.

39. Id. In 2002, IDRF provided $719,000 for development projects; $88,000 for Orissa Super-Cyclone Rehabilitation Projects; and has raised $1,679,000 for Gujarat Earthquake and Rehabilitation Projects since 2001, including $462,000 in 2002. IDRF's annual report for 2002–2003 is available at www.idrf.org.

40. *The Foreign Exchange of Hate: IDRF and the American Funding of Hindutva* (Mumbai: Sabrang Communications & Publishing, 2002), http://pluralism.in/2011/03/the-foreign-exchange-of-hate-idrf-and-the-american-funding-of-hindutva/.

41. Ramesh N. Rao, *Let The Facts Speak* (IDRF, 2003).

42. www.ekalvidya.org.

43. www.hssworld.org.

44. www.vhp-america.org.

45. www.hscnet.org.

46. www.gopio.net. The author served as the first chair of the GOPIO Human Rights Commission.

47. www.hinduamericanfoundation.org; www.hicad.org.

48. www.hinduamericanfoundation.org.

49. See, e.g., Policy Briefings, *Genocide and Ethnic Cleansing of Hindus from Bangladesh*, available at www.Hinduamericanfoundation.org/policy_bangladesh; Policy Briefings, *Discrimination and Persecution: The Plight of Hindus in Pakistan,* available at www.hindumaericanfoundation.org/policy_pakistan; *Pakistan and Al-Qaeda Sponsored Islamist Terrorism in Kashmir: Hindu Victims and Refugees,* available at www.hinduamericanfoundation.org/policy_kashmir.

50. See, e.g., Hindu American Foundation, *Hindus in Bangladesh, Pakistan and Kashmir—A Survey of Human Rights (2005),* available at www.hinduamericanfoundation.org.

51. *Hindus and Jews Unite on Capital Hill in Rare Meeting of Spiritual Leaders*, available at www.hinduamericanfoundation.org.

52. *HAF Receives Hindu Renaissance Award at Annual Meet*, available at www.hinduamericanfoundation.org.

53. Hindu American Foundation, Press Release, Tampa, Feb. 7, 2006, HAF Newsletter, March 3, 2006.

54. Hindu American Foundation, Press Release, "Hindu Americans Shocked by Alabama Church Burnings," Tampa, February 11, 2006, http://www.hafsite.org/issues?q=/media/pr/20060211_alabama.

55. "Rama Shoes Removed from Market," *Hinduism Today,* January–February–March 2006, 7.

56. www.sulekha.com/expressions/column.asp?cid=305890.

57. "Textbooks Get it Wrong," *Hinduism Today,* January–February–March 2006, 60. www.hinduismtoday.com.

58. Id.

59. Maria Glod, "Wiping Stereotypes of India off the Books; Fairfax Parents Win Fight for Nuanced Teachings on Homeland," *Washington Post*, April 17, 2005, C1.

60. For a report of this meeting see "California Textbook Corrections Result of Broad-Based Coalition of Hindus," *Hindu Press International*, March 2, 2006, available from hpi.list@hindu.org (based on a joint press release of the HEF and the Vedic Foundation, available at www.hindueducation.org.).

61. Id.

62. Id.

63. Ashfaque Swapan, "Panel Accepts Some Textbook Edits After Compromise," *India West*, March 6, 2006, available at www.indiawest.com (hereinafter Textbook Edits). See also "Outcome Known on California Texts," *Hinduism Today*, April–May–June 2006, 58–63.

64. Textbook Edits, *supra* note 65.

65. See "California Educational Books Lawsuit Settled," available at www.capeem.org.

66. See Hindu Student Council, "Biases Against Hinduism in Academia," 2004, available at www.hscnet.org.

67. Abhijit Bagal, "Biases in Hinduism Studies," May 13, 2005, available at www.swaveda.com. The writer stated that he was not affiliated with any political or religious organization and was writing the article in his individual capacity.

68. See Monika Joshi, "Religious Leaders Meet to Advance Interfaith Relations," *India Abroad*, February 17, 2006, C6.

69. Led by Pastor Paul Kottke of the University Park Methodist Church, Denver.

70. See, e.g., Roula Khalaf, et al., "Danish Producers Feel Heat of Cartoon Boycott," *Financial Times*, February 11, 2006, 7; Ralph Atkins et al., "Radical Forces in Middle East Ensure Cartoon Backlash Turns Explosive," *Financial Times*, February 6, 2006, 6; Martin Arnold et al., "Cartoons Spark Islamic Rage," *Financial Times*, February 3, 2006, 1.

71. Roula Khalaf et al., "UN, EU and Muslims Link in Call to Curb Protests," *Financial Times*, February 8, 2006, 9.

72. Id.

73. Special Report 1, "Mutual Incomprehension, Mutual Outrage—Islam and Free Speech," *The Economist*, February 11, 2006.

INDEX